FEDERAL
JOBS

THE ULTIMATE GUIDE

THIRD EDITION

Dana Morgan

Robert Goldenkoff

THOMSON
ARCO

Australia • Canada • Mexico • Singapore • Spain • United Kingdom • United States

An ARCO Book

ARCO is a registered trademark of Thomson Learning, Inc., and is used herein under license by Peterson's.

About The Thomson Corporation and Peterson's

With revenues of US$7.2 billion, The Thomson Corporation (www.thomson.com) is a leading global provider of integrated information solutions for business, education, and professional customers. Its Learning businesses and brands (www.thomsonlearning.com) serve the needs of individuals, learning institutions, and corporations with products and services for both traditional and distributed learning.

Peterson's, part of The Thomson Corporation, is one of the nation's most respected providers of lifelong learning online resources, software, reference guides, and books. The Education Supersite[SM] at www.petersons.com—the Internet's most heavily traveled education resource—has searchable databases and interactive tools for contacting U.S.-accredited institutions and programs. In addition, Peterson's serves more that 105 million education consumers annually.

For more information, contact Peterson's, 2000 Lenox Drive, Lawrenceville, NJ 08648; 800-338-3282; or find us on the World Wide Web at: www.petersons.com/about

Contents

PART I

THE FEDERAL
CAREER SEARCH PROCESS

Trying to land a federal job can be sort of like fishing on the ocean. You have this huge mass of murky water, and while you know that somewhere in the depths there are probably hungry fish that may bite, you can't predict when, where, or even if they will.

The federal government is like the ocean. With 3 million employees, it's huge. And like the dark ocean waters, it is rather difficult to understand because it offers few real glimpses into its inner workings. As a job seeker, you cast your line blindly into the turbid mass, only to lose the bait, pull up an old boot, or let a tempting nibble get away.

If the waters were suddenly crystal clear, wouldn't that make all the difference? Then you could actually *see* the fish swimming down below. All you would have to do is size them up, choose your favorite fish, and dangle the line in front of his nose. If he's hungry and the bait is right, he'll bite.

Federal Jobs: The Ultimate Guide attempts to take the murky federal waters and make them clear. It provides a vision of how the government agencies are structured, whom they hire, and how they hire. All you have to do is size them up, choose your favorite agency or agencies, and get the bait right!

Federal Jobs: The Ultimate Guide is intended to help federal job seekers go about a job search in the simplest fashion, by breaking down the massive federal monolith into workable subunits. Not only does this make the search more manageable, it also allows job seekers to follow their interests and apply their backgrounds to specific agencies of interest. Thus, they lead *targeted* job searches that are likely to reach a successful conclusion more quickly than a random shot-in-the-dark approach.

By beginning with the Career Search Index in the back of this book, a job seeker first discovers how many federal agencies there are that might fit his or her needs in terms of types of positions offered, the mission of the agency, and the location of the agency. The job seeker can then focus his or her search on these target agencies rather than browsing blindly through job listings.

Other aspects of *Federal Jobs: The Ultimate Guide* can be incorporated into a successful federal job search. This book teaches you to:

★ Understand where the best federal opportunities might be

★ Learn how special hiring programs might work for you

★ Compute the salary you might expect to get upon entering federal service

★ Use the power of "information networking" to help you avoid the lengthy application process

★ Write a federal resume, OF 612, or SF 171 that stands out from the crowd and wins you a job

Good luck in your job search. Take control of your own destiny, and reel in a big one!

CHAPTER 1

SO YOU WANT A FEDERAL CAREER?

So you're thinking you might like to work for the federal government? Good choice! From astronaut to zoologist, the federal government is the largest, most broad based, and perhaps the most multifaceted employer in the nation. One look at the scope of its work will tell you why: the government's responsibilities range from highways to human rights, from pollution control to arms control, from the ocean floor to outer space. In short, federal employees ensure the safety, health, and quality of life of all Americans.

Surveys indicate that the majority of federal employees enjoy their jobs. And, while many workers transfer from agency to agency within the government, few are willing to trade federal employment for a private sector job in corporate America. What does the federal government have to offer that makes it such a great place to work?

Ten Good Reasons to Start a Federal Career

1. **Stability.** Today's world of work is quite different than it was in our fathers' and grandfathers' generation. Back then, the "company man" mentality was the status quo, and it was typical for a person to work for only one company from graduation day to retirement. In today's world, the thought of spending one's entire career with a single corporation seems entirely unrealistic. Organizations are so busy reorganizing and acquiring and downsizing and *changing,* that jobs are constantly fluctuating and are in danger of being eliminated or restructured. Because of this, people's career paths must often be restructured too, whether they like the idea or not.

   While change is rampant in the corporate world, the federal workforce is relatively stable. Private-sector industries respond to fluctuations in the economy in a constant quest to strengthen the bottom line, while the federal government operates in response to a payroll budget that is set by Congress and the President prior to each fiscal year. Thus, the federal government runs a steady course, adhering to a preset payroll budget, while the corporate world must constantly adjust to meet profit targets.

A federal agency is not going to be "bought out" by another agency, or gobbled up in a hostile takeover. As a federal employee, you are not nearly as likely to experience "career turbulence" as you are in the corporate workplace. The peace of mind that the federal work world offers is an important aspect to any job—just ask anybody who has experienced a sudden and unwanted separation from a job they had planned to keep.

2. **Challenging work.** Federal employees often work at the cutting edge of science, technology, and public policy. The Commerce Department's National Institute of Standards and Technology, for example, performs some of the world's most advanced research in computer-automated manufacturing, semiconductor processing, and mechanical behavior. Similar state-of-the-art work is conducted (and in some cases may *only* be conducted) at federal labs across the country. Knowledge gained from such pursuits is applied to curing diseases such as cancer and AIDS, creating heartier crops, designing transatmospheric space planes, and finding new sources of energy.

If you don't have a technical degree, there's still plenty of challenging work. Specialists in law enforcement, education, housing, and economics are formulating, implementing, and evaluating public policies designed to alleviate crime, drug abuse, illiteracy, homelessness, and poverty.

3. **Location.** Working for the federal government means your choice of work sites is virtually unlimited. Contrary to popular belief, most federal jobs are *not* located in Washington, DC. In fact, 85 percent of all federal civilian jobs are located *outside* of the nation's capital. What this means for prospective employees is that federal jobs can be found in the largest cities and the smallest towns all across the U.S., and even around the world. The Interior Department's National Park Service provides a good example. From New York City's Gateway National Recreation Area to Alaska's Noatak National Preserve, Park Service employees can be found in the most and least densely populated areas of the nation.

4. **Responsibility.** Federal employees tend to get considerable responsibility early in their careers. Promotions usually come quickly, and new employees may find themselves managing programs after just three years on the job. But you may not even have to wait that long. In many instances, you're given important assignments from the first day on the job. New attorneys at the Justice Department, for example, may immediately find themselves arguing motions in court, taking depositions, and cross-examining witnesses.

5. **Job mobility and diverse career paths.** Finding your niche in the federal government can be fairly easy. Its size gives you upward mobility to advance within a particular field and lateral mobility to explore different occupations. Many federal employees transfer between regional and headquarters offices or to different agencies altogether.

6. **Flexible hours.** Many federal agencies offer flexible work schedules. While you must work 80 hours in a two-week pay period to be considered a full-time employee, how you allocate those hours is up to you. For example, some federal employees work 10-hour days, four days a week.

7. **Good benefits.** Federal benefits are quite generous. Federal employees receive paid time off for ten national holidays and receive twenty days of vacation per year after just three years of employment. Retirement benefits, health insurance, and sick leave are also generous. And one of the best aspects of federal employment is that employees have the opportunity to change jobs, offices, and agencies and still retain their full federal benefits and service years.

8. **Workforce diversity.** The federal workforce across the nation is extremely diverse. In fact, more than 30 percent of employees in non postal executive branch agencies are members of minority groups. Equal employment laws, merit principles, and well-defined grievance procedures help ensure fairness in hiring and promotions and protect employees from arbitrary and capricious decisions on the part of supervisors.

9. **Workplace environment.** While the federal government may not be known for having the cushiest offices or the most upscale surroundings, many agencies offer such amenities as on-site fitness centers and child-care facilities. Even smaller federal agencies can offer these perks because they are a part of the government system.

10. **Public Service.** When working for the federal government, you're not just catering to your personal interests—you're serving the greater good of the nation. Many federal employees derive satisfaction by knowing that a group of people or a particular program is better off because of their work. In the years ahead, the country will face some extraordinary challenges: poverty, global pollution, racism, terrorism, nuclear proliferation, and much more. Your time and talent will help ensure successful outcomes. The hours may be long, and the tasks enormous, but one thing is clear: You can make a difference!

Organization of the Federal Government

The first three articles of the Constitution divide the federal government into three branches:

1. the legislative

2. the executive

3. the judiciary

   This division results in the separation of powers that ensures our democratic system of government. Simply put, the *legislative* branch makes the laws, the *executive* branch implements them, and the *judiciary* enforces them.

   With about 3 million employees, the executive branch is the largest branch of the federal government. This includes 1,946,684 executive nonpostal employees and 867,863 postal employees. This is followed by the legislative and judicial branches, which have a combined total of about 62,000 employees.

Competitive vs. Excepted Service

About 80 percent of federal jobs fall under the Competitive Service and are filled on the basis of an applicant's education and work experience. An applicant's qualifications are assessed based on a standard application form (such as an OF 612 or SF 171), an applicant's resume, or a written examination required for particular positions. Only a relative handful of federal jobs require applicants to take a written examination. Competitive Service jobs are regulated by the U.S. Office of Personnel Management (OPM) and must conform to certain merit principles ensuring that all federal employees are treated fairly and are protected from arbitrary treatment by supervisors. These merit principles help form the government-wide standards by which Competitive Service job vacancies are written and announced, and how job applicants are evaluated, hired, and paid.

Most of the remaining federal positions make up what is known as the Excepted Service. Agencies in the Excepted Service are excepted from Competitive Service regulations, and have the authority to develop their own hiring policies. Though excepted from OPM's regulations, many positions in the Excepted Service are governed by merit principles and have the same protections as those positions in the Competitive Service.

The agencies and occupations comprising the Excepted Service include:

* Agency for International Development

* Board of Governors of the Federal Reserve System

* Central Intelligence Agency

* Defense Intelligence Agency

* Federal Bureau of Investigation

* General Accounting Office

* Library of Congress

* National Security Agency

* Nuclear Regulatory Commission

* Postal Rate Commission

* State Department (Foreign Service positions)

* Tennessee Valley Authority

* U.S. Postal Service

* Attorney positions throughout the government

* Chaplain positions throughout the government

There are more than 200 federal agencies, departments, bureaus, and other organizations that make up the federal government. Some of these are small, such as the Postal Rate Commission, with only about 50 permanent employees. Others, such as the Social Security Administration and the Department of Veterans Affairs, are huge, with more than 200,000 employees located throughout the nation. Because of the massive size and scope of the federal government, it is wise to narrow your job search to only those agencies that fit your needs. A quick search through the Career Search Index in the back of this book will enable you to identify the agencies you are interested in according to mission, location, and skills or interests. Chapter 3 gives details on how to go about your federal job search beginning with the Career Search Index and taking easy steps through the application process. Happy hunting!

CHAPTER 2

THE FEDERAL EMPLOYMENT OUTLOOK: WHERE THE JOBS ARE LIKELY TO BE

With the tragic events of September 11, 2001, came a shift in emphasis in federal priorities. While past administrations focused attention on such important national policies as education, health care, or winning the drug war, our country no longer has the luxury to concentrate attention on single national issues. The federal government must now shift its gaze to the global community, with a new focus on national and international security issues, emergency preparedness, intelligence gathering, and preventive screening.

New Needs for Security Organizations

The new focus can be seen in the creation of many bold new departments, organizations, and hiring initiatives. The Department of Transportation's *Transportation Security Administration (TSA)* provides security and safety at our nation's ports, airports, railways, and other critical assets that are key to the free movement of passengers and goods throughout the country. This new agency is creating tens of thousands of new federal positions for airport baggage screeners, as well as special agent and law enforcement positions.

Even more special agent and law enforcement positions are needed to staff the *Department of Homeland Security (DHS)*, a cabinet-level organization with a potential workforce of 170,000. This new department is responsible for the prevention of terrorist attacks within the U.S., the reduction of American vulnerability to terrorism, and assisting in the recovery from terrorist attacks if they do occur in the United States.

Both of these organizations are in need of personnel such as *Intelligence Analysts* and *Special Agents*. And, since virtually everything in these two new organizations must be built from scratch, thousands of new federal jobs will open up in all areas of support work, such as administrative staff, human resources personnel, and IT employees. A complete list of the most common support positions, which tend to be in demand throughout the government, is found in Chapter 00, including details on the duties these federal positions entail.

Growth in Current Agencies

In conjunction with the two newly formed security organizations, our nation's current security and intelligence agencies, such as the *FBI, CIA,* and *NSA,* plan to increase their staff of *Intelligence Analysts, Cryptologists,* and *Special Agents.* Agencies responsible for our country's borders, such as *U.S. Customs and Immigration and Naturalization* are also expected to beef up their numbers, hiring more *Border Patrol Officers* and *Immigration Agents.* Such tremendous growth in the federal government has not been seen for generations.

Critical Shortage of Language Skills

Also related to our nation's newfound sense of urgency for national security is a need for people with foreign language skills. Job titles such as *Linguist, Translator,* and *Interpreter* are in huge demand. More than 70 agencies require employees with foreign language skills, and many of these agencies are experiencing a critical shortage of employees with the required abilities. Agencies with a focus on intelligence, law enforcement, and diplomacy all require such individuals. Specific agencies include the *FBI,* the *CIA,* the *Foreign Commercial Service,* the *Department of Defense,* and the *State Department.*

Diplomatic Security

The *U.S. Capitol Police,* the *Secret Service,* and the *Bureau of Diplomatic Security* (part of the *State Department),* are also likely to be increasing the size of their workforce in response to government and national security needs. These agencies work to protect the President, the Vice President, and other high-level government staff and their families, as well as visiting diplomats and their families.

Countering Bioterrorism

To guard against the threat of bioterrorism, the *Food and Drug Administration* introduced a Hiring Initiative for Countering Bioterrorism. The *National Institutes of Health (NIH)*, the *FDA*, and the *Centers for Disease Control (CDC)* are looking for physicians and scientists to help the nation guard against potential bioterrorist attacks.

Air Safety

Sky Marshals are returning to the skies to keep air transportation safer for the millions of travelers who fly aboard American commercial aircraft. Now called *Federal Air Marshals*, this elite corps of employees is hired by the *Federal Aviation Administration (FAA)*, and must pass rigorous selection and training programs before flying a mission.

National Preparedness

Related to homeland security is our newly recognized need for national preparedness. In response to this need, the *Federal Emergency Management Agency (FEMA)* will be hiring *Emergency Management Specialists* to assist state, local, and tribal governments in planning and coordinating disaster response efforts.

Health-Care Workers

While homeland security issues currently have the overriding attention of our nation and our government, there are other aspects of our nation that fall under the scope of the federal government that must remain in focus. For example, there is an ongoing strong demand for *Nurses* in the federal workforce, especially at the *Department of Veterans Affairs*, which has more than 200,000 health-care workers in hundreds of medical centers and facilities across the nation.

Shortage at the Federal Aviation Administration (FAA)

Air Traffic Controllers, already one of the largest positions in the federal government with more than 30,000 workers nationwide, will soon be in great demand as more than half of all frontline controllers will be eligible for retirement in the next 10 years. According to a recent report from the General Accounting Office, the *FAA* will need to hire thousands of *Air Traffic Controllers* over the next decade to replace the 15,000 frontline controllers who are eligible for retirement by 2010. Also, 2,000 additional controllers will need to be in place by 2010 due to increased air traffic.

The Securities and Exchange Commission (SEC)

Due to recent high-profile accounting scandals and growing concerns regarding corporate accounting practices, the Securities and Exchange Commission will likely be beefing up its enforcement side by hiring additional accountants and attorneys as well as compliance examiners with backgrounds in accounting or finance. These positions will be located in Washington, DC, and in regional offices nationwide.

Other Ongoing Needs

Throughout the federal government, there is an ongoing need for *Attorneys*. Continuing efforts to contract out federal activities may also mean an increasing need for *Contracting and Procurement Specialists*. Attorney and contracting positions are found in nearly every federal agency across the nation; you will find details on these positions in Chapter 00.

Growth at Entry Levels

The greatest demand for these positions and other professional positions in the federal government is likely to be at the entry levels (GS-5, -7, and -9), due to the fact that most agencies tend to promote internally. However, this may change over time, given the administration's efforts to encourage agencies to open up more jobs to people outside the federal government.

Job Outlook Strong

This tremendous current surge in federal employment makes it a great time to be searching for a federal job. The job outlook is strong, and the prospects for employment are excellent. If you have the skills, motivation, and commitment that federal jobs require, you are likely to find a rewarding and meaningful career with Uncle Sam.

CHAPTER 3

HOW TO LAND A FEDERAL JOB

Just beginning the federal job search process? Take heart! Landing a federal job today is much easier than it was just a short time ago. The notorious centralized "register" system has all but disappeared, so job seekers can now apply directly to the agencies for which they'd like to work. This new system empowers job seekers to choose where they'd like to work and grants agencies the power to choose whom they'd like to hire. Also, many federal examinations have been done away with, so that fewer than 20 percent of all nonpostal service jobs require civil service tests. This speeds up and simplifies the federal hiring process to a great degree. All you need is a little time, a little energy, and a bit of determination to be on your way to a federal career.

Don't jump into your job search blindly, however. It is wise to gather information and develop a strategy before you enter into the federal job search arena. Following the tips contained in these chapters will help you narrow your focus and give you a solid step-by-step game plan to guide you to the federal job that is right for you.

The Federal Job Search

Most people are painfully familiar with searching for a job in corporate America. They know all about shuffling through the want ads and wandering door-to-door, resume in hand. But how do you go about finding those elusive *federal* jobs? Does a federal job search resemble a private-sector search?

Consider the typical job search in corporate America. Most job seekers start with the classified ads, a convenient, inexpensive, low-risk way to look for job openings. There is nothing wrong with browsing through the classifieds—people do land jobs this way. Unfortunately, applying to jobs that announced their openings to the general public puts you in the midst of a huge amount of competition. If you are reading the ad, it is likely that many other qualified candidates are reading it too. This "front door" approach to job hunting can be frustrating, because it puts you in the middle of the stiffest competition for the job.

Other private-sector job seekers try the "back door" approach to job hunting. They try tapping into the "hidden" job market. They search for the jobs that have not yet been advertised, that perhaps have not yet solidified in the minds of the hiring managers. These are the jobs for which they figure they can stand alone as qualified candidates because no one else knows the jobs exist. Tapping into the "hidden" job market involves networking, making telephone and personal contacts, and involves more risk to the ego than simply reading the morning newspaper.

How do these standard job-hunting approaches compare to a *federal* job search? Surprisingly, a federal job search is quite similar to a private-sector job search, and in many ways, federal searches are even easier. Although most people don't realize it, both the front door and back door job search strategies can work in the federal sector just as they do in the private sector. Most people, however, are not sure how to find the "classified ads" for federal jobs (they aren't usually listed in the daily paper), and they are unaware that a "hidden" job market exists for federal jobs.

This book gives you the know-how to navigate the federal hiring system effectively. It shows you how to find those elusive federal job announcements, how to sift through them to find the ones that fit you best, and how to interpret the complex government hiring terminology that can be confusing and misleading. It also helps you to explore the opportunities that can be found through networking, and provides practical tips on how to network in the federal government effectively.

> **TIP: A wise federal job seeker will work both methods concurrently. While he will not ignore the "front door" job announcements that appeal to him, he will also pick up the telephone and make important "back door" contacts that may help him unearth jobs that he wouldn't otherwise have found.**

In the following chapters, we explore both the front door and back door federal job search strategies. Whichever you use, the first thing you must do is get focused on what you want to do and where you want to work.

The Front Door: 5 Simple Steps

A basic federal job search is easy as long as you know where to look! Follow these simple steps to target your search to the agencies where you want to work.

Step 1: Explore the Charts

As you begin your federal job search, realize that the federal government is a huge entity. With more than 2,700,000 employees working for about 200 federal agencies across the country and around the globe, it is by far the largest single employer in the United States. Each year, the federal government hires an average of over 300,000 new employees to replace workers who are leaving. These positions are spread across the nation, from quiet rural hamlets to the biggest bustling cities. In order to make sense of such a giant conglomerate, you must first break the federal government down into manageable, distinct parts. This is easy to do by using the Career Search Index in the back of this book.

Suppose you know you want to do environmental research on the northern West Coast, but you wonder if there is a federal agency there that is involved in your field. Or maybe you want to work in Boston, developing policy for an agency with an international scope, but you aren't sure which local agencies have such a mission. Maybe you simply want to know which federal agencies have offices in Denver, or which agencies hire people with a background in criminal justice.

There's no better place to find the answers to such questions than the Career Search Index on pages 00 through 00. This series of charts provides a complete list of the federal agencies, their missions, where they are located, and what kinds of people they hire.

How to Use the Charts

The Career Search Index contains three charts that allow you to cross-reference your skills, experiences, values, interests, and geographic preferences to determine which federal agencies and what positions within those agencies appeal to you. Here is a quick guide to the charts:

1. The Occupational Interest Chart. Begin with the Occupational Interest Chart that starts on page 00. Read down the left column to find an Occupational Interest that fits your experience, education, skills, and/or interests. Maybe your background is in chemical engineering, economics, or marketing. Follow the chart horizontally from your occupational interest to reach a series of

dots. Follow the dotted columns up to find the acronym of a federal agency that *tends to hire people with education/experience in that field.* Write down the page numbers for those agencies on a sheet of paper. Later, when you look up the agency profiles, you'll explore those agencies in detail.

2.   The Agency Mission Chart. Now turn to the Agency Mission Chart beginning on page 00. Read down the left column to find the mission description of various agencies. Perhaps you want to work for an agency devoted to scientific research, or perhaps for one that focuses on environmental issues. Or maybe an international emphasis appeals to you. Jot down the page number of each agency that the chart lists as having a mission of interest to you.

3.   The Agency Locations Chart. Finally, take a look at the Agency Locations Chart beginning on page 00. Maybe you have in mind a specific part of the country in which you'd like to work. Do you want to stay out west where your family is? Have you always dreamed of moving to New York City? Do you hope to live by the ocean somewhere? Refer to the Locations Chart. Jot down the page numbers of those agencies that fit your location preferences.

Cross-Reference

Now check to see if any of those page numbers from the three charts coincide. Do any agencies show up on all three of them? If they do, that means that the agency profiles found on those pages meet your needs in terms of occupational interest, agency mission, and location. These are the agency profiles that you should explore first.

Positions in Demand

There are certain positions in the federal government that are very common. They exist in almost every agency and are intrinsic to its internal administrative functions. For example, you could find a *Program Analyst, Human Resources Specialist,* or *IT Specialist* at almost any agency, and the job description at each would be very similar to the others.

It is important to note that because these positions are universal, we have not addressed them individually in the charts or in the agency profiles. Instead, you can find a list and a standard description of these positions in demand in Chapter 8.

Step 2: Explore the Profiles

Begin your exploration of the agencies that suit you best by turning to the agency profiles on pages 00 through 00. These profiles provide specific details on each federal agency, including job descriptions for the positions they hire most, departmental divisions, locations of regional offices, and telephone numbers and addresses of agency personnel offices. Explore the profiles a bit to see if any look especially enticing. Review each agency carefully. Check to see if there are job titles that interest you. Do you like the size of the agency? Does it seem to offer what you are looking for in a work setting? Does it have regional offices in the locations you prefer?

High Five

Choose about five of the federal agencies that are highest on your list in terms of your needs and interests. Write them down so that you remember them. With these five agencies firmly in mind, you are now ready to move your job search forward another step.

Step 3: Locate Job Openings

The five agencies that you identified as your "best fit" agencies probably have job listings on their Web site. The agency Web site located just under the agency name of each profile is the best way to find job openings at your five agencies of top interest.

When it comes to the federal hiring process, the Internet is tailor-made. While Internet job searches in the private sector may not always yield results, it is the number one place to conduct a job search for federal employment. Why does it work so well? Here are a few reasons:

1. The federal government generally does not advertise its job openings in the local newspaper, as so many private-sector corporations do. Thus, the Internet is nearly a single-source outlet for federal job announcements.

2. Every sizeable agency in the federal government has a Web site, and nearly all provide a list of current vacancies within their agency (or a link to current vacancies).

3. You can find out about openings in a timely manner, rather than having to wait for (and pay for) a biweekly publication of federal job openings.

4. Many agencies even provide online application forms so that the application writing and mailing processes are greatly simplified.

5. You never have to leave your home to find federal job listings. No trips to the library or federal personnel center!

6. Job announcements are available 24 hours a day, 7 days a week, so you can search for them at your convenience.

7. Since federal jobs are located throughout the nation, the Internet is a great way to reach a national audience easily.

> *TIP: Make sure to give the agency Web sites a generous review. Don't simply rush directly to the current job listings without first reading more information about what the agency does and how it accomplishes its goals. Most agency Web sites are full of details that will help you gain a clearer perspective of the agency's mission and goals, and this knowledge will likely help you to write a more impressive and targeted resume or federal application.*

Internet Sites with Federal Job Information

Besides individual agency Web site job listings, there are other sites that offer helpful information and some have government-wide job listings in a searchable database. Many sites are available free of charge, and others offer various services on a subscription or fee basis. Here's a list of some of the biggest and best:

✮ www.usajobs.opm.gov

An excellent source of current federal listings, this Office of Personnel Management's (OPM) centralized federal jobs site provides access to full-text job announcements, electronic and hard copy application forms, and a resume builder that can create and email federal resumes. It also allows you to conduct searches and create a profile, so that USAJOBS will notify you by e-mail when new job listings are posted that meet your search criteria. This is a must-stop site for any federal job seeker.

While this site has much to offer, keep in mind that it is not a complete listing of all federal jobs across the nation. Only those job listings that have been submitted by the hiring agencies will be accessible on OPM's site.

✳   www.firstgov.gov

This is the official U.S. government Web portal. It provides links to many of the federal agencies in the three branches and provides an overview of federal government organization.

✳   www.StudentJobs.gov

Loaded with information you need if you are looking for a student job in the federal government. Learn about co-ops, internships, summer jobs, the Outstanding Scholars Program, volunteer opportunities, and plenty of part-time and full-time jobs.

✳   The Federal Web Locator (www.infoctr.edu/fwl/)

Provided by the Villanova Center for Information Law and Policy, this Web site provides links to hundreds of government agency Web sites.

✳   www.fedworld.gov

FedWorld is a searchable database that is updated weekly, allowing you to search for open federal jobs by series, grade, and state. It uses the same jobs database as the OPM's USAJOBS, so be aware that this is not a complete listing of all federal job openings.

✳   www.fedjobs.com

A searchable job database compiled by the Federal Research Service (FRS) in Vienna, VA, the job listings on this site are accessible only by subscription. While it claims to have the most complete listing of federal job openings, remember that most of these openings are available for free through the various agency Web sites. For subscription rates, contact 1-800-822-JOBS. Note that the FRS also publishes a biweekly job listing called Federal Career Opportunities. Subscriptions are offered on a daily, 3-month, or unlimited basis.

✳   http://jobsfed.com

In addition to federal job listings, this site provides information on federal employment, a resume builder, and a job-matching service, all available for a fee.

✳   http://federaljobs.net

This site provides links to some agency Web sites and gives brief information and statistics on federal employment topics.

✯ www.attorneyjobs.com

An online listing of attorney and law-related jobs with the federal government and other employers, it is available by subscription from Federal Reports, P.O. Box 3709, Georgetown Station, Washington, DC 20007; (202) 393-3311.

✯ www.govexec.com

As the online edition of *Government Executive* magazine, it contains many articles on current federal issues and a section called "jobs and careers," which targets federal hiring needs and trends. A must-stop informational site for serious job searchers.

✯ www.aspanet.org

This is the Web site for the American Society for Public Administrators. It has links to federal and state government jobs, as well as links to public service–oriented jobs in the private sector.

> **TIP: If you don't have access to the Internet at home, consider making a visit to your local library, schools, community college, or state unemployment office for a chance to log on and review the Web sites. Another option is to visit a USAJOBS touch-screen computer kiosk, which are located at OPM offices and in most federal buildings nationwide.**

Printed Sources of Federal Job Listings

If you aren't able to find Internet access, there are still other ways to identify federal job openings:

State Unemployment Agency

State unemployment agencies are required to post federal job listings. Visit your local agency and ask for assistance if you don't see the listings posted. Look in the blue pages of your local phone book for the nearest agency location.

Federal Career Opportunities (FCO)

Federal Career Opportunities
Federal Research Service
P.O. Box 1059
Vienna, VA 22183
Toll Free: (800) 822-5627
E-mail: *info@fedjobs.com*

A biweekly publication listing thousands of open federal jobs. Log on to their Web site at www.fedjobs.com for subscription rates. FCO may offer the most complete list of current federal job openings, but be aware that many of the same federal vacancy listings are now easily available for free at the OPM Web site. FCO is commonly available in libraries and bookstores, so try browsing through a copy before subscribing.

Federal Jobs Digest (FJD)

Breakthrough Publications
P.O. Box 594
Millwood, NY 10546
Toll Free: (800) 824-5000
http://jobsfed.com

FJD offers federal job listings on a biweekly basis. It's a good resource for news on federal employment happenings, trends, etc., but it may provide a slightly less extensive list of current job openings. Widely available in libraries or by subscription. FJD also offers a job matching service that compares your background to federal job requirements, and tells you which job titles match your qualifications. You learn job titles and grade levels, but not current vacancies.

The Federal Times

6883 Commercial Drive
Springfield, VA 22159
Toll Free: (800) 368-6718
http://www.federaltimes.com

A weekly newspaper with current information about various federal topics. Because its target audience is current federal employees, it offers good inside information on federal trends. The list of current job opportunities is not extensive, but this is a solid resource for federal job seekers from the GS-7 level through SES positions.

Other Sources of Federal Job Listings

Agency Recruitment Offices

People often assume that federal agencies are completely unapproachable when it comes to walk-in job seekers. But many federal recruitment or personnel offices are accessible to walk-in visitors, posting current job openings on bulletin boards and providing vacancy announcements and blank application forms to take home.

Agency Job Hotlines

Job hotline numbers are located at the end of many agency profiles. These automated telephone messages give information on current vacancies within specific agencies. Often they allow you to request that vacancy announcements be sent to you for details on particular positions.

USAJOBS Automated Telephone System

Telephone: (912) 757-3000 or (202) 606-2700
TDD: (912) 744-2299

An interactive voice response system that provides job seekers with access to government-wide current job vacancies, employment information and a chance to order employment forms and applications. Available 24 hours a day.

FEDFAX

Using a Touch-Tone phone or fax machine, you can choose to have certain employment-related documents or forms faxed to you. Note that it does not contain current job listings. Available 24 hours a day at these numbers: Atlanta: (404) 331-5267; Denver: (303) 969-7764; Detroit: (313) 226-2593; San Francisco: (415) 744-7002; Washington, DC: (202) 606-2600.

Federal Executive Boards (FEBs)

FEBs provide information on all federal offices within the local geographic area. They are located in major metropolitan areas throughout the U.S., offering job seekers a chance to grasp the potential federal employment possibilities that are in the local area. Call your local FEB and request listings of federal offices in your area:

Albuquerque–Santa Fe, NM
www.albuquerque-santafe.feb.gov
(505) 845-4238

Atlanta, GA
http://r4.gsa.gov/febatlanta.htm
(404) 331-4400

Baltimore, MD
www.baltimore.feb.org
(410) 962-4047

Boston, MA
www.boston.feb.gov
(617) 565-6769

Buffalo, NY
www.buffalo.feb.gov
(716) 551-5655

Chicago, IL
www.chicago.feb.gov
(312) 353-6790

Cincinnati, OH
www.cincinnati.feb.gov
(513) 684-2101

Cleveland, OH
www.grs.nasa.gov/WWW/OHR/FEB
(216) 433-9460

Dallas–Ft. Worth, TX
www.dallas-fortworth.feb.gov
(817) 684-5370

Denver, CO
www.denver.feb.gov
(303) 676-7009

Detroit, MI
(313) 226-3534

Honolulu-Pacific, HI
www.honolulu-pacific.feb.gov
(808) 541-2637

Houston, TX
www.houston.feb.gov
(713) 209-4524

Kansas City, MO
http://kcfeb.gsa.gov
(816) 823-5100

Los Angeles, CA
www.losangeles.feb.gov
(562) 980-3445

Miami, FL
www.miami.feb.gov
(305) 536-4344

St. Paul, MN
www.minnesota.feb.gov
(612) 713-7200

Newark, NJ
www.newark.feb.gov
(973) 645-6217

New Orleans, LA
www.nfc.usda.gov/feb
(504) 255-5420

New York, NY
www.newyorkcity.feb.gov
(212) 264-1890

Oklahoma City, OK
www.oklahoma.feb.gov
(405) 231-4167

Portland, OR
www.portland.feb.gov
(503) 326-2060

Philadelphia, PA
(215) 597-2766

Pittsburgh, PA
www.pittsburgh.feb.gov
(412) 395-6220

St. Louis, MO
www.stlouis.feb.gov
(314) 539-6312

San Antonio, TX
www.sanantonio.feb.gov
(210) 308-4520

San Francisco, CA
www.gsa.gov/r9feb
(510) 637-1103

Seattle, WA
www.seattle.feb.gov
(206) 220-6171

Step 4: Read the Vacancy Announcement

A federal job seeker who spots a job opening must never apply to that job without first reading the vacancy announcement. This extra step to the federal search process is often overlooked by job seekers because vacancy announcements don't exist in the private sector.

Thus, the private-sector front door job search looks something like this:

Discover job listing > Send in resume > Interview for job

While the federal front door job search looks like this:

Discover job listing > Get vacancy announcement > Send in application (SF 171, OF 612, or Federal Resume) > Interview for job

The vacancy announcement is a written statement published by a federal agency describing one or more vacant positions within that agency. It gives detailed specifics on what the position entails, what qualifications an applicant must have in order to be considered for the job, and information on how to apply for the job.

The vacancy announcement tells you in quite specific terms whether or not you are qualified, in terms of years, type of experience, and educational background for the job you saw listed. It also tells you who can be considered for the position. These facts will not be spelled out in the original job listing but are sure to be detailed in the vacancy announcement. It is, therefore, important to read the vacancy announcement before sending in an application to avoid wasting your time applying to jobs for which you will not be considered.

Perhaps most importantly, a vacancy announcement is your best source of information on exactly what type of candidate the hiring manager is looking for to fill a position. Reading the vacancy announcement gives you insight that will help you highlight those particulars of your work experience that are most crucial to the job you are applying for. See Chapter 5 for more details on Vacancy Announcements.

> **TIP:** *For positions that offer multiple openings at several grade levels, it doesn't hurt to send in applications for each GS level you think you may qualify for. This way, you increase your chances of landing a job. While you may be disqualified at the GS-9 level, you can still be considered at the GS-7 level. Your multiple applications may be identical, except for indicating the different GS levels for which you are applying.*

Step 5: Send in Your Application

When you read the vacancy announcement for the position you have interest in, you learn the method for submitting your application. Some agencies still prefer that you send a hard copy of your resume or OF 612 application form through the postal system. Many agencies, however, are now turning to electronic alternatives such as e-mail for their hiring needs. Federal employers are learning that electronic applications provide a quicker way to review an applicant's qualifications.

Each agency has its own preferred submission method, and those may change with time or according to the position you are applying for. The main point is that you must check the vacancy announcement for instructions on how to apply and then follow those instructions to the letter. Always make sure that your application arrives by (or is postmarked by) the closing date stated on the vacancy announcement. There is no room for error here. If you miss the closing date, you miss the job.

> **TIP:** *Continue to send in application packages as vacancy announcements become available. Keep checking the Web sites of your top agencies of interest to discover the latest job listings, and stay updated on federal trends by logging on to some of the other sites listed earlier. The more connected you are, the better your chances of catching your opportunity when it comes!*

CHAPTER 4

THE INSIDE SCOOP: USE THE BACK DOOR TO LAND A JOB FAST

The five steps in Chapter 3 describe the "front door" approach to landing a federal job. While this method is certainly effective, it can be quite slow and laden with paperwork. If you are serious about getting a job, you should fortify the straightforward front-door approach with a back-door networking campaign.

Rather than waiting for the wheels of the federal vacancy system to grind slowly forward and patiently awaiting new job postings to apply to, consider taking control of the job search game yourself. Knock on the back door and start talking to people *before* a vacancy is announced. After all, if you are responding to a posted job listing, chances are that other people saw it and are responding to it too. Stand out from the crowd of applicants by knocking on the back door and letting the federal hiring officials create a job just for you.

Consider This

Who would you lay your money on to find a job faster? Would it be Hank, who writes up a terrific OF 612, then mails it in to a few agencies and sits at home awaiting the magic phone call? Or would it be Phil, who is busy making friends and establishing contacts with important people in the agencies he likes? No contest! Phil wins hands down because he will hear about hiring needs in the agency before the jobs are ever posted to the general public. This way, Phil short-circuits the competition by putting himself in the right place at the right time and grabbing up the job he wants before the competition even enters the picture.

Although it is tempting to conduct a job search while sitting at your home computer in your sweatpants and slippers, you just can't manage a successful search without putting some energy into talking to people. A written summary of your skills simply isn't a good enough substitute for the real thing—yourself, live and in person, creating an impression on the people with whom you hope to work.

The reason that networking is so vital to the job search is that the human factor is such a big part of every job. It doesn't matter how impressive your genius in engineering is; if you can't get along with your coworkers, you won't be able to do your job well. And hiring managers know this. They figure they can teach an employee the practical, detail stuff. But they can't teach someone with an abrasive personality to have a harmonious relationship with the other people in the office. And if you don't have harmony in the office, you can't produce results.

So hiring managers, whether consciously or subconsciously, often base their hiring decisions not so much on practical skills as on interpersonal skills. For them, determining whether a person is qualified for a job includes determining whether that person "fits in" with others in the office. So if you, as a job seeker, manage to establish rapport with someone who has hiring authority, you have just dramatically increased your chances of getting the job you want.

Think about it. If you had the responsibility to hire someone, wouldn't you prefer to know as much as possible about the person you want to hire? Hiring officials do know how to make the system work for them. They know how to avoid the impersonal, rigid application process if they have in mind a talented candidate whom they want to hire.

Help Good Things Happen

Remember those five or so agencies that you targeted when you looked through the Career Search Index charts? Review those again for a minute because they will be the heart of your back-door entry into the federal government.

As opposed to the front-door application system, the back-door job search doesn't begin with the lists of current federal job openings. It begins with a clear decision about where you want to work. It begins with your own efforts to make a good job happen.

Opening the Back Door

> *My friend Mia has a wonderful job at an agency within the Department of the Interior. When I asked her how she got hired, she told me that she knew someone at the agency who recommended her for the job. That probably doesn't come as a big surprise to you. Many of my clients say to me with a touch of*

discouragement, "To get a job, it doesn't matter what you know, but whom you know." But when I pressed Mia for more information, it turns out that she didn't know a soul at the Department of the Interior until she decided she wanted to work there. Then she made it a point to establish professional contacts there, to get to know people who could give her the inside scoop on Interior occupations in her field. Basically, she networked her way in.

So if you are discouraged that you don't know someone with connections to federal agencies, *get* to know someone. Are we suggesting that you pick up the phone and beg some stranger who works at a federal agency to help you get a job? Not at all. There is an easy, painless way to make connections in the federal government that is a solid first step in landing a job there. We call it "Information Networking." Here's what you do.

Information Networking

Start with the five agencies you've chosen from the Career Search Index. As you look at them, think of yourself not as a job seeker but as an information gatherer, a researcher, a journalism student, perhaps, who is writing a paper on certain positions at certain federal agencies. You are out to dig up information about the agencies and occupation titles that appeal to you. Why do you want to do that? Because as a smart job seeker, you don't decide to spend your time pursuing a job until you know whether or not that occupation is really something you'd be happy with. So the more information you have about the occupations, the fields, related positions, and related agencies that pique your interest, the better.

Therefore, begin by gathering information about federal occupations, not by looking for actual job openings. This approach might do two things for you:

1. It might open your eyes to positives or negatives about the occupation or related occupations.

2. As you conduct your research, it might give you federal contacts who will refer you to other contacts until eventually you may find someone who refers you to an actual job opening. Yes, it sounds like networking. But it's easier, because it's networking as an information gatherer rather than as a job seeker.

As an example, let's pretend that you used the Career Search Index and located an interest in the Agricultural Marketing Service (AMS), especially the *Market News Reporter* position title. From the Career Search Index, you know that the

OUACHITA TECHNICAL COLLEGE

AMS hires people as Market News Reporters, but there are no job openings at this time. (It's okay if there are no current openings—you are an information gatherer now, not a job seeker.)

From the agency profile, you determine that a Market News Reporter appears to have an interesting occupation, but you would like to know more about it. So how do you find out more? The best way is to ask someone who does the very work you have interest in. Call a Market News Reporter, and ask! What have you got to lose?   Introduce yourself in this way:

> *"Hi. My name is James Wilson, and I am doing some occupational exploration. I know that the AMS (it's okay to use acronyms with them, it'll make you sound like more of an insider) has people called Market News Reporters, and I was hoping to speak with a Market News Reporter to get some information."*

Notice that you are not identifying yourself as a job seeker. Be very careful to steer clear of verbiage that puts you in the job seeker category, even when you are simply speaking to a secretary and are not yet talking with your targeted contact. Don't use words like "opportunities," "positions," and "job openings." For example, the following would not be likely to get you through to your intended contact:

> *"Hi. My name is Jim Carson, and I am hoping to find a job with the government. Your agency looks particularly intriguing, especially the Policy Analyst positions, which fit very well with my background. Is there a Policy Analyst there with whom I could speak?"*

Jim Carson did several things wrong here.

> ✷   First, he said up front that he is seeking a federal job. This is an instant invitation for the person on the other end of the line to suggest Jim get in touch with Personnel and file an application (the equivalent of "go away and leave me alone").

> ✷   Second, he used the phrase "Policy Analyst positions" which seems to imply that there are specific positions currently open. This invites the listener to reply that there are, in fact, no Policy Analyst positions currently open and to suggest again that Jim refer his plight to the Personnel office. (In other words, "get lost.")

☆   Third, Jim sounds a bit too "salesmanlike" when he tells the secretary that his background is well suited to the Policy Analyst positions. Even if he hadn't so clearly identified himself as a job seeker, this last phrase is a dead giveaway. The secretary is likely to suspect that Jim is a job seeker and to steer him toward the Personnel office (the black hole).

Don't be concerned that you are being devious. This is absolutely not the case. Yes, you may be looking for a job, but you aren't looking for a job *from them at that moment*. What you are doing is approaching your job search in an intelligent fashion by exploring different career paths and gathering information before you make any long-term job choices.

Match Your Job Title

To be successful, try to gather your information from someone who has the actual title of the position in which you are interested. Don't try to garner knowledge from the personnel office. There are several reasons why they are not likely to be of much help:

☆   They are not program area managers with authority to hire. They usually don't have that power. Developing rapport with personnel doesn't do you as much good as developing rapport with professional colleagues within the department or division where you want to work.

☆   Staffing specialists are trained to be screeners. They handle incoming employment calls so that the hiring managers are not interrupted. Talking to them doesn't influence the hiring decision.

☆   Staffing specialists are not likely to know much about the occupation you are interested in. What they know a lot about is how to be a staffing specialist. They might write the job descriptions for certain positions, but that is usually the extent of their knowledge.

Attempting to reach the division head or department manager isn't the wisest move either. Division heads often have secretaries who are trained to screen out extraneous calls like yours, and your attempts at reaching them are likely to be foiled.

Whatever the occupation you are interested in, call someone who has that very job title. He or she will be able to give you perspective on the field.

TIP: Agencies often experience a swell in hiring needs during the months of July, August, and September. This is because they frequently put off hiring throughout the year due to budgetary concerns. When the end of the fiscal year (September 30) approaches, however, they must be staffed at 100 percent or risk losing any unfilled positions the next fiscal year. In other words, from July through September, agencies often have money to spend and positions that need to be filled. This is one of the best times of year to search for a federal job!

Finding the People You Want to Talk To

So how do you find these people who can help you, the ones who would be your colleagues if you were to get hired by an agency? It's simple, and it's all right here in the agency profiles.

Look up the profile of the agency that appeals to you most. You'll see that the profile has several sections: Agency Mission, Job Descriptions, etc. Now refer to the section "Major Activities and Divisions." This gives you an idea how the agency is subdivided and offers some clues as to which occupations might be found under which departments or divisions. Once you decide which division employs people with the position title that interests you, call that division and ask to speak to someone with that title.

Another easy way to find current names and phone numbers at an agency is on their Web site. Note that site addresses are listed under the agency name of each profile. Most Web sites have directory listings of the entire agency staff. Regional and local offices sometimes have their own directories, so at the main menu page, try clicking on the office location where you'd like to work for a directory specific to that office.

There are also several easily accessible resources found in your local library's reference section that can give you current names and telephone numbers of professionals within those agency divisions. Two of the best are:

*   *The Federal Yellow Book* (Leadership Directories, Inc., Washington, DC)

*   *The Federal Staff Directory* (Staff Directories, LTD; Mt. Vernon, VA)

Let's say you are interested in being an Intelligence Research Analyst with the Department of Energy. Turn to the Department of Energy agency profile on page 00. Look at the section called Major Activities and Divisions. You'll notice nine discrete divisions, each with its own mission area. As you review them, decide which division you think would be most likely to employ Intelligence Research Analysts. In this case, the Defense Intelligence Programs Division seems the most likely choice. Thus, choose the office or division that seems to fit and call the division directly. Ask the person who answers the phone for that office if there is an Intelligence Research Analyst handy to speak with.

What Do I Say Now?

You've just reached a helpful, informed person who has a job title the same as or similar to the one you are interested in pursuing. If the person seems receptive, tell him or her that you'd like to spend just a few minutes talking together to get that person's perspective of the field and to understand a bit more about what the occupation entails. Basically, you are hoping for an "information interview," a face-to-face meeting where you ask occupation-related questions and establish a solid contact with the person so that if a position comes open in the future, that person will think of you for the job. That person might also be familiar with the hiring needs of other agencies and may point you to specific job openings or hiring managers with vacancies to fill.

People will remember you much better if they have seen you than if you are just another voice on the phone, so a face-to-face meeting is preferable. Of course, if you live far away from the agency you are contacting, a face-to-face meeting may not be possible. If you can make a personal appearance at the agency, it makes a much stronger and longer-lasting impression when your potential employers can match your name with a face. To set up the meeting, say something like this:

> *"Hello. My name is Jerome Greene and I am exploring the federal government as a possible career move. I'm just beginning my research, however, and I'm hoping to gather advice and information from people in the field. Since you are a Program Analyst, I'd appreciate your perspective on program analysis. Could I ask for about 10 minutes of your time? I'll be in town next Tuesday, and I'd like to come and talk with you if you can set aside a few minutes for me."*

The Meeting

The networking meeting should be brief and focused. Don't forget that you, as the person who requested the meeting, are running the show. Make sure to do your homework ahead of time so that you know what you want to ask before you arrive. Research the agency before your meeting so that you appear confident, knowledgeable, and prepared.

> **TIP: A great place to find background information on the agency is in the "about us" or "agency history" section of the agency Web site. Or, try reading the U.S. Government Manual, an excellent resource compiled by the Office of the Federal Register. This can be found at your local library, and contains updated agency and contact information.**

Begin by explaining up front that you do not expect the person to know of any specific current vacancies and are not looking for a job from him. This prevents him from fidgeting in his seat throughout the meeting, wondering when you are going to ask for a job. Make it clear that you are there to gather information and to expand your contacts in the field.

Next, introduce your background and offer a bit of career history. Just a bit—if it's too long, you've lost him. One to 2 minutes should be the maximum. This helps your contact to understand what your areas of expertise are and gives him a better idea of how you might fit into certain occupations.

Take the time to establish rapport. A relaxed atmosphere is more enjoyable for everyone involved. Remember, this is not a job interview. You can be less formal than at a job interview, but don't get off the subject so far that your contact person begins to glance at the clock.

Enter the meeting with a prepared list of questions you hope to have answered. Below are ten sample questions you may want to ask, depending upon your level of experience and your knowledge of the field.

1. Could you explain to me the typical duties of the Auditor position?

2. About how many people with that job title are employed by your agency?

3. Do these people usually work at headquarters or at a field office?

4. Does the work that you do cause you to travel extensively?

5. Tell me about a typical day in the life of an Auditor here at this agency.

6. What do you like best about your job?

7. What do you like least about your job?

8. Would you recommend federal employment as a good career choice? Why or why not?

9. My research also pointed me to XYZ Agency, and I was thinking of talking with some Auditors there also. Can you recommend anyone there with whom I might speak?

10. Can you recommend anyone else I might talk to in this agency or at another agency who might give me another perspective on the field?

Be sure that your questions are focused and clear. Do not, for example, ask for advice on what career you should pursue. The following does not sound impressive:

"My background in the private sector involves eight years in systems analysis and design. Can you suggest how I might apply my experience to the federal government?"

This is simply too unfocused and leaves the impression that you didn't bother to do your own research. Don't take up someone's important time asking questions that you should have answered for yourself before you called.

Impress with your directed, sure-footed approach to the job search by asking questions that show forethought. This, for example, sounds impressive:

"I was reading about the massive changes to the Department of Agriculture over the past several years. The new Natural Resources Conservation Service caught my eye, and I was hoping to talk with someone over there. Do you know someone in Conservation Operations with whom I might speak?"

This indicates a clear goal orientation and shows that you're smart enough to do your research. It is a simple, direct question for your network contact to answer.

> **TIP: Do not leave the networking meeting without asking for names of other people in the federal government whom you might contact. The most important aspect of the meeting is to keep the web of contacts growing until you eventually hit the one that leads to the job you want.**

Remember that the goal of your information interview is not to land a job offer, but to simply gather information in your quest for a federal position. Always seek out the names of additional contacts. Success is defined by the quantity and quality of new acquaintances you have made and the names you have gathered to contact in the future.

Once you get the ball rolling, you'll be surprised at how easy it is to make connections with people and how receptive they are to talking with you.

> **TIP:** *Be sure to ask the people who offer you new contact names if you can refer back to them when calling the new contact. For example, you can say, "Hello, Mrs. Smith. My name is Sean Taylor. Carl Lee suggested that I call you." This "name dropping" opens doors and eases your introduction to each new contact.*

Keep All Doors Open

Working both the front door and back door of the job search concurrently should keep you busy. Develop your list of target agencies and begin the networking process. Remain open to the various traditional channels so no job openings of interest pass you by, yet continue to establish new relationships with people in the agencies that interest you most.

There are more possibilities to explore than you had ever imagined. And the professional contacts you make along the way will be useful to you for years to come.

CHAPTER 5

THE APPLICATION PROCESS

Last year, Lisa decided she might like to try her hand at landing a federal job. Then she saw that she would have to ignore her hard-wrought resume and start over on a new and lengthy form. In frustration, she asked me why the government was making her life so difficult by requiring special application formats. "Why can't I just use my corporate resume, which I've worked so hard on and have already completed?" she asked. I can see her point.

In this instance, we see the other side of the coin, too. The purpose of the federal application form is to ensure that all applications coming in to personnel contain the same information. In this way, applications are rated against a job standard and can then be numerically ranked against each other, with the "best-qualified" applicant (the highest numerical score) first in line for the job. It is all a part of the "competitive" process that is the heart of the federal hiring system: the jobs go to the applicants who are the best qualified, as evidenced by previous experience and academic credentials. The standardization of federal applications is an attempt to rid the federal hiring process of discrimination.

Federal Application Forms

On January 1, 1995, the federal government decided to accommodate frustrated would-be federal employees like Lisa. It began to allow applicants an option: to submit a federal employment application form such as the OF 612 or the older SF 171, or to submit a self-designed federal resume instead. See the list below for details about the application forms.

✶ The SF 171. For years, the Standard Form 171 was the ruling king of the federal application process. It is no longer printed or distributed by the feds, but it is still accepted by personnel offices as an official government application form. Since it has now been out of print for many years, the newer form may be a better bet at striking a familiar chord with personnel specialists.

✴ The OF 612. This is the federal application form that replaces the SF 171. It's a bit shorter than its predecessor and a bit less involved in the general information areas, but it still requires a lot of time and energy to get it done right. Much to the delight of all federal job seekers, this form is now available in screen-fillable, printable form (the Adobe Acrobat PDF/F format) at OPM's Web site at www.opm.gov.

✴ The Federal Resume. The resume is a tempting substitute for the preprinted application forms since you can design it yourself. You must make it much longer and more detailed than a traditional resume, however, so it may not save as much time as you think. Federal resumes work well when they are the requested format used by the agency, but they can be confusing to staffing specialists who are familiar with standardized forms and must search varied resume formats for the information they seek. Resumes do have the advantage of being available online at the USAJOBS Web site online resume builder (www.USAJOBS.opm.gov). This allows you to store, edit, and print your resume from the system as needed or to submit it electronically for specific positions at federal agencies.

Both the OF 612 and the federal resume format require basically the same information. The most important thing to note is that whatever form you choose, all applications to the federal government *must* include the following information, or you may lose consideration for the job:

Job Information

✴ Announcement number and the title and grade(s) of the job for which you are applying (if you are answering a specific vacancy)

Personal Information

✴ Full name, mailing address (with zip code), and day/evening phone numbers (with area code)

✴ Social security number

- ★ Country of citizenship (most federal jobs require U.S. citizenship)

- ★ Veterans' Preference, if any (attach DD-214; submit SF-15 if claiming 10-point preference)

- ★ Reinstatement eligibility (if you previously worked for the federal government and have achieved career or career-conditional status)

- ★ Highest federal civilian grade held (if you previously worked for the government)

Education

- ★ High school (name, city, and state; zip code if known); date of diploma or GED

- ★ Colleges and universities (name, city, and state; zip code if known); majors; type and year of any degrees received (if no degree, show total credits earned and indicate whether semester or quarter hours)

- ★ Send a copy of your college transcript only if the job vacancy announcement requests it or if you are qualified for the job solely on the basis of your academic background.

Work Experience

Give the following information for all paid and nonpaid work experience related to the job for which you are applying: (never send generic job descriptions).

- ★ Job title (series and grade if federal job)

- ★ Description of job duties and accomplishments

- ★ Name and address of current/former employer(s)

- ★ Supervisor's name and phone number

- ★ Starting and ending dates of positions (month and year)

- ★ Average number of hours worked per week

- ★ Salary

- ★ Indicate if your current supervisor may be contacted

Other Qualifications

* ✶   Job-related training courses (title and year)

* ✶   Job-related skills such as other languages, computer software/hardware, tools, machinery, typing speed

* ✶   Job-related certificates and licenses (current only)

* ✶   Job-related honors, awards, and special accomplishments; for example, publications, memberships in professional or honor societies, leadership activities, public speaking, and performance awards (give dates but do not send documents unless requested)

The Inside Scoop

Have you ever wondered what happens to your application once it enters the federal personnel office? From an outsider's perspective, federal personnel offices can seem inefficient and rigidly uncommunicative. What in the world takes them so long to review your application?

It is wise to take a peek at what goes on behind the scenes in the federal application process, because if you know the rules of the game, you know how to play to win.

> *Maria, who has been a personnel specialist with the Interior Department for 22 years, says that times have changed greatly for her. In the old days, she would merely call the Office of Personnel Management (OPM) and request a list of eligibles for a certain position she had to fill. Job hopefuls would have sent their applications to OPM to be put on a centralized job list called a "register," for consideration in all federal agencies. Now, the applications are sent directly to her agency, and Maria herself collects, rates, and ranks all the incoming applications for a position.*

The following sections explain the new federal application process in general terms from the point at which the screening process begins.

Rating

After the closing date of a particular position, when all the applications have been collected by the agency announcing the job, the personnel specialist who has been handling this particular vacancy makes an initial review of all applications to ensure that applicants meet the minimal qualifications. Thus the applications are initially rated, and those that are not minimally qualified are screened out. Some agencies send the candidates a notice at this stage, advising them of their rating: either they have passed the initial screening or they haven't.

This rating is based upon a numerical scoring process that staffing specialists use to compare your application to a job standard. Do you have the level of education that you need to qualify for the job? Do you have enough years of related or general experience (paid or unpaid)? Do you have related training? Do you have special accomplishments that apply? Are you a veteran? These are the items that actually earn you points, and if you chalk up enough of them you pass the initial screening. It is vital, therefore, to write a very complete and thorough application. If you leave off important information, you won't get the credit you deserve, and you might not pass the screening.

If you don't hear from an agency right away after sending in an application, don't be alarmed. It could be that the position has been put on hold, or things are moving along slowly. If you want to call the personnel office to check on the status of your application, you can, but don't waste time trying to "sell yourself" to personnel employees as a winning candidate since they typically don't have the power to influence the hiring decision. Generally, staffing specialists simply write vacancy announcements, screen incoming applications, and assist in upholding federal hiring policy. They do not decide who will get the job.

Ranking

After the initial screening, the personnel office or the hiring office may name a number of people to form a "panel of experts" to review the applications in depth. These experts should have at least the same grade level as the announced job and are usually in the same field. The panel reviews the information on each application and any supplements (such as the KSA) and considers it in relation to the announced criteria for the job. In this way, the panel comes up with a "best qualified" list, again assigning numerical scores. This is called ranking.

The hiring office has determined in advance exactly what factors should be evaluated and specifically what weight the panel should give to each factor. This is very different from the way a private sector organization reviews job applications. The private sector hiring process is not usually as specific, allowing hiring officials to fill a position based more on gut instinct and personal rapport with the candidates in the initial interviews. The federal job search usually does not involve interviewing until the final three "best qualified" candidates have already been selected. Choosing the top three most highly ranked job candidates is called the "rule of three."

Because of this detailed numerical evaluation system, federal job applicants have a tough time standing out from the crowd of other applicants. Since large numbers of qualified candidates are likely to apply for an advertised federal vacancy, and because only the top three candidates are likely to be interviewed, it is difficult to land an interview with the hiring official and to impress him or her with intelligence and charm. Federal applicants who are going through the front door must rely heavily on their paperwork—their federal application—to win the job for them.

Eight Keys to the Federal Application System

Before getting into the details of applying, there are a few key points to remember about the federal application system:

1. If the job you are applying for is a current job opening, be sure to read the vacancy announcement before sending any employment forms to the agency. The vacancy announcement tells you the preferred method of submitting your application and what additional information they require.

2. If the vacancy announcement lists knowledge, skills, and abilities (KSAs), be sure to address them very carefully and thoroughly—these are often the "make or break" points for federal job candidates (these are discussed later in this chapter).

3. OPM's Web site, www.usajobs.opm.gov, allows you access to electronic and hard copy application forms, and it provides a resume builder that lets you edit, save, and print a federal-style resume. The key is not to write one good resume or OF 612 and then send it away without saving it. Either save it on the computer or make hard copies of it first, so that you don't have to redo all that work to fill out another. If you plan to use the postal service, remember that a copy of a federal application will be accepted just as quickly as an original, so make several copies of your completed application before you send it off in the mail (each copy must be *signed* in ink, however).

4. Some people argue that they want to individualize each resume or application to the particular job for which they are applying. But, after you've filled out one OF 612 or federal resume, you won't want to fill out another. To work

efficiently, write one good application template and then customize your credentials to fit a particular job via the KSA supplement (more on that later in this chapter). If you are working with a hard copy that you plan to send through the mail, leave certain spaces on your template blank:

> **TIP:** On the OF 612 form, leave blank spaces 1 (job title in announcement), 2 (grade applying for), 3 (announcement number), and 18 (signature and date). This way, you can write in information appropriate to the job for which you are applying and can sign/date the application in original ink.

5. Besides the federal government's USAJOBS site, which provides free fillable OF 612 forms in Word or Adobe® Acrobat® PDF, there are software programs available for a fee that provide additional services. For example, the *Quick and Easy Federal Jobs Kit Version 6.0* (put out in 2001 by the Federal Research Service, Vienna, VA) allows you to search for a job, fill out application forms or resumes, then print, fax, or e-mail the application from within the program. *Quick and Easy* handles Resumix resumes and includes additional application formats used by various agencies. The cost is $49.94 plus shipping. Call 800-782-7424 or log on to www.fedjobs.com. You can also check with your local library or community college to see if either has this program available for public use.

6. Federal agencies generally do not accept unsolicited applications. They simply don't know what to do with them. Certain job openings are assigned to certain staffing specialists, and if an application comes in that doesn't belong to a particular opening, no one knows where it should go. The chances of sending in an application to a federal agency out of the blue and landing a chance job slot are pretty slim. Also, you should not expect to be considered for a wide range of positions at an agency based on a single application submission. Unless you see information that specifically states otherwise, your application will probably be considered only for the particular job opening for which you are applying, and then it will be discarded.

7. Federal staffing specialists place you into a salary or grade category according to an "eligibility system." They review your experience, education, etc., to

determine what grade you are qualified for within a certain job series. So if you wish to be a soil scientist with the U.S. Soil Service, a staffing specialist will review your background according to that job standard and will qualify you as a GS-5, GS-7, GS-9, etc. You can find these job standards in the book *Qualification Standards Operating Manual*, which can be accessed from the OPM Web site at www.opm.gov. A look at these standards helps you determine which jobs you qualify for and at what grade level. These standards are also often spelled out on the vacancy announcement.

8. Again, read the vacancy announcement before you send in your application. Often the vacancy announcement lists supplemental information that you must submit along with your application. Your application will be dismissed as incomplete without it, no matter how qualified you are.

The Vacancy Announcement

Let's explore a typical vacancy announcement. Figure 5-1 is a rather standard-looking sample from the Federal Aviation Administration. Although vacancy announcements come in all shapes and sizes, there are several vital elements that you will find on almost all announcements.

1. Vacancy announcements begin by indicating the title of the position and the grade at which the agency is hiring. It may say something like "GS-401-5." The middle digits are a series code the government uses for classification purposes; 401, for example, is the code for biologist. The last digit is the grade, in this case, GS-5. Sometimes a vacancy is open at multiple grades. In such a case, the grades are shown with slash marks. As an example, GS-5/7 means you can apply at either grade 5 or 7 or both.

2. Many announcements list the position's "promotion potential." This tells you how high your salary can climb (through which grade level) before you have to bid competitively for the next grade.

3. Also look for the announcement number toward the top of the page. Be sure to use this number when filling out your resume or application and any supplemental forms.

4. Most vacancy announcements indicate a precise starting and closing date, called the "open period." Federal jobs are usually posted as open for about two to three weeks, and applications are accepted only during that time. If

your application is not received by the closing date, it will probably not be considered for the job. Some announcements say "Open Continuously." This means that applications are accepted for this position throughout the year, and they are likely to fill many such positions under this announcement.

4.   Federal announcements include an "Area of Consideration" section, also known as the "Who Can Apply" section. This explains, usually in tough-to-decipher federal lingo, who can and who cannot be considered for the position which is being announced. For example, it might say *"status candidates only."* Status candidates are those who have previously worked for the government for three years as career employees or those currently working for the government. If you have status, you probably know it. *"Non-status candidates"* are everybody else. Vacancies that are advertised for current federal employees only might also say *"merit promotion."* Those open to the general public might say *"all sources."* If you aren't able to make sense of it all, call the agency and ask. You'll usually find a name and number of a contact person at the end of the announcement.

6.   The location line tells where the job is located geographically. It also indicates the office or division in which the job is held.

7.   A "Duties and Responsibilities" section offers an overview of the job description. It is important to read this carefully because it gives a clear idea exactly what the position entails and helps you to write a strong description of your background and tailored KSAs.

8.   Announcements might describe the *"Selective vs. Quality Ranking Factors."* Quality ranking factors are those which the hiring officials would like to see you have. Selective ranking factors are the basic qualifications you must have in order to be considered for the job. If you don't have all of the selective factors, you probably will not pass the first round of screening, so you may want to turn your attention to other job openings. But, if you don't have all of the quality factors, go ahead and give the job a shot. You can still be considered for the job without having the quality ranking factors as long as you have all of the selective factors. You might also see the terms "basic requirements" and "other requirements." Generally, the basic requirements, like the "selective ranking factors," are those that you must have in order to be considered qualified for the job. The "other requirements" are a nice bonus if you have them, and they may help you to be considered for a higher starting grade level or step.

Figure 5-1 Sample Vacancy Announcement

Department Of Transportation

Promotional and Career Opportunities

ORGANIZATION: FEDERAL AVIATION ADMINISTRATION   ANNOUNCEMENT NO.
1-APO-2002-1921

POSITION: ECONOMIST, GS-110-5/7   OPENING DATE: AUGUST 28, 2002

PROMOTION POTENTIAL: GS-13   CLOSING DATE: SEPTEMBER 18, 2002

LOCATION: Assistant Administrator for Policy,
Planning, and International Aviation, Planning
Analysis Division, Statistics and Forecast Branch,
Washington, DC

AREA OF CONSIDERATION: NATIONWIDE STATUS/NONSTATUS CANDIDATES

NOTE: Certain handicapped individuals and disabled veterans eligible for
special appointing authorities may also apply. Ingrade/downgrade
applicants will be considered.

NOTE: THIS ANNOUNCEMENT MAY BE USED TO FILL OTHER SIMILAR
POSITIONS SUBJECT TO THE PRIOR APPROVAL OF THE HUMAN RESOURCE
MANAGEMENT DIVISION.

Equal Opportunity through Affirmative Action: The Federal Aviation
Administration is committed to a multicultural environment. Minorities
and women are strongly encouraged to apply.

Duties: Performs economic duties under the general guidance of a senior
economist. Develops and maintains databases using standard computer
software. Assists senior economists in the compilation, collection, and
mathematical manipulation of data. Assist in developing national,
regional, and airport-specific aviation forecasts. Assists in performing
preliminary data analysis and preparing statistical and written reports
related to special request. Forecasts aviation activity under the supervision
of senior economists. Uses standard economic research methods to assist
senior analysts in completing complex economic studies.

Qualifications: All applicants *must have* at least 21 semester hours in
economics and 3 semester hours in statistics, accounting, or calculus. All

---

applicants must demonstrate at least one year of specialized experiences to the next lower grade in the Federal government. Specialized experience is that which is directly related to the line of work of the position to be filled and which has equipped the applicant with the particular knowledge, skills, and abilities to successfully perform the duties of the position. To be creditable, specialized experience must have been at least equivalent to the next lower grade in the normal line of progression for occupation in the organization.

PRIVACY ACT REQUIREMENTS (P.L. 93-579)

The referenced forms are used to determine qualifications for promotion and are authorized under Title 5 of the U.S. Code, Sections 3302 and 3361. Each specified form must be submitted in order for you to be considered for promotion to the position being advertised. The social security number is not required for this purpose and may be deleted from the forms submitted. Your servicing personnel office or the office named in this announcement will be able to provide information on specific Privacy Act requirements.

CANDIDATES WHO FAIL TO SUBMIT THE REQUIRED FORMS WILL NOT BE CONSIDERED. NONE OF THESE FORMS WILL BE SUBSEQUENTLY LOANED OR RETURNED TO THE APPLICANTS.

CANDIDATE WILL BE EVALUATED ON BASIS OF EXPERIENCE AND EDUCATION, PERFORMANCE APPRAISAL, TRAINING, AND AWARDS.

DOT IS AN EQUAL OPPORTUNITY EMPLOYER

ALL QUALIFIED CANDIDATES WILL BE CONSIDERED REGARDLESS OF RACE, COLOR, RELIGION, SECT, OR NATIONAL ORIGIN

FORM DOT F 3300.6 (Rev. 1-88) SUPERSEDES PREVIOUS EDITION

ANNOUNCEMENT NO.: 1-APO-2002-1921 (Cont'd.)

Rating and Ranking Process: Qualified applicants will be rated and ranked based on the following Knowledge, Skills, and Abilities (KSAs):

1. Knowledge of general economics theory, principals, and practices.

2. Knowledge of general statistical theory, principals, and practices.

3. Ability to collect, analyze, and evaluate data with the use of generally used personal computer software.

4. Ability to effectively communicate both orally and in writing.

How to Apply: See attached "Here's What Your Resume or Application Must Contain." In addition, the submission of the following supplemental forms/information is encouraged. ALL APPLICATION MATERIALS MUST BE SUBMITTED AS A COMPLETE PACKAGE, AND RECEIVED OR POSTMARKED BY THE CLOSING DATE OF THE ANNOUNCEMENT.

1. WA Form 3330-8, Acknowledgment & Status of Application (or equivalent), for acknowledgment of application and final selection notification.

2. WA Form 3330-9, Evaluation of Knowledge, Skills, and Abilities (or equivalent), completed by supervisor (current or former).

3. Response to Evaluation Criteria. A supplemental statement for each KSA is highly recommended.

4. Latest performance appraisal.

5. Current SF-50, Notification of Personnel Action, to verify competitive status or reinstatement eligibility.

6. SF-181, Race and National Origin Identification.

*Applications must be postmarked by the closing date of the announcement and received by the close of business on the fifth working day after close of announcement.

**Applicants must have completed one year of service at the next lower grade as of the closing date of the announcement

***We are prohibited from considering applications received in penalty and/or interoffice mail or in any other government envelope.

Where To Send Application:

Federal Aviation Administration
Human Resource Management Division
Operations Team 1, AHR-19A
800 Independence Avenue, SW
Washington, DC 20591

Applications may be hand-delivered to Room 109.

Please call 267-8007 for further information or forms.

9. Almost all federal vacancy announcements include a "Knowledge, Skills, and Abilities" (KSA) section. The KSAs are also called "ranking factors." They denote the specific qualification areas that are carefully screened when your application is being considered.

The KSA Supplement

The KSAs are of vital importance. Let's take a closer look at them.

The KSA requirement is a growing trend in the world of federal employment. In fact, there are very few vacancy announcements that do not request a KSA supplement from the applicant. What is it?

The KSA is a request on the vacancy announcement for the applicant to address, independently of the OF 612, SF 171, or federal resume, several questions or important factors regarding career experience as it relates to the vacancy duties. The applicant simply uses a blank piece of paper which he or she attaches to the resume or application and, in paragraph form, answers the KSA questions.

KSA questions can be as general as requesting the applicant to "Address your experience regarding written and oral communication skills." Or, they can be very specific, such as "Describe your ability to oversee procurement and contracting procedures as well as grant activities." In other cases, as in the sample vacancy announcement on page 00, they may not be posed in question format at all, but simply listed as important qualification factors.

Often, the final hiring decision comes down to the KSA supplemental answers you supply. While the resume or application is used merely to determine that the applicant meets the basic qualifications ("rated for eligibility"), the KSAs are used to determine the strength of the applicant *in the most important areas of the job*. The hiring office has already determined exactly what factors should be evaluated on incoming applications and how much weight each factor should be given, and the KSAs are numerically scored ("ranked") against these factors.

Therefore, do not scrimp on your KSA supplement. Give examples from past work or nonwork experiences that lend credence to your having the qualities the hiring officials are searching for. Use the full-length allowance given. If no length is specified, each KSA answer should be about two full paragraphs, or one-half to one full page. When in doubt, don't leave anything out. Refer your examples back to the OF 612 or resume to help the staffing specialists cross-reference.

Tips for a Well-Written KSA

Here are four tips to help you write an outstanding KSA supplement.

1. For each KSA, provide *several examples* of your experience as it relates to the responsibilities of the position for which you are applying. Describe your experience in terms of the *context* of your responsibilities, the *challenges* you faced, the *action* that you took in response to these challenges, and the *results* of your actions. Your narrative should contain enough representative examples to provide a sound basis for staffing specialists and hiring officials to assess the breadth and depth of your qualifications.

2. Don't generalize. Address each KSA with as much *detail* as possible. Describe your experience in terms of *specific* job-related activities, focusing on key skills and strengths such as leadership, budgeting, researching, and writing.

3. Each KSA answer should include the *context* or environment in which you performed your job duties. Was it a large office setting? How many people were involved? What was the volume of sales? How many regions or districts were involved? Quantify whenever possible.

4. Demonstrate your competence not only through professional experience, but also:

   ★ Volunteer experience
   ★ Education
   ★ Training
   ★ Special accomplishments
   ★ Awards
   ★ Potential for growth

The following are examples of weak and strong KSA supplements:

Question: Identify your ability to develop and implement policy and define procedural guidelines.

Weak Example

As a Fiscal Analyst for BTI International, I review internal and external fiscal policy to develop plans and procedures for implementing programs and projects. I maintain solid working relationships with internal and external fiscal managers to ensure uniformity of programs and policies.

This KSA is weak because it does not prove its case:

★ No specific examples are given to illustrate the assertions made.

★ There is no detail regarding *how* solid working relationships are maintained or *how* uniformity is ensured.

★ No context is given.

★ No challenges are described for which action could be taken.

★ No outcomes are described.

Strong Example

As a Policy Analyst and member of BTI International's Fiscal Strategy Committee, I directed the development of the BTI External Fiscal Strategy Plan. This subcommittee's charter was to provide a comprehensive external fiscal strategy and 5-year efficiency plan to ensure the corporation's effectiveness in the global marketplace. I designed a strategic planning process which involved the review and analysis of all appropriate existing internal and external fiscal policy and procedures, incorporating the participation of more than six national offices and 50 employees at all levels of the organization.

As a result of the plan, the committee, through my direction, made difficult cost-saving decisions to reduce funding to ongoing external programs. In one instance, I directed the committee to reduce funding to a partnership program by 50%, which saved the organization more than $1 million over a two-year period. Subsequently, program managers made major reorganizations to align BTI's vision and direction with the new fiscal and economic realities. The plan has been in place for four years and has reduced external spending by 20% overall, saving the organization more than $6 million. Our committee's External Fiscal Strategy Plan continues to provide a successful fiscal framework for BTI. (See Job Block A and Question 31.)

This example is strong because:

★ It provides a *specific example,* which proves successful development and implementation of procedures and policies.

★ It uses the challenge-action-results model. This paints the applicant as a problem-solver who can take action and achieve results.

★ It describes details of the activity, including context and outcome.

★ It refers the reader to the portions of the application that relate to the KSA question.

Certainly, the applicant could have provided even more examples related to the KSA question, and may have chosen to tie in related education or training.

A powerful KSA hammers home the point by providing plenty of examples of past successes.

The Federal Application: Acceptable vs. Exceptional

While you can probably write an acceptable application simply by following the directions on the form, below are several bits of "inside information" that will help your federal application be exceptional. When writing the OF 612, consider these guidelines:

Guideline #1: Never Stay within the Allotted Space on the Work Experience Blocks

On the current OF 612 form, there is a certain amount of blank or lined space for you to fill in information about a past or current employer. If you fill up the allotted space but do not run beyond it, your job description is probably too short. Be sure to use an additional sheet of paper to give you the space you need to include all the details that can earn you points in the rating and ranking process. Simply type the additional information on a blank sheet of paper and attach it to the form. Make sure each added page includes your name, social security number, and the job title or vacancy announcement number you are applying for. Label it as a "continuation sheet for Job Block –". See the example of a continuation sheet in Figure 5-3.

Be careful not to let the mind-set of a private-sector job search influence the length of your job description information. While private-sector job searches stress brevity on the resume, federal applications are meant to be very thorough and specific. The fact of the matter is that you can't lose points for a federal application that is too long (unless all the important information gets swallowed up in a bunch of gobbledygook), but you will *not* get points for information that is not on the application form.

Guideline #2: Give Them the Details

Think of it this way: in the federal hiring process, your application form (or federal resume) serves as the equivalent of the first interview. This is very different from a private sector job search.

In a corporate job search, your resume serves to pique the interest of the hiring officials. They think, "Hmm. This person looks interesting. Let's call her in and interview her to find out if she really is qualified."

In the public sector, hiring officials determine whether or not you are qualified from your paperwork alone. There is no initial screening interview, and there are no second chances. Put it all on your application: don't let your application be screened out erroneously simply because you didn't tell them enough about your background!

Guideline #3: Do Not Generalize

This again is different from the way you write a corporate resume.

A good corporate resume can make statements such as "Prepared reports," and the reader can pick up the gist of things and will ask for details if need be in the interview. But a good SF 171 or OF 612 or *federal* resume cannot make such a generalized statement without costing the applicant dearly.

Suppose the staffing specialist is screening the applications for experience in researching and writing scientific reports. An application that states "I prepared scientific reports" will probably lose significant points, because the word "prepared" does not give the staffing specialist any idea what the applicant actually did. Did he type reports? Edit them? Collate them? Research them? Write them? The word "prepared" is much too vague.

And how did he accomplish his work with reports? If he researched them, did he gather information by telephone? From whom? Did he read trade journals? Did he collect data from other reports? How many? How long did it take him to do this?

"Reports" is also too vague. What kind of reports were these that the applicant "prepared"? Were they financial reports? Status reports? Technical reports? And how long were they? One page? Five pages? Fifty pages? How often were they "prepared"? Weekly? Monthly? Daily? Were they computerized? And to whom were they distributed? What was their purpose?

As you can see, while "prepared reports" is fine as two words on a resume, it should be about two paragraphs on a federal application.

You can be sure your application is detailed enough if you always answer for yourself the question *how*. We recently worked on a federal application with a man who kept writing that he "monitored foreign affairs in target countries." Well, how did he do that? Did he visit the foreign countries? Did he talk to correspondents there? Did he watch CNN? Did he read journals or newspapers? Always answer the question *how*.

Considering the above suggestions, compare the following two work experience blocks.

Figure 5-2 shows an example of a poorly done work experience block. Aside from being much too short, it is also much too vague. "Handled correspondence" is vague. What does "handled" mean, for example? And what type of correspondence? "Entire office" is also vague. How many people were in the office? Was it an office of one or 100? And "responded to inquiries" is vague. We need to know *how* she responded.

Without being privy to more details, a staffing specialist couldn't determine whether this is the application of an entry-level clerk typist in a single-person office or of the CEO of a large corporation.

Figure 5-3 shows an example of a work experience block that is done correctly to maximize staffing specialist points.

Notice not only the clarity of detail but also the easy-to-read format:

★ She starts with a brief introductory paragraph that provides an overview of her experience.

★ She then bullets out her responsibilities and accomplishments in separate easy-to-read descriptive statements.

★ She first describes her job duties, then focuses on her particular accomplishments beyond her daily responsibilities. She tells not just what she did and how she did it but how successful she was at it.

★ She quantifies whenever possible, not just in terms of how she saved her organization money but also how she worked efficiently to save time.

★ She separates out her two discrete responsibilities (Client Coordinator and Training Associate). One might choose instead to use two separate job blocks for these, even if they are concurrent responsibilities within the same organization.

★ She uses action statements such as "designed," "developed," and "conducted." Remember, staffing specialists are looking for initiative.

★ She quantifies the amount of time she spent performing particular tasks.

★ She refers the reader to related information on her KSA supplement so the staffing specialist is able to cross-reference.

Figure 5-2 Poorly Done Work Experience Block

Form Approved

OMB No. 3206-0219

OPTIONAL APPLICATION FOR FEDERAL EMPLOYMENT - OF 612

You may apply for most jobs with a resume, this form or other written format. If your resume or application does not provide all information requested on this form and in the job vacancy announcement, you may lose consideration for a job.

1 Job title in announcement	2 Grades(s) applying for	3 Announcement number
Program Analyst	GS-11	2-ATO-02-345

4 Last name	First and middle names	5 Social Security Number
Wilson	Margaret Lynn	001-01-001

6 Mailing address

540 Boone Blvd.

7 Phone number (include area code)

Daytime (301) 555-9092

City	State	Zip Code
Newington	VA	00001

Evening (301) 555-3629

WORK EXPERIENCE

8 Describe your paid and nonpaid work experience related to the job for which you are applying. Do not attach job descriptions.

1) Job title (if Federal, include series and grade)   Client Coordinator/Training Facilitator

From (MM/YY)	To (MM/YY)	Salary	per	Hours per week
8/97	6/02	$ 41,126	year	40

Employer's name and address

Shel-Flor, Inc.
2964 James Pike, Nye, IN 45062

Supervisor's name and phone number

James Miller
(301) 555-7877

Describe your duties and accomplishments

As Client Coordinator and Training Administrator for Shel-Flor, Inc., I was responsible for various administrative duties, including handling correspondence for the entire office. I responded to inquires from clients regarding Shel-Flor products and directed problems and concerns to the appropriate supervisors. My duties often required me to travel to

Shel-Flor's regional office, where I trained administrators and lower-level officers on policy formulation and implementation techniques. To improve efficiency, I designed a streamlined system of correspondence with clients, so that problems could be dealt with on a more timely basis.

2) Job title (if Federal, include series and grade)

From (MM/YY)   To (MM/YY)   Salary   per   Hours per week

$

Employer's name and address   Supervisor's name and phone number

Describe your duties and accomplishments

50612-101   NSN 7540-01-351-9178   Optional Form 412 (September 2001)

Figure 5-3 Correctly Done Work Experience Block

Form Approved
OMB No. 3206-0219

OPTIONAL APPLICATION FOR FEDERAL EMPLOYMENT - OF 612

You may apply for most jobs with a resume, this form, or other written format. If your resume or application does not provide all information requested on this form and in the job vacancy announcement, you may lose consideration for a job.

1 Job title in announcement	2 Grades(s) applying for	3 Announcement number
Program Analyst	GS-11	2-ATO-02-345

4 Last name	First and middle names	5 Social Security Number
Wilson	Margaret Lynn	001-01-001

6 Mailing address

540 Boone Blvd

7 Phone number (include area code)

Daytime   (301) 555-9092

City	State	Zip Code	
Newington	VA	00001	Evening (301) 555-3629

WORK EXPERIENCE

8 Describe your paid and nonpaid work experience related to the job for which you are applying. Do not attach job descriptions.

1) Job title (if Federal, include series and grade) Client Coordinator/Training Facilitator

From (MM/YY)	To (MM/YY)	Salary	per	Hours per week
8/97	6/02	$ 41,126	year	40

Employer's name and address	Supervisor's name and phone number
Shel-Flor, Inc. 2964 James Pike, Nye, IN 45062	James Miller (301) 555-7877

Describe your duties and accomplishments

From August 1997 to June 2002, I acted as Client Coordinator and Training Administrator for Shel-Flor, Inc., an independent sheet metal manufacturer with 4,000 employees nationwide. During this five-year period, I conducted various policy-setting functions, as well as public relations, customer service, administrative, and training duties of increasing responsibility:

Margaret Lynn Wilson   SS# 001-01-001
Announcement # 2-ATO-02-345
Continuation sheet for work experience block 1, page 2

As Shel-Flor's front-line representative, I maintained professional and courteous relationships with current clients and potential customers. I evaluated requests, concerns, and needs and acted as company liaison to solve problems and build rapport in the corporate community. (See KSA Statement #1)

I responded to approximately 40 inquiries per week from a client base of nearly 150 corporations and independent buyers. Inquiries and requests related to Shel-Flor products, such as sheet laminates, bulk metal, and availability of various consumer goods. I responded to approximately 60% of client inquiries by telephone or fax and 40% through on-site visits with the client.

Throughout all client interactions, I assessed whether client concerns warranted supervisory involvement, and, if so, reported all details of the transaction to the appropriate supervisor by personal briefing and by memorandum

I created policy and procedural guidelines to standardize the client interaction activities of the 3 Midwest regional offices. These new policies improved efficiency by 40% by reducing duplication of effort and increasing interoffice communication.

I coordinated all written correspondence received from clients, which included the formulation of standard letters for consistent inquiries and individual response letters for specific requests and inquiries. I reviewed and evaluated all incoming letters, ascertained the level of response needed, and coordinated and authorized all outgoing correspondence.

SPECIAL ACCOMPLISHMENTS

• I designed and implemented a computerized departmental daily log, in which clerks recorded all client interaction. This detailed the client firm, name, the nature of the concern, and the action that was taken to respond. The new log I created improved departmental efficiency and communication. (See KSA Statement #4)

Margaret Lynn Wilson   SS# 001-01-001
Announcement # 2-ATO-02-345
Continuation sheet for work experience block 1, page 3

• In 1993, I developed a proactive approach for reaching our growing base of potential new clients in the mid-Atlantic region, by coordinating with five separate Shel-Flor departments in the design of several informative letters and brochures highlighting Shel-Flor and its products. This strategy, which is partly responsible for Shel-Flor's 40% increase in new customer growth, is still being used three years later.

• I developed and implemented a streamlined client response system, which improved efficiency of response by 50% and allowed our officers to deal with clients in a 24-hour period. This involved a computerized system whereby client names were earmarked for action if they had not had a response from a Shel-Flor officer within one day of the request.

TRAINING ADMINISTRATOR/FACILITATOR (12/97 to 6/02)

As one of three people chosen to design, coordinate, and lead training in the Midwest region, I traveled approximately once a month to Shel-Flor's Cincinnati regional office to train administrators and officers on effective policy setting and tracking implementation techniques as systems changed and improved. The training program consisted of a two-day workshop, which I researched and designed in conjunction with a team of senior-level officers.

The goal of these workshops was to alleviate the effects of sloppy tracking techniques that had become outdated and ineffective in itemizing vital statistics. In order to train regional administrators and officers on the new programs to be implemented, I employed such training devices as role-playing, team-building group interaction, and the RMS Management-Style Indicator. These techniques helped to assure a smooth transition from the old tracking system to the redesigned system.

SPECIAL ACCOMPLISHMENTS

• Officers who attended my sessions reported a 40-60% increase in efficiency and productivity from their administrators. (See KSA Statement #2)

• I was chosen to receive an Outstanding Performance Award for Workshop Design and Presentation, September 2001.

Guideline #4: Add More Job Blocks

★ The OF 612 form only offers two job blocks in which you can detail your past experience. Don't be afraid to add extra blocks to include all jobs from your career history that have relevance to the job you are applying for. Simply use an additional sheet of paper and label it a "continuation sheet." Include your name, social security number, and the vacancy announcement number at the top of the page, as in the Shel-Flor example in Figure 5.3.

Guideline #5: Use Key Words and Phrases from the Vacancy Announcement

★ Make sure that the information on your application clearly matches the skills and experience that are listed on the vacancy announcement as vital to the job. Remember that agency staffing specialists will be looking for key words and phrases that match the job requirements outlined on the vacancy announcement. The closer the match, the more points you will earn in the evaluation process.

Guideline #6: Include Volunteer Work and Military Experience

★ A staffing specialist reviews your application to see if you have accrued a certain amount of time doing or learning things related to the job for which the agency is hiring. The staffing specialist does not care whether or not you got paid while you were doing or learning those things. In many cases, *volunteer experience is equivalent to paid experience*. This same theory applies to active duty military experience and experience in the military reserves.

Guideline #7: Pay Attention to Sections on Training Courses and "Special Skills" Question #13 (OF 612)

★ These sections ask the applicant to list any training courses taken or special skills, awards, honors, certificates, etc. that are job related. These items are very important to almost all federal applications and they are often point-getters. The rule to follow: do not stay within the allotted space when answering these questions. It is fine to run on to an additional page in order to include all of the courses and awards you have taken or received. List all training courses even if they were very informal. Don't overlook informal awards and special recognition. All special accomplishments inside and outside of the job should be listed briefly here.

Do not be modest. This is your chance to let it be known how hard you've worked and what a talented person you are. If you don't say it here, you may miss your chance at the job.

The Federal Resume

The federal resume is a popular choice for many federal job candidates who prefer the less rigid structure of a self-designed resume compared to the OF 612 application form. If the rules are followed very carefully, a federal resume can earn as many points with staffing specialists as an application form like the OF 612 can. However, federal resumes are a bit riskier. Here's why:

✶ Many job applicants mistakenly assume that their two-page corporate resume is a fine form to submit for a federal job. They hear the word "resume" and think that they already have one written. But a federal resume is vastly different from a corporate resume. Submitting a corporate resume for a federal job generally results in the applicant being disqualified.

✶ Federal staffing specialists screen an awful lot of applications. They like to have forms that they are familiar with so they can screen them quickly and easily. Federal resumes don't require a standardized format and thus aren't reader friendly, especially for quick screenings. This might cause staffing specialists to miss important information.

✶ With a federal resume, it is up to the applicant to do a thorough job and include all required information for the application process. This is more difficult than using a federal form like the OF 612, which has all the required information listed on the pages.

If you do decide to use a federal resume, however, simply remember to include all the information listed on pages 00 when writing it. The following is an example of a well-written federal resume. This resume follows the guidelines for federal resumes outlined by OPM. Another example of a federal resume can be found at OPM's www.USAJOBS.opm.gov Web site. Click on "resume builder" to take you to the sample resume prompt. (You may also build a resume at this site that can be sent electronically in response to some job openings).

TYRONE C. WILLIAMS

429 Seventh Street
Washington, DC 21220
(301) 000-0000 (work)
(202) 000-0000 (home)
E-mail: tcwilliams@pbj.net

Social Security Number:	123-45-6789
Country of Citizenship:	United States of America
Veterans' Preference:	No
Highest Grade:	No past federal employment
Contact Current Supervisor:	Yes

VACANCY INFORMATION

Announcement Number: 02-201-06B

Job Title: Policy Analyst

Grade(s): GS-12

SKILLS SUMMARY

Auditing large organizations, conducting investigations and reviews, financial management, writing reports, project planning, project management, survey techniques, presentation skills, management techniques, information gathering and research, leading meetings, team leadership, writing proposals and presenting recommendations, evaluating and assessing growth and economic impact.

PROFESSIONAL EXPERIENCE

Karnes Group, Inc.   Dates Employed: May 1998–Present
221 Southland Rd. Suite 50   Hours Per Week: 40+
Rockville, MD 00100
Senior Auditor, Government Affairs Division
Salary: $00,000 per year
Supervisor: Ms. Sabina Wirth, (301) 000-0000

Directed a team of four auditors to investigate the financial status of three of the state of Maryland's largest environmental awareness and pollution control programs.

• Planned, coordinated, and conducted seven major audits of Maryland state air pollution, toxic substance, and water pollution control programs.

- Conducted personal and telephone interviews and gathered financial data from more than 40 senior government officials.

- Investigated findings through on-site follow-up with six offices throughout the state.

- Wrote monthly status reports and segments of congressional testimony on state pollution control issues.

- Presented audit findings to senior corporate and state officials and to congressional staff.

Selected Accomplishments:

- Identified unnecessary costs in Maryland wastewater treatment programs, which led to $4M reduction in contract expenditures.

- Selected for five-month special assignment with State Government Operations Subcommittee on Environment, Energy, and Natural Resources to plan and hold hearings on statewide hazardous waste enforcement.

Butler County Department   **Dates Employed: June 1994–May 1998**
of Economic Development   **Hours Per Week: 40+**
629A Swank Road, Hamilton, IN 46069
Program Analyst
Salary: $00,000 per year, 40 hours per week

Supervisor: Mr. Roger Tanimere (219) 000-0000

Conducted reviews of county and state economic programs to evaluate efficiency and effectiveness. Studied projected growth patterns and assessed incentive programs.

- Assisted senior-level program analysts in conducting reviews of state-funded economic programs.
- Made recommendations regarding zoning, status, tax base, and environmental restrictions to facilitate healthy growth patterns.
- Assessed potential growth in terms of infrastructure and environmental impact.

Selected Accomplishments:

- Special Commendation Award for the design of two statewide economic growth surveys.
- Made recommendations for preventative $2-million infrastructure revisions, which saved the county $16 million in long-term costs.

EDUCATION

B.S. in Business Administration, 1994
Miami University, Oxford, OH, 45000
GPA: 3.8
Honors: Magna Cum Laude, Phi Beta Kappa
High School: Tylertown High School, Tylertown, OH 45001; Diploma, 1990

HONORS, AWARDS, MEMBERSHIPS

Exceptional Performance Bonus Award—For excellence and thoroughness in
developing congressional testimony on water pollution control issues, April 2002

Special Commendation Award—For economic growth survey design,
March, 1996

PUBLICATIONS

Contributed to the following county Economic Outlook reports:

• Environmental Impact of Allen Road Interchange, August 2001

• The Tylersville Road Business Corridor, February 1997

JOB-RELATED TRAINING

Training Course	Hours	Date Completed
Lotus 1-2-3	03	02/12/98
Business Writing	03	08/04/99
dBASE III	03	03/15/00
TQM	06	10/30/02

JOB-RELATED SKILLS

Excel Spreadsheets
PowerPoint
Windows Applications
Coaching and Mentoring Skills
Writing Reports
Some knowledge of Spanish Language

JOB-RELATED CERTIFICATES AND LICENSES

None

SUPPLEMENTAL INFORMATION

Additional information that may be required as indicated on a vacancy
announcement may be listed here.

Federal Resume Checklist

Be sure to include the following information not found on typical private-sector resumes. Otherwise, your application may be considered incomplete.

1. Social security number

2. Country of citizenship

3. Veterans' Preference status (see chapter 00 if you are not sure if you qualify)

4. Highest grade worked (if you have worked in the federal government before)

5. Indicate if the reader may contact your current supervisor

6. The vacancy announcement number, job title, and grade to which you are applying

7. The mailing address of your current and past employers

8. The names and phone numbers of your supervisors from all past and present employers

9. The number of hours you worked per week

10. The dates you were employed, including month and year

11. Your high school name, city and zip code; indicate diploma or GED

12. Academic honors information from college no matter how distant your graduation

13. Training courses taken: they can earn you points in the review process

14. A list of job-related skills. In case they missed them in the body of your resume, staffing specialists are likely to see them listed succinctly here. A little extra insurance.

15. A list of honors, awards, memberships, certificates, and licenses that may apply to the job you want. If you aren't sure whether they apply, include them and let the staffing specialists decide.

Resume Tips

1. Use 8.5" x 11" white bond paper and print only on one side.

2. Read the vacancy announcement thoroughly. Are there any special requests that must be added to your resume format?

3. Don't worry about keeping it to two pages, unless the vacancy announcement specifies a length. Four or five pages (or even six or seven or more, if necessary) are fine. Do not consider this an open invitation to ramble aimlessly, however.

4. Stay focused on the job you are applying for and keep it relevant. Include everything that you think might relate to the duties and skills described in the vacancy announcement. Recite this mantra: If in doubt, DON'T leave it out!

5. Don't try to cram too many words onto the page. Keep the format neat and consistent throughout the resume, with plenty of white space to make it easy to follow. Use a standard 10-, 11-, or 12-point font, such as Courier, Ariel, or Times New Roman.

6. At the top of each additional page, include your name, social security number, and the announcement number to which you are applying.

Scannable Resumes, Agency E-Forms, and Electronic Submissions

A quick visit to a few agency Web sites demonstrates how much the hiring procedures vary depending upon the agency and its hiring needs. Some organizations use their own online application system for application submissions. Some state that they accept only e-mailed applications; others refuse emailed submissions and prefer to use the postal service. The Department of Defense, the Air Force, and the Veterans Administration use a system for current federal employees called Resumix, which uses a computer database to read and identify skills and information from scanned resumes.

To navigate this ever-changing sea of application and resume systems and their particular requirements, log on to agency Web sites and gather information on preferred application techniques. Or, check the bottom of the vacancy announcement you wish to reply to. It will probably give specific instructions on the application submission format the agency prefers.

Your Masterpiece

Although the task of writing a federal application may seem daunting, don't be intimidated. Not only will you have a biographical masterpiece when you're finished, but you'll learn quite a bit about yourself as you review your career history and think about all the successes you've had. The process of writing your application will boost your confidence and increase your self-awareness, making you a more articulate interviewer and a stronger candidate for the federal job you choose to pursue.

CHAPTER 6

SALARY AND BENEFITS

Federal Salaries

Excellent pay and benefits are one outstanding aspect of federal employment. The average annual salary for all full-time federal employees now exceeds $51,000, and many employees earn beyond the standard wages of the basic pay system. Most white-collar federal employees are paid according to a system known as the General Schedule or GS. It consists of a series of grade levels ranging from GS-1 at the lowest level to GS-15 at the top level. There is a series of ten steps under each grade that an employee moves through, although at the GS-5, -7, -9, and -11 levels, employees often jump directly to the next grade rather than progressing through the steps. Federal employees who are not under the General Schedule pay system include Postal Service employees who are paid under the Postal Service rates; upper-level executives and political appointees, who fall into the Senior Executive Service (SES); and hourly wage earners, who are paid according to the Prevailing Rate Schedule Wage Grade (WG) classification. We focus our attention on the General Schedule pay system since most entry-level and mid-level professional positions fall into this system.

Each position in the General Schedule pay system falls into a structured occupational group and has been assigned a particular job series classification. For example, General Schedule Groups include the Social Science, Psychology, and Welfare Group (GS-100 series) or the Biological Sciences Group (GS-400 series). Within the larger groupings is a set of more specific job series. For example, under the Biological Sciences Group there are the Forestry Series (GS-460), the Agronomy Series (GS-471), and the Fishery Biology Series (GS-482), among many others. In all, there are about 442 different white-collar occupations that fall into this classification system.

A set of grade levels for each position is determined by the education and experience they require, as well as by the duties, skills, responsibilities, and other factors they entail. So when you apply for a particular position, staffing specialists determine whether you are qualified for the position and what pay level you qualify for by matching your credentials against a set of "qualifications standards." These standards are written by OPM and are contained in a book referred to as the *Qualifications Standards Operating Manual.* These standards can also be found online at www.opm.gov/qualifications/index.htm. A review of the standards gives you a sense of which positions you qualify for and at what grade level. Because the job standards are prewritten and government-wide, competitive service agencies normally have very little flexibility to negotiate salaries.

Excepted Service agencies, such as the CIA, the FBI, and the Postal Service are not required by law to follow the OPM standards and can establish their own evaluation criteria to fill internal vacancies. These agencies have more hiring flexibility than the competitive service agencies. Take note that these agencies are not required to advertise their job openings through OPM, so their vacancies may not be listed on the USAJOBS Web site.

General G-S Qualifications

Typically, new employees with bachelor's degrees and no experience in a career field start at the GS-5 level, or the GS-7 level if a B average was maintained. A relevant master's degree will earn you a GS-9 position, and a doctorate qualifies you for a GS-11 if the degree is directly related to the job to be filled. Career experience can also qualify you for higher salary grades. The general rule is that the career experience must be equivalent to the requirements for the next lower salary grade. For example, in order to qualify for a GS-12 position, you must have one year of related experience equivalent to GS-11.

Base salaries for 2002, not including locality pay, which is allocated to workers in a number of major cities, are shown in the following table.

GS	1	2	3	4	5	6	7	8	9	10
1	14757	15249	15740	16228	16720	17009	17492	17981	18001	18456
2	16592	16985	17535	18001	18201	18736	19271	19806	20341	20876
3	18103	18706	19309	19912	20515	21118	21721	22324	22927	23530
4	20322	20999	21676	22353	23030	23707	24384	25061	25738	26415
5	22737	23495	24253	25011	25769	26527	27285	28043	28801	29559
6	25344	26189	27034	27879	28724	29569	30414	31259	32104	32949
7	28164	29103	30042	30981	31920	32859	33798	34737	35676	36615
8	31191	32231	33271	34311	35351	36391	37431	38471	39511	40551
9	34451	35599	36747	37895	39043	40191	41339	42487	43635	44783
10	37939	39204	40469	41734	42999	44264	45529	46794	48059	49324
11	41684	43073	44462	45851	47240	48629	50018	51407	52796	54185
12	49959	51624	53289	54954	56619	58284	59949	61614	63279	64944
13	59409	61389	63369	65349	67329	69309	71289	73269	75249	77229
14	70205	72545	74885	77225	79565	81905	84245	86585	88925	91265
15	82580	85333	88086	90839	93592	96345	99098	101851	104604	107357

To read the table, follow the numbers 1–15 down the left side of the chart. These are the grades. The shaded numbers 1–10 across the top of the chart are the steps. All grade promotions typically begin at Step 1.

Two-Grade Promotions

A glance at the chart may give you some sense of what your starting federal salary may be. Don't add up the figures just yet, however, because the chart can be deceiving. There are many positive aspects of the federal GS system that the salary table doesn't make clear. For example, for professional positions, there are two-grade promotion intervals between grades 5 and 11, allowing you to skip a grade in between. Thus, promotions progress from GS-5, to GS-7, to GS-9, to GS-11. With satisfactory performance, it takes about a year to go from a GS-5 to a GS-7 and another year to be promoted from a GS-7 to a GS-9. One to two years are usually required to progress from a GS-9 to a GS-11. From grades 11 to 15, promotions progress at one-grade intervals. Clerical positions also use one-grade promotion intervals.

Moreover, because each grade level is divided into ten steps, pay increases are possible without promotions. Movement between steps is determined automatically by years of service. Generally, as you can see from the chart, the salary at the Step 10 level is about 30 percent higher than that at the Step 1 level in each grade.

Cost-of-Living Adjustments

The federal government grants its employees cost of living adjustments each year. So while a GS-11 Step 1 (without locality pay) would earn $41,684 in 2002, a GS-11 Step 1 would likely earn about 42,700 in 2003. Therefore, each year of federal employment promises two salary increases: the step or grade increase *and* the cost-of-living increase. While these increases vary from year to year, recent adjustments have been about 2.7 percent.

Hard-to-Fill Occupations

Workers in hard-to-fill occupations, such as engineers, accountants, and doctors, are paid at special salary rates. These positions are often designated as "excepted service positions" to allow the agency more flexibility in hiring.

Locality Pay Increases

Likewise, special salary rates are paid to employees in high-cost-of-living areas, such as San Francisco, Los Angeles, and New York. Thirty-two cities are now designated as high-cost-of-living areas. Employees in these areas earn from 8.64 to 19.04 percent more than the base chart salary figures. These pay adjustments are called "locality pay." You can find an updated locality pay chart and a complete list of locality pay metropolitan areas at www.usa.opm.gov.

Other Pay Systems

There are other major pay systems in the federal government that cover specialized groups of employees. The Foreign Service Pay System covers Foreign Service employees. The Department of Veterans Affairs has its own pay system for physicians, dentists, nurses, podiatrists, optometrists, and certain executive positions. The Federal Wage System covers most employees in "blue-collar" jobs, including trade, craft, and labor occupations. The pay for these employees is set in accordance with locally prevailing wage rates. The Executive Schedule is a pay system for top-level managers. SES salaries in 2002 range from $113,000 to $130,000.

Career Progression in the Federal Government

When entering federal service, your grade level and base pay (salary) are determined by your education level and your amount of work experience. As noted earlier, entry-level professional positions are normally filled at the GS-5 or GS-7 levels. New employees usually come in at the Step 1 rate for a given grade; however, people in shortage positions, such as engineers, physicists, chemists, metallurgists, and other scientific occupations, may be allowed to come in at a higher step level. Either your experience or a combination of experience and education can qualify you for a position.

Progression in many professional positions occurs according to what is known as a "career ladder." In a typical career ladder, you would be promoted accordingly: GS-5, GS-7, GS-9, GS-11, GS-12. GS-5 and GS-7 amount to an apprenticeship for gaining experience in a particular position. GS-9 and GS-11 are journeyman positions in which the employee is more experienced but still not completely capable of performing all the functions required for that position. At the GS-12 level, the employee is considered "full-performance," that is, experienced in all aspects of the job.

Promotions along the career ladder for professional positions below GS-12 come relatively quickly, about one promotion every year or two, assuming good performance. These promotions are normally noncompetitive in that the employee is not competing against anyone else—they occur automatically.

Promotions above a GS-12 are usually competitive. That is, all interested candidates have to formally apply for the position and a slot at that level must exist.

Supervisors and managers in grades 13 through 15 are under a pay-for-performance system. You can identify the positions covered by this system because they have a GM rather than a GS designation on the vacancy announcement.

Vacation, Sick Leave, and Holiday Benefits

Vacation days are earned according to the length of time you've been with the federal government. You earn 13 days a year for the first 3 years, 20 days a year for the next 12 years, and 26 days a year after 15 years. A maximum of 30 days may be accumulated and carried forward from year to year. Thirteen days of sick leave are earned each year with no limitation on the total accumulation. Federal employees also receive paid time off for ten national holidays.

Health Benefits and Insurance Plans

Federal employees are offered a choice of hundreds of medical health plans that are administered by private insurers. Workers can thus select the plan that best suits them. The federal government pays a share of the premiums. Low-cost group term life insurance, the Federal Employee's Group Life Insurance program (FEGLI), is also available.

Retirement Benefits

The federal government has an excellent retirement system that is based on Social Security and employee contributions. You may choose to contribute up to 12 percent of your salary into a THRIFT savings 401k plan. This amount increases to 15 percent in 2004. The government matches the contributions you make up to 5 percent. These contributions are tax deferred and reduce your taxable income by the amount you have contributed.

Work Schedules

At the discretion of agency management, several schedule options are offered. These include full-time, part-time, flexible, and compressed schedules. Flexible work schedules, commonly called flextime, allow workers to vary their arrival and departure times. Compressed schedules allow employees to complete the basic work requirement of 80 hours in a two-week pay period in less than 10 working days. The government considers home-based employment options as well.

CHAPTER 7

SPECIAL HIRING PROGRAMS

Many job seekers enter into the federal job search with trepidation. They worry that all federal hiring is done through one massive centralized system that they must learn to navigate, or that each of the hundreds of federal job titles has its own particular and complicated application process.

In fact, neither one of these perceptions is true. Thanks to a recent reorganization and streamlining of the federal employment process, almost all federal hiring is done directly by the individual agencies, and most agencies follow a fairly simple and similar system for hiring, much like organizations in the private sector.

Even though federal hiring has been simplified, it is important to be aware of several government-wide hiring programs that target specific groups such as top-level managers, current students, or disabled veterans. These programs sometimes provide the hiring manager with special authority to hire outside the traditional federal hiring rules or may involve certain changes to the usual application procedures. The most prevalent special hiring programs are described below.

Senior Executive Service

The Senior Executive Service is a corps of men and women who administer public programs at the top levels of government. The positions are usually managerial and supervisory in nature and follow the SES pay rates, which range from $113,000 to $130,000 per year.

Each agency determines the qualifications required for its SES positions. Some positions are open only to *status candidates* (basically, those who have three years or more of government service); others are open to all applicants.

How to Apply

Most SES positions are included in the agency's Web site job listings (see agency profiles, pages 00-00 for agency Web site addresses). These listings often include full position descriptions, qualification requirements, and application procedures. SES positions are highly competitive, and, of the nearly 3 million federal jobs across the nation, only about 7,000 of them are Senior Executive Service. Many vacancy announcements request the submission of a full executive application package, including an Executive Federal Resume, Executive Core Qualifications, Technical & Managerial Factors (similar to the KSA statement), and a cover letter. The total package can be twenty to thirty pages.

Other Sources of SES Vacancy Announcements

An excellent resource for any SES job seeker is the Senior Executive Service Web site of the Senior Opportunity And Resume System (SOARS). This system is designed to bring together SES members and agencies to fill the top leadership positions in government. SES members, and OPM-Certified Candidate Development Program Graduates (CDP Grads) can post resumes and/or view current job opportunities posted by agencies. Agencies can post opportunities and/or view resumes. The Web address is https://sesmobility.opm.gov/ses.asp.

Another site to try is www.seniorexecs.org, which is the Web site of the Senior Executives Association. Many of the sources for traditional federal vacancy listings also list SES openings. These sources of job listings can be found in Chapter 2.

Clerical Job Seekers

Clerical jobs are widely available throughout the federal government at the 2, 3, 4, 6, 8, and 10 levels, depending upon experience and education. Some agencies require that you take the federal clerical and administrative support exam in order to be considered eligible for clerical positions within their agency, although government-wide mandatory testing for administrative careers has been eliminated. Other agencies administer their own tests, and others require no test at all, depending upon the needs of the agency and the requirements of the particular position. Contact the personnel office of the agency in which you would like to work. A staff member can provide you with the local testing schedule and answer your questions regarding clerical positions with the agency.

Federal clerical and administrative support positions can vary widely, depending upon the agency and the types of duties required. For example, at the GS-2/4 level, a huge and varied list of job titles exists, such as Business Clerk, Teletypist, Purchasing Agent, Legal Clerk, Telephone Operator, Messenger, Fingerprint Identification Clerk, and Language Clerk.

How to Apply

With these many variations in mind, the best bet for clerical job seekers is to follow these steps:

1. Identify an appealing job vacancy announcement through one of the federal job listings outlined in Chapter 2.

2. Read the vacancy announcement carefully to ensure that you are qualified for the position.

3. Carefully follow the application procedures listed on the vacancy announcement to ensure that you have followed all necessary steps to be considered for the position. Keep an eye out for typing proficiency and testing requirements, and be sure to submit all necessary supplemental forms with your application package.

Additional information on federal clerical positions can be found at www.USAJOBS.opm.gov/ei63.htm.

Overseas Employment

In 2001, there were 89,431 federal civilian workers stationed overseas in more than 140 countries. Although federal employment abroad had recently been on the decline, our country's new interest in global intelligence gathering and national and international security is likely to spark a resurgence in overseas employment.

Who Hires Overseas Workers?

The Defense Department is by far the largest overseas employer, with more than 53,000 civilian workers stationed abroad. Other agencies with a large overseas presence include the State Department (over 17,000), Veterans Affairs (over 3,000), the Justice Department (over 2,500), the Treasury Department (over 1,300), and the Department of Agriculture (over 1,200). The Department of Commerce, the Department of Health and Human Services, and the Department of Transportation also have a large number of overseas workers.

How to Apply

Overseas opportunities are varied, and positions are filled in different ways. Many overseas jobs are filled locally. In some cases, the agency hires citizens of the host country, which helps the local economy. In other cases, the agency gives hiring preference to U.S. citizens who are currently residing in that country, such as military dependents and students. Some overseas positions might be classified as temporary employment, others are permanent positions that may last for several years. Generally, overseas assignments experience high turnover as employees are rotated back to the States, creating a consistent but competitive cache of available overseas positions.

Overseas employment information for the individual agencies is listed in the agency profiles. There you will find Web site addresses, telephone numbers, and general employment information for specific positions overseas.

The Foreign Service

The Foreign Service is a relatively small cadre of federal employees who represent the United States overseas in diplomatic, consular, commercial, cultural, and informational activities. The largest foreign service position, in terms of numbers, is that of Foreign Service Officer (FSO). About 4,200 FSOs work for the State Department, while 950 are employed by the United States Information Agency (USIA). About 150 FSOs work for the Commerce Department's U.S. and Foreign Commercial Service. Supporting the work of FSOs are Foreign Service Specialists, who supply clerical, administrative, technical, financial, medical, and other types of expertise.

All Foreign Service positions are in the Excepted Service, which means they are not subject to the same hiring procedures and principles as most federal jobs, which fall under Competitive Service rules.

Becoming an FSO is a multistep, yearlong process that requires passing a written examination, an oral assessment, and later, a thorough background investigation. (Foreign Service Specialists need not take the written exam—only the oral exam is required.)

How to Apply

Refer to the specific agency entries that list positions in the Foreign Service— the Department of State (page 00), the USIA (page 00), and the U.S. Foreign and Commercial Service (page 00)— for application instructions.

Non-Appropriated Fund Instrumentalities (NAFI) Employment

More than 140,000 employees work for the Department of Defense in Non-Appropriated Fund Instrumentalities (NAFI) jobs in post exchanges, military clubs, and recreation services. These positions are not in the competitive service, and applications for these positions must be submitted directly to the agency of interest. For more information, contact the NAFI personnel office in Arlington, VA, at (703) 696-3318, or visit their Web site at www.cpms.osd.mil/nafppoindex.html.

Temporary and Term Employment

Temporary and term appointments are used to fill positions when there is not a continuing need for the job to be filled. Neither type of appointment is a permanent one, so they do not give the employee competitive status or reinstatement eligibility. However, qualifying experience gained while employed in a temporary or term position is considered when applying later for a permanent position.

A temporary appointment usually lasts one year or less, and has a specific expiration date. Temporary employees are eligible to earn leave and are covered by Social Security and unemployment compensation, but do not receive the other fringe benefits provided to career civil service employees.

A term appointment is of a nonpermanent nature and lasts for a limited period of time, usually more than one year but not exceeding four years. Term employees are eligible to earn leave and generally have the same benefits as permanent employees, including health and life insurance, within-grade increases, and Federal Employees Retirement System and Thrift Savings Plan coverage.

How to Apply

Most temporary and term vacancies are filled through open competitive examination procedures, much like other typical federal jobs. Check with agencies directly regarding temporary and term opportunities.

Veterans' Programs

Veterans' Readjustment Appointment (VRA) Authority

The VRA is a special authority by which agencies can, if they wish, hire an eligible veteran without competition. This means that while the VRA veteran must meet the basic qualifications required for a position, he or she does not have to be ranked among other job candidates. An agency's use of the authority is entirely discretionary, and no one is automatically entitled to a VRA appointment.

VRA appointees are initially hired for a two-year period. Successful completion of the two-year VRA appointment leads to a permanent civil service appointment. Agencies can use the VRA authority to fill white-collar positions up through GS-11 and equivalent jobs under other pay systems.

Service Requirements

Generally, the VRA appointee must have served on active duty for a period of more than 180 days, which occurred after August 4, 1964, and must have received other than a dishonorable discharge. For more information, call the USAJOBS Automated Telephone System at (202) 606-2700 or log on to the USAJOBS Web site.

If you are eligible for a VRA appointment, contact the personnel office of the federal agency for which you are interested in working to find out about VRA opportunities.

Direct Hire of Severely Disabled Veterans

Federal agencies have the authority, by law, to give noncompetitive appointments to any qualified disabled veteran. This authority is discretionary with the agency.

In order to qualify, one must be a disabled veteran with a compensable service-connected disability of 30 percent or more. One must have the disability rating by the VA dated within the preceding year. The veteran must also meet the minimum requirements for the position and must serve under any appropriate temporary authority not limited to 60 days or less.

Veteran's Preference Credit

Preference is given to veterans in competitive examinations, in appointments to positions, and in retention during reductions-in-force. When an agency advertises a job vacancy, it must examine the submitted applications according to selected criteria and rate the applicants according to the score they receive from this review. Actual numerical scores are assigned to the applicants according to how closely their abilities, skills, and experience relate to the job being advertised.

After the applicants have been rated and ranked, the agency must select from the top rated applicants on the list. The agency may not skip over a Veteran's

Preference candidate to appoint a non-preference job candidate lower on the list without providing sufficient reason.

To provide a uniform method by which special consideration is given to qualified veterans seeking federal employment, 5 additional points may be added to a passing score on federal applications for a nondisabled veteran, and 10 additional points may be added for a disabled veteran. Thus, if a nondisabled veteran's application received a score of 90, his 5 preference points bring his score up to a 95.

How to Apply

If you think you may qualify for Veteran's Preference, visit OPM's "Vet Guide" at www.opm.gov/veterans/html/vetguide.htm. This Web site provides detailed eligibility information for the various programs for veterans, their spouses, and their dependents.

Applicants applying for 10-point preference must submit form SF-15, Application for 10-Point Veteran Preference, with their application package. This form can be downloaded from the OPM Web site.

Job Opportunities for Persons with Disabilities

Special Appointing Authorities

An agency may avoid typical competitive appointment procedures to meet the needs of those who have severe physical impairments or mental disabilities. The agency may use a variety of special appointing authorities to bring a disabled person on board.

How to Apply

If you are interested in being considered under these special hiring authorities, you must contact either a state vocational or Department of Veterans Affairs rehabilitation counselor and request their assistance. They review and prepare the necessary documents. They should be asked to provide you with a "certification" statement that describes your ability to perform the essential duties of the position in which you are interested.

Special Accommodations on the Job

The federal government makes reasonable accommodations in the duties of a job or in the work site to make it easier for a disabled person to perform the duties of a position. This includes providing interpreters for persons with hearing impairments, readers for persons with visual impairments, alteration of work schedules to match specific needs, and special equipment or furniture as needed.

For more information, persons with disabilities should contact the personnel office or Selective Placement Program manager of the federal agency of interest. Selective Placement managers work with supervisors and managers to match the skills and qualifications of disabled persons to available job openings.

Affirmative Employment Programs

The federal government has established special recruitment programs to attract qualified women, Hispanics, African Americans, American Indians, Alaska Natives, Asians, and Pacific Islanders into the federal service. See the agency profiles section of this book for information on specific programs, or contact federal agencies of interest for information on particular programs.

Bilingual/Bicultural Program

This program permits federal agencies to directly hire individuals who are proficient in the Spanish language or who have knowledge of the Hispanic culture to fill positions that require these skills in the course of performing job-related tasks. See the OPM's USAJOBS Web site for more information on this program.

How to Apply

Apply directly to the agency of interest at any time throughout the year. A test may be required to determine eligibility.

Student Employment

Most federal agencies use the standard government-wide Student Educational Employment Program (SEEP) to attract students into the public sector. These programs offer on-the-job experience in government agencies and allow the students to gain insight into government employment while gaining contacts within specific agencies. Some agencies also have their own intern, fellowship, or other student programs that are specific to their particular organization in addition to the government-wide programs.

To find information on particular agencies and the student-hiring programs they use, refer to the Alternative Employment Programs section of the individual agencies in the Agency Profiles portion of this book. The profiles give details about the student hiring programs the agency uses, and contact information for learning more.

The Student Educational Employment Program (SEEP)

Students who would like to work for the federal government as researchers, computer scientists, policy analysts, or in any type of career can work across the country in federal settings such as offices, laboratories, parks, and hospitals. Student employees have the opportunity to earn money, to train with people who manage the day-to-day business of the national government, and to get on-the-job, career-related experience.

The federal government has recently redesigned its student employment program to include two components: Student Temporary Employment and Student Career Experience. Both are available to all levels of student, including high school, vocational and technical, associate degree, baccalaureate degree, graduate degree, and professional degree. To be eligible for either one, you must be at least a half-time student at an accredited school or university. Both programs allow a qualified student to be hired, without competition, at any grade in a full-time, part-time, or seasonal capacity.

Student Temporary Employment Program (STEP)

The temporary program is intended to allow students an opportunity to earn income and gain work experience during the school year or vacation periods. The work may or may not be related to the student's field of study. These temporary appointments can be extended indefinitely as long as the student remains a student. However, these jobs do not become permanent positions, and there is no commitment on the part of the agency to provide continued employment.

Student Career Experience Program (SCEP)

The Student Career Experience component of SEEP is the more structured part of the program. These positions will reflect the student's field of study and provide direct experience in work related to the student's career goals. The Student Career Experience Program may also offer the opportunity for the student to become a permanent employee after graduation without competition.

How Do I Find a Student Position?

Student positions are now easier than ever to find, thanks to the Internet. Many agencies announce their openings on one of several job sites (listed below), and students from across the country can respond to those job announcements on a timely basis. Remember that if you want to work for an agency during the summer months, you must begin your search of agencies that appeal to you long before the summer nears. Many agencies have specific open and close dates for their student position announcements, and any applications arriving past the closing date will be considered ineligible.

Federal agencies are not required to post their student job openings publicly, and they are not required to rate and rank the incoming student applications competitively. Some agencies, therefore, have a more informal system of hiring, and may not conduct a structured student-hiring program. This is especially true of the smaller agencies that do not hire large numbers of students each year. Rather than waiting for the student programs to be formally announced, try to get a jump on the process by conducting your own job search. Here's what to do:

1. Use the Career Search Index at the back of this book to discover the agencies in which you would like to work and target them individually. Pay particular attention to agencies that have positions that are related to your career goals.

2. Turn to the agency profiles section and learn more about the agencies you identified in the Index. Explore the job titles, regional locations, overseas travel opportunities, and other aspects of the agency. Check in the "Alternative Employment" section for information about specific student hiring programs at each agency.

3. Go to the agency Web site listed in the profile and find out more details about the agencies that appeal to you most. Many agencies offer information on student hiring programs throughout the year. Look up the details of their programs and find out what the open dates are for applications to be accepted. Look for contact information: names, e-mail addresses, and telephone numbers.

4. If your information is still incomplete, call the personnel office and ask to speak with the student employment director to gather any information that wasn't covered in the book or on the agency Web sites.

5. Send the student employment director a federal resume or application with a cover letter telling about your career pursuits and your interest in a student position. Be sure to read the vacancy announcement carefully, if one is available, to see if other forms such as school transcripts are requested as part of the application package.

6. Most importantly, make some connections with people inside the agency. Call the specific division or department within each agency in which you would like to work and ask an employee who has a job title similar to the one you are interested in if you might have an information interview with him or her. This way, you might learn more about your field of interest and you will be establishing connections with important insiders who may be able to recommend you to the hiring manager when it comes time to hire. Competition for student positions is keen, and establishing personal connections will help you to stand out from the other applicants.

How Do I Find the Job Sites that List Student Job Openings?

The best plan is to identify the agencies that appeal to you, then look up the agency Web site listed in the profiles section of this book, as described above.

But there are also many other Web sites that list federal student jobs. OPM's Web site is a good bet; try www.USAJOBS.gov, click on job openings, and then choose the "student" category, which will take you to current listings. Or, try www.studentjobs.gov. This site is full of information about student jobs, and lists job openings across the country and throughout the year. It allows you to search the site according to the types of positions you would like, salary expectations, geographic preferences, and the time frame of announcements you would like to see. It also allows you to create a resume that can be printed or sent out electronically, and create a profile so that you will be notified of future postings that match your job criteria.

The Outstanding Scholar Program

Many agencies focus a part of their recruiting programs on individuals who qualify for the Outstanding Scholar Program. This program allows students to be hired at the GS-5 or GS-7 level for professional and administrative career positions, with excellent opportunities for advancement. These students may be hired noncompetitively, so that the hiring process is simplified and less time consuming.

To qualify, you must be a graduate of an accredited college or university, have a grade point average of 3.5 or higher for all undergraduate course work, or have graduated in the top 10 percent of your class or major university subdivision. If you qualify for the Outstanding Scholar Program, you can be hired on the spot at career fairs across the country. This special hiring authority is restricted to grade levels GS-5 and GS-7. Positions in accounting, auditing, engineering, physical sciences, biological sciences, and mathematics are not currently covered by this program.

How to Apply

Students who are eligible for the Outstanding Scholar Program may apply directly to the agencies of interest at any time throughout the year. No special application or test is required.

Presidential Management Intern Program

The Presidential Management Intern (PMI) Program is a highly competitive program designed to be a starting point for individuals who wish to pursue management careers in the federal service. PMI positions provide graduate degree holders with a special means of entry into the federal service. The positions focus upon combining the development of management skills with a thorough knowledge of many facets of an agency. Through a variety of rotational assignments, seminars, discussion groups, and other activities, PMI provides a unique training experience that prepares the interns for future positions as managers.

Most PMI positions are located in Washington, DC. Interns typically start at Grade 9, Step 1, and receive full federal benefits.

What Is the Work Schedule?

Presidential Management Interns receive two-year Excepted Service appointments. PMIs work the same type of schedule as regular full-time employees at that agency. However, because of rotational assignments and special PMI activities, an intern's daily schedule tends to be somewhat more flexible.

Who Is Eligible for these Positions?

Students who complete or expect to complete an advanced degree focusing on the analysis or management of public policies and programs from an accredited

U.S. college or university during the current academic year are eligible to be nominated for the program. Nominations should be made by the college or university official who has an appropriate knowledge of the nominee's abilities and achievements. Nominations should come from the school dean, academic program director, or departmental chairperson. Nominations from individual professors, advisers, or placement counselors are not accepted. Presidential Management Internships cannot be used to fulfill a degree requirement. All degree requirements must have been met at the time of appointment to an internship.

How to Apply

Application materials are made available to graduate schools in the early fall. Application packages include complete information on the PMI program as well as further eligibility requirements.

Further information on the PMI program is available at www.pmi.opm.gov/PMIMAIN.HTM. This site gives specifics on qualifications criteria, application forms and deadlines, and other information on the scope of the PMI program. Or, contact by telephone, fax, or e-mail the PMI program office, which has government-wide oversight responsibility for the program.

Phone: 215-861-3027
Fax: 215-861-3030
E-mail: pmi@opm.gov
Philadelphia Service Center
William J. Green, Jr. Federal Building
600 Arch St., Room 3400
Philadelphia, PA 19106-1596

Summer Employment Program

The summer employment program creates work opportunities for those who are available to work only during the summer months. Positions range from office support to trade labor to professional opportunities. Positions usually begin mid-May and end September 30.

How to Apply

Apply directly to the agency for which you would like to work. Or visit OPM's USAJOBS Web site and search by "summer jobs" or "job series 9999."

Student Volunteer Services

A variety of opportunities exist throughout the federal government for students willing to gain experience through volunteer efforts. Some colleges and universities have included volunteer service internships in their public administration curricula so that students can earn college credit by being student volunteers.

How to Apply

Use the agency profiles to contact agencies of interest directly.

CHAPTER 8

POSITIONS IN DEMAND

There are fourteen cabinet-level departments and more than 200 separate agencies in the federal government employing nearly 3 million people nationwide and overseas. Many of these entities are behemoth in size, each employing hundreds of thousands of employees. Others are smaller, with more modest staff numbers perhaps only in the hundreds.

Yet every one of these agencies, whether large or small, needs a core staff of employees to keep the office operations running smoothly and to support the administration of the agency mission. These core employees are the people who keep the government running and they are integral to every federal agency, from NASA to the U.S. Mint, from the CIA to the National Park Service. As diverse as they are, every federal agency calls upon the same core positions to keep their internal operations in order.

This foundational group of jobs, which are at the heart of virtually every federal agency in the U.S. government, are discussed in this chapter. Because they are so abundant, the core federal positions are not listed separately under each agency profile in this book. To address them in each profile would be redundant.

The good news is that these essential federal positions are everywhere. They can be found in almost every agency in every state across the country. If the position you desire is described in this chapter, you can assume with confidence that the list of government agencies that have career opportunities you'd be interested in is very long and very broad.

Occupational Groupings

The federal government assigns related positions to common occupational groupings. Each occupational group contains several position titles, each with an assigned series number. There are nearly 450 federal occupations that have been grouped into the following 24 groups:

GS-000   Miscellaneous Occupations Group

GS-100   Social Science, Psychology, and Welfare Group

GS-200   Personnel Management and Industrial Relations Group

GS-300   General Administrative, Clerical, and Office Services Group

GS-400   Biological Sciences Group

GS-500   Accounting and Budget Group

GS-600   Medical, Hospital, Dental, and Public Health Group

GS-700   Veterinary Medical Science Group

GS-800   Engineering and Architecture Group

GS-900   Legal and Kindred Group

GS-1000   Information and Arts Group

GS-1100   Business and Industry Group

GS-1200   Copyright, Patent, and Trademark Group

GS-1300   Physical Sciences Group

GS-1400   Library and Archives Group

GS-1500   Mathematics and Statistics Group

GS-1600   Equipment, Facilities, and Service Group

GS-1700   Education Group

GS-1800   Investigation Group

GS-1900   Quality Assurance, Inspection, and Grading Group

GS-2000   Supply Group

GS-2100   Transportation Group

GS-2200   Information Technology Group

GS-2300   Postal Operations Group

These groupings encompass all of the typical federal general schedule occupations. Additional details on federal occupational groupings and series codes can be found in the Office of Personnel Management's *Position Classification Standards*, which is available on their Web site at www.opm.gov. These standards give generalized job descriptions for each of the federal occupations. This resource can also be found at some public libraries.

Another resource, the *Qualification Standards Operating Manual,* provides a look at the specific qualification requirements used by federal staffing specialists when determining the eligibility of applicants for employment in General Schedule (GS) positions.

Core Professional Positions

The following list contains the core federal professional positions that tend to be common throughout the government and that are found in at least 50 percent of the federal agencies. Unless indicated otherwise, all of those listed below follow the GS pay scale for professional positions, beginning at the GS-5 level for recent graduates of bachelor degree programs with no work experience in the appropriate field. Since the job descriptions vary only slightly from agency to agency, one general position description is given here.

Economist (GS-110)

Economists do professional work or provide professional consultation involving research into economic phenomena. They analyze economic data and prepare special or continuing reports on economic activities.

There are nearly 5,000 federal positions in the Economist series. These jobs are found throughout the government.

Human Resources Specialist (GS-201)

Human Resources Specialists provide a variety of human resources services. They apply merit principles to attract, develop, and retain a high-quality and diverse workforce. HR Specialists sustain features of the employer-employee relationship, such as employee benefits. Functional areas may include compensation, classification, employee benefits, recruitment and placement, or military.

There are more than 11,400 federal Human Resources Specialist and related positions.

Information Technology (IT) Specialist (GS-2210)

IT Specialists perform work necessary to design or implement systems for solving problems or accomplishing work by the use of computers. Specializations within the Information Technology series include:

★   IT Specialist: Develops policies and standards that establish the framework for the management of all IT programs.

★   Information Systems Security Specialist/Analyst: Ensures the confidentiality, integrity, and availability of networks, systems, and data through the planning, analysis, development, and implementation of information systems security programs.

★   Computer Programmer: Performs work that involves the design, documentation, development, modification, testing, installation, implementation, and support of new or existing applications software.

★   Systems Analyst: Consults with customers to refine functional requirements and translates functional requirements into technical specifications.

★   Systems Engineer: Performs work that involves the planning, installation, configuration, testing, implementation, and management of the systems environment in support of the organization's IT architecture and business needs.

★   Network Administrator: Performs work that involves the planning, analysis, design, development, testing, quality assurance, configuration, installation, implementation, integration, maintenance, and/or management of networked systems used for the transmission of information in voice, data, and/or video formats.

★   Database Administrator: Plans, develops, and implements systems for the acquisition, storage, and retrieval of data.

★   Web Developer: Applies technical knowledge of Internet systems, services, and technologies toward systems/applications development and technical management of web sites.

★   Systems Administrator: Installs, tests, operates, troubleshoots, and maintains hardware and software systems.

★   Technical Support Specialist: Delivers customer support services, including installation configuration, troubleshooting, and customer assistance and/or training.

There are more than 57,000 federal IT Specialist positions throughout the government.

Management/Program Analyst (GS-343)

Management/Program Analysts provide advice and service to management in such areas as planning, policy development, work methods and procedures, manpower utilization, organizational structures, information management, or similar areas with the objective of improving managerial effectiveness. The paramount qualifications required are a high order of analytical ability and a knowledge of the principles of management.

Management/Program Analysts may also evaluate the actual or potential effectiveness of current or projected operating programs in achieving their objectives. This includes such duties as analyzing the objectives of operating programs, identifying problem areas, trends, and areas of imbalance, and evaluating alternative actions in terms of effect on the program.

There are more than 43,000 federal Management/Program Analyst positions throughout the government.

Logistics Management Specialist (GS-346)

Logistics Management Specialists typically perform staff work in planning and coordinating logistical support activities to provide the money, manpower, material, facilities, and services needed to support a specific mission at the time and place they are needed. The Logistics Management Specialist identifies the activities involved and integrates the efforts of each activity into a comprehensive logistical plan.

There are more than 11,300 federal Logistics Management Specialist positions and related occupations.

Accountant (GS-510)/Auditor (GS-511)

Accountants and Auditors perform professional work in any of several capacities depending upon the accounting system involved, the organizations and operating programs served, and the financial data sought.

Accountants classify and evaluate financial data; record transactions in financial records, develop and install new accounting systems, and prepare financial statements.

Auditors evaluate accounts for the purpose of certifying that various financial statements accurately represent the financial position of the activity audited in terms of assets, liabilities, net worth, and income and expenses.

There are nearly 25,000 federal Accountant/Auditor positions located throughout the government.

Budget Analyst (GS-560)

Persons in positions in this series perform work in the phases or systems of budget administration currently in use in the federal service. Budget Analysts evaluate the relative costs and benefits of alternate courses of budget and program action, check the propriety of obligations and expenditures, establish standard rates and charges to customers, or develop budgetary policy.

There are nearly 13,000 federal Budget Analyst positions nationwide.

Public Affairs Specialist (GS-1035)

Employees in the Public Affairs series perform work to establish and maintain mutual communication between federal agencies and the general public. They identify communications needs and develop informational materials and require skills in written and oral communication, analysis, and interpersonal relations.

There are nearly 6,000 federal Public Affairs Specialist and related positions.

Writer-Editor (GS-1082)/Technical Writer-Editor (GS-1083)

Employees in this series write or edit articles, news releases, pamphlets, reports, brochures, speeches, scripts, or other similar items. Writer-Editors acquire information about the subject involved through library research, background interviews, and reading. They then select the pertinent information and write or edit the final drafts of manuscripts.

Technical Writers draw on a substantial knowledge of a particular subject area to write or edit technical materials such as reports of research findings, scientific or technical articles, technical manuals and specifications, or speeches on scientific or technical subjects.

There are nearly 2,500 federal Writer-Editor and Technical Writer/Editor positions.

Contract Specialist, Procurement Analyst (GS-1102)

Other titles in this series are Contract Negotiator, Contract Administrator, Contract Termination Specialist, Contract Price/Cost Analyst, and Supervisory Contract Specialist (GS-9-15).

Those in positions in this series perform work involving the procurement of supplies, services, construction, or research using formal advertising or negotiation methods. They evaluate contract price/cost proposals by applying knowledge of the legislation, regulations, and methods used in contracting, business, and industry practices.

Contract Specialists plan and conduct the contracting process from the initial description of the requirements through contract delivery.

Procurement Analysts plan and evaluate procurement programs, and review contractual actions for conformance with regulatory requirements and procurement practices.

There are more than 27,000 federal Contract/Procurement positions throughout the government.

Training Specialist, Training Instructor (GS-1712)/General Education and Training (1701)

Training Specialists and Instructors perform work involved in a program of instructional training in an occupation or other subject. They may be instructors in specific subject areas; may develop or review special subject-matter course materials, training aids, and manuals for training programs; or may administer training programs. The duties of some positions include demonstration in the use of equipment, techniques, and principles of the subject being taught.

There are more than 17,000 federal positions related to education and training.

Secretary (GS-318)

Other titles in this series include Administrative Officer (GS-341), and Support Services Administration (GS-342).

Secretaries assist an individual or the staff of that individual by performing general office work auxiliary to the work of the organization. The duties require a knowledge of clerical and administrative procedures and various office skills.

More than 54,000 secretaries work for federal organizations across the nation. Secretary positions often begin at the GS-3/4 level.

Attorney (GS-905)

This series includes professional positions involved in preparing cases for trial and/or the trial of cases before a court or an administrative body. Attorneys render legal advice and services regarding matters falling within the purview of a federal government agency.

More than 27,000 attorneys work throughout the federal government.

Other Positions in Demand

There are other positions in demand in the federal government that are not found throughout all the agencies. For example, the federal government has more than 24,000 Air Traffic Controllers working for a single agency (the FAA). More than 44,000 nurses are federally employed, nearly all of them at the Department of Veterans Affairs.

The following is a chart of these positions in demand that are not necessarily located throughout the government agencies but are still some of the largest occupational groupings in the federal government:

Positions in Demand:

White-Collar Occupations with 15,000 or More Employees

Title	Employment 2000
Misc. Clerk and Assistant	77,148
Misc. Administration	63,218
IT Specialist	57,143
Secretary	50,983
Management/Program Analyst	43,135
Nurse	44,523
Criminal Investigation	35,907
General Attorney	27,237
Contracting	27,149
Social Insurance Administration	26,702
Contact Representative	25,848
Air Traffic Controller	24,071
Medical Officer	21,932
Electronics Engineering	21,018
Engineering Technicians	17,165
General Education and Training	17,067

PART II

AGENCY PROFILES

Welcome to the *Agency Profiles*, created especially for people who are searching out where they might fit in to the massive federal government structure. This portion of the book contains a brief profile of every federal agency that employs about 200 people or more. It is the only resource of its kind that describes every agency in the federal government in terms of the positions they hire (including specific job descriptions for each position), special hiring programs they use, and other core career information. It also offers a look at how the agencies are set up, where their regional offices are located, how to apply for a job with them, and how to find out more information about them. Here are a couple of things to keep in mind as you browse through:

Surf the Charts to Chart Your Course through the Profiles

The Agency Profiles section is an incredible overview of the nearly 200 federal agencies: who they are, what they are, and what types of people they hire. But without a sense of direction and focus, a search through the profiles can be pretty overwhelming. Rather than simply flipping through the profiles aimlessly, try checking out the Career Search Index charts on pages 00 in the back of this book. These charts break the agencies down according to their mission areas, the locations they are in, and the types of people they hire. This will allow you to narrow your focus to only those agencies that appeal to you most. Be bold. Check out as many agencies as you like, and who knows what hidden career possibilities you may dig up. Enjoy the quest!

Common Positions are Listed Elsewhere

Some federal positions, such as Policy Analyst, Budget Analyst, Human Resources Specialist, IT Specialist, and the various administrative and clerical jobs, are very common throughout the federal service and can be found in almost every government agency across the nation. To avoid redundancy, these positions are not included in this section, but can be found in full detail in Chapter 8, *Positions in Demand.* Try referring to Chapter 8 first, then check the Career Search Index in the back to locate your agencies of interest.

Generally, Only Professional Positions Are Listed

The positions covered in this section focus on those at the professional level. Wage-grade positions, and those that start below the GS-5 level, such as technician and clerical jobs, are generally not included, unless those positions are an integral part of the agency's mission, such as firefighters in the U.S. Forest Service.

Yet even within these more focused parameters, you'll be amazed at how broad the range of federal positions is and just how many choices are out there. A thorough search of the Index and the Profiles will surely yield a number of exciting opportunities for you to pursue.

☆ Department of Agriculture (www.usda.gov)

Agricultural Marketing Service (AMS)
www.ams.usda.gov

Nature of Work: Agriculture, consumer protection, marketing, scientific research, trade, wages/prices/rates

Number of Employees: 3,100

Headquarters: Washington, DC

Regional Locations: None

Typical Background of New Hires: Agriculture, agronomy, business, marketing

Mission

AMS promotes the orderly and efficient marketing of agricultural products from the farm gate to the consumer's table. In carrying out its mission, AMS is responsible for providing market news, commodity standards, and grading and inspection services for various agricultural commodities, including cotton, tobacco, dairy products, fruits and vegetables, livestock, meat, poultry, and egg products.

Job Descriptions

Agricultural Commodity Grader: Examines and evaluates agricultural products to determine their official U.S. grade and to evaluate their quality in accordance with official standards. Inspects or monitors the conditions under which the product is processed, stored, or transported to determine the effect of these conditions on product quality.

Agricultural Marketing Specialist: Incorporates a knowledge of the commodity exchanges and markets, agricultural statutory provisions, and agribusiness operations to analyze, manage, and regulate the marketing of agricultural commodities.

Market News Reporter: Gathers, analyzes, and disseminates current information on available supplies, demand, prices, marketing trends, and other facts relating to the marketing of agricultural products.

Microbiologist: Conducts microbiological examinations of food and other agricultural products to determine the presence, numbers, and/or species of microorganisms.

Major Activities and Divisions

Commodity Programs: The AMS is divided into six commodity programs: cotton, dairy, fruit and vegetable, livestock and seed, poultry, and tobacco. The programs employ specialists who provide standardization, grading, and market news services for these commodities.

Science and Technology Program: Provides centralized scientific support to AMS programs, including lab analysis, lab quality assurance, coordination of scientific research, and statistical and mathematical consulting services.

Transportation and Marketing Program: Works to ensure an effective transportation system to move agricultural products through the nation's highways, railroads, airports, and waterways, and into the domestic and international marketplace.

Alternative Employment Programs

AMS has a student Career Experience program that provides hands-on training for students who have completed at least their sophomore year of college. These positions are located nationwide. For more information, see "internship programs" at the AMS Web site.

Application Procedures

AMS lists current job openings on its Web site at www.ams.usda.gov. Read the instructions on the vacancy announcement for application instructions for particular job openings or direct inquiries to the AMS program area in which you are interested:

Cotton: (202) 720-3193
Compliance and Analysis: (202) 720-6766
Dairy: (202) 720-4392
Fruit and Vegetable: (202) 720-4722
Livestock and Seed: (202) 720-5705
Poultry: (202) 720-4476
Science and Technology: (202) 720-5231
Tobacco: (202) 205-0567
Transportation: (202) 690-1300

AMS headquarters mailing address:

Agricultural Marketing Service
Department of Agriculture Division
South Bldg.
14th St. and Independence Ave. SW
Washington, DC 20250
Information: (202) 720-8999

Agricultural Research Service (ARS)
www.ars.usda.gov

Nature of Work: Agriculture, scientific research

Number of Employees: 8,500

Headquarters: Washington, DC

Regional Locations: Albany, CA; Athens, GA; Beltsville, MD; College Station, TX; Ft. Collins, CO; Peoria, IL; Philadelphia, PA; Stoneville, MS

Typical Background of New Hires: Agriculture, agronomy, biological sciences (animal science, entomology, genetics, plant science), biology, chemistry, engineering, physical sciences (physiology), soil science, veterinary medicine

Mission

ARS is responsible for planning and conducting research that provides new knowledge and technologies to ensure an adequate supply of food and fiber for the nation's population. The agency's objectives include research and development in the area of natural resources, crop and animal quality and productivity, commodity conversion and delivery, and human health.

Job Descriptions

Agronomist: Performs research on breeding, production, and culture of aquatic, field, and horticultural crops. Studies relationships of plants and soil, weed control, and plant adaptation.

Animal Scientist: Studies the classification, structure, ecology, parasitological phenomena, and the evolutional history of livestock animals. Performs research in the areas of animal quality and productivity.

Chemist: Performs research in the areas of analytical chemistry, biochemistry, and organic chemistry. Investigates agricultural commodities in terms of composition, molecular structure, and chemical properties. Examines the effects of chemical applications and chemical transformations.

Entomologist: Investigates plant-eating insects for the control of weeds and evaluates insect-resistant plant varieties. Studies chemical and nonchemical methods of control of insect pest populations. Classifies and examines the geographical distribution of insects and mites, and investigates the role of insects as vectors of diseases affecting crops, animals, and humans.

Engineer (Agricultural, Chemical, Civil, Electrical, Hydraulic, Industrial, Mechanical): Depending upon the area of specialization, an ARS engineer can focus on a certain agricultural research area: soil and water conservation; the design of specialized equipment and facilities; the design of farmsteads; the development of farm machinery; the use of electricity in agriculture; or agricultural marketing procedures.

Geneticist: Performs research in inheritance and interaction of genetic characters, their environment, and basic physiological principles. Develops breeding methods and selection procedures.

Microbiologist: Studies the characteristics and life process of microorganisms and their relationships to plant and animal life forms. Conducts research into such fields as immunology, medical parasitology, physiology, genetics, and cytology. Develops scientific microbiological methods in the investigation and use of microorganisms in agriculture.

Physiologist: Performs research on the physiological processes of plants, including photosynthesis, mineral element nutrition, absorption, and the effects of chemicals, light, and moisture.

Plant Pathologist: Performs research on plant diseases caused by parasitic or nonparasitic microorganisms and viruses. Studies the life cycles of disease-producing organisms and host-parasite relationships, and explores methods for disease prevention and control. Examines the effects of diseases on the culture, harvest, transportation, and storage of plants.

Plant Physiologist: Performs research on physiological processes in plants, including photosynthesis, respiration, mineral element nutrition, water relations, and absorption. Studies the effects of light, temperature, moisture, and chemicals on the growth, ripening, and quality of plants.

Soil Scientist: Studies the relationship between plants and soil. Examines effects of various soil mixtures and mineral components on maturity, ripening, and quality of plants and plant processes.

Veterinary Medical Officer: Conducts research into the breeding, feeding, and hygienic management of livestock and poultry. Studies diseases that affect livestock, such as tuberculosis, cattle-tick, and scabies and examines methods of prevention or eradication of such diseases.

Major Activities and Divisions

ARS is divided into twenty-two National Programs, which coordinate ARS's 1200+ research projects. These include:

* ☆ Animal Production, Product Value, and Safety: Includes food safety, nutrition, animal health, and food animal production.

* ☆ Natural Resources and Sustainable Agricultural Systems. Includes water quality and management, air quality, soil resource management, and global change.

* ☆ Crop Production, Product Value, and Safety: Includes plant, microbial, and insect genetic resources; plant diseases, crop protection, and quarantine; and energy alternatives.

The National Agricultural Library (NAL): NAL houses the world's largest collection of printed materials on agriculture and related sciences. It collects technical information on agriculture and related subjects from all over the world and makes it available to scientists, educators, and farmers in printed form and on computer databases. Their Web site is www.nal.usda.gov.

Alternative Employment Programs

ARS maintains an active co-op program that focuses on life science majors. Positions typically filled are Biological Aid/Technician and Physical Science Aid/Technician. ARS hires co-ops at the GS-3 or GS-9 levels, depending upon education and experience. Contact your school placement office for more information. ARS also conducts an extensive volunteer program for students.

Remarks

Research activities are carried out at 121 domestic locations, including Puerto Rico and the Virgin Islands, and in eight foreign countries.

Application Procedures

ARS lists current job openings at their Web site at www.ars.usda.gov. Because they are part of the REE (Research, Education, and Economics) portion of the Department of Agriculture, this Web site also provides a list of current job openings for the Economic Research Service, the National Agricultural Statistics Service, and the Cooperative State Research, Education, and Extension Service. Follow the application directions on the vacancy announcement you have interest in. Or, contact the regional office in which you have interest:

Beltsville Area
USDA, REE, Agricultural Research Service
Human Resources Division
5601 Sunnyside Avenue
Beltsville, MD 20705
(301) 504-1482 (Job Line)

Midsouth Area
Experimental Station and Lee Roads
P.O. Box 225
Stoneville, MS 38776
(662) 686-5265

Northern Plains Area
1201 Oakridge Rd., Suite 150
Ft. Collins, CO 80525-5562
(662) 686-5265

North Atlantic Area
600 East Mermaid La.
Philadelphia, PA 19118
(215) 233-6593

Pacific West Area
800 Buchanan St.
Albany, CA 94710
(510) 559-6060

South Atlantic Area
College Station Rd.
P.O. Box 5677
Athens, GA 30604
(706) 546-3311

Southern Plains Area
7607 East Mark Dr.
Suite 230
College Station, TX 77840
(409) 260-9346
(301) 344-2288 (Job Hotline)

Midwest Area
1815 North University St.
Peoria, IL 61604
(309) 681-6600

National Agricultural Library
10301 Baltimore Ave.
Beltsville, MD 20705
(301) 504-5248
Dial-a-Vacancy: (301) 504-1482

Animal and Plant Health Inspection Service (APHIS)
www.aphis.usda.gov

Nature of Work: Agriculture, biotechnology, import/export, plant/animal health

Number of Employees: 7,500

Headquarters: Washington, DC

Regional Locations: Employees work at ports of entry across the U.S. and in several foreign countries.

Typical Background of New Hires: Biological sciences (botany, microbiology), biology, environmental sciences, veterinary medicine (DVM), wildlife biology

Mission

APHIS protects the animal and plant resources of the nation from disease and pests to preserve the marketability of U.S. agricultural products in this country and abroad. In cooperation with state governments, APHIS administers federal laws and regulations pertaining to animal and plant health and quarantine, humane treatment of animals, and the control and eradication of pests and diseases.

Job Descriptions

Microbiologist: Conducts scientific research into the characteristics and life processes of microorganisms and their relationships to other living forms. Studies the distribution of microorganisms in agricultural and animal commodities and products, their reaction to physical and chemical factors in the environment, their role as pathogenic and immunizing agents, and their isolation, cultivation, identification, and classification.

Plant Protection and Quarantine Officer: Inspects passengers, commerce, baggage, and cargo entering the U.S. to ensure it is free of prohibited pests and organisms. Inspects and certifies domestic commodities for export, regulates the import and export of endangered plant species, ensures that imported seed is free of noxious weeds, and regulates genetically engineered organisms that present a plant pest risk. Conducts domestic control and eradication programs on established insect pest populations. May work at any major port of entry in the U.S. or overseas.

Veterinary Medical Officer: Maintains inspection and quarantine service at designated ports of entry for imported animals and birds. Determines the existence or extent of outbreaks of disease and pests affecting livestock and poultry. Organizes control and eradication programs in cooperation with state officials and cooperates with animal health officials in other countries in planning and conducting disease control efforts. Monitors the handling of livestock and poultry to assure humane treatment, and ensures that laws governing the transportation, sale, and handling of dogs, cats, and circus and zoo animals are obeyed.

Wildlife Biologist: Conducts professional scientific biological work in the conservation and management of wildlife. Applies biological facts and procedures necessary for the conservation and management of wildlife in order to ensure compatibility with human demands and needs.

Major Activities and Divisions

Inspection Activities: APHIS conducts inspection and quarantine activities at U.S. ports of entry to prevent the introduction of exotic animal and plant diseases and pests.

Regulatory Activities: APHIS develops standards for veterinary biologics and inspects establishments that handle animals intended for research or exhibition.

Wildlife Control: APHIS carries out cooperative operational programs to control wildlife damage.

Alternative Employment Programs

APHIS hires approximately 10 to 20 co-op students per year. Students typically begin at the GS-5 or 7 levels and are often hired during their junior year in school. APHIS also hires Stay-in School students for clerical positions and numerous summer interns in scientific, technical, and administrative fields nationwide.

Application Procedures

APHIS hosts a job site for all USDA MRP (Marketing and Regulatory Programs) agencies. These agencies have a job system called PEARS, which allows prospective employees to browse through job listings. Log on to the main APHIS Web site and look for the PEARS link.

For further information on positions in the U.S., contact:
Field Personnel Services
APHIS
Human Resources
Butler Square West
100 North 6th St.
Minneapolis, MN 55403
Toll free: (800) 762-2738

For further information on job positions abroad, contact:
Resources Management Staff
APHIS
International Services Unit 65
4700 River Rd.
Riverdale, MD 20737-1228
(301) 734-7550

Cooperative State Research, Education, and Extension Service (CSREES)
www.reeusda.gov

Nature of Work: Agriculture, education, scientific research, volunteers

Number of Employees: 210

Headquarters: Washington, DC

Regional Locations: Federal employees work in the DC headquarters only. Cooperative Extension Service employees (state or county employees) work across the country in conjunction with CSREES.

Typical Background of New Hires: Agriculture, agronomy, biological sciences (animal science, horticulture), education, home economics

Mission

CSREES is the educational agency of the Department of Agriculture and the federal partner in the Cooperative Extension System, integrating federal, state, and county governments. All three partners share in financing, planning, and conducting CSREES's educational programs that link research, science, and technology to the needs of people.

Job Descriptions

Agricultural Extension Specialist: This is a very broad title encompassing all of the CSREES program area employees who may specialize in a certain area of agriculture or home economics such as horticulture, animal science, or agronomy. Agricultural Extension Specialists in Washington are responsible for disseminating information on research, trends, marketing, and other agricultural or home economics issues through the nationwide educational network. They also provide national-level policy formulation, program leadership, and evaluation systems in support of the Cooperative Extension System.

Major Activities and Divisions

There are currently seven educational program areas at CSREES. They are agriculture; natural resources and environment management; Community Resources and Economic Development; Family Development and Resource Management; 4-H and Youth Development; Nutrition, Diet, and Health; and Leadership and Volunteer Development.

Alternative Employment Programs

The CSREES maintains a student employment program in its Washington office.

Remarks

The Cooperative Extension Services at the land-grant universities have professional staff located at the state, county, and area level. They work in cooperation with CSREES in Washington to assess clientele needs and develop educational programs to assist farmers, families, individuals, and communities in cultivating problem-solving and decision-making skills. They apply new communications technologies, including computers, video, satellites, and teleconferencing in producing and delivering educational programs.

Application Procedures

Direct inquiries to:
    CSREES
    Personnel and Management Services Division
    Cooperative Management Staff, USDA
    South Bldg.
    14th St. and Independence Ave. SW
    Washington, DC 20250
    (202) 720-6130
    E-mail: CSREES@reeusda.gov

> ### The Economic Research Service (ERS)
> ### www.ers.usda.gov
>
> **Nature of Work:** Agriculture, economic policy, information, scholarly research
>
> **Number of Employees:** 500
>
> **Headquarters:** Washington, DC
>
> **Regional Locations:** None
>
> **Typical Background of New Hires:** Agriculture, economics, geography, history, law, mathematics, media communications, political science, social work/sociology, statistics

Mission

The Economic Research Service generates economic and social information that agricultural decision makers use to measure and improve the performance of agriculture and rural America.

Job Descriptions

Agricultural Economist: Monitors and analyzes U.S. and world agricultural production and demand for agricultural commodities. Evaluates the economic performance of U.S. agricultural production and marketing and estimates the effects of Government policies on farmers, rural communities, and natural resources. There are 397 Agricultural Economists at ERS. Positions may be filled in any one of the four program divisions at ERS headquarters.

Economist: Conducts economic research into issues such as agricultural supply, demand, consumption patterns, international trade, and domestic policy. Conducts situation and outlook reporting activities and prepares interpretive reports.

Geographer: Collects and analyzes information regarding geographical issues such as land ownership, use, and value. Monitors the nation's land and resource base and analyzes the interrelationships between land resources, economic returns, and the competition for agricultural land.

Historian: Performs historical research on agricultural, economic, and policy issues. Collects historical facts on such things as the effects of government programs on farmers and the economic performance of U.S. agricultural production. Analyzes current agricultural and rural issues for the view of the U.S. and world economies and provides a historical view on the forces shaping those economies.

Mathematician: Performs research using basic mathematical principles and methods. Develops mathematical techniques in the solution of agricultural economic, marketing, and production problems and issues.

Sociologist: Performs research and scientific study into the culture, structure, and functioning of agricultural communities. Assesses rural areas in terms of demographics and agricultural production. Monitors trends in rural populations, employment, income, and farm ownership.

Statistician: Gathers and interprets quantified information. Prepares situation and outlook reports on agricultural issues, including supply, demand, trade, and production.

Major Activities and Divisions

Commodity Economics Division (CED): Carries out a program of analysis designed to improve understanding of U.S. and world markets for agricultural products.

Agriculture and Trade Analysis Division (ATAD): Provides research information on agricultural trade and development relationships between the U.S. and foreign countries.

Resources and Technology Division (RTD): Provides economic analyses of agricultural resource and technology issues at both national and regional levels.

Agriculture and Rural Economy Division (ARED): Conducts a program of research to increase understanding of national and regional trends in agriculture and rural areas.

Alternative Employment Programs

ERS offers summer internship positions for both graduate and undergraduate students, principally in agricultural economics, economics, and information technology. See the ERS Web site for details.

Remarks

ERS publishes several magazines and periodicals, including *Farmline*, *Rural Development Perspectives*, and *National Food Review*.

Application Procedures

ERS often has openings for economists and agricultural economists, and therefore maintains a standing register (open job announcement) for these positions. All other positions are announced as they arise.

Direct inquiries to:
Economic Research Service
1800 M St. NW
Washington, DC 20250
(202) 694-5110

Farm Service Agency (FSA)
www.fsa.usda.gov

Nature of Work: Agriculture, disaster assistance, environmental protection, forestry/wildlife, marketing, trade

Number of Employees: 6,700 (also 12,000 nonfederal employees)

Headquarters: Washington, DC

Regional Locations: Billings, MT; Dallas, TX; Indianapolis, IN; Jackson, MS; Kansas City, MO; Oklahoma City, OK; Puerto Rico; Raleigh, NC; Sacramento, CA; Salt Lake City, UT; Spokane, WA; Springfield, IL; St. Paul, MN; Topeka, KS; Valdosta, GA. FSA also has field offices in each state and in most counties.

Typical Background of New Hires: Accounting, agriculture, agronomy, business, economics, marketing, mathematics, soil science, statistics, transportation

Mission

FSA administers agricultural commodity, conservation, environmental protection, and emergency programs. Its primary goals are establishing commodity price stability, orderly marketing, and resource conservation programs. Administration of the farm programs authorized by the Congress is handled through a system of state and county committees throughout the fifty states.

FSA is also responsible for developing and administering crop insurance programs in a way that provides as many producers as possible the opportunity to protect their crop investments against losses due to natural disasters. It also provides financial and other assistance to family farmers who are unable to obtain credit from regular commercial lenders.

Job Descriptions

Agricultural Economist: Analyzes and interprets economic data relating to agricultural trends. Prepares special reports on economic facts and agricultural activities as they affect the market balance. Trainee positions are available.

Agricultural Management Specialist: Acts on debt settlement matters and assists or provides credit counseling for borrowers. This position requires a working knowledge of farm business organization, agricultural credit, rural housing, and farm management practices. Position can grow into a County Supervisor post.

Agricultural Marketing Specialist: Conducts research and makes recommendations concerning the marketing of one or more agricultural commodities or marketing facilities and services. Works with various agricultural trade groups in the sale, exchange, purchase, and disposition of agricultural commodities. Trainee positions are available.

Agricultural Program Specialist: Assists in formulating policy by making recommendations for consideration of state committees on current and proposed services. Directs the grain storage programs of the Commodity Credit Corporation (CCC). Assists in program operations and conducts meetings with county and community committee members, farmers, growers' associations, warehouse workers, and processors on various programs. Also conducts the state and county office manager training programs. Trainee positions are available.

Area Claims Specialist: Establishes and maintains a program for claims processing and quality assurance. Assigns work to Loss Adjustment Contractors. No degree is required, but an applicant should have experience with or knowledge of crops, farming practices, agricultural marketing trends, and natural crop hazards.

Compliance Investigator: Conducts independent, on-site compliance reviews. Evaluates general FSA program activities and the operations of private insurance companies under contract with or reinsured by FSA. Performs reviews to ensure compliance with policies, procedures, and guidelines. No degree is needed, but requirements for the position include knowledge of investigative techniques and agricultural practices of the farming industry.

County Executive Director: Works with the elected county committee in managing the day-to-day operations of one of the 2,600 County Offices. County Executive Directors are not federal employees but receive federal benefits. Director trainee positions are filled at a level comparable to a GS-5. Service as a County Executive Director is a stepping stone to federal positions in field and Washington FSA offices.

Crop Insurance Underwriter: Assists in establishing county actuarial structures by analyzing soil capabilities and limitations, farming practices, production, and climatological data. Assigns premium rates and crop coverage in a specified region according to regulations. Requires a bachelor's degree in agriculture or experience that demonstrates knowledge of agricultural principles such as herbicide and insecticide requirements, planting dates, drainage, and soils.

Insurance Management Specialist: Plans and directs the operation of contract service programs. Develops and recommends FSA policies and practices related to sales and contract servicing. Requires a broad knowledge of crops, farming practices, crop hazards, and crop insurance policies.

Loan Specialist: Provides supervised credit to family farmers, rural residents, and small communities. Reviews applications and assesses borrower eligibility and soundness of loan proposals. These positions are available in field locations.

Loss Adjustment Contractor: Visits farms to inspect damaged or destroyed crops. Appraises potential crop production, measures acreage, and explains contractual responsibilities to the insured. Determines time and cause of loss, and measures farm-stored production. Promotes the crop insurance program and maintains positive relationships with people who are insured. NOTE: Loss Adjustment Contractor positions are NOT federal positions. Because they work closely with FSA, however, you may inquire with FSA personnel for further information.

Statistician: Develops coverage and premium rates using various statistical methods. Requires a bachelor's degree.

Traffic Management Specialist: Plans and develops traffic management programs by formulating policies, evaluating programs and operations, and conducting special studies. Furnishes technical traffic-management advisory services. Trainee positions are available.

Major Activities and Divisions

Commodity Programs: FSA administers the CCC's commodity stabilization programs.

Emergency Assistance: In the aftermath of a natural disaster, FSA assists farmers with cost-sharing to carry out emergency conservation practices on damaged farmland.

Conservation Programs: FSA conservation programs target such environmental concerns as soil erosion, water pollution, wetland protection, and timberland improvement.

Commodity Purchases and Donations: FSA employees are the administrative agents for CCC, which provides financing for farm programs and for the purchase, storage, and disposal of commodities in federal stocks.

Other FSA Programs

FSA offers insurance through two basic delivery systems: sales and service agencies (Master Marketers) and private insurance companies that it reinsures. Master Marketers provide management, supervision of at least 25 agents, and contract servicing. Reinsured companies offer crop insurance under their own brand names and provide marketing, distribution, servicing, and loss adjustment functions. FSA carries out all other activities, such as loss adjustment and claims functions on policies sold by Master Marketers, training for agents and loss adjusters, marketing services, and quality control.

FSA's credit delivery system is carried out through a network of local offices that serve every rural county or parish in the fifty states. The network includes 46 state offices, 260 district offices, and about 1,930 county offices.

Alternative Employment Programs

FSA hires co-op students at the high school and college (undergraduate and graduate) levels, targeting agriculture and business administration majors. Contact your school's placement or cooperative education office for more information.

Remarks

FSA has regional offices across the U.S.:

State Offices: Each state FSA office has an administrative staff and agricultural program specialists.

County Offices: The agency has a locally administered office in most counties headed by a county committee and a County Executive Director.

Area Offices: There are two FSA offices in Kansas City, each with a separate function. The Kansas City Commodity Office (KCCO) is responsible for acquiring, storing, and disposing of bulk and processed commodities. The Kansas City Management Office (KCMO) is the processing office for FSA and CCC programs. There is also a Caribbean area office in Puerto Rico.

The Aerial Photography Field Office: Houses aerial photographs covering all of the nation's major cropland areas. The photos provide visual information for local planning groups and are widely sold to other agencies and to the public.

Application Procedures

Direct inquiries to either office:
USDA-FSA, Personnel Division
South Bldg.
Washington, DC 20013
(202) 720-5237

Or

USDA-FSA-KCMO, Personnel Division
Kansas City, MO 64141-0205
(816) 926-6647

Grain Inspection, Packers, and Stockyards Administration (GIPSA)
www.usda.gov/gipsa/

Nature of Work: Agriculture, import/export

Number of Employees: 1,000

Headquarters: Washington, DC

Regional Locations: GIPSA has an office in almost every state.

Typical Background of New Hires: Agriculture, business, economics

Mission

Facilitates the marketing of livestock, poultry, meat, cereals, oilseeds, and related agricultural products, and promotes fair and competitive trading practices for the benefit of consumers and American agriculture.

Job Descriptions

Agricultural Commodity Grader: Examines and evaluates products to determine their official U.S. grade and/or their acceptability in terms of quality or condition. Inspects or monitors the conditions under which the product is stored, processed, or transported.

Agricultural Marketing Specialist: Conducts research and analysis into the marketing of one or more agricultural commodities or products. Incorporates a knowledge of marketing practices, the commodity exchanges and markets, agricultural trade, and statutory provisions to establish agricultural marketing programs.

Scales and Weighing Specialist: Provides official weighing services at export port locations and at inland locations for domestic grain. Provides oversight, guidance, and assistance to nonfederal agencies performing official weighing activities. These positions are typically not filled at the entry level.

Major Activities and Divisions

GIPSA comprises two major divisions:

✶ Federal Grain Inspection Service: Establishes official U.S. standards for grading grain and sees that these standards are uniformly applied.

✶ Packers and Stockyards Programs: A regulatory entity that ensures open and competitive markets for livestock, meat, and poultry.

Alternative Employment Programs

GIPSA hires approximately 1 to 10 co-op students per year. They typically begin at the GS-4 level and fill the position of Physical Science Technician. Contact your school placement office for more information.

Application Procedures

Address inquiries to:
USDA, GIPSA
1400 Independence Ave SW
Washington, DC 20250
(202) 720-0219

Kansas City Technical Center
USDA, GIPSA, TSD
10383 N. Ambassador Dr.
Kansas City, MO 64153

Food and Nutrition Service (FNS)
www.fns.usda.gov

Nature of Work: Education, food/nutrition, health, social services

Number of Employees: 1,900

Headquarters: Alexandria, VA

Regional Locations: Atlanta, GA; Burlington, MA; Chicago, IL; Dallas, TX; Denver, CO; Robbinsville, NJ; San Francisco, CA

Typical Background of New Hires: Business, health sciences, home economics, public administration

Mission

The Food and Nutrition Service administers USDA's numerous food assistance programs, which are designed to provide access to a more nutritious diet for persons with low incomes and to encourage better eating patterns among the nation's children.

Job Descriptions

Food Program Specialist: (Comprises half of the employees of FNS) Develops, evaluates, and promotes programs concerned with providing food to low-income households, schools, and nonprofit institutions through food assistance programs. Examines state and local operating programs, drafts regulations and instructions that put program legislation into effect, and develops national models to improve program effectiveness.

Investigator: Conducts confidential reviews of firms and individuals suspected of committing Food Stamp Program violations. Travels extensively to visit sites and conduct interviews.

Public Health Nutritionist: Provides technical expertise in the areas of food and nutrition. Develops nutrition education materials, and administers national nutrition education programs.

Major Activities and Divisions

FNS oversees several food assistance programs operated in cooperation with states and local governments.

The Food Stamp Program: Provides food coupons and Electronic Benefits Transfer cards to needy persons to increase their food purchasing power.

Child Nutrition: Designed to improve the nutrition of children, especially those from low-income families, by providing nutritious school meals and nutrition assistance for day-care programs.

The Food Distribution Program: Makes food available to low-income families, the elderly, and on Indian reservations.

The WIC Program/ Farmer's Market: Provides specified nutritious food supplements to low-income pregnant and nursing women.

Team Nutrition: Provides schools with nutrition education materials for children and families.

Alternative Employment Programs

FNS participates in an employment program for college students with appropriate majors. It offers a summer intern program, targeting sophomore-level college students and filling about 20–25 positions nationwide. The closing date for the summer intern application is usually in mid-March. FNS also participates in the PMI program.

Remarks

FNS was formerly named the Food and Consumer Service.

Application Procedures

FNS lists current vacancy announcements at OPM's USAJOBS site. Or, direct inquiries to the regional office in which you would like to work:

Headquarters Address
USDA Food and Nutrition
Service Personnel Division
Operations Branch, Room 614
3101 Park Center Dr.
Alexandria, VA 22302
(703)-305-2326

Regional Offices
Food and Nutrition Service
Mid-Atlantic Regional Office
300 Corporate Blvd.
Robbinsville, NJ 08691
(609) 259-5025

Southeast Regional Office
61 Forsyth St., SW; Room 8T36
Atlanta, GA 30303
(404) 562-1800

Southwest Regional Office
1100 Commerce St., Room 5-A-6
Dallas, TX 75242
(214) 290-9800

Western Regional Office
550 Kearney St. Room 400
San Francisco, CA 94108
(415) 705-1310

Northeast Regional Office
10 Causeway St. Room 501
Boston, MA 02222-1069
(617) 565-6370

Midwest Regional Office
77 West Jackson Blvd., 20th Floor
Chicago, IL 60604
(312) 353-6664

Mountain Plains Regional Office
1244 Speer Blvd., Suite 903
Denver, CO 80204
(303) 844-0300

Food Safety and Inspection Service (FSIS)
www.fsis.usda.gov

Nature of Work: Consumer protection, food/nutrition, health/health care

Number of Employees: Approx. 11,000

Headquarters: Washington, DC

Regional Locations: Alameda, CA; Atlanta, GA (Inspection Office and Lab); Dallas, TX; Des Moines, IA; Minneapolis, MN (Servicing Personnel Office); Philadelphia, PA; Lawrence, KS; Madison, WI; Omaha, NE; Albany, NY; Beltsville, MD; Boulder, CO; Chicago, IL; Jackson, MI: Pickerington, OH; Raleigh, NC; Salem, OR; Springdale, AR

Typical Background of New Hires: Food science, veterinary medicine (D.V.M.)

Mission

FSIS is responsible for assuring that federal health standards are met in the processing of meat, poultry, and egg products. It also conducts research projects to devise ways of improving meat products in terms of nutritional value, cholesterol levels, and other health-related aspects.

Job Descriptions

Food Inspector: Inspects the slaughter and processing of food animals in meat or poultry plants and/or inspects processed meat and poultry products. Over 6,000 positions exist nationwide.

Food Technologist: Monitors compliance with regulations concerning proper formulation and labeling of processed products, authorized levels of food additives, sanitation, and packaging. Technologists are assigned to meat packing plants in various cities throughout the U.S. Technologist positions offer rotational or stationary work options. These positions are technical rather than professional in nature and do not require a college degree.

Veterinary Medical Officer: (Requires a D.V.M. from an accredited veterinary school.) Performs antemortem and postmortem inspection of food animals. Acts as resident pathologist, parasitologist, and epidemiologist at one or several packing plants. Identifies and removes from the food-processing cycle those carcasses that are unfit for human consumption. Also ensures that plants and facilities meet federal standards of cleanliness and that processed foods are truthfully labeled according to federal law.

Major Activities and Divisions

The FSIS is divided into five regional offices, three laboratories, and twenty-six small area offices. The bulk of FSIS employees are stationed in meatpacking plants throughout the country.

Alternative Employment Programs

The FSIS participates in both the STEP program, which enables students to earn a salary while continuing their education, and the Student Career Experience Program, which offers students work experience in their field.

Application Procedures

FSIS has online job announcements at their Web site. They also have a toll-free, 24-hour information request line: 800-370-3747. Or, see FSISCAREERS@usda.gov.

All hiring for FSIS field positions is done through the Minneapolis national personnel office. Direct inquiries in writing to:

For field positions:

USDA
Food Safety and Inspection Service
Butler Square West, 4th Floor
100 North Sixth St.
Minneapolis, MN 55403
(612) 370-2400

For headquarters positions:

U.S. Department of Agriculture
Food Safety and Inspection Service
Human Resources Division
Room 3161, South Bldg.
14th St. and Independence Ave. SW
Washington, DC 20250
(202) 720-6617
Information: (202) 720-7943

Foreign Agricultural Service (FAS)
www.fas.usda.gov

Nature of Work: Agriculture, import/export, international affairs, marketing, trade

Number of Employees: 800

Headquarters: Washington, DC

Regional Locations: 75 American embassy and consulate locations around the world, covering 130 countries

Typical Background of New Hires: Agriculture, economics, marketing

Mission

The Foreign Agricultural Service helps American farmers and traders take maximum advantage of increased opportunities to sell U.S. agricultural commodities abroad and helps increase U.S. farm income. The agency operates an information and market development program that serves U.S. agricultural communities and government decision makers.

Job Descriptions

Agricultural Economist: Analyzes and advises on the agricultural economy, developments, and trends in the U.S. and foreign countries. Conducts economic analyses in connection with the development of international markets for U.S. agricultural commodities.

Agricultural Marketing Specialist: Evaluates production and consumption trends and food and fiber requirements of foreign countries. Researches and designs international market development programs. Conducts competition studies and examines international marketing trends.

International Economist: Analyzes the trade policies and practices of foreign countries to ensure conformance with international treaty negotiations. Maintains an ongoing effort to reduce foreign trade barriers and practices that discourage the export of U.S. farm products. Conducts overseas travel for export promotion programs. Participates in international trade negotiations, and administers agricultural import quotas and regulations.

Agricultural Attaché: See *Remarks* below.

Major Activities and Divisions

FAS maintains a worldwide agricultural intelligence and reporting system through its attaché service. It also has a continuing marketing development program, and, through the Office of the General Sales Manager, manages agricultural functions under the Public Law 480 Program.

Alternative Employment Programs

FAS hires college students for its co-op program. Typical majors are economics, marketing, computer science, and international business. Typical titles are Economist Assistant and Marketing Assistant.

Remarks

FAS does not place entry-level personnel directly into overseas positions. Agricultural Economists and Marketing Specialists enter into the Professional Development Program, which prepares candidates for tours in the worldwide Agricultural Attaché Service after one to three years in Washington. The Agricultural Attaché monitors international agricultural markets and reports to Washington on matters of trade, analysis of supply and demand, market opportunities, and export programs.

Before being assigned overseas, most employees must pass an examination process for entry into the Foreign Service. Overseas assignments typically last 2–4 years.

Application Procedures

Current job opportunities are listed on the FAS Web site, including positions for the Risk Management Agency and the Farm Service. Or, direct inquiries to:

Recruitment Officer

Foreign Agricultural Service, USDA
FAS Personnel, Room 5627, South Bldg.
1400 Independence Ave. SW
Washington, DC 20250-1004
(202) 720-7115 (Public Affairs)

U.S. Forest Service
www.fs.fed.us/

Nature of Work: Environmental protection, forestry/wildlife, recreation

Number of Employees: Over 30,000

Headquarters: Washington, DC

Regional Locations: Albany, CA; Albuquerque, NM; Asheville, NC; Atlanta, GA; Berkeley, CA; Radnor, PA; Fort Collins, CO; Juneau, AK; Lakewood, CO; Madison, WI; Milwaukee, WI; Missoula, MT; New Orleans, LA; Ogden, UT; Portland, OR; Rio Piedras, PR; St. Paul, MN (List includes regional offices and some experiment stations.)

Typical Background of New Hires: Archaeology, biological sciences (entomology, fisheries, wildlife biology, zoology), biology, botany, earth sciences (hydrology), education (outdoor education), engineering, environmental sciences, forestry, geology, soil science

Mission

The Forest Service is responsible for managing the nation's almost 200 million acres of National Forest land, which contain vast reserves of timber and water resources and are home to many species of wildlife. Farmers and ranchers use its pastures for grazing their livestock, and industry buys its timber to produce wood products. The Forest Service also develops human resources through such programs as the Job Corps and the Youth Conservation Corps.

Job Descriptions

Archaeologist: Performs research or other professional or scientific work in archaeology, including the study of historic and prehistoric cultures. Conducts field studies, laboratory analyses, and library research. Prepares reports for publication and advises on historic preservation issues.

Engineer (Civil, Mechanical, Agricultural, Electrical): Engineers provide technical expertise in forest resource management. Civil engineers work in systems, planning design and construction for roads, bridges, buildings, waste treatment systems, and other facilities. Mechanical and agricultural engineers develop, test, and select mechanical equipment for use in tree planting, brush cutting, fire control, chemical spreading, timber harvesting, and other forest management projects. Electrical engineers analyze and make recommendations on the effects of power-line and waterpower usage on national forests. They also design and select remote telephone systems and microwave and electrical transmission systems.

Entomologist: Examines the geographical distribution of insects and investigates chemical and nonchemical methods of insect control. Studies the role of insects as carriers of diseases affecting plants and wildlife.

Firefighter: Works with an interagency team and interdisciplinary specialists to prevent the outbreak of forest fires and fight uncontrolled fires. Specialty areas include Hotshot, Helitack, Handcrew, Helishot, Engine, and Fire Prevention/Patrol. Permanent and temporary positions exist.

Fishery Biologist: Conducts studies in the development, conservation, and management of fishery resources. Develops spawning beds for fish, stabilizes stream channels, and develops fishing lakes. Consults and cooperates with state fish agencies in the maintenance and improvement of fish habitats and the conservation of endangered aquatic species.

Forester: Develops, conserves, and manages the natural resources of forests, including timber, soil, land, water, wildlife, and fish habitats. Protects resources against fire, insects, disease, floods, and erosion. Interprets and implements legislation on the management of forestland.

Fuels Planner: Assists in the prevention of forest fire outbreaks by detecting and reducing hazardous buildups of fire fuel. This includes thinning, shrub treatments, gravel piling, and prescribed burns. Strategies must take into account the effect treatments might have on wildlife habitat, watersheds, forage and coverage, and ingress and egress for emergency vehicles.

Geologist: Determines geologic history, rock types, rock structure, the classification of landforms, and groundwater conditions. Applies data from geologic mapping, aerial photography, and seismic and electrical resistivity geophysical methods to solve problems concerning soil stability, landslides, road construction, and bridge sites. Conducts broad geologic surveys for planning road nets, timber harvesting, watershed studies, and soil inventories.

Hydrologist: Determines and analyzes watershed conditions in terms of management potential and possible hazards. Recommends and designs flood control, watershed, and soil conservation practices. Examines the effects of recreation use, minerals management, grazing, timber harvest, waste disposal, and road construction on the water resources.

Landscape Architect: Assists in the planning and design of outdoor recreation facilities. Conducts land-use planning and feasibility studies and makes recommendations on such projects as timber harvesting, transportation systems, fire control facilities design, and watershed improvements. Usually works as part of an interdisciplinary team made up of scientists and other professionals.

Plant Pathologist: Performs scientific research into the cause, nature, prevalence, and severity of parasitic, nonparasitic, and virus diseases attacking plants. Investigates the relation of such diseases to the propagation, planting, location, cultivation, and transportation of plants and plant products.

Range Conservationist: Analyzes the range resource on one or more of approximately 11,000 National Forest grazing allotments. Adjusts the number of game and livestock animals to the forage supply and determines the proper grazing seasons and how much grazing the forage plants and soil can withstand. Determines the modification or replacement of low-value brush and plans the construction of trails, range seeding, water developments, and fencing.

Remote Sensing Analyst: Conducts analyses of short-term and long-term changes to Forest Service soil and habitat environments using infrared technology, aerial and satellite data, ground "truthing," and computer analysis with algorithms.

Soil Scientist: Conducts soil inventories on forestlands to determine the distribution of areas having similar characteristics. Maps soil area boundaries on aerial photographs and determines the significance of basic differences in soil capability to forest management projects.

Special Agent (Criminal Investigator): Acts as a front-line investigator in cases of theft, vandalism, violent crime, or other offenses on Forest Service property. Cases might include timber theft, contract fraud, arson, narcotics production on federal lands, or theft of archaeological artifacts.

Teacher: Works to develop environmental education skills of resource professionals, educators, and citizens' groups. Informs the public on how it can use National Forest System lands, resources, and facilities. Works with environmental education and public participation programs.

Wildlife Biologist: Cooperates with state wildlife agencies and with the U.S. Fish and Wildlife Service in ensuring that state fish and game laws are effective and operative. Coordinates forest resource activities, such as timber harvest and minerals management, with the habitat needs of wildlife. Protects and improves habitat for both game and nongame species.

Major Activities and Divisions

Recreation: The Forest Service maintains 99,468 miles of trails, more than 6,000 picnic and campgrounds, 320 swimming sites, 1,106 boating sites, and 307 winter sports sites. More than 25,000 cultural, historical, and archeological sites have been identified in the National Forest System.

Timber: Of the 191 million acres of National Forests, 86.5 million acres are classified as commercial forests, land that is available for timber harvest. The forest service annually sells about 11 billion board feet of timber. The agency reforests an average of 400,000 acres per year.

Water: The Forest Service's watershed management programs work to assure adequate yields of high-quality water and continuing soil productivity.

Forage: The Forest Service manages more than 14 percent of the nation's 1.2 billion acres of forest range. The rangeland is managed to conserve the land and its vegetation while providing food for both domestic livestock and wildlife.

Wildlife and Fish Habitat: The Forest Service manages fish and wildlife habitat on the National Forests and National Grasslands in cooperation with the fish and game departments of the states.

Minerals and Energy: Responsibility for regulating and managing mineral activities on National Forest System lands is shared by the Forest Service and the Department of the Interior. The Forest Service administers mining claims on public domain lands.

Fire Management: The Forest Service has one of the world's largest wildland fire-fighting forces and provides fire protection for National Forest System lands.

Forest Pest Management: Forest insect and disease prevention is carried out by the Forest Service on National Forest Lands, and it provides technical and financial assistance to support these activities on other forested lands.

Research: Research is conducted at eight Forest and Range Experiment Stations and the Forest Products Laboratory, plus seventy-five research labs throughout the U.S., Puerto Rico, and the Pacific Trust Territories. The principal areas of Forest Service research are land and resource protection, resource management, and wood utilization.

Human Resource Programs: The agency administers programs that provide work, training, and education to members of minority groups, the economically depressed, the elderly, the handicapped, and youth. Examples are the Youth Conservation Corps, the Forest Service Volunteers program, the Touch America Project, and the Senior Community Service Employment Program.

Alternative Employment Programs

The Forest Service participates in the Federal STEP and SCEP hiring programs.

Application Procedures

See the Forest Service Web site or OPM's USAJOBS Web site for current job listings. Or, see www.fs.fed.us/intro/directory/orgdir.html for a listing of forest service offices and stations. You may also direct inquiries to the regional office listed here.

Headquarters:
Forest Service
U. S. Department of Agriculture
Sidney R. Yates Federal Building
201 14th Street, SW at Independence
Ave. SW
Washington, DC 20250

Offices also in:
Franklin Court Building
1099 14th St., NW, Suite 5500 W
Washington, DC 20005-3042
Rosslyn Plaza, Bldg. E
1621 N. Kent Street
Arlington, VA 22209
and
Rosslyn Plaza, Bldg. C
1601 N. Kent Street
Arlington, VA 22209

USDA, Forest Service
Staffing Branch
RPE Room 913
P.O. Box 9060
Washington, DC 20090-6090
(703) 605-5245

Southwestern Region
U.S. Forest Service
333 Broadway, SE
Albuquerque, NM 87102
(505) 842-3292

Southern Region
U.S. Forest Service
1720 Peachtree Rd, NW
Atlanta, GA 30367
(404) 347-3842

Alaska Region
U.S. Forest Service
Federal Office Bldg.
P.O. Box 21628
Juneau, AK 99802
(907) 586-8863

Rocky Mountain Region
U.S. Forest Service
740 Simms St.
Box 25127
Lakewood, CO 80225
(303) 275-5350

Eastern Region
U.S. Forest Service
310 West Wisconsin Ave.
Milwaukee, WI 53203
(414) 297-3601

Northern Region
U.S. Forest Service
Federal Bldg.
P.O. Box 7669
Missoula, MT 59807
(406) 329-3347

Intermountain Region
U.S. Forest Service
Federal Bldg.
324 25th St.
Ogden, UT 84401
(801) 625-5127

Pacific Northwest Region
U.S. Forest Service
333 SW First Ave.
P.O. Box 3623
Portland, OR 97208
(503) 808-2600

Pacific Southwest Region
U.S. Forest Service
1323 Club Drive
Vallejo, CA 94592
(707) 562-USFS

National Agricultural Statistics Service (NASS)
www.nass.usda.gov

Nature of Work: Agriculture, statistics

Number of Employees: 1,050

Headquarters: Washington, DC

Regional Locations: There are 46 state Statistical Offices under NASS. Refer to address listing for locations and phone numbers.

Typical Background of New Hires: Agriculture, economics, mathematics, statistics

Mission

NASS prepares estimates and reports on production, supply, price, and other items necessary for the orderly operation of the U.S. agricultural economy. Information is gathered through a complex system of sample surveys of producers, processors, buyers, and others associated with agriculture. Data is collected by mail, telephone, personal interviews, and field visits. NASS also prepares periodic reports for free distribution to the news media and Congress.

Job Descriptions

Agricultural Statistician: Selects samples for survey purposes, develops crop and livestock estimates, and writes technical explanatory reports supporting estimates. Prepares and disseminates estimates to the news media.

Mathematical Statistician: Analyzes estimates and conducts statistical research to improve estimating procedures. Designs mathematical methods related to statistical processes. Develops crop and livestock estimates through information-gathering techniques and ensures statistical integrity of numerical data.

Major Activities and Divisions

The national office and the 46 State-Federal offices prepare weekly, monthly, annual, and other periodic reports for distribution to the news media, Congress, and survey respondents.

Alternative Employment Programs

The Agricultural Research Service hires students in various roles throughout the organization during the school year and each summer. Contact the office listed below for the state in which you're interested:

Beltsville Area *(MD, DC):* (301) 504-6507

Midsouth Area *(AL, KY, LA, MS, TN):* (662) 686-5201

Midwest Area *(IL, IN, IA, MI, MN, MO, OH, WI):* (309) 681-6632

North Atlantic Area *(CT, DE, MA, MD, ME, NH, NJ, NY, PA, RI, VT, WV):* (215) 233-6402

Northern Plains Area *(CO, KS, MT, NE, ND, SD, UT, WY):* (970) 229-5502

Pacific West Area *(AK, AZ, CA, HI, ID, NV, OR, WA):* (510) 559-6076

South Atlantic Area *(FL, GA, NC, PR, SC, U.S. Virgin Islands, VA):* (706) 446–3614

Southern Plains Area *(AR, NM, OK, TX):* (979) 260-9416

International Locations

Montpellier, France; Buenos Aires, Argentina; Brisbane, Australia; Beijing, China: (301) 504-4539

National Agricultural Library *(Beltsville, Maryland)*: (301) 504-6575

Headquarters Contacts (Washington, DC, and Maryland)

Eastern Services Branch, Human Resources Division, (301) 504-1400
   For general information on student or summer employment, you may also contact:
   Student Employment Program Coordinator
   Human Resources Division
   (301) 504-1434

Remarks

Entry-level employees can begin their careers at a field office or at headquarters in Washington. Statisticians typically travel extensively throughout the U.S.

Application Procedures

Contact the State Statistician for more information about a career with NASS (see addresses below) or direct inquiries to:

Washington Headquarters

USDA/NASS
Field Operations, HR
Rm. 4143 South Building
1400 Independence Avenue SW
Washington, DC 20250-2000
Toll free: (800) 832-4180

Alabama
nass-al@nass.usda.gov
(334) 279-3555
Toll free: (800) 832-4181

Alaska
nass-ak@nass.usda.gov
(907) 745-4272
Toll free: (800) 478-6079

Arizona
nass-az@nass.usda.gov
(602) 280-8850
Toll Free (800) 645-7286

Arkansas
nass-ar@nass.usda.gov
(501) 296-9926
Toll Free: (800) 327-2970

California
nass-ca@nass.usda.gov
(916) 498-5161
Toll Free: (800) 851-1127

Colorado
nass-co@nass.usda.gov
(303) 236-2300
Toll Free: (800) 392-3202

Delaware
nass-de@nass.usda.gov
(302) 698-4537
Toll Free: (800) 282-8685

Florida
nass-fl@nass.usda.gov
(407) 648-6013
Toll Free: (800) 344-6277

Georgia
nass-ga@nass.usda.gov
(706) 546-2236
Toll Free: (800) 253-4419

Hawaii
nass-hi@nass.usda.gov
(808) 973-2907
Toll Free: (800) 804-9514

Idaho
nass-id@nass.usda.gov
(208) 334-1507
Toll Free: (800) 691-9987

Illinois
nass-il@nass.usda.gov
(217) 492-4295
Toll Free: (800) 622-9865

Indiana
nass-in@nass.usda.gov
(765) 494-8371
Toll Free: (800) 363-0469

Iowa
nass-ia@nass.usda.gov
(515) 284-4340
Toll Free: (800) 772-0825

Kansas
nass-ks@nass.usda.gov
(785) 233-2230
Toll Free: (800) 258-4564

Kentucky
nass-ky@nass.usda.gov
(502) 582-5293
Toll Free: (800) 928-5277

Louisiana
nass-la@nass.usda.gov
(504) 922-1362
Toll Free: (800) 256-4485

Maryland
nass-md@nass.usda.gov
(410) 841-5740
Toll Free: (800) 675-0295

Michigan
nass-mi@nass.usda.gov
(517) 324-5300
Toll Free: (800) 453-7501

Minnesota
nass-mn@nass.usda.gov
(651) 296-2230
Toll Free: (800) 453-7502

Mississippi
nass-ms@nass.usda.gov
(601) 965-4575
Toll Free: (800) 535-9609

Missouri
nass-mo@nass.usda.gov
(573) 876-0950
Toll Free: (800) 551-1014

Montana
nass-mt@nass.usda.gov
(406) 441-1240
Toll Free: (800) 835-2612

Nebraska
nass-ne@nass.usda.gov
(402) 437-5541
Toll Free: (800) 582-6443

Nevada
nass-nv@nass.usda.gov
(702) 784-5584
Toll Free: (888) 456-7211

New Hampshire
nass-nh@nass.usda.gov
(603) 224-9639
Toll Free: (800) 642-9571

New Jersey
nass-nj@nass.usda.gov
(609) 292-6385
Toll Free: (800) 328-0179

New Mexico
nass-nm@nass.usda.gov
(505) 522-6023
Toll Free: (800) 530-8810

New York
nass-ny@nass.usda.gov
(518) 457-5570
Toll Free: (800) 821-1276

North Carolina
nass-nc@nass.usda.gov
(919) 856-4394
Toll Free: (800) 437-8451

North Dakota
nass-nd@nass.usda.gov
(701) 239-5306
Toll Free: (800) 626-3134

Ohio
nass-oh@nass.usda.gov
(614) 728-2100
Toll Free: (800) 858-8144

Oklahoma
nass-ok@nass.usda.gov
(405) 522-6190
Toll Free: (888) 525-9226

Oregon
nass-or@nass.usda.gov
(503) 326-2131
Toll Free: (800) 338-2157

Pennsylvania
nass-pa@nass.usda.gov
(717) 787-3904
Toll Free: (800) 498-1518

Puerto Rico
nass-pr@nass.usda.gov
(787) 723-3391

South Carolina
nass-sc@nass.usda.gov
(803) 765-5333
Toll Free: (800) 424-9406

South Dakota
nass-sd@nass.usda.gov
(605) 330-4235
Toll Free: (800) 338-2557

Tennessee
nass-tn@nass.usda.gov
(615) 781-5300
Toll Free: (800) 626-0987

Texas
nass-tx@nass.usda.gov
(512) 916-5581
Toll Free: (800) 626-3142

Utah
nass-ut@nass.usda.gov
(801) 524-5003
Toll Free: (800) 747-8522

Virginia
nass-va@nass.usda.gov
(804) 771-2493
Toll Free: (800) 772-0670

Washington
nass-wa@nass.usda.gov
(360) 902-1940
Toll Free: (800) 435-5883

West Virginia
nass-wv@nass.usda.gov
(304) 345-5958
Toll Free: (800) 535-7088

Wisconsin
nass-wi@nass.usda.gov
(608) 224-4848
Toll Free: (800) 789-9277

Wyoming
nass-wy@nass.usda.gov
(307) 432-5600
Toll Free: (800) 892-1660

Natural Resources Conservation Service (NRCS)
www.ncrs.usda.gov

Nature of Work: Agriculture, environmental protection, forestry/wildlife, mining, recreation, regional development, waterways

Number of Employees: 15,500

Headquarters: Washington, DC

Regional Locations: There are over 3,000 field locations throughout the U.S.

Typical Background of New Hires: Agriculture, agronomy, biological sciences (animal science, aquatic biology, plant science, wildlife biology), cartography, engineering, environmental sciences (natural resources management, range management), forestry, geology (hydrology), landscape architecture, recreation, soil science

Mission

The NRCS is responsible for developing and carrying out a national soil and water conservation program in cooperation with landowners and other land users. It assists in agricultural pollution control, environmental improvement, and rural community development.

Job Descriptions

Engineer: Job assignments for engineers vary and may include work with water-supply systems, concrete and earthen dams, and/or stream-bank erosion. NRCS engineers can either specialize or conduct work involving several fields. These include erosion control, water management, structural design, construction, hydraulics, soil mechanics, and environmental protection.

Range Conservationist: Assists ranchers in managing their rangeland in an efficient and productive way, whether the land is used for supporting livestock or wildlife or for recreational purposes. Helps plan grazing systems that increase production and prevent overgrazing. Suggests ways to control brush and offers advice on water management and better ways to produce forage.

Soil Conservationist: Offers technical help and conservation planning to land users, such as family farmers, ranchers, land developers, and local government offices. Suggests ways to conserve the soil, build a farm pond, or cut down on water pollution. Assists teachers in starting outdoor laboratories for their students and gives talks and slide programs to clubs and organizations.

Soil Scientist: Provides information on soils to farmers, commercial developers, and state and local planners. Maps and classifies soils and identifies such problems as erosion and dampness. Writes soil descriptions and identifies soil borders on aerial photographs. Spends time both in the field and in the office.

Major Activities and Divisions

Conservation Operations: NRCS provides assistance to landowners and operators in carrying out soil and water conservation programs.

River Basin Surveys and Investigations: NRCS, along with the Economic Research Service and Forest Service, studies the watersheds of rivers and other waterways.

Watershed Planning: NRCS has responsibility for administering investigations and surveys of proposed small watershed projects in response to local requests.

Watershed and Flood Prevention Operations: NRCS cooperates with local sponsors to reduce erosion, floodwater, and sediment damage.

Great Plains Conservation Program: NRCS promotes conservation and agricultural stability in the Great Plains area.

Resource Conservation and Development Program: NRCS assists in planning and developing land and water resources in multiple-county areas.

Rural Abandoned Mine Program: The NRCS assists land users in reclaiming abandoned or inadequately reclaimed coal-mined lands and water.

Alternative Employment Programs

The NRCS maintains a co-op program for current college students. These typically begin at the GS-3 level for college sophomores, and the GS-4 level for juniors. Positions include Student Trainee–level Soil Conservationists, Soil Scientists, Engineers, and Range Conservationists. There is a Standard Announcement (No. 445) that reopens annually. Applications are typically accepted from September to December. For more information, contact NRCS headquarters or the NRCS office in which you are interested.

Remarks

Entry-level opportunities exist at headquarters and in the many field locations.

Application Procedures

Summary and full-text vacancy announcements are posted each Monday at www.nrcs.usda.gov. Or, direct inquiries on entry-level positions to:

Special Examining Unit
Natural Resources Conservation Service
P.O. Box 37636
Washington, DC 20013

You can also contact the NRCS offices in the localities in which you would like to work. NRCS offices are listed in telephone directories under U.S. Government, Agriculture, Natural Resources Conservation Service.

For information about jobs in Hawaii and the Pacific overseas areas, contact:

Office of Personnel Management
Honolulu Area Office
Prince Kuhio Federal Bldg.
300 Ala Moana Blvd.
P.O. Box 50028
Honolulu, HI 96850
(808) 541-2603

Risk Management Agency (RMA)
www.rma.usda.gov

Nature of Work: Agriculture, education, insurance

Number of Employees: 500

Headquarters: Washington, DC

Regional Locations: RMA has offices in all 50 states that are overseen by 9 regional offices: Raleigh, NC; Topeka, KS; Davis, CA; Jackson, MS; Oklahoma City, OK; Billings, MT; St. Paul, MN; Valdosta, GA; Spokane, WA

Typical Background of New Hires: Agriculture, Economics

Mission

The RMA administers a crop insurance program to help farmers survive a major crop loss. Crop insurance is widely available for major commodities such as corn, wheat, soybeans, and cotton. RMA also provides training to farmers to help them acquire the risk management skills needed in the global marketplace.

Job Descriptions

Actuary: Performs actuarial and underwriting duties. Assists in implementing the various crop insurance and risk management programs.

Compliance Officer: Assures compliance and uniformity in sales and loss adjustment policies and underwriting procedures.

Economist: Conducts applied and theoretical research pertaining to the crop insurance programs.

Risk Management Specialist: Performs underwriting duties regarding the crop insurance programs. Implements and promotes risk management strategies.

Major Activities and Divisions

RMA is divided into four major areas:

* Research and Development: Includes the actuarial division as well as product development and research and evaluation.

* Insurance Services: Includes Reinsurance Services, Risk Management Services, and the Risk Management Education Division.

* Compliance: Includes Risk Operations. There are six regional compliance offices serving the fifty states and Puerto Rico.

* Alternative Employment Programs: RMA participates in FDA's Summer Intern Program (SIP), which is a paid internship open to currently enrolled college students.

Application Procedures:

RMA lists current job openings on their Web site and at the Foreign Agriculture Service Web site. Or, direct inquiries to:

RMA_mail@wdc.usda.gov
USDA/RMA/Stop 0801
Room 3053-South
1400 Independence Ave. SW
Washington, DC 20250
(202) 690-2803
Fax: (202) 690-2818

> ## Rural Business-Cooperative Service (RBS)
> ## www.rurdev.usda.gov/rbs/
> **Nature of Work:** Agriculture, business, funding, marketing
> **Number of Employees:** 400
> **Headquarters:** Washington, DC
> **Regional Locations:** Area offices in every state
> **Typical Background of New Hires:** Accounting, agronomy, banking/finance, business, economics, management, marketing

Mission

The Rural Business Service makes loans to rural businesses to ensure development in rural agricultural communities and works with state and local governments to develop local businesses.

Job Descriptions

Agricultural Economist: Monitors and analyzes regional agricultural production and demand for agricultural commodities.

Agricultural Marketing Specialist: Analyzes the marketing practices of agricultural commodities and products. Works to design and establish local and regional agricultural marketing programs.

Agricultural Statistician: Gathers information on agricultural trends and market outlooks. Applies statistical theories to interpret and quantify data.

Loan Specialist: Analyzes credit risk factors and lending principles regarding loans that are granted or insured by RBS. Evaluates financial structures and practices of businesses concerned with RBS loans.

Rural Development Specialist: Analyzes and monitors local and regional business trends. Develops cooperative services and works with state and local governments to develop area businesses.

Major Activities and Divisions

The RBS is divided into three major operating divisions:

★ *Business Programs:* Oversees loan processing and specialty lending.

✯   *Cooperative Services Programs:* Offers cooperative services and marketing to state and local governments to develop local businesses. Also is involved with the empowerment and enterprise zone project.

✯   *Community Development:* Comprises the Empowerment Program and community outreach divisions.

Alternative Employment Programs

RBS hires several co-op students annually.

Remarks

RBS is part of the Rural Development Mission Area, which includes the Rural Utilities Service and the Rural Housing Service.

Application Procedures

Links to online job listings through the OPM USAJOBS Web site can be found on the RBS site. Click on "job opportunities." Or, you may contact the Washington, DC, office for jobs in the headquarters location or the St. Louis office for field positions. State offices also have their own human resources personnel and often conduct their own hiring.

Rural Development Mission Area:

RBS
AG Box 0703
14th St. and Independence Avenue
Washington, DC 20250
Attn.: Human Resources
(202) 720-6903 (Office of Communications)

Rural Development Mission Area:

RBS
1520 Market St.
St. Louis, MO 63103
Attn.: Human Resources
(314) 539-2488

Rural Housing Service (RHS)
www.rurdev.usda.gov/rhs/

Nature of Work: Funding, materials/facilities

Number of Employees: 6,400

Headquarters: Washington, DC

Regional Locations: Area offices in every state

Typical Background of New Hires: Accounting, banking/finance, business, economics, realty

Mission

The Rural Housing Service ensures community development by making loans to finance the development of single-family housing, multiunit housing, and community facilities.

Job Descriptions

Loan Specialist: Evaluates and analyzes credit risk factors and lending principles regarding loans that are granted or insured by RHS.

Realty Specialist: Offers real estate expertise on contractual documents and in the buying, selling, and management of local properties.

Statistician: Gathers information on housing trends, real estate industry outlooks, and other pertinent data. Applies statistical theories to interpret and quantify data.

Major Activities and Divisions

The RHS is divided into three lending divisions: Single Family Housing; Multi-Family Housing; and Community Programs.

Alternative Employment Programs

RHS hires several co-op students annually.

Remarks

RHS is part of the Rural Development Mission Area, which includes the Rural Utilities Service and the Rural Business Service.

Application Procedures

Contact the Washington, DC, office for jobs in the headquarters location or the St. Louis office for field positions. State offices also have their own human resources personnel and often conduct their own hiring.

Rural Development Mission

Area: RHS
  AG Box 0703
  14th Street and Independence Avenue
  Washington, DC 20250
  Attn.: Human Resources
  (202) 720-6903 (Office of Communications)

Rural Development Mission Area:

RHS
1520 Market St.
St. Louis, MO 63103
Attn.: Human Resources
(314) 539-2488

Rural Utilities Service (RUS)
www.rurdev.usda.gov/rus/

Nature of Work: Funds/funding

Number of Employees: 530

Headquarters: Washington, DC

Regional Locations: None

Typical Background of New Hires: Accounting, business, engineering (electrical, electronic), finance/banking

---

Mission

RUS makes or guarantees loans to finance the provision of electric and telephone service to persons in rural areas. More than 26 million rural residents in 46 states benefit from these services. RUS also sponsors a guaranteed loan program that makes available funds from non-RUS sources available to finance large-scale electric and telephone projects.

Job Descriptions

Electrical Engineer: Plans and designs systems for electric distribution and generation. Prepares construction standards and conducts research into rural electric systems and needs.

Electronic Engineer: Provides technical assistance on construction and operation of rural telephone systems. Coordinates with private industry in the preparation of technical standards, construction practices, and equipment specifications.

Financial Analyst: Coordinates and conducts studies of corporate financial and power supply arrangements of large utility systems. Reviews financial and managerial operations of electric and telephone systems.

Loan Specialist: Analyzes and evaluates credit risk factors and lending principles involved in loans that are granted, insured, or guaranteed by RUS. Evaluates financial structures and practices of business organizations concerned with REA loans. Keeps abreast of pertinent statutory, regulatory, and administrative provisions.

Major Activities and Divisions

Electric Program: Assists rural electric utilities in obtaining financing for construction projects.

Telecommunications Program: Makes loans to create public-private partnerships to finance the construction of the telecommunications infrastructure in rural America.

Water and Environmental Programs: Provides loans, grants and loan guarantees for drinking water, sanitary sewer, solid-waste and storm-drainage facilities in rural areas and cities and towns of 10,000 or less.

Alternative Employment Programs

RUS offers a co-op program, hiring one to ten students per year. Co-ops are typically in their junior year of college, and work as computer specialists at the GS-4 level. Contact your school office for more information.

Remarks

Engineers enter into a six-month training program upon employment with RUS. Although newly hired engineers are based in the Washington, DC headquarters, some travel with an RUS field engineer is likely. Travel opportunities will exist throughout an engineer's term of employment at RUS.

RUS recruits on college and university campuses throughout the country.

Application Procedures

Direct inquiries to:
Director, Personnel Management Division
Rural Utilities Service
U.S. Department of Agriculture
14th Street and Independence Avenue SW
Room 40325
Washington, DC 20250-1500
(202) 720-1255 (Public Affairs)

☆ Department of the Air Force (www.af.mil)

> ## Air Force Materiel Command—Air Logistics Centers
> ## www.af.mil/sites/afmc.shtml
>
> **Nature of Work:** Aviation/space program, military affairs, scientific research, weapons
>
> **Number of Employees:** 73,000
>
> **Headquarters:** Wright-Patterson Air Force Base, OH
>
> **Regional Locations:** Hill Air Force Base, UT; Kelly Air Force Base, TX; McClellan Air Force Base, CA; Robins Air Force Base, GA; Tinker Air Force Base, OK
>
> **Typical Background of New Hires:** Chemistry, engineering

Mission

Provides worldwide logistical support to the Air Force, ensuring that weapon systems are constantly ready by repairing and modifying missiles, engines, support equipment, and aircraft.

Job Descriptions

Aerospace Engineer: Designs airframes, power plants, and flight and environmental control systems.

Chemist: Synthesizes new industrial coatings to protect equipment in severe environments using gas chromatography, X-ray diffraction, and mass spectrometers.

Civil Engineer: Plans and designs roads, airfields, buildings, drainage systems, and water treatment plants.

Electrical Engineer: Designs, installs, and reconfigures generation and distribution systems and oversees contractor work on such systems.

Electronics Engineer: Designs and services aircraft navigation and control systems, infrared detection systems, radars, and laser bombing devices.

Industrial Engineer: Recommends improved ways of integrating people, machines, materials, and computers. Designs repair facilities, hangars, and warehouses.

Materials Engineer: Studies the behavior of materials under flight conditions and develops materials that resist fatigue and corrosion.

Mechanical Engineer: Oversees the development of heating and air-conditioning systems and pneumatic and hydraulic systems for aircraft and develops and modifies jet engines.

Metallurgist: Develops special purpose alloys for aircraft, jet engines, missiles, and rocket nozzles.

Major Activities and Divisions

Each Air Logistics Center (ALC) repairs, modifies, and integrates specific weapons systems. For example, the Ogden ALC at Hill Air Force Base supports the F-16 and F-10 fighters and the Minuteman III and Peacekeeper ballistic missiles. The Oklahoma City ALC maintains the B-1B bomber, C-135 transport/tanker, and engines used on various fighters. The Warner Robins ALC at Robins Air Force Base is responsible for the F-15 fighter and C-141 and C-130 transport aircraft. For more information on the specific ALCs, visit their Web sites (listed under application procedures).

Alternative Employment Programs

Engineering majors may work as engineering technicians during the summer. Co-op positions are available to engineering students with one or more years of college. Some ALCs also participate in the STEP and SCEP student employment programs.

Remarks

The ALCs are just one component of the Air Force Logistics Command but they hire the greatest number of employees.

Application Procedures

Direct inquiries to the ALC where you would like to work.

Oklahoma Air Logistics Center
4028 Hilltop Rd.
Tinker Air Force Base, OK 73145
(405) 739-3272
www.tinker.af.mil

(A New Job Information Center is located outside the Lancer Gate on Douglas Blvd. This provides access to job information and applications without having to enter restricted base areas.)

Ogden Air Logistics Center
2849 ABS/DPCSE
Hill Air Force Base, UT 84056
www.hill.af.mil

Job Information Hotline: (801) 777-3762 or DSN 777-3762.

Warner Robins Air Logistics Center
Employment Office
Robins Air Force Base, GA 31098
www.robins.af.mil

Information about positions open to the general public may be obtained by calling a 24-hour recording at (478) 926-5661 on the 1st and 15th of each month. Information about positions restricted to reinstatements, transfer eligibles, or Veterans Employment Opportunities Act (VEOA) only may be obtained by calling (478) 926-6666 on the 1st and the 15th of each month. All job listings are posted at the Robins AFB Employment Office, Building 1524, located adjacent to the Museum of Aviation.

☆ Department of the Army (www.cpol.army.mil)

Visit the Army Web site listed above for links to overseas employment information, online vacancy listings, information on applying for civilian positions with the U.S. Army, RESUMIX online application forms, and other employment topics.

U.S. Army Audit Agency
www.hqda.army.mil/aaaweb/

Nature of Work: Accounting/auditing, military affairs

Number of Employees: 6,100

Headquarters: Alexandria, VA

Regional Locations: Atlanta, GA; Hanover, MD; Philadelphia, PA; Sacramento, CA; San Antonio, TX; St. Louis, MO; Frankfurt, Germany. These regional offices oversee operations at more than 24 field offices, including 3 overseas.

Typical Background of New Hires: Accounting

Mission

Evaluates the effectiveness and efficiency with which the Army's resources are controlled and managed.

Job Descriptions

Auditor: Examines financial and property records as well as research and development, procurement, logistics, readiness, training activities, and computer systems. As each field office covers a large geographic area, auditors travel frequently. Assignments are available in Europe and the Far East after the first year of employment.

Major Activities and Divisions

The U.S. Army Audit Agency is divided into four agency operations: Acquisition and Materiel Management, Forces and Financial Management, Installations Management, and Policy and Operations Management.

Alternative Employment Programs

Student work-study programs exist that allow current college juniors or seniors to work flexible part-time or full-time schedules as Student Trainee Auditors.

Remarks

During the first six months of employment, auditors attend a one-week training program at the Auditor Trainee School. This is followed up later in the auditor's career with training at the Intermediate Auditor and Senior Auditor Schools.

Application Procedures

Direct inquiries to:

U.S. Army Audit Agency
Human Resources
393 Llewellyn Ave.
Ft. George G. Meade, MD 20755-5375
(301) 677-7743/7586/7584

Army Corps of Engineers (USACE)
www.usace.army.mil/

Nature of Work: Environmental protection, military affairs, waterways

Number of Employees: 34,600 civilians and 650 military

Headquarters: Washington, DC

Regional Locations: 8 Regional Business Centers, 41 District Offices, and field offices throughout the world.

Typical Background of New Hires: Engineering, environmental science, science

Mission

Provides military and civil engineering support for the Army and Air Force and protects and maintains the nation's navigable waters and wetlands.

Job Descriptions

Architect: Designs and develops plans for new construction or improvement of existing structures and buildings.

Cartographer: Plans, designs, researches, develops, constructs, and modifies mapping and charting systems.

Chemist: Performs research and development, investigations, analysis, and interpretations in support of Corps projects.

Civil Engineer: Designs and builds military housing, dams, river channels, missile sites, space-launching facilities, pipelines, and air bases. Is also involved with soil and water conservation, hydroelectric power, recreation, and related projects.

Computer Scientist: Applies theoretical foundations of computer science, such as computer system architecture and system software organization; has specialized knowledge of design characteristic and potential applications.

Electrical Engineer: Plans and supervises construction of major communications facilities.

Environmental Engineer: Designs, operates, and maintains equipment and facilities used in reducing or preventing air, land, and water pollution.

Hydrologist: Performs basic and applied research in water and water resources.

Mechanical Engineer: Designs heating, ventilation, and air-conditioning systems as well as energy production systems.

Park Ranger: Performs work in the conservation and use of Corps of Engineers' parklands and recreational facilities.

Safety Engineer: Develops and analyzes safety standards that reduce hazardous conditions at industrial and construction sites, recreational areas, and offices.

Major Activities and Divisions
The USACE has eight divisions (also called Regional Business Centers) throughout the U.S., with 41 district offices in the U.S., Asia, and Europe and field offices throughout the world.

The Army Corps of Engineers is divided into several centers, divisions, and directorates: Programs Management Division; Military Engineering and Construction Division; Environmental Programs Division; Installation Support Division; Directorate of Real Estate; Directorate of Research and Development; the Marine Design Center; the Transatlantic Programs Center; and the Engineering and Support Center.

Alternative Employment Programs
The Army Corps of Engineers maintains an extensive student and summer employment program.

Remarks
The Army Corps of Engineers is the world's largest public engineering and construction organization.

Application Procedures

Each of the 41 district offices has its own Web site, linked to the main Army Corps Web site. Most of these list employment opportunities in their district and throughout the Corps. Go to http://www.usace.army.mil/where.html#State to find the links to district office information.

Headquarters
U.S. Army Corps of Engineers
441 G St. NW
Washington, DC 20314-1000
(202) 761-1767

Army Communications/Electronics Command (CECOM)
www.monmouth.army.mil/cecom/cecom.html

Nature of Work: Communications, intelligence, scientific research

Number of Employees: 5,800

Headquarters: Fort Monmouth, NJ

Regional Locations: Fort Belvoir, VA; Fort Huachuca, AZ; Fort Leavenworth, KS; Fort Sill, OK; Lakehurst, NJ

Typical Background of New Hires: Computer science, engineering (industrial, mechanical, electronics, electrical, chemical)

Mission

Oversees research, development, and testing of communications and electronics equipment for the Army.

Job Descriptions

Intelligence Research: Collects, analyzes, evaluates, interprets, and disseminates information on political, economic, social, cultural, physical, geographic, scientific or military conditions, trends, and forces in foreign and domestic areas that directly or indirectly affect national security.

Computer Engineer: Develops hardware and software for signals processing, fire support, and electronic warfare systems.

Electronics Engineer: Conducts research on electronic warfare systems, electrooptics, and command and control systems.

Other Engineering Positions: CECOM also hires many mechanical, industrial, electrical, and chemical engineers to work in one of the technology areas listed below.

Major Activities and Divisions

The Information Systems Engineering Command (ISEC) serves as the Army's engineer and integrator for infrastructure/force projection information systems. www.hqisec.army.mil/

Software Engineering Center: Provides life-cycle software products and services that enhance Army/Joint war fighting, business, management, and support capabilities. www.sed.monmouth.army.mil/

Tobyhanna Army Depot: (Located in PA) A full-service repair, overhaul, and fabrication facility. www.tobyhanna.army.mil/

Research, Development, and Engineering Center: Conducts research and development of night vision and electronic sensor technology, signals intelligence, and other technologies.

Logistics Readiness Center: (Locations in NJ, VA, MD, and AZ) Provides communications electronics logistical support to the U.S. Army.

CECOM Acquisition Center: Visit the Web site at www.monmouth.army.mil/ cecom/acq/index.html. For more information on careers with the Acquisition Center, call 732-532-3028 or 1503.

Program Executive Office Enterprise Information Systems: Acquires and fields information management systems that assist with the accession and training of soldiers, tracks the Army's personnel, provides and maintains the war fighters' equipment, and plans the movement of supplies and assets.

Alternative Employment Programs

CECOM maintains a co-op program with part-time or full-time summer positions in its business and technology areas for students at the high school, vocational/ tech school, and college levels. CECOM actively recruits on college campuses across the U.S. They publish their campus recruiting schedule on their Web site.

Remarks

International assignments lasting two years are available to employees with one to five years of experience.

Application Procedures

Submit a resume to the address below, which will be circulated by the Personnel Office to managers who are hiring, or apply for a specific position. Please note that a copy of your college transcript is required if you are interested in a co-op position or an entry-level technical position. Specify in your cover letter the business or technology area(s) and geographic location(s) you are interested in. Or, direct inquiries to: cecomjobs@mail1.monmouth.army.mil.

Deputy Chief of Staff for Personnel
Civilian Personnel Advisory Center-CECOM JOBS
Bldg. 901, Murphy Drive
Fort Monmouth, NJ 07703-5000

U.S. Army Training and Doctrine Command (TRADOC)
www.tradoc.monroe.army.mil

Nature of Work: Education, military affairs

Number of Employees: 23,000

Headquarters: Fort Monroe, VA

Regional Locations: Nationwide

Typical Background of New Hires: Accounting, business, computer science, education, engineering, international affairs, languages

Mission

Administers the Army school system, which trains Active Army and Army Reserve soldiers. There are 27 facilities in this school system, each responsible for a different specialty.

Job Descriptions

Computer Specialist: Provides automated data processing and programming services for TRADOC staff.

Education Services Officer: Operates each installation's Army Education Center and is responsible for management, administration, counseling, and staff work.

Educator: Teaches the courses used to train Army personnel, develops curricula, and tests and evaluates students.

Engineer (all fields): Designs and operates new equipment and processes. Engineers involved with construction provide engineering and management expertise for operating, maintaining, altering, and building plant facilities.

Housing Management Specialist: Manages housing projects at TRADOC facilities, identifies housing requirements, monitors all contractual services, and facilitates repairs.

Information Security Specialist: Protects classified information, processes requests for disclosures of military information to foreign governments, and reviews accreditation of foreign visitors.

Intelligence Analyst: Gathers intelligence data on foreign armies, which is then incorporated into U.S. Army training doctrine.

Manpower Management Specialist: Determines training needs at TRADOC installations by analyzing mission, workload, personnel, and equipment utilization.

Motor Pool Manager: Operates and maintains vehicles that support the local transportation needs of TRADOC facilities.

Personnel Security Specialist: Administers programs that provide security clearances for TRADOC employees and contractors.

Physical Security Specialist: Inspects and evaluates security measures protecting TRADOC facilities and equipment, determines security needs, and recommends corrective measures.

Procurement Officer: Purchases all supplies, services, and construction necessary to operate TRADOC facilities.

Safety And Occupational Health Manager: Organizes and directs comprehensive loss prevention programs.

Safety Specialist: Identifies hazards, assesses risks, and recommends solutions to workplace safety problems.

Major Activities and Divisions

TRADOC involves 15 major installations, 27 schools, and more than 9,000 instructors.

Alternative Employment Programs

TRADOC maintains co-op programs for many of its positions. Inquire with the civilian personnel office at the installation where you would like to work.

Remarks

Each TRADOC installation accepts employment applications directly. A complete list of facilities may be obtained from TRADOC headquarters at the address below.

Application Procedures

Direct inquiries to:

Civilian Intern and Student Program Coordinator
Army Training and Doctrine Command
Fort Monroe, VA 23651-6000
Attn.: ATPL-C
757-788-3514 (Operations)

Military Traffic Management Command
www.mtmc.army.mil

Nature of Work: Military affairs, transportation

Number of Employees: approx. 3,500 military and civilian

Headquarters: Alexandria, VA

Regional Locations: Nationwide (4 subordinate commands: Ft. Eustis, VA; Newport News, VA; Oahu, HI; Rotterdam, the Netherlands)

Typical Background of New Hires: Accounting, business, economics, finance/banking, statistics

Mission

Provides global surface transportation and traffic management services for the military to meet national security objectives in peace and war.

Job Descriptions

Traffic Management Specialist: Plans transportation systems consisting of distribution patterns, site locations, and special handling equipment. Also arranges the shipment, handling, and receiving of military equipment and household goods.

Transportation Specialist: Moves military personnel and supplies throughout the world. This is accomplished by scheduling transportation services, negotiating rates, and working with a variety of legal matters.

Contract Specialist: Performs pre-award and post-award functions for procurements involving complex contracts of specialized information technology, transportation, and transportation services.

Major Activities and Divisions

The Military Traffic Management Command (MTMC) serves as one of the three transportation component commands of the United States Transportation Command (USTRANSCOM). MTMC is staffed with representation from the Army, Navy, Air Force, Marines, Coast Guard, and Canadian Armed Forces. It comprises a headquarters and four major subordinate commands:

    ✫   Deployment Support Command, Fort Eustis, Virginia

    ✫   Transportation Engineering Agency, Newport News, Virginia

    ✫   598th Transportation Group, Rotterdam, the Netherlands

    ✫   599th Transportation Group, Wheeler Army Airfield, Hawaii

MTMC assets include 10,400 containers, 2,100 railcars, and 142 miles of government railroad track. Additionally, MTMC has an active presence at 22 ports worldwide. MTMC executes its mission through three core processes:

    ✫   *Surface Movement*: The Joint Traffic Management Office develops best-value transportation options and manages the transportation of freight such as tanks, fuel ammo, vehicles, and food to locations around the world.

    ✫   *Passenger and Personal Property*: Moves household goods and vehicles.

    ✫   *Deployability Engineering*: The Transportation Engineering Agency conducts research and analyzes systems for defense transportation, weapons, unity, and force deployability.

Alternative Employment Programs

The Command maintains a co-op program for students depending on the availability of funding.

Application Procedures

Direct inquiries to:

Career Program Administrator
Military Traffic Management Command
5611 Columbia Pike
Falls Church, VA 22041-5050
Attn.: MT-PEC

Tank-Automotive & Armaments Command (TACOM)
www.tacom.army.mil

Nature of Work: Military affairs, scientific research, transportation, weapons

Number of Employees: 12,000

Headquarters: Warren, MI

Regional Locations: Picatinny Arsenal, NJ; Rock Island, IL; Anniston, AL; Texarkana, TX; Warren, MI

Typical Background of New Hires: Business, engineering

Mission

Researches, develops, fields, and supports mobility and armament systems.

Job Descriptions

Electronics Engineer: Develops instruments such as sensors, communications systems, and laser range finders.

Materials Scientist: Formulates new materials used in compounding armor to reduce its vulnerability.

Mechanical Engineer: Designs turbine and piston engines, drive systems, and other vehicular components.

Major Activities and Divisions

Anniston Army Depot: A maintenance facility with the capability to overhaul any military vehicle, test and overhaul turbine engines, design and fabricate components, and repair and rebuild small arms and weapons hardware. Anniston's 2400 employees possess skills in engine and vehicle maintenance, welding and metal work, electrical and electronics repair, artillery and small arms repair, and engineering and science.

Red River Army Depot: Repairs and overhauls the Army's light tracked combat vehicle fleet. Red River's 1300 employees are skilled in electrical and electronics repair, machining, welding and metal work, equipment and vehicle maintenance, and hydraulics systems maintenance.

Picatinny Arsenal: Involves research and development, and fielding and logistics support for the Army's armament and munitions systems. Career fields at Picatinny include Computer Science, Computer Engineering, Electronics Engineering, Electrical Engineering, Industrial Engineering, Chemistry, Chemical Engineering, Mechanical Engineering, and Metallurgical Engineering.

Detroit Arsenal: Manages vehicle system acquisition planning and contract management, worldwide fielding and support of military vehicle systems, research and development of wheeled and tracked vehicle systems, and armor and crew stations. The 3500 employees at the Detroit Arsenal work in fields such as logistics management, engineering, science, mathematics, and contract management.

Rock Island Arsenal: Plans and executes armament and chemical defense systems acquisition, and life-cycle management. The 1,000 employees at Rock Island are skilled in logistics management, purchasing, quality assurance, and engineering and science.

Alternative Employment Programs

TACOM has a co-op program for engineering and computer science students and internships for engineering students. Also, there are internships for other specialties such as business and management.

Application Procedures

The TACOM Web site allows job seekers to submit an informal application to one of the five regional locations, but does not list current job openings. You can find a list of current vacancies by visiting the employment section at Army Civilian Personnel On-Line (CPOL) at www.cpol.army.mil. Or, direct inquiries to:

U.S. Army Tank-Automotive and Armaments Command
Personnel Staffing Specialist
AMSTA-RM-PS
6305 East 11 Mile Rd.
Warren, MI 48397-5000

☆ Commerce Department (www.home.doc.gov/)

Bureau of Economic Analysis (BEA)
www.bea.gov

Nature of Work: Business, economic policy, statistics

Number of Employees: 400

Headquarters: Washington, DC

Regional Locations: None

Typical Background of New Hires: Accounting, computer science, economics, statistics

Mission

Provides policy makers and business leaders with information on the U.S. economy by preparing and interpreting data on economic indicators such as the gross national product.

Job Descriptions

Accountant: Maintains the nation's economic accounts, such as the national income and product accounts, U.S. balance of payments, and related international investment accounts.

Computer Scientist: Provides programming and systems analysis support.

Economist: Creates econometric models of the U.S. economy, and develops systems of leading, coincident, and lagging economic indicators.

Statistician: Compiles and analyzes data on the nation's economic accounts, such as domestic production, distribution, and consumption of goods and services.

Major Activities and Divisions

The accounts that BEA compiles include:

National economic accounts: Provide an aggregated view of the final uses of the nation's output and the income derived from its production; two of its most widely known measures are gross domestic product (GDP) and gross domestic income (GDI).

Industry economic accounts: Provide detailed information on the flows of goods and services to industries for the production of gross output and on the contributions by private industries and government to the nation's gross domestic product.

Regional economic accounts: Provide estimates and analyses of personal income, population, employment, and gross state product.

International economic accounts: Encompass the international transactions accounts and the estimates of U.S. direct investment abroad and foreign direct investment in the U.S.

Alternative Employment Programs

BEA maintains a co-op program for certain occupations depending on funding availability.

Application Procedures

Direct inquiries to:

Office of Personnel Operations
Bureau of Economic Analysis
1441 L St. NW
Room #3009
Washington, DC 20230
(202) 606-9900

Bureau of the Census
www.census.gov

Nature of Work: Statistics

Number of Employees: 12,700

Headquarters: Suitland, MD

Regional Locations: Atlanta, GA; Boston, MA; Charlotte, NC; Chicago, IL; Dallas, TX; Denver, CO; Detroit, MI; Kansas City, KS; Los Angeles, CA; New York City, NY; Philadelphia, PA; Seattle, WA (addresses listed on Web site)

Typical Background of New Hires: Accounting, cartography, computer science, economics, finance, geography, mathematics, statistics

---

Mission

Collects, tabulates, and publishes statistical data about the people and economy of the United States. These data are used to apportion legislative districts and allocate federal funds. Census reports are also used by state and local governments, business, industry, and nonprofit organizations.

Job Descriptions

Computer Specialist—System Analysis: Analyzes system processes or designs applications for accomplishing work through information technology. Analyzes system requirements and alternative solutions, develops system specifications, and analyzes existing systems to correct problems or improve performance.

Computer Specialist—Programming and Analysis: Develops and maintains application systems. Creates detailed systems flow, program specifications, and structured programs.

Computer Specialist—Networks: Designs and manages local area networks and their interconnection with wide area networks. Manages network servers and network software, identifies and corrects network problems, and optimizes network performance.

Mathematical Statistician: Designs, develops, and adapts mathematical statistical techniques to statistical processes. Performs research in basic statistical theories.

Statistician: Applies statistical theories, techniques, and methods to gather and/or interpret quantifiable data.

Survey Statistician: Works in Census Bureau field offices to recruit and train survey interviewers and supervise the various surveys.

Major Activities and Divisions

The Census Bureau collects data on population, housing, agriculture, state and local governments, industry, foreign trade, and transportation.

Alternative Employment Programs

The Census Bureau supports the Student Educational Employment Program (formerly the Co-operative Education Program) for the following positions: statistician, mathematical statistician, computer specialist, geographer, and cartographer.

Part-time Field Representative positions are often available. Field Reps conduct Census Bureau surveys in regional locations. Contact the regional location of interest directly.

International consultant two-year assignments are available for computer specialists, statisticians, and economists.

Remarks

The International Programs Center, part of the Population division of the U.S. Bureau of the Census, assists counterpart governments throughout the world in collecting, analyzing, and using statistics. See their Web site at www.census.gov.ipc.www. It lists current job openings.

Application Procedures

Go to the Bureau of the Census Web site (www.census.gov/hrd/www/vacancy/2region.htm) and click on field office jobs. Each regional office has its own Web site with employment data specific to that region. Or, direct inquiries to:

U.S. Bureau of the Census
Human Resources Division
Washington, DC 20233
(301) 457-8353
Fax: (301) 457-1906

Economic Development Administration (EDA)
www.doc.gov/eda/

Nature of Work: Economic policy, employment

Number of Employees: 350

Headquarters: Washington, DC

Regional Locations: Atlanta, GA; Austin, TX; Chicago, IL; Denver, CO; Philadelphia, PA; Seattle, WA. These regional offices oversee about three dozen sublocations. (addresses and phone numbers on Web site)

Typical Background of New Hires: Business, economics, engineering (civil), finance/banking

---

Mission

Provides loans, grants, and technical assistance to states, cities, American Indian reservations, and private nonprofit firms in order to increase employment and stimulate economic growth.

Job Descriptions

Civil Engineer: Develops industrial parks, access roads, water and sewer lines, harbors, airports, and other public facilities necessary for industrial and commercial growth.

Economist: Studies the economic feasibility of resource development to establish jobs, assists in planning and implementing economic development programs, and determines the impact of existing and alternative programs.

Financial Management Specialist: Coordinates budget, accounting, and managerial financial reporting; evaluates program accomplishments.

Major Activities and Divisions

Program areas include public works grants to help build or expand public facilities essential to commercial growth, technical assistance and grants for feasibility studies, planning grants to fund economic development programs, and economic and trade adjustment assistance.

Alternative Employment Programs

EDA maintains several co-op positions depending on availability of funding.

Application Procedures

Direct inquiries to:

Office of Personnel Operations
Economic Development Administration
14th Street and Constitution Avenue NW
Room #7417
Washington, DC 20230
(202) 482-2309 (for information)

International Trade Administration (ITA)
www.ita.doc.gov/

Nature of Work: International affairs, trade

Number of Employees: 2,140

Headquarters: Washington, DC

Regional Locations: 48 district offices nationwide

Typical Background of New Hires: Business, economics, international affairs, law, marketing

Mission

Strengthens the nation's international trade and investment position by formulating foreign policy, monitoring international agreements, and developing markets for U.S. products.

Job Descriptions

Economist: Compiles extensive commercial and economic information on specific countries and regions. Forecasts international economic trends and reports on trade information and foreign investment.

Foreign Commercial Service Officer: Promotes U.S. exports, resolves trade and investment disputes, and organizes trade promotion programs and events.

Import Compliance Specialist: Enforces U.S. antidumping and countervailing duty laws and related agreements, administers foreign-trade zone operations, and implements statutory import programs.

International Trade Specialist: Develops trade and export strategies, counsels businesses on overseas trade missions, analyzes and interprets trade date, negotiates agreements, and formulates policy.

Major Activities and Divisions

International Economic Policy: Analyzes and implements international economic policies.

Import Administration: Develops and executes policies and programs concerning the administration of antidumping and countervailing duty law.

Supervises programs dealing with foreign trade zones, quotas, and other statutory import programs.

Trade Development: Provides advice on international trade and investment policies; oversees programs promoting U.S. participation in foreign markets; and manages federal participation in international expositions held in the U.S.

Market Access and Compliance: Obtains market access for American firms and works to achieve full compliance with trade agreements by other nations.

U.S. Commercial Service: Promotes the export of goods and services from the U.S.

Trade Compliance Center: Helps American exporters overcome foreign trade barriers and ensures compliance to U.S. agreements.

Alternative Employment Programs

ITA typically hires several co-ops annually at the GS-4, -5, and -7 levels to work as International Trade Specialists. PMI, internship, and Stay-in-School positions are also available.

Remarks

Foreign Commercial Service Officers, as members of the Foreign Service, must pass the "Commercial Service Assessment" that consists of a written test and oral examination. See the ITA Web site for application information.

Application Procedures

For all occupations except Foreign Commercial Service Officer, direct inquiries to:

Office of Human Resources
International Trade Administration
14th Street and Constitution Avenue NW
Washington, DC 20230
Human Resources: (202) 482-3505
For internships and co-ops: (202) 482-3301
Information: (202) 482-3809

Minority Business Development Agency (MBDA)
www.mbda.gov/

Nature of Work: Business, minorities/women

Number of Employees: 200

Headquarters: Washington, DC

Regional Locations: Atlanta, GA; Chicago, IL; Dallas, TX; New York, NY; San Francisco, CA; Washington, DC. There are also four district offices located in Boston, MA; Los Angeles, CA; Miami, FL; and Philadelphia, PA. (Addresses available on Web site).

Typical Background of New Hires: Business, economics, finance/banking, marketing, public administration

Mission
Strengthens the capabilities of minority businesses by providing technical and management expertise.

Job Descriptions
Economist: Participates in economic, fiscal, and budgetary planning, forecasting, and analysis.

Financial Management Specialist: Examines the financial statements of minority-owned businesses and recommends ways of improving cash flow.

Program Analyst: Determines whether a program is fulfilling its intended mission and recommends improvements.

Major Activities and Divisions
Management and technical assistance is provided on request to minority firms through a network of business development centers funded by MBDA. The agency also helps funnel resources and business toward minority firms.

Alternative Employment Programs
MBDA maintains several co-op positions depending on availability of funding.

Remarks
MBDA has minority Business Development Centers and Native American Business Development Centers across the U.S. See the MBDA Web site for more information.

Application Procedures

Direct inquiries to:

Minority Business Development Agency
14th Street and Constitution Avenue NW
Washington, DC 20230
Information: (202) 482-5061

National Institute of Standards and Technology (NIST)
www.nist.gov/

Nature of Work: Scientific research

Number of Employees: 3,000

Headquarters: Gaithersburg, MD

Regional Locations: Boulder, CO

Typical Background of New Hires: Chemistry, computer science, engineering, mathematics, physical sciences

---

Mission

Provides basic physical measurement standards for science, industry, and government and performs research that increases U.S. industrial productivity.

Job Descriptions

Chemist: Investigates the composition, structure, and properties of different materials.

Computer Scientist: Helps federal agencies solve specific computer application problems and develops standards for protecting sensitive information processed, stored, and transmitted by computer.

Electrical Engineer: Studies the applications of electrical energy, develops standards for electrical equipment, and devises or modifies electrical devices, materials, and procedures.

Materials Scientist: Characterizes the structure and properties of metals, polymers, ceramics, composites, and glasses and assesses their performance under service conditions.

Mechanical Engineer: Evaluates the durability, quality, and strength of materials and products.

Physicist: Develops accurate and uniform physical standards and measurement methods through research in fields such as atomic and molecular physics, radiation research, chemical kinetics, and thermodynamics.

Major Activities and Divisions

NIST carries out its mission in four cooperative programs:

* ✶ The NIST Laboratories: Conducts research that advances the nation's technology infrastructure and is needed by U.S. industry to improve products and services.

* ✶ The Baldrige National Quality Program: Promotes performance excellence among U.S. manufacturers, service companies, educational institutions, and health-care providers; conducts outreach programs and manages the annual Malcolm Baldrige National Quality Award.

* ✶ The Manufacturing Extension Partnership: A nationwide network of local centers offering technical and business assistance to small manufacturers.

* ✶ The Advanced Technology Program: Accelerates the development of innovative technologies for broad national benefit by cofunding R&D partnerships with the private sector.

Alternative Employment Programs

Summer Undergraduate Research Fellowship (SURF): NIST offers 12-week fellowships for undergraduate students in science and engineering. This intensive, hands-on lab experience is designed to encourage students to pursue doctoral degrees in science and engineering.

NIST hires about 50 postdoctoral researchers annually through the NIST/NRC Postdoctoral Research Associates Program.

Application Procedures

Direct inquiries to the personnel office where you would like to work.

Personnel Officer
Administration Bldg., Room A-123
National Institute of Standards and Technology
Gaithersburg, MD 20899
(301) 975-3007
Information: (301) 975-6478
E-mail: inquiries@nist.gov

Personnel Officer
Mountain Administrative Support Center
U.S. Department of Commerce
325 Broadway
Boulder, CO 80303
(303) 497-6615
(303) 497-6332 (Job Line)

National Oceanic and Atmospheric Administration (NOAA)
www.noaa.gov/

Nature of Work: Environmental protection, scientific research, waterways

Number of Employees: 12,000

Headquarters: Silver Spring, MD

Regional Locations: Many locations nationwide

Typical Background of New Hires: Biology, cartography, computer science, earth sciences, hydrology, mathematics, meteorology, oceanography, physics

Mission

Gathers scientific data on the oceans, atmosphere, space, and sun, which is then used to forecast the weather, manage ocean resources, produce nautical and aeronautical charts, and safeguard marine and estuarine sanctuaries.

Job Descriptions

Cartographer: Constructs aeronautical and nautical charts. Also produces maps of earthquake zones, bathymetric charts, and other cartographic products.

Computer Scientist: Analyzes, archives, and disseminates environmental data.

Engineer: General, electrical, electronic, and mechanical engineers develop, test, and maintain instruments and equipment used in NOAA research.

Diver: Works throughout the oceans and inland waters of the world. Deploys and retrieves scientific instruments, documents the behavior of fish and other marine animals, performs emergency and routine ship repair and maintenance, assesses the impact of man on the environment, and locates and charts submerged objects.

Fishery Biologist: Studies the problems of growth and reproduction of fish and shellfish.

Hydrologist: Analyzes river flow, studies and forecasts floods, and issues flood warnings.

Meteorologist: Analyzes weather data and prepares forecasts for the public, mariners, aviators, and farmers.

Oceanographer: Studies the chemical composition of the water as well as the contours, structure, and composition of the ocean floor.

Major Activities and Divisions

National Weather Service: Collects weather observations from surface and upper air stations, radars, ocean buoys, ships, satellites, and volunteers and incorporates this information into atmospheric models.

National Ocean Service: Surveys and charts the nation's navigable coastal waterways and maintains the National Geodetic Reference System which provides a precise geographic framework for all mapping and charting. Monitors the environmental health of the nation's coastline and oversees a system of marine sanctuaries and estuarine research reserves.

National Environmental Satellite, Data, and Information Service: Operates the nation's earth observation satellites and global data centers that collect information on meteorology, land sciences, oceanography, solid-earth geophysics, and solar-terrestrial sciences.

National Marine Fisheries Service: Manages coastal fishing, protects marine mammals and endangered species, and gathers information on the safety, quality, and nutritional value of seafood. Also maintains a nationwide system of fishery laboratories that performs diverse tasks such as resource assessment, experimental biology, pathobiology, fishery engineering, conservation engineering, and aquaculture research.

Office of Oceanic and Atmospheric Research: Performs environmental research at numerous laboratories and supports university research examining national and global problems of the oceans and atmosphere.

Office of Marine and Navy Operations (OMAO): Operates a wide variety of specialized aircraft and ships to complete NOAA's environmental and scientific missions.

NOAA Commissioned Corps: Operates NOAA's fleet of research and survey ships and flies its aircraft.

Marine Operations Centers: Operates an assortment of hydrographic survey, oceanographic research, and fisheries research vessels. Centers are located in Norfolk, VA (East Coast fleet) and Seattle, WA (West Coast fleet). See www.omao.noa.gov/ for more information, including job listings.

Aircraft Operations Center: Maintains a fleet of aircraft to support NOAA's atmospheric and hurricane surveillance/research programs. Located at MacDill Air Force Base, Tampa, FL.

Diving Center: Located in Seattle, WA. The NOAA Diving Program trains and certifies scientists, engineers, and technicians to perform underwater tasks that support NOAA's mission. NOAA has more than 300 divers and averages more than 9,000 dives per year. See www.hdc.noaa.gov/dd.html.

Alternative Employment Programs

NOAA occasionally offers co-op and summer employment to high school and college students interested in its mission-related occupations.

Commissioned Corps: Commissioned Corps Officers typically have science or engineering backgrounds. NOAA Corps Officers operate ships, fly aircraft, lead mobile field parties, conduct diving operations, manage research projects, and serve in staff positions throughout NOAA. For a full list of NOAA Corps entrance requirements and other information, see www.noaacorps.noaa.gov/corpsrecruiting/index.html.

NOAA Marine Operations regularly has openings for shipboard personnel. For civilian jobs in the NOAA fleet, you must apply on line on the Commerce Opportunities On-Line (COOL) Web site at www.jobs.doc.gov.

Application Procedures

NOAA's office of Human Resources can be found at http://hr.noaa.gov.

A listing of all current job openings in NOAA can be found at www.usajobs.opm.gov/a9noaa.htm

Or, direct inquiries to:

Human Resources Management Office, 0FA4
National Oceanic and Atmospheric Administration
1305 East-West Highway
Silver Spring, MD 20910
(301) 713-0534
Information: (202) 482-2985

For Corps Positions:

NOAA Corps Recruiting Unit
1315 East-West Highway
Room 12100, SSMC 3
Silver Spring, MD 20910-3282
E-mail: NOAACorps.Recruiting@noaa.gov
Toll Free: (800) 299-6622
Fax: (301) 713-4140

National Technical Information Service (NTIS)
www.ntis.gov

Nature of Work: Communications/media, computers, libraries

Number of Employees: 385

Headquarters: Springfield, VA

Regional Locations: None

Typical Background of New Hires: Computer science, finance/banking, marketing

Entry-Level Job Titles: Technical Information Specialist

Mission
Catalogs and sells to the public U.S. government-sponsored research, development, and engineering reports as well as international technical reports and other analyses produced by national and local government agencies.

Job Descriptions
Technical Information Specialist: Analyzes the content of reports and prepares indices, bibliographies, and abstracts. Responds to requests for information from universities, industry, government agencies, and the general public.

Major Activities and Divisions

In addition to selling documents and microforms, NTIS summarizes current U.S. and foreign research reports in various publications. These include weekly newsletters, a biweekly journal, an annual index, and other formats. NTIS also maintains an online database at http://grc.ntis.gov, which allows detailed subject searches.

NTIS also operates FEDWORLD, a government information Web site.

Alternative Employment Programs

Co-op opportunities may be available depending on funding. Contact the personnel office.

Remarks

NTIS is funded entirely by sales of its documents and microforms.

Application Procedures

Direct inquiries to:

Office of Personnel
National Technical Information Service
5285 Port Royal Rd.
Springfield, VA 22161
Toll Free: (800) 553-NTIS (Information)

National Telecommunications and Information Administration (NTIA)
www.ntia.doc.gov

Nature of Work: Business, Technology, Information, International Affairs, Scientific Research

Number of Employees: 300

Headquarters: Washington, DC

Regional Locations: Boulder, CO (Institute for Telecommunications Sciences)

Typical Background of New Hires: Engineering, computer science, political science, public policy, law, economics, telecommunications

Mission

NTIA works to spur innovation, encourage competition, help create jobs, and provide consumers with more choices and better quality telecommunications products and services at lower prices. It negotiates with foreign governments to ensure adequate spectrum for national defense, public safety, and U.S. business needs, and it encourages the development of emerging telecommunications technologies.

Job Descriptions

Telecommunications Policy Analyst: Assists in the analysis of issues related to the domestic and/or international telecommunications industry, telecommunications policy and Internet policy, with an emphasis on domain name systems and e-commerce.

Engineering Positions (located at ITS; Boulder, Co): Conducts telecommunications research and development, including interoperability testing of heterogeneous telecommunication networks and end-user devices (requiring a base knowledge of Internet and telephony protocols and test equipment/ procedures), advancement of procedures and tools (e.g., analytical models, simulation, prototype system development) useful for interoperability analysis (both functional and performance) of advanced information systems and services (especially hybrid wireless/wireline networks), and development of telecommunication planning tools, including network management and system administration tools.

Telecommunication Specialist (Office of Spectrum Management): Establishes plans and policies for the management of spectrum assignments and their use by stations operated by the Federal government, and assists in the development of international telecommunications policies.

Major Activities and Divisions

Office of Policy Analysis and Development: OPAD's goal is to enhance public interest by generating policies and programs in the telecommunications and information sectors that enhance service and competition. Information: (202) 482-1880.

Office of International Affairs: Acts as an advocate of U.S. commercial interests overseas.

Office of Spectrum Management: Manages the Federal Government's use of the radio frequency spectrum.

Institute for Telecommunications Sciences: ITS is the research and engineering branch of NTIA.

Office of Telecommunications and Information Applications: Administers grant program to assist state and local governments, educational and health care entities, libraries, public service agencies, and other groups in using telecommunications and information technologies.

Alternative Employment Programs

The Institute for Telecommunication Sciences (ITS) provides internships for students with engineering and/or computer science backgrounds. These are full-time or part-time paid or volunteer internship positions. Typically, full-time positions are held during the summer and often continue as part-time positions during the fall and spring semesters. ITS targets students in undergraduate engineering programs or graduate students with an undergraduate engineering degree. Look for current information on http://www.its.bldrdoc.gov/home/intern/intern.html.

The Office of International Affairs hosts volunteer internships for students with backgrounds in telecommunications, political science, public policy, economics, law, or engineering/technology policy. Internships take place in the spring, summer, or fall semesters or year-round. Call (202) 482-1890 for more information.

OPAD hires volunteer interns for a semester or longer to assist in policy development and research applications, providing an opportunity to write as well as conduct research on cutting-edge policy issues. Call (202) 482-1880 for more information.

Application Procedures

Current vacancies are listed by NTIA at the main Web site (click on the office that interests you) and at the Institute for Telecommunications Sciences at www.its.bldrdoc.gov/Home.html.

Or, contact:

Department of Commerce, NTIA
1401 Constitution Ave. NW
Washington, DC 20230
(202) 482-7002

For the Institute for Telecommunication Sciences, contact:

NTIA/ITS (Boulder)
U.S. Department of Commerce
325 Broadway
Boulder, CO 80305-3328
(303) 497-5216
Fax: (303) 497-5993

Bureau of Industry and Security
www.bxa.doc.gov

Nature of Work: National security, business, defense, international affairs, law enforcement, import/export

Number of Employees: 385

Headquarters: Washington, DC

Regional Locations: Boston, MA; New York, NY; Washington, DC; Miami, FL; Chicago, IL; Dallas, TX; Los Angeles, CA; San Jose, CA

Typical Background of New Hires: Engineering (chemical, nuclear), physical science, criminal justice

Mission

Works to advance U.S. national security, foreign policy, and economic interests by regulating the export of sensitive goods and technologies and enforcing export control, anti-boycott, and public safety laws.

Job Descriptions

Special Agent (enforcement): Works with the export industry to detect and prevent illegal shipments, and works with other U.S. agencies and foreign governments on export enforcement issues.

Engineer: Conducts technical and scientific reviews of export licensing and makes recommendations regarding the propriety of licensing for overseas exporting.

Major Activities and Divisions

BIS is divided into two major areas:

✭ Export Administration

The Office of Nonproliferation Controls and Treaty Compliance: Administers the Commerce Department's multilateral export control responsibilities. (202) 482-3825

The Office of Strategic Trade and Foreign Policy Controls: Implements U.S. foreign policy controls such as crime control, antiterrorism, and regional stability, and is responsible for controls on exports to terrorist countries. (202) 482-0092

The Office of Exporter Services: Counsels exporters, conducts export control seminars, and drafts changes to the Export Administration Regulations. (202) 482-0436

The Office of Strategic Industry and Economic Security: Ensures the U.S. defense industries can meet national security requirements and provides advocacy assistance to U.S. Defense exporters. (202) 482-4506

✭ Export Enforcement

Office of Export Enforcement (OEE): investigates violations of the export administration regulations and the fastener quality act and apprehends violators. (202) 482-2252

Office of Export Enforcement, Intelligence and Field Support Division: Located at Headquarters office, and is staffed by OEE special agents. This office receives information from various sources and disseminates it to special agents in the field. (202) 482-1208

Office of Enforcement Analysis (OEA): Makes licensing recommendations to BIS licensing officers based on intelligence information and input received from special agents in the field. (202) 482-4255

Office of Anti-Boycott Compliance (OAC): Implements the anti-boycott provisions of the Export Administration Regulations. (202) 482-5914

Alternative Employment Programs

Limited student hiring may occur depending on funding.

Application Procedures

BIS does not currently list job openings on their Web site. Contact the regional location in which you would like to work.

Bureau of Industry and Security
14th Street and Constitution Avenue NW
U.S. Department of Commerce
Washington DC 20230
(202) 482-2721 or (202) 482-1900

Boston Field Office
Room 350
10 Causeway Street
Boston, MA 02222
(617) 565-6030
Fax: (617) 565-6039
New York Field Office
Suite 104
1200 South Avenue
Staten Island, NY 10314
(718) 370-0070
Fax: (718) 370-0826

Washington Field Office
Suite 1125
381 Elden Street
Herndon, VA 20170
(703) 487-9300
Fax: (703) 487-9463

Miami Field Office
Suite 2060
200 E. Las Olas Blvd.
Fort Lauderdale, FL 33301
(954) 356-7540
Fax: (954) 356-7549

Chicago Field Office
High Point Plaza
4415 West Harrison Street
Suite 530
Hillside, IL 60018
(312) 353-6640
Fax: (312) 353-8008

Dallas Field Office
Room 622
525 South Griffin Street
Dallas, TX 75202
(214) 767-9294
Fax: (214) 767-9299

San Jose Field Office
Suite 250
96 North Third Street
San Jose, CA 95112-5519
(408) 291-4204
Fax: (408) 291-4320

Los Angeles Field Office
Suite 310
2601 Main Street
Irvine, CA 92714-6299
(949) 251-9001
Fax: (949) 251-9103

Patent and Trademark Office (PTO)
www.uspto.gov

Nature of Work: Business, law/justice

Number of Employees: 6,300

Headquarters: Crystal City, VA

Regional Locations: None

Typical Background of New Hires: Biological sciences, biology, chemistry, engineering, law, physics, computer science

Mission

Protects U.S. inventions, products, and corporate logos by issuing patents and trademarks, publishing patent and trademark information, maintaining public search files of domestic and foreign patents and trademarks, and providing copies of patents and trademarks to the public.

Job Descriptions

Patent Examiner: Determines the patentability of an invention or discovery by assessing whether it will perform as claimed and whether any previous inventions exist that may be comparable to it.

Major Activities and Divisions

Examiners with backgrounds in biology, chemistry, microbiology, and related sciences judge the patentability of inventions relating to chemical or biotechnological products and processes.

Examiners with a physics background normally assess the patentability of inventions in such fields as semiconductor physics, radiant energy, atomic and nuclear physics, optics, and lasers.

Examiners with engineering backgrounds judge the patentability of inventions in fields as diverse as photography, data processing, optics, aeronautics, surgery, heat generation, metallurgy, plastics, medicine, and phase separation.

Alternative Employment Programs

A summer employment program exists at PTO. See the PTO Web site for current information.

Remarks

New employees receive training at the Patent Academy. Training covers patent examining practice and procedures and the legal concepts required for these activities.

Application Procedures

The USPTO Web site maintains an online Patent Examiner application format at www3.uspto.gov/go/jars/index.html.

Or, direct inquiries to:

Office of Human Resources
U.S. Patent and Trademark Office
2011 Crystal Dr. CPK1-707
Arlington, VA 22202
Personnel: (703) 305-8231
Vacancies: (703) 305-4221
TDD: (703) 305-8586

U.S. Commercial Service (CS)
www.usatrade.gov

Nature of Work: Business, import/export, international affairs, marketing

Number of Employees: 1,800

Headquarters: Washington, DC

Regional Locations: 105 Export Assistance Centers throughout the U.S. and 151 international offices in 83 countries.

Typical Background of New Hires: Business, international affairs, marketing

---

Mission

Facilitates U.S. exports by identifying agents and distributors for U.S. and foreign companies. Locates sources of financing for businesses and conducts market research for U.S. firms.

Job Descriptions

Foreign Service Officer (FSO): Introduces U.S. exporters to foreign businesses interested in representing their products. Assists in the resolution of trade and investment disputes and organizes trade promotion programs. Candidates for Foreign Service Officer positions with CS must pass the Commercial Service Assessment, a competitive oral and written examination, which is used to recruit new, tenure-track Foreign Service Officers into the Commercial Service.

Major Activities and Divisions

Market Research: CS offers international market information on specific industries that can help determine market potential, market size, and identify competitors.

International Partnerships: CS helps identify potential business partners in a targeted export market, as well as business prospects for products and services.

Consulting and Advocacy: CS assists exporters in determining the best markets for products and services, developing an effective export strategy, and identifying and complying with legal and regulatory issues.

Alternative Employment Programs

CS offers co-op positions and internships at their centers throughout the U.S. Contact directly the office in which you wish to work (contact information can be found at www.usatrade.gov/Website/website.nsf/WebBySubj/Main_Employment#interns). Or, call (202) 482-3301.

Remarks

Candidates must be available for worldwide assignment. All FSO candidates receive several weeks of orientation at the State Department's Foreign Service Institute in Washington, DC. All candidates must pass the Foreign Service Examination to be considered for employment as a Foreign Service Officer. See the profile on the State Department for more information about the examination.

Application Procedures

Direct inquiries to:

U.S. Commercial Service
Human Resources Office
14th Street and Constitution Avenue NW
Washington, DC 20044-0688
(202) 482-3505

☆ Department of Defense (www.dod.mil or www.defenselink.mil)

Defense Contract Audit Agency (DCAA)
www.dcaa.mil

Nature of Work: Accounting/auditing, military affairs

Number of Employees: 4,000

Headquarters: Ft. Belvoir, VA

Regional Locations: Irving, TX; Los Angeles, CA; Smyrna, GA; Philadelphia, PA; La Mirada, CA; Lowell, MA. These regional offices oversee operations at over 350 domestic and international audit sites.

Typical Background of New Hires: Accounting

Mission

Audits Defense Department contractors, reviewing and reporting on costs incurred. Annually reviews more than 10,000 businesses and issues about 60,000 audit reports.

Job Descriptions

Auditor: Evaluates management policies and decisions, financial records, and the internal controls of defense contractors.

Major Activities and Divisions

DCAA advises government procurement officials on analyzing and negotiating contractors' bids, renders opinions on contractors' financial capabilities, validates contractors' claimed costs, and engages in operational audits that assess the adequacy of internal control systems.

Alternative Employment Programs

DCAA participates in the STEP and SCEP student hiring programs. Contact the regional office in which you would like to work. DCAA engages in campus recruitment nationwide.

Remarks

Entry-level auditors are trained at DCAA's Defense Contract Audit Institute in Memphis, TN. DCAA also encourages auditors to take the CPA exam and helps them pass by sponsoring CPA review courses.

Application Procedures

Current jobs are listed online at www.dcaa.mil. Or, direct inquiries to:

Headquarters
Defense Contract Audit Agency
8725 John J. Klingman Rd. Suite 2135
Ft. Belvoir, VA 22060-6219
(703) 767-2200

Central Region
6321 Campus Circle Drive East
Irving, TX 75063-2742
(972) 753-2526

Eastern Region
2400 Lake Park Drive, Suite 300
Smyrna, GA 30080-7644
(770) 319-4494

Mid-Atlantic Region
615 Chestnut Street, Suite 1000
Philadelphia, PA 19106-4498
(215) 597-6085

Northeastern Region
59 Composite Way
Lowell, MA 01851-5150
(978) 551-9780

Western Region
16700 Valley View Ave, Suite 300
La Mirada, CA 90638-5833
(714) 228-7016

> ### Defense Intelligence Agency (DIA)
> ### www.dia.mil
>
> **Nature of Work:** Defense/national security, intelligence, military affairs
>
> **Number of Employees:** 7,000
>
> **Headquarters:** Washington, DC (Pentagon)
>
> **Regional Locations:** Arlington, VA; Frederick, MD; Huntsville, AL
>
> **Typical Background of New Hires:** biology, chemistry, computer science, economics, engineering (aerospace, chemical, computer, electrical, electronic, nuclear, and systems), geography, languages, international affairs, microbiology, pharmacology, physics, political science, and toxicology.

Mission

Gathers, analyzes, and disseminates intelligence information on the capabilities and intentions of foreign military forces.

Job Descriptions

Computer Specialist: Assesses systems capabilities in relation to intelligence requirements, evaluates technology and applies it to enhance the agency's systems capabilities, develops technical standards and specifications, and creates and maintains computer based systems and applications programs. May require deployment to foreign regions.

Intelligence Officer: Interprets photographic, electronic, technical, and other types of information gathered from satellites, aerial reconnaissance, and ground observations and develops data on foreign military forces.

Major Activities and Divisions

The Directorate for Analysis and Production: Provides rapid and responsive all-source military intelligence in response to the needs of the needs of the Secretary of Defense, the Joint Chiefs of Staff, the military services, other government agencies, and the commanders in the field.

The Directorate for Intelligence Operations: Directs and manages Department of Defense all-source collection requirements and conducts DoD human intelligence (HUMINT) operations.

The Joint Military Intelligence College (JMIC): JMIC is an accredited college, which is congressionally authorized to award a Bachelor of Science in intelligence and a Master of Science in strategic intelligence. Visit the JMIC section of the DIA Web site for more information, or call (202) 231-3299.

Alternative Employment Programs

Undergraduate Training Assistance Program (UTAP): A select number of high school seniors are employed by DIA and are offered tuition assistance for an undergraduate degree, provided summer employment, and guaranteed a job in their field of study upon graduation.

Graduate Training Assistance Program (GTAP): Recipients of the GTAP will begin their employment with DIA with full-time enrollment in the Joint Military Intelligence College, leading to the Master of Science in strategic intelligence degree.

Summer Intern Program: Undergraduate and graduate students, pursuing degrees critical to the agency's mission, are assigned jobs relating to their area of study. Interns are appointed for a 10-week period—early June to mid-August—as full-time, temporary employees.

Cooperative Education Program: Undergraduate and graduate students who are enrolled in their institution's cooperative education program are offered paid work experience relating to their area of study.

Remarks

DIA is headquartered at the Pentagon in Washington, DC, with major operational activities at the Defense Intelligence Analysis Center (DIAC), Washington, DC; the Armed Forces Medical Intelligence Center (AFMIC), Frederick, MD; and the Missile and Space Intelligence Center (MSIC), Huntsville, AL.

Because of intensive pre-employment screenings, interested candidates should apply to DIA at least six months prior to intended start date.

Application Procedures

The DIA Civilian Employment and Classification Division reviews and processes applications from individuals interested in a career with DIA. Applicants are placed in a candidate pool for consideration against current and/or future openings. Resumes remain in the candidate pool for one year. To submit your resume directly to the candidate pool, e-mail it to dia@alexus.com, referencing source code EMLP in the subject line.

For student opportunities or positions at the grade level GG-14 or above, review the vacancy announcements at www.dia.mil and apply directly online.

Or, direct inquiries to:

Defense Intelligence Agency
Civilian Staffing and recruitment Branch
7400 Defense Pentagon
Washington, DC 20301-7400
(202) 231-8228
E-mail: www.careers@dia.mil

Defense Security Service (DSS)
www.dss.mil

Nature of Work: Defense/national security, law enforcement

Number of Employees: 2,800

Headquarters: Alexandria, VA

Regional Locations: Linthicum, MD; Ft. Meade, MD; Long Beach, CA; Smyrna, GA; field offices are located nationwide, as well as in Brussels, Belgium and Manheim, Germany. (addresses and phone numbers are listed on the Web site)

Typical Background of New Hires: Criminal justice, liberal arts

Mission

Conducts personnel security investigations of Defense Department employees and other federal workers requiring security clearances. Also oversees industrial security programs for Defense Department contractors.

Job Descriptions

Industrial Security Representative: Conducts security surveys and inspections of defense industrial contractor facilities possessing classified information/ material. Assists industrial contractors in developing security measures and assesses facilities' vulnerability to terrorism and sabotage.

Special Agent: Confirms birth and citizenship; verifies education and employment claims; reviews local criminal justice and credit records; interviews friends, neighbors, and relatives of federal personnel requiring security clearances.

Major Activities and Divisions

DSS conducts personnel security investigations under the Personnel Security Investigations Program (PSI). These investigations are used by DoD adjudicative facilities to determine an individual's suitability to enter the armed forces, to access classified information, or to hold a sensitive position within the DoD.

The DSS Industrial Security Program (ISP) includes the Defense portion of the *National Industrial Security Program (NISP)*, which was established to ensure that private industry and colleges and universities while performing government contracts or research and development and safeguarding classified information in their possession.

The DSS Academy provides security education and training programs to support DSS components, DoD agencies, and DoD Military Departments and Contractors.

Alternative Employment Programs

DSS participates in a co-op program depending on the availability of funding.

Remarks

DSS was formerly called the Defense Investigative Service.

Application Procedures

Apply online with a resume at https://storm.psd.whs.mil/cgi-bin/apply.pl. Or call (703) 617-0652 to have a copy of the HRSC job kit faxed to you. You can also mail your resume to:

Resume
Washington Headquarters Services
NCR Human Resources Services
5001 Eisenhower Avenue, Room 2E22
Alexandria, VA 22333-0001

Defense Logistics Agency (DLA)
www.dla.mil

Nature of Work: Inventory/supply, military affairs

Number of Employees: 24,000

Headquarters: Fort Belvoir, VA

Regional Locations: Atlanta, GA; Battle Creek, MI; Columbus, OH; Los Angeles, CA; New Cumberland, PA; Philadelphia, PA; Richmond, VA; Stockton, CA

Typical Background of New Hires: Business, computer science, engineering

Mission

Purchases equipment, supplies, and services for the military services. This includes virtually all of its food, medicine, and clothing, as well as a large portion of its chemical, construction, electronics, and industrial supplies.

Job Descriptions

IT Specialist: Provides ADP and digital telecommunications support to DLA activities worldwide.

Contract Specialist: Prepares solicitations; analyzes proposed costs; and negotiates, awards, and administers contracts for supplies, equipment, and services.

Engineer: In nearly all disciplines, performs professional engineering work in the design, evaluation, and improvement of purchased materials, ensuring products meet the specifications and needs of the military end-user.

Environmental Protection Specialist: Develops and monitors environmental protection programs to facilitate the safe demilitarization and disposal of excess military property and facilities.

Industrial Property Management Specialist: Approves contractors' property control systems and ensures they meet prescribed requirements.

Industrial Specialist: Assesses the ability of contractors to produce a particular item and monitors its production ensuring that it meets technical specifications.

Inventory Management Specialist: Manages, regulates, and coordinates DLA-managed items to determine how much stock to purchase to assure adequate stock availability when and where needed.

Property Disposal Specialist: Oversees the use, donation, merchandising, or disposal of excess or surplus property.

Quality Assurance Specialist: Ensures that supplies comply with contractual performance standards.

Supply Management Specialist: Supervises the movement of freight and passengers from industrial plants and depots to installations, ocean/air terminals, and overseas locations.

Major Activities and Divisions

Defense Supply Center Columbus: Supplies weapon systems spare parts and end items.

Defense Supply Center Richmond: The lead center for aviation weapon systems and environmental logistics support.

Defense Supply Center Philadelphia: Supplies and services U.S. service members by providing them food, clothing, and medicines, and supports U.S. humanitarian and disaster relief efforts.

Defense Distribution Center: Stores and provides worldwide transportation of supplies.

Defense Energy Support Center: Purchases and manages DoD energy products.

Defense National Stockpile Center: An international commodity broker of strategic and critical materials.

Defense Reutilization and Marketing Service: Provides DoD with worldwide reuse, recycling, and disposal solutions that focus on efficiency, cost avoidance, and compliance.

Defense Logistics Information Service: Involved in the creation and dissemination of logistics information to military and government customers.

Document Automation and Production Service: The single manager for all DoD printing and duplicating.

DLA Europe: Serves as a focal point for DLA matters in Europe.

DLA Pacific: Provides liaison and logistics support to the U.S. Pacific Command.

Alternative Employment Programs

DLA maintains a co-op program and intern program for sophomores and juniors. About 20 of each are hired each year at the GS-3 and -4 levels and work in a variety of occupations. PMIs are hired as well.

Application Procedures

The preferred method for submitting a resume and supplemental data is through the resume builder on the HROC Web page at www.hroc.dla.mil. You can also e-mail your resume to resume@hroc.dla.mil or mail a hard copy of your resume to:

DLA Human Resources Operations Center
HROC-AS (Stairs Unit)
P.O. Box 182662
Columbus, OH 43218-2662
Direct inquiries to: (614) 692-5975

Department of Defense Educational Activity (DoDEA)
www.odedodea.edu/

Nature of Work: Education, military affairs

Number of Employees: 8,800 teachers; approximately 15,000 employees overall

Headquarters: Arlington, VA

Regional Locations: Ft. Rucker, AL; Ft. Benning and Ft. Knox, KY; West Point, NY; Camp Lejuene and Ft. Bragg, NC; Laurel Bay, SC; Quantico, VA. Other locations include Guam, Puerto Rico, Bahrain, Belgium, Cuba, England, Germany, Greece, Iceland, Italy, Japan, Korea, the Netherlands, Portugal, Spain, and Turkey.

Typical Background of New Hires: Education

Mission

Provides schools for children of military members stationed at various bases in the United States and around the world.

The schools are organized into two separate but parallel systems: the Department of Defense Dependents Schools (DoDDS) overseas, and the Department of Defense Domestic Dependent Elementary and Secondary Schools (DDESS) in the United States. In 1994, the two systems were brought together under an umbrella agency, the Department of Defense Education Activity (DoDEA).

Job Descriptions

All tours of duty are 1 or 2 school years depending on the area of assignment. One-year tour areas include Bahrain, Cuba, Iceland, Italy (Sigonella and La Maddalena), Korea, Japan (Misawa and Okinawa), Portugal (Azores), and Turkey. Two-year tour areas include Belgium, England, Germany, Greece, Italy (other than Sigonella and La Maddalena), Japan (other than Misawa and Okinawa), the Netherlands, and Spain.

For more details on all positions, including qualifications standards, visit www.odedodea.edu/pers/employment/application/positions.html.

Elementary School Positions (Grades Prekindergarten–6): All educators applying for elementary classroom teaching positions must possess 24 semester hours of elementary education course work. No second category is required, except where noted. A valid state or territory certificate/license may be accepted in lieu of meeting the minimum qualification requirements when issued a 2-year Provisional License. Elementary teaching positions are available in prekindergarten, kindergarten, language immersion, art, music, physical education, reading recovery, and more.

Middle School Positions (Grades 6–8): DoDDS operates middle schools and combination middle/secondary schools. Specific qualifications requirements for positions at these schools are listed on their Web site. Teaching positions include English, speech, journalism, social studies, general science, health, and math.

Secondary School Positions (Usually Grades 7–12): DoDDS operates a variety of school configurations. Secondary school teachers may be required to teach at the middle and senior high school levels. A second teaching category is required for most secondary positions. Details regarding academic qualifications are listed on their Web site. Teaching positions include English, speech, journalism, drama, computer science, languages, business, humanities, and more.

Training Instructors, Certified: One year of teaching experience is required and may be in an adult education program, middle or secondary school, college, or industrial establishment in the particular occupational field(s) for which applying.

Training Instructors, Noncertified: Noncertified training instructor applicants must have a high school diploma or equivalent certificate. Additionally, they must complete a formal program at or above the high school level (or vocational high school level), trade school, or military/Peace Corps training program in the specialty area. Specialty areas include automotive technology, cosmetology, graphic arts, small engine repair, dental technology, fashion design, welding, and others.

Junior Reserve Officers Training Corps (JROTC) Instructor: Must be retired from active duty military at least 180 days prior to appointment. Must be certified to teach JROTC from respective headquarters services. Retired officers must have bachelor's degree. A second category is not required.

Pupil Personnel Services Positions: Some positions may require the educator to provide services to more than one school or school complex (itinerant position). Position titles include *Dormitory Counselor, School Psychologist, School Social Worker, Educational Prescriptionist*, and *Guidance Counselor*.

Educational Support Positions: Many of these positions require the educator to provide services to more than one school or school complex and involve travel to various locations. Special education positions may require teaching children at any age level with a variety of disabilities ranging from mild to severe. In addition, most special education teachers are expected to participate on multidisciplinary assessment teams. Position titles include *Teacher, Talented and Gifted; Teacher, Emotionally Impaired; Teacher, Moderately to Severely Learning Impaired; Teacher, Hearing Impaired; School Nurse; Teacher, English as a Second Language;* and more.

Major Activities and Divisions

The Department of Defense Education Activity (DoDEA) is a civilian agency of the U.S. Department of Defense. It is headed by a director who oversees all agency functions from DoDEA headquarters in Arlington, Virginia. DoDEA's schools are divided into three areas, each of which is managed by an area director. Within each of these three areas, schools are organized into districts headed by superintendents. DoDEA operates 224 public schools in 21 districts located in 14 foreign countries, 7 states, Guam, and Puerto Rico. All schools within DoDEA are fully accredited by U.S. accreditation agencies. Approximately 8,800 teachers serve DoDEA's 106,000 students.

Alternative Employment Programs

The DoDDS participates in a Student Teaching Opportunities Overseas Program that places student teachers around the globe for their student teaching experience. To qualify, a student must be enrolled in a degree or teacher education program with an accredited institution and, there must be a student teacher agreement between DoDDS and the college or university. If the institution does not currently have a student teaching agreement with DoDDS, a student may still apply by requesting that the school enter into a DoDDS agreement. For more information, visit www.odedodea.edu/pers/employment/studentteaching/studentteacherpage_links.htm.

Remarks

Proof of near-native language proficiency is evidenced by submitting a rating of an "Advanced Plus" or "Superior" rating from the American Council on the Teaching of Foreign Languages, Inc. (ACTFL). ACTFL may be contacted at (914) 963-8830 to make arrangements for an Oral Proficiency Interview (OPI).

Housing: Living quarters may be provided without charge in some areas. These quarters may be in college dormitories, apartments, old hotels, converted office buildings, or newly built facilities.

DoDDS employs the best-qualified professional staff to implement its program of learning. These special selection factors are applied to determine the best-qualified and suitable applicants.

* Academic preparation

* Information secured through employment references and sources

* Recommendation from interviewer

* Recent experience as an educator

* Possession of personal qualifications and traits such as stability and ability to adapt to unusual and sometimes stressful situations, which are essential for successful performance in an overseas assignment

* Academic preparation to teach more than one subject or grade level (*Note:* This flexibility is critical to meet the needs of the ever-changing population of students.)

* Special achievements or awards related to the position(s) for which being considered

Application Procedure

While applications are accepted at any time, applicants are encouraged to apply by early January to be considered for the next school year.

To find specifics on certification and licensure requirements, visit www.odedodea.edu/pers/employment/application/requirement.html.

DoDEA has an online application system at www.odedodea.edu/pers/employment/application.

Contact the DoDEA at:

4040 North Fairfax Drive
Arlington, VA 22203-1634
Recruitment: 703-696-3067
Fax: 703-696-2699
www.odedodea.edu/pers/employment
E-mail (link on Web site): recruitment@hq.odedodea.edu

Defense Threat Reduction Agency (DTRA)
www.dtra.mil

Nature of Work: Defense, intelligence, international affairs

Number of Employees: 2,100 civilian and military

Headquarters: Ft. Belvoir, VA

Regional Locations: Alexandria and Dulles, VA; Albuquerque, NM. Overseas offices in Frankfurt, Germany; Moscow; Russia; and Yokota Air Base, Japan.

Typical Background of New Hires: Biology, chemistry, physical science, physics (nuclear), intelligence

---

Mission

The DTRA safeguards America and its friends from weapons of mass destruction (chemical, biological, radiological, nuclear, and high explosives) by reducing the present threat and preparing for the future threat.

Job Descriptions

Intelligence Research Specialist: Collects and analyzes information on political or military conditions, trends, and forces in foreign and domestic areas that directly or indirectly affect national security.

Subject Matter Experts: DTRA hires people with backgrounds in the sciences to serve as subject matter experts (SME) on weapons of mass destruction threat reduction. Titles include Physical Scientist, Nuclear Physicist, Chemist, and Biologist.

Major Activities and Divisions

DTRA performs four essential functions to accomplish its mission: combat support, technology development, threat control, and threat reduction.

Combat Support: responsible for the Defense Department's stockpile stewardship duties and provides technical support for all nuclear weapons in DOD custody.

Technology Development: Evaluates the lethality of conventional, biological, chemical, and other advanced weapons against a broad spectrum of target types in war fighting and terrorist scenarios.

Threat Control: Conducts on-site inspection activities to ensure compliance under an increasing number of arms control treaties and agreements.

Threat Reduction: Manages the Cooperative Threat Reduction (CTR) program, which is designed to help the countries of the former Soviet Union destroy nuclear, chemical and biological weapons of mass destruction and associated infrastructure and establish verifiable safeguards against the proliferation of those weapons.

Alternative Employment Programs

DTRA participates in the PMI program, a summer hiring program, and the federal STEP and SCEP student hiring programs.

Application Procedure

Applicants for DTRA jobs must submit a three-page resume. Applicants not currently serviced by the HRSC must also submit an additional supplemental page.

All DTRA jobs require at least a *secret* security clearance. As appropriate, interim clearances may be granted. Be sure to annotate your resume if you currently have or previously had a clearance.

For additional information on DTRA Job Opportunities, contact the DTRA Civilian Personnel Operations Branch at (703) 767-0174 or the Special Recruitment Programs Branch at (703) 767-0171.

E-mail: rm@dtra.mil

National Imagery and Mapping Agency (NIMA)
www.nima.mil

Nature of Work: Defense/national security, maritime activities, military affairs, scientific research

Number of Employees: 7,360

Headquarters: Washington, DC

Regional Locations: Components are located in Bethesda, MD; Fairfax, VA; Fort Belvoir, VA; Reston, VA; St. Louis, MO. Many sublocations worldwide.

Typical Background of New Hires: Cartography, geography, geology

---

Mission

Provides geospatial intelligence to the U.S. armed forces in support of national security. NIMA also produces nautical charts and marine navigational data for the merchant marine and private boaters.

Job Descriptions

Aeronautical Information Specialist: Gathers data necessary for producing precise aeronautical and space charts and flight information publications.

Cartographer: Determines position, elevation, and shapes of geomorphic and topographic features and prepares charts for aerial navigation.

Geodesist: Uses observations and measurements to determine the exact positions of points and areas on the earth's surface.

Geospatial Analyst: Acquires and analyzes geospatial intelligence and other information from a variety of sources in support of national security objectives.

Imagery Analyst: Analyzes and interprets imagery to monitor military leadership, operating tactics, and infrastructure of foreign countries.

Marine Information Specialist: Conducts hydrographic surveys and determines the physical characteristics of bodies of water for navigation charts.

Physical Scientist: Studies earth-related phenomena such as gravitational and magnetic fields used in navigation and mapmaking.

Major Activities and Divisions

Aerospace Center (St. Louis Air Force Station, MO): Provides mapping, charting, and geodesy services for aerospace missions.

Combat Support Center (Washington, DC): Distributes NIMA products to military and civilian users.

National Imagery and Mapping College (Fort Belvoir, VA): Trains members of the armed forces and other government employees in mapping, charting, and geodesy.

Hydrographic/Topographic Center (Washington, DC): Furnishes nautical and topographic products.

Telecommunications Services Center (Reston, VA): Operates NIMA's telecommunications systems and maintains the long-haul equipment linking major production centers and field activities.

Reston Center (Reston, VA): Produces geodetic, mapping, and charting products.

Systems Center (McLean, VA): Enhances NIMA's output using softcopy or computerized production techniques.

Alternative Employment Programs

NIMA maintains a co-op program for students majoring in the physical sciences.

Remarks

NIMA was established in 1996. when the Defense Mapping Agency, the Central Imagery Office, and other programs were consolidated. It is a combat support agency.

Application Procedures

NIMA lists current job openings on its Web site. Or, direct inquiries to:

NIMA Human Resources Office
HR Central Operations Center
Central Staffing and Classification Branch
3200 South Second St.
St. Louis, MO 63118-3399
Toll Free: (800) 777-6104 or (314) 263-4888
E-mail resume to: hrjobs@nima.mil

National Security Agency (NSA)
www.nsa.gov

Nature of Work: Defense/national security, intelligence, international affairs, scientific research

Number of Employees: 38,000

Headquarters: Fort Meade, MD

Regional Locations: Classified

Typical Background of New Hires: Computer science, engineering, languages, mathematics, physical sciences

---

Mission

Intercepts and analyzes foreign telecommunications to protect U.S. national security. NSA also protects U.S. communications and information systems from eavesdropping by foreign countries.

Job Descriptions

Computer Scientist: Supports NSA's data collection and analysis functions by designing database management, real-time programming, distributed processing, and other systems.

Cryptanalyst: analyzes encrypted information to identify basic elements in a cipher code to lead to its solution. NSA hires college graduates with a variety of backgrounds and academic majors for these positions.

Electrical Engineer: Designs equipment used in collecting and analyzing foreign communications. Equipment may include antennas, computers, and devices that recognize telemetric patterns. You may also be involved with signal analysis, optics, and microelectronics.

Intelligence Analyst: Summarizes and interprets raw data and reports on the capabilities and intentions of foreign governments and military forces.

Linguist: Translates material into English, develops glossaries and handbooks, and participates in the development of computer-aided voice translation systems.

Mathematician: Applies probability theory, statistics, algebra, matrix theory, stochastic processes, and other concepts to cryptography.

Signals Analyst: Works to identify, recover, and derive intelligence from all manner of foreign signals. NSA targets people with backgrounds in computer science, math, engineering, and related technical disciplines for these positions.

Major Activities and Divisions

NSA is the nation's cryptologic organization and employs this country's premier code makers and code breakers. A high-technology organization, NSA is on the frontiers of communications and data processing. In addition, NSA is one of the most important centers of foreign language analysis and research within the government.

Alternative Employment Programs

NSA has five unique student hiring programs:

College Summer Employment Program (CSEP): Open to students following their junior year who are majoring in math, computer science, or electrical and computer engineering.

Director's Summer Program (DSP): An intense 12-week program that gives math students the opportunity to learn and develop cryptomathematical theory and to apply the theory to operational problems.

Summer Network Evaluation Intern Program (SNEIP): Offers students in engineering or computer science an opportunity to apply their knowledge in the area of network security.

Summer Program for Research Technology (SPORT): Summer opportunities for operations research (OR) students to engage in real-world applications at NSA.

National Physical Science Consortium (NPSC): The National Physical Science Consortium is an organization of leading universities, national laboratories, and corporations that provide scholarly career paths to help further the education of minority students and women in the physical sciences.

Remarks

Because of intensive preemployment screenings, interested candidates should apply to NSA at least four months prior to graduation. New employees are trained at the National Cryptologic School, which is located at NSA's headquarters. The school offers technical, linguistic, and managerial courses.

Application Procedures

NSA engages in campus recruitment across the country, and their recruiting schedule is listed on their Web site. Direct career inquiries to:

Office of Civilian Personnel
Recruitment Branch
National Security Agency
Attn.: M322
Fort Meade, MD 20755-6000
Toll Free: (800) 255-8415
Information: (301) 688-6524

☆ Department of Education (www.ed.gov)

Department of Education
www.ed.gov

Nature of Work: Education, funds/funding

Number of Employees: 4,900

Headquarters: Washington, DC

Regional Locations: Atlanta, GA; Boston, MA; Chicago, IL; Dallas, TX; Denver, CO; Kansas City, MO; New York, NY; Philadelphia, PA; San Francisco, CA; Seattle, WA

Typical Background of New Hires: Accounting, economics, education, finance, law, public administration

Mission

The Department of Education administers and coordinates most federal assistance to education.

Job Descriptions

Education Program Specialist: Maintains a working knowledge of the legislation and regulations relating to assigned educational programs. Provides technical assistance to officials whose organizations are eligible for federal funds. Evaluates effectiveness of programs through review of reports, on-site reviews, audit reports, and educational surveys. Makes recommendations for program policy.

Computer Specialist: Designs and programs computer systems.

Equal Opportunity Specialist: Performs work to ensure that recipients of federal financial assistance comply with nondiscrimination legislation. Investigates individual and class-action complaints and conducts compliance reviews. Monitors compliance agreements and attempts conciliation using negotiation and mediation.

Grant Specialist: Develops objectives for the accomplishment of assigned grants programs and activities. Conducts evaluations and identifies problems related to assigned programs. Exercises signatory authority to enter into or modify grants and cooperative agreements on behalf of the government.

Institutional Review Specialist: Conducts program reviews of postsecondary education institutions to determine whether institutions are complying with regulations and to provide assistance to improve administration of the program.

Lender Review Specialist: Conducts program reviews of lenders and guarantee agencies to determine whether such institutions are in compliance with the federal provisions of the Student Financial Assistance Programs, such as the Guaranteed Student Loan (GSL) Program and the Parent Loan to Undergraduate Student (PLUS) Programs. Prepares program review reports offering recommendations for improvement of the administration of the programs. Follows up on all discrepancies noted in the program review.

Major Activities and Divisions

Bilingual Education and Minority Languages Affairs: Ensures access to equal educational opportunity and improves the quality of programs for limited English proficiency and minority languages populations.

Civil Rights: Responsible for the administration and enforcement of civil rights laws related to education and the handicapped.

Education Research and Improvement: Involved in research, statistics, development, and assessment.

Vocational and Adult Education: Administers programs of grants, contracts, and technical assistance for vocational and technical education.

Special Education and Rehabilitative Services: Responsible for special education programs designed to meet needs and develop the full potential of handicapped children.

Postsecondary Education: Coordinates programs for assistance to postsecondary educational institutions and students pursuing a postsecondary education.

Elementary and Secondary Education: Provides financial assistance to state and local education agencies for both public and private preschool, elementary, and secondary education.

Alternative Employment Programs

The Department of Education offers a co-op, Stay-in-School, and summer hire program for students of all ages.

Remarks

Approximately 8,000 postsecondary education institutions and $12 billion in SFA funds are subject to monitoring and compliance activities. This work is divided geographically among ten regional offices and three Regional Divisions.

Application Procedures

Direct inquiries to the office in which you'd like to work.

Headquarters:

Department of Education
Personnel Management Service
600 Independence Ave. SW
Washington, DC 20202
Human Resources: (202) 401-0553
Employment: (202) 205-3885
800-USA-LEARN

Regions:

U.S. Department of Education
Attn.: Personnel
540 McCormack Courthouse
Boston, MA 02109-4557
(617) 223-9317

The Wannamaker Building
100 Penn Square East, Suite 505
Philadelphia, PA 19107
(215) 656-6010

111 North Canal St.
Suite 1094
Chicago, IL 60606
(312) 886-8222

10220 N. Executive Hills Blvd.
7th Floor, Suite 720
Kansas City, MO 64153
(816) 880-4000

50 United Nations Plaza
Room 205
San Francisco, CA 94102-4987
(415) 556-4120

75 Park Place
12th Floor
New York, NY 10007
(212) 264-7005

61 Forsyth St., SW
Suite 19T40
Atlanta, GA 30303
(404) 562-6225

1999 Bryan St.
Suite 2700
Dallas, TX 75202-6817
(214) 880-3011

1244 Speer Blvd.
Suite 310
Denver, CO 80204
(303) 844-3544

Jackson Federal Bldg.
915 2nd Ave., Rm. 3362
Seattle, WA 98174-1099
(206) 220-7800

☆ Department of Energy (www.energy.gov)

> ### Department of Energy (DOE)
> ### www.energy.gov
>
> **Nature of Work:** Defense and national security, disaster assistance, energy, hazardous materials, nuclear energy, scientific research
>
> **Number of Employees:** 16,000
>
> **Headquarters:** Washington, DC
>
> **Regional Locations:** Albuquerque, NM; Chicago, IL; Las Vegas, NV; Oak Ridge, TN; Richland, WA; San Francisco, CA; Savannah River, GA; Idaho Falls, ID (Operations Offices); Miamisburg, OH
>
> **Typical Background of New Hires:** Accounting, architecture, biological sciences, business, earth sciences, engineering, English (journalism), environmental sciences, finance/banking, physical social sciences

Mission

Through scientific research and the implementation of programs and projects, the Department of Energy works to move the U.S. from its current state of energy management to the energy environment of tomorrow. The DOE is responsible for foreseeing the future energy demands of the U.S. and for developing more efficient means of energy usage today.

Job Descriptions

Accountant: Examines documents such as payrolls, invoices, and vouchers to ascertain that the transactions of companies subject to the jurisdiction of the DOE are properly supported. Typically an FERC position.

Architect: Designs, evaluates, performs research on, and advises on the construction or rehabilitation of buildings with consideration toward conservation of energy and the use of renewable resources such as solar or geothermal energy. Typically a Conservation and Renewable Energies position.

Auditor: Works individually or participates as a member of a field audit team engaged in examination and verification of the books, records, plant inventories, and other data supporting financial statements of licensees, electric utilities, and natural gas pipeline companies. Typically an FERC or Inspector General position.

Biologist: Assesses the effects of change or the introduction of new phenomena on biological ecosystems. Makes recommendations to conserve biological environments. Typically a Conservation and Renewable Energies position.

Botanist: Conducts botanical research, including plant taxonomy, morphology, ecology, and ethnobotany. Typically a Conservation and Renewable Energies position.

Chemist: Investigates and assesses the composition, molecular structure, and properties of nuclear, fossil, or other energy systems and substances. Examines the transformations that they undergo and the amount of matter and energy included or generated in these transformations.

Community Planner: Identifies community needs, resources, and energy problems and assists citizens to make decisions that reflect energy conservation practices. Typically a Conservation and Renewable Energies position.

Ecologist: Assembles and analyzes complex data on water quality, in-stream flows, and aquatic biology using limnological techniques. Makes recommendations regarding the effects of energy projects on ecological systems.

Economist: Prepares analyses on complex, long-term energy trends and the microeconomic and macroeconomic impacts of energy trends on regional and industrial sectors. Analyzes rate contracts and system operations of utilities. Prepares studies to determine the most economical sources of power. May specialize in industrial or mineral economics. Typically an FERC or EIA position.

Electric Power Industry Analyst: Conducts analyses into the electric power industry. Measures trends, assesses competition within the electric power industry, and analyzes the capital/financial structure of electric power companies. Typically an EIA position.

Energy Conservation Program Specialist: Develops programs and policies designed to broaden the use of renewable energies and to conserve nonrenewable resources.

Engineer (chemical): Researches, develops, evaluates, and improves processes, equipment, methods, or products relating to renewable resources and energy conservation practices, as well as other energy issues.

Engineer (civil): Plans and designs structures and facilities that provide shelter, support transportation systems, and control natural resources. Surveys and maps the earth's physical features and phenomena. Applies a knowledge of hydraulics, mechanics, and solids (particularly soils), strength of materials, theory of structure, and surveying to the use of renewable resources and other energy issues.

Engineer (electrical): Works with and conducts research related to electrical circuits, circuit elements, and associated phenomena concerned with electrical energy for purposes such as motive power, heating, illumination, chemical processes, or the production of localized electric or magnetic fields.

Engineer (mechanical): Applies a knowledge of thermodynamics, mechanics, and other physical, mathematical, and engineering sciences to problems concerned with the production, transmission, measurement, and use of energy, especially mechanical power.

Environmental Protection Specialist: Conducts studies and collects data on how the public use of land and water resources affects and is affected by the construction and operation of hydropower projects and natural gas pipelines. Works with such issues as air and water pollution and quality, endangered species protection, oil spill prevention and control, and hazardous waste management. Prepares testimony and exhibits for use at meetings and evidentiary hearings. Typically an FERC position.

Environmental Safety Specialist: Takes remedial action to treat or stabilize radioactive wastes at DOE surplus sites. Conducts technical analyses and provides advice concerning nonproliferation and radioactive waste decontamination. Typically a Nuclear Energy position.

Federal Financing Specialist: Administers federal financing programs related to the conservation of energy. Typically a Conservation and Renewable Energies position.

Fishery Biologist: Examines the effects of hydropower projects and natural gas pipelines on the spawning of anadromous fish, fish passage, and other limnological phenomena.

Industrial Hygienist: Collects and analyzes safety, health, and quality assurance data from field facilities. Provides advice concerning the industrial hygiene aspects peculiar to facilities, equipment, or experiments involving the use of nuclear reactors or sources of ionizing radiation.

Intelligence Research Analyst: Performs analysis of intelligence provided by national level collection agencies regarding nuclear and general science issues.

Metallurgist: Studies the properties and behavior of metals extracted from their ores as affected by the composition, treatment in manufacture, and conditions of use. Develops environmentally efficient methods of extraction and refinement.

Natural Gas Industry Analyst: Conducts analyses into the natural gas industry. Measures trends, assesses competition within the natural gas industry, evaluates interfuel substitution, and analyzes the capital/financial structure of natural gas companies.

Physical Scientist: With no one area of specialization, conducts research involving the physical sciences relating to conservation and energy.

Physicist: Conducts research and other scientific work in the applications of energy in the areas of mechanics, sound, optics, heat, electricity, magnetism, radiation, or atomic phenomena.

Public Utilities Specialist: Analyzes rate contract and system operations of utility companies to determine whether service under contracts is subject to the FERC's jurisdiction. Evaluates data to determine the most economical sources of power generation. Typically an FERC position.

Radiological Scientist: Conducts research on a wide range of radiological and fission energy projects, such as nuclear applications to the space program, nuclear reactor development, and decontamination strategies.

Statistician/Mathematical Statistician: Gathers information on energy trends, national energy resource levels, energy industry outlooks, energy production, and technology. Conducts mathematical analyses and applies statistical theories to interpret and quantify energy data.

Wildlife Biologist: Plans and conducts field investigations at existing and proposed hydropower projects or natural gas pipelines. Determines the nature and extent of probable impact of the projects on wildlife and surrounding terrestrial environments.

Major Activities and Divisions

Policy and International Affairs: Coordinates cooperative international energy programs with foreign governments and international organizations such as the International Energy Agency and the International Atomic Energy Agency.

Energy Efficiency and Renewable Energy: Works to increase the production and utilization of renewable energy (solar, biomass, wind, geothermal, alcohol fuels, etc.) and to improve the energy efficiency of transportation, buildings, industrial systems, and related processes through support of long-term, high-risk research and development activities.

Defense Programs: Researches, develops, tests, manufactures, and retires all U.S. nuclear weapons. Produces all nuclear materials needed for the weapons program and manages defense-related nuclear wastes.

Nuclear Energy, Science, and Technology: Conducts research and development programs relating to nuclear reactor development, nuclear fuel cycle, space nuclear applications, and uranium enrichment. Performs decontamination and decommissioning at DOE surplus radioactive waste sites.

Fossil Energy: Conducts research and development programs involving fossil fuels (coal, petroleum, and gas).

Energy Information Administration (EIA): Responsible for the collection, processing, and publication of data in the areas of energy resource reserves, energy production, demand, consumption, distribution, and technology.

Environmental Safety and Health: Addresses community concerns in the areas of environmental safety and health factors.

Federal Energy Regulatory Commission (FERC): Ensures the nation's consumers have adequate energy supplies at reasonable rates, while providing regulatory incentives for increased productivity, efficiency, and competition. Regulates certain aspects of the natural gas, electric utility, hydroelectric power, and oil pipeline industries.

Civilian Radioactive Waste Management: Manages programs for recommending, constructing, and operating repositories for disposal of high-level radioactive waste and spent nuclear fuel.

Alternative Employment Programs

The Community College Institute: Offers opportunities to participate in educational training and research relating to energy production, use, and conservation to community college students from across the country. Location: Oak Ridge National Laboratory (Oak Ridge, TN)

The DOE sponsors thousands of student internships and fellowships across the U.S. Some states where large numbers of interns are hired include CA, ID,

IL, NM, SC, NY, TN, WA, and DC. See www.energy.gov/careers/sub/
internships.html for more information or call the Office of Science Education at
(202) 586-7174 or 0987.

Application Procedures

The DOE Job Site, where you can find information on vacant positions within the
department, is at www.energy.gov/careers/index.html. Jobs can be searched based
upon location, occupational series, location or DOE organization. A link is
provided to the Department's "DOE JOBS ONLINE", which allows applicants to
apply for certain DOE jobs online. DOE Jobs ONLINE also allows applicants to
receive e-mail notifications of job openings.

DOE has Operations Offices and other sites across the U.S. For a list of
regional locations with addresses and phone numbers, go to www.ma.doe.gov/
phonebook/field.html.

Many DOE locations prefer to have applications and resumes submitted via
the DOE QUICKHIRE system. See specific vacancy announcements for
instructions on how to apply.

For more information, contact:

U.S. Department of Energy
Headquarters Personnel Services Division
ME50/Room 4H-08
1000 Independence Ave. SW
Washington, DC 20585
Human Resources: (202) 586-8591
Vacancy Hotline: (202) 586-4333
Information: (202) 586-5000
People Locator, Toll Free: (800) DIAL-DOE

Federal Energy Regulatory Commission (FERC)
www.ferc.fed.us

Nature of Work: Energy, environmental protection

Number of Employees: 1,300

Headquarters: Washington, DC

Regional Locations: Atlanta, GA; Chicago, IL; New York, NY; Portland, OR; San Francisco, CA

Typical Background of New Hires: Accounting, agriculture, biological sciences, business, chemistry, economics, engineering (civil), environmental sciences (natural resource management)

Mission

The Federal Energy Regulatory Commission's primary goal is to ensure the nation's consumers have adequate energy supplies at just and reasonable rates, while providing regulatory incentives for increased productivity, efficiency, and competition.

Job Descriptions

Accountant: Examines documents such as payrolls, invoices, and vouchers to ascertain that the transactions of companies subject to the jurisdiction of FERC are properly supported.

Auditor: Participates as a member of a field audit team engaged in examination and verification of the books, records, plant inventories, and other data supporting financial statements of licensees, electric utilities, and natural gas pipeline companies. Position requires extensive travel for extended periods (3-6 months).

Civil Engineer: Prepares engineering studies to determine the stability of various types of dams, powerhouses, and other project structures. Develops graphs, charts, tables, and statistical curves.

Ecologist: Assembles and analyzes complex data on water quality, in-stream flows, and aquatic biology using limnological techniques. Makes recommendations regarding the effects of energy projects on ecological ecosystems.

Economist: Applies basic economic principles and skills to analyze rate contracts and system operations of utilities. Prepares economic studies to determine most economical sources of power. May specialize in industrial or mineral economics.

Environmental Protection Specialist: Conducts studies and collects data on how the public use of land and water resources affects and is affected by the construction and operation of hydropower projects and natural gas pipelines. Prepares testimony and exhibits for use at evidentiary hearings and public meetings.

Fishery Biologist: Examines the effects of hydropower projects and natural gas pipelines on the spawning of anadromous fish, fish passage, and other limnological phenomena.

Public Utilities Specialist: Analyzes rate contracts and system operations of utility companies to determine whether service under contracts is subject to the Commission's jurisdiction. Also involves analyzing data to determine the most economical sources of power generation.

Wildlife Biologist: Plans and conducts field investigations at existing and proposed hydropower projects or natural gas pipelines. Determines the nature and extent of probable impact of the projects on wildlife and surrounding terrestrial environments.

Major Activities and Divisions

* Natural Gas: FERC regulates the transmission and sale of natural gas for resale in interstate commerce.

* Oil: FERC regulates the transmission of oil by pipeline in interstate commerce.

* Electricity: FERC regulates the transmission and wholesale sales of electricity in interstate commerce.

* Hydroelectricity: FERC licenses and inspects private, municipal and state hydroelectric projects.

* Environment: FERC oversees environmental matters related to natural gas, oil, electricity and hydroelectric projects.

* Financial Reporting: FERC administers accounting and financial reporting regulations and conduct of jurisdictional companies.

* Site Approval: FERC approves site choices as well as abandonment of interstate pipeline facilities.

Alternative Employment Programs

The FERC maintains a co-op program for students pursuing an associate degree and for students enrolled in a baccalaureate or graduate program.

Application Procedures

Direct inquiries to:

The Federal Energy Regulatory Commission
Division of Human Resources
888 First St. NE
Washington, DC 20426
Information: (202) 208-0055
Personnel: (202) 219-2991

✮ Executive Office of the President (www.whitehouse.gov)

Office of the United States Trade Representative
www.ustr.gov

Nature of Work: Commerce, international affairs

Number of Employees: 175

Headquarters: Washington, DC

Regional Location: Geneva, Switzerland

Typical Background of New Hires: Economics, law

Mission

Directs all trade negotiations for the U.S. and formulates U.S. international trade policy.

Job Descriptions

Attorney: Advises trade negotiators on the legality of agreements and renders legal opinions on specific policy, trade, and commodity matters.

International Economist: Conducts trade negotiations with other countries and international organizations and gathers and interprets international trade data used in setting policy.

Major Activities and Divisions

The U.S. Trade Representative represents the U.S. at meetings of the World Trade Organization and the Organization for Economic Cooperation and Development. The agency also has primary responsibility for negotiating bilateral and multilateral trade agreements.

Alternative Employment Programs

The student intern program at USTR is a volunteer program where undergraduate and graduate students gain knowledge and experience on U.S. trade policy and, in many cases, earn college credit at the same time.

Assignments range from research, analyses, statistics, briefing books, report preparation, meeting and conference planning, letter writing, to covering Hill meetings, hearings, and markups as necessary. USTR generally receives approximately 300 applications each semester.

Students may be placed in such offices as: General Counsel; Congressional Affairs; Western Hemisphere; Europe and the Mediterranean; Japan; China; Asia Pacific Economic Cooperation; World Trade Organization and Multilateral Affairs; Industry, Agricultural Affairs; Public Affairs; Intergovernmental Affairs; Environment and Natural Resources; Services, Investment, and Intellectual Property; and the Geneva headquarters.

Twenty to 30 interns are chosen annually. Students are required to submit a resume, a writing sample, and a letter stating period of availability. For more information, see the USTR Web site at www.ustr.gov or call USTR Human Resources at (202) 395-7360.

Submit written applications to:

Office of the U.S. Trade Representative
Human Resources, Intern Coordinator
Winder Building
600 17th Street, NW
Washington, DC 20508

Remarks

The Office of the United States Trade Representative is a cabinet-level agency. The head of the organization, his or her three deputies, and two other senior officials all hold the rank of Ambassador.

Application Procedures

The USTR Web site lists current job openings. See www.ustr.gov for job information, and follow the application instructions on specific vacancy announcements. Or, direct inquiries to:

Office of the United States Trade Representative
Office of Personnel
600 17th St., NW
Washington, DC 20508
(202) 395-7360
Toll Free: (888) 473-USTR (8787)
E-mail: contactustr@ustr.gov

Office of Management and Budget (OMB)
www.omb.gov

Nature of Work: Accounting, budgeting, management

Number of Employees: 550

Headquarters: Washington, DC

Regional Locations: None

Typical Background of New Hires: Accounting, business, finance, management

Mission

Develops, coordinates, and evaluates management procedures and program objectives within and among federal agencies. OMB also controls the administration of the federal budget.

Job Descriptions

Budget Preparation Specialist: Participates in the preparation, execution, and analysis of the President's budget. The work encompasses problem identification and resolution; compilation and analysis of program and budgetary information; technical and substantive review of budgetary data, appropriations language, and related Congressional reports.

Legislative Analyst (or Attorney): manages the central legislative clearance process, which ensures that Presidential policies are reflected correctly on legislative matters before the Congress.

Policy Analyst: Oversees the federal regulatory system so that agencies' regulatory actions are consistent with economic principles, sound public policy, and the goals of the President. Review requests by agencies for approval of collections of information (including surveys, program evaluations, and applications for benefits). Major topic areas include the environment, agriculture, rural development, energy, labor, education, immigration, health, welfare, housing, finance, and criminal justice.

Program Examiner: Serves as a focal point in OMB with responsibilities for the formulation and execution of the budget in an assigned area. The Examiner performs policy, program management, and regulatory analyses; reviews issues identified as needing special attention; reviews and clears legislative proposals and testimony; and reviews executive orders and other documents.

Major Activities and Divisions

Most of OMB's work is organized into management activities and budget activities. OMB's management units review agency regulations, management structures, paperwork requirements, proposed legislation, and other management procedures to ensure they are as efficient as possible and consistent with the President's objectives. OMB's budget units examine agency budget requests and pass back revisions so that the President's budget is in line with fiscal, policy, and program goals.

Alternative Employment Programs

Each spring a limited number of students are hired as summer interns. Opportunities are best for graduate students seeking a master's degree in public policy, public administration, business, information systems, computer science, economics, law, or a related field.

Remarks

OMB conducts annual spring recruiting visits to many graduate business and public policy schools for entry-level permanent and summer positions.

Application Procedures

OMB lists current job openings on their Web site. See specific vacancy announcements for application information, or contact:

Executive Office of the President
Office of Management and Budget
Administration Office, Room 4013
725 17th St. NW
Washington, DC 20503
(202) 395-7250
Fax: (202) 395-3504
EOP Job Line: (202) 395-5892
E-mail: OMB_Recruitment@omb.eop.gov.

✮ Department of Health and Human Services (www.hhs.gov)

Agency for Healthcare Research and Quality (AHRQ)
www.ahrq.gov

Nature of Work: Health/health care, scientific research

Number of Employees: 265

Headquarters: Rockville, MD

Regional Locations: None

Typical Background of New Hires: Economics, epidemiology, health policy, medicine, nursing, sociology, statistics

Mission

AHRQ is the lead agency charged with supporting research designed to improve the quality of health care, reduce its cost, improve patient safety, decrease medical errors, and broaden access to essential services.

Job Descriptions

Economist: Conducts research or evaluates research on various health-care cost effectiveness issues.

General Health Scientist: Conducts health-related research or provides guidance to researchers in health science studies. Most hires for this position hold a Ph.D.

Grants Specialist: Reviews and evaluates proposed research to determine scientific merit and program relevance.

Programs and Divisions

AHRQ is divided into these mission-oriented offices and centers:

The Center for Cost and Financing Studies (CCFS): Conducts and supports studies of the cost and financing of health care and develops data sets to support policy and behavioral research and analyses.

The Center for Organization and Delivery Studies (CODS): Conducts, supports, and manages studies of the structure, financing, organization, behavior, and performance of the health-care system and providers within it.

The Center for Outcomes and Effectiveness Research (COER): Conducts and supports studies of the outcomes and effectiveness of diagnostic, therapeutic, and preventive health-care services and procedures.

The Center for Practice and Technology Assessment (CPTA): CPTA was established to serve as a single contact for organizations and individuals searching for comprehensive evidence reviews on health conditions, treatments, and technologies.

The Center for Primary Care Research (CPCR): Conducts and supports studies on primary care and clinical, preventive, and public health policies and systems.

The Center for Quality Improvement and Patient Safety (CQuIPS): Conducts and supports research on the measurement and improvement of the quality of health care and enhancement of patient safety.

The Office of Health Care Information (OHCI): Designs, develops, implements, and manages programs for disseminating the results of agency activities.

The Office of Priority Populations Research (OPPR): Coordinates, supports, manages and conducts health services research on priority populations.

The Office of Research Review, Education, and Policy (ORREP): Directs the scientific review process for grants and Small Business Innovation Research (SBIR) contracts, the assignment of applications to agency centers, manages agency research training programs, and evaluates the scientific contribution of proposed and ongoing research, demonstrations, and evaluations.

Alternative Employment Programs

AHRQ participates in the summer internship program. Contact the agency for more information.

Remarks

AHRQ employs a large number of computer scientists for agency-related and mission-specific projects.

Application Procedures

The AHRQ Web site lists current job openings. Identify a position of interest and submit an application according to the vacancy announcement directions.

Direct inquiries to:

Agency for Healthcare Research and Quality
2101 East Jefferson St., Suite 501
Rockville, MD 20852
(301) 594-2408 or (301) 443-3201
Fax: (301) 594-2283

Send applications to:

Division of Personnel Operations
Parklawn HRS/PSC
P.O. Box 5375
Rockville, MD 20848-5375
Fax: (301) 480-3864
E-mail: psc_staffing@psc.gov

Applications may also be submitted by hand to:

Parklawn Building
5600 Fishers Lane, Room 17A-20
Rockville, MD 20847

Administration for Children and Families
www.acf.dhhs.gov

Nature of Work: Families/children, funds/funding, handicapped, low-income people, Native Americans, refugees

Number of Employees: 1,500

Headquarters: Washington, DC

Regional Locations: Atlanta, GA; Boston, MA; Chicago, IL; Dallas, TX; Denver, CO; Kansas City, MO; New York, NY; Philadelphia, PA; San Francisco, CA; Seattle, WA

Typical Background of New Hires: Psychology, public administration, social sciences, social work/sociology

Mission

The Administration for Children and Families (ACF) is responsible for federal programs that promote the economic and social well-being of families, children, individuals, and communities.

Job Descriptions

Program Analyst/Specialist: Administers the Child Support Enforcement; Office of Community Services; Office of Refugee Resettlement; Administration for Children, Youth, and Families; Administration for Native Americans; and Administration on Developmental Disabilities programs. Develops and evaluates program policies and guidelines and assesses their effectiveness. Prepares reports concerning program outcomes, impact, and projections. Provides guidance and information. Develops objectives for national programs to aid runaway and homeless youth, abused and neglected children, disabled persons, Native Americans, and others. Interprets discretionary and service grant solicitations and conducts on-site reviews of the operations of related programs.

Major Activities and Divisions

ACF oversees about sixty programs that provide funds to state, local, and tribal organizations, both public and private. These programs are overseen by the following offices and bureaus:

Children's Bureau

Administration on Children, Youth and Families
330 C St. SW, Room 2422
Washington, DC 20201
(202) 205-8618
E-mail: cbcomments@acf.dhhs.gov

Provides preventive intervention services to children and their families such as foster care and adoption assistance, child abuse and neglect prevention, child welfare services, and the abandoned infants assistance program.

Office of Community Services

Demonstration and Special Projects Division
370 L'Enfant Promenade, SW
Washington, DC 20447
(202) 401-4807

Administers block grants and discretionary grant programs. Also carries out the Low Income Home Energy Assistance Program and the REACH program.

Child Care Bureau

Administration on Children, Youth and Families
330 C St. SW, Room 2046
Washington, DC 20201
(202) 690-6782
E-mail: ccb@acf.dhhs.gov

Assists low-income families in obtaining child care so they can work or attend training/education.

Office of Child Support Enforcement

370 L'Enfant Promenade SW
Washington, DC 20447
(202) 401-9370

Coordinates the Child Support Enforcement programs and activities, which require states to enforce support obligations owed by absent parents to their children.

Administration on Developmental Disabilities

200 Independence Ave. SW, Room 300-F
Washington, DC 20201
(202) 690-6590
E-mail: add@acf.dhhs.gov

Increases the provision of quality services to persons with developmental disabilities.

Head Start Bureau

330 C St. SW, Room 2018
Washington, DC 20201
(202) 205-8572
E-mail: askus@hskids-tmsc.org

Provides comprehensive developmental services for America's low-income, preschool children ages 3 to 5 and social services for their families.

Administration for Native Americans

200 Independence Ave. SW, Room 348-F
Washington, DC 20201
Help Desk: (202) 690-7776 or 877-922-9ANA

Represents the concerns of American Indians, Alaska Natives, and Native Hawaiians.

Office of Refugee Resettlement

370 L'Enfant Promenade SW, 6th Floor
Washington, DC 20447
(202) 401-9246
Fax: (202) 401-5487
E-mail: rmunia@acf.dhhs.gov

Administers the Refugee Assistance Program, which is designed to assimilate refugees into American society.

Family and Youth Services Bureau

330 C St. SW
Washington, DC 20201
(202) 205-8102
Fax: (202) 260-9333
E-mail: FYSBComments@acf.dhhs.gov

Provides comprehensive services for youth in at-risk situations such as emergency shelters and crisis intervention programs.

Office of Family Assistance

370 L'Enfant Promenade SW
Washington, DC 20447
(202) 401-5139
Fax: (202) 205-5887
E-mail: tanf@acf.dhhs.gov

Provides time-limited assistance to needy families with children to promote work, responsibility and self-sufficiency.

Alternative Employment Programs

The Family Support Administration hires approximately 20–30 people annually for its summer employment program, offering both clerical and professional positions. It also accepts volunteers for positions related to their college majors.

Application Procedures

ACF lists current job openings on its Web site. Follow directions on specific vacancy announcements when applying for a position. Or, direct inquiries to the regional location in which you'd like to work:

Headquarters Location:
Department of Health and Human Services
Administration for Children and Families
5600 Fishers Lane
Rockville, MD 20857
Administration: (202) 401-9238
Information: (202) 401-9200

Or, you may visit the posted job board at the Program Support Center:

Switzer Building
330 C St. SW, Room 1100
Washington, DC 20201
(202) 260-6885 (personnel/program support)

Region I - Boston: CT, ME, MA, NH, RI, VT
Administration for Children and Families
JFK Federal Building
Room 2000, 20th Floor
Boston, MA 02203-0001
(617) 565-1020

Region II - New York: NY, PR, VI, NJ
Administration for Children and Families
26 Federal Plaza, Room 4114
New York, NY 10278-0022
(212) 264-2890, Ext. 103

Region III - Philadelphia: DE, MD, PA, VA, WV, DC
Administration for Children and Families
150 S. Independence Mall West, Suite 864
Philadelphia, PA 19106-3499
(215) 861-4000

Region IV - Atlanta: AL, FL, GA, KY, MS, NC, TN, SC
Administration for Children and Families
Atlanta Federal Center
61 Forsyth St. SW, Suite 4M60
Atlanta, GA 30303-8909

Region V - Chicago: IL, IN, MI, MN, OH, WI
Administration for Children and Families
233 N. Michigan Avenue, Suite 400
Chicago, IL 60603
(312) 353-4237, Ext. 102

Region VI - Dallas: AK, LA, NM, OK, TX
Administration for Children and Families
1301 Young St., Room 914
Dallas, TX 75202
(214) 767-9648

Region VII - Kansas City: IA, KS, MO, NE
Administration for Children and Families
Federal Office Building, Room 276
601 E. 12th St.
Kansas City, MO 64106- 2898
(816) 426-3981

Region VIII - Denver: CO, MT, ND, SD, UT, WY
Administration for Children and Families
Federal Office Building, Room 924
1961 Stout Street, Denver, CO 80294-1185
(303) 844-3100 Ext. 301

Region IX - San Francisco: AZ, CA, HI, NV, Guam, American Samoa, Trust Territory of Pacific Islands
Administration for Children and Families
50 United Nations Plaza, Room 450
San Francisco, CA 94102-4988
(415) 437-8400

Region X - Seattle: AK, ID, OR, WA
Administration for Children and Families
Blanchard Plaza
2201 Sixth Avenue, Suite 600
Seattle, WA 98121-1827
(206) 615-2547

The Centers for Disease Control and Prevention, and Agency for Toxic Substances and Disease Registry (CDC and ATSDR)
www.cdc.gov

Nature of Work: Education, food/nutrition, health/health care, safety, scientific research, statistics

Number of Employees: 8,500

Headquarters: Atlanta, GA

Regional Locations: Anchorage, AK; Cincinnati, OH; Fort Collins, CO; Morgantown, WV; Pittsburgh, PA; Research Triangle Park, NC; San Juan, PR; Spokane, WA; Washington, DC

Typical Background of New Hires: Biology, chemistry, education (health), environmental sciences, health sciences, medical sciences, psychology, sociology, statistics

Mission

The Centers for Disease Control and Prevention conducts a wide range of health-related activities both domestically and internationally. CDC's mission includes chronic and environmentally related diseases, injuries and disabilities, healthy lifestyles, occupational safety, laboratory science, health training and education, health statistics, epidemiology and surveillance, and general prevention services.

Job Descriptions

Behavioral Health Scientist: Conducts behavioral research and community interventions to promote health, control chronic diseases and infant and maternal mortality, and develop health education techniques.

Chemist: Conducts scientific research into the composition, molecular structure, and properties of certain substances. Relates findings to medical uses and purposes.

Environmental Health Specialist: Investigates, evaluates, and provides information on sanitation practices, techniques, and methods for the purpose of identifying, preventing, and eliminating environmental health hazards. May assist local public health officials at the scene of natural or manmade disasters. Reviews environmental impact statements to assure that major federally supported development projects are reasonably safe. Conducts research to prevent harm from toxic chemicals and natural and man-made radiation.

Epidemiologist: Conducts investigations into the causes of prevalent and rapidly spreading or contagious diseases. Works to control newly discovered infectious diseases such as AIDS, toxic shock syndrome, and Legionnaires' disease, as well as old diseases that are resistant to drugs. Control programs can include public education and vaccination. May involve travel or extended assignments in foreign countries.

Medical Officer: Performs or advises on professional or scientific work in one or more fields of medicine. Requires a current license to practice medicine and a degree of Doctor of Medicine or Doctor of Osteopathy.

Microbiologist: Applies a medical application to the study of microorganisms, especially in the fields of immunology, medical parasitology, physiology, serology, and genetics. Studies the role of microorganisms as pathogenic and immunizing agents through isolation, cultivation, identification, and systematic classification.

Public Health Associate/Advisor: Performs disease intervention and prevention activities typically in the areas of sexually transmitted diseases. Interviews patients to obtain information regarding the source and possible spread of the disease and conducts follow-up activities to prevent further spread. Involves routine contact with health professionals. After one to two years as a Public Health Associate, an individual converts to Public Health Advisor, taking on more managerial responsibilities.

Public Health Educator: Plans health education programs designed to meet the needs of particular individuals, groups, or communities. Selects specialized education methods and prepares educational materials. Consults with state and local health departments and with national and local voluntary agencies. Studies health problems and methods of disease prevention and assists in coordinating mass health programs.

Statistician: Collects and analyzes vital and health statistics in the U.S. Makes data available to health professionals and the public in published reports. Quantifies such information as the nature and economic impact of illness and disability in the U.S.; the availability of hospital and nursing home care; and births, deaths, marriages, and divorces.

Toxicologist: Conducts scientific research into toxic substances. Determines their chemical and physical properties, examines their effects on the body, and explores possible antidotes and detoxifying agents.

Major Activities and Divisions

National Center on Birth Defects and Developmental Disabilities: Provides national leadership for preventing birth defects and developmental disabilities and for improving the health and wellness of people with disabilities.

National Center for Chronic Disease Prevention and Health Promotion: Uses surveillance, epidemiologic and laboratory studies, behavioral research, and community interventions to promote health and control chronic diseases.

National Center for Environmental Health: Promotes health and quality of life by preventing and controlling disease, injury, and disability caused by or related to the interactions between people and their environment outside of the workplace.

National Immunization Program: Prevents disease, disability, and death from vaccine-preventable diseases in children and adults.

National Institute for Occupational Safety and Health: Works closely with employers, labor unions, and other government agencies to provide world leadership in the prevention of work-related injury, illness, and death. Provides a scientific approach to gathering information and translates it into products and services.

National Center for Infectious Diseases: Investigates outbreaks of infectious disease within the U.S. and internationally and develops programs to prevent their spread.

National Center for Injury Prevention and Control: Reduces morbidity, disability, mortality, and costs associated with injuries outside the workplace.

National Center for Health Statistics: Collects the full spectrum of the nation's vital and health statistics.

Epidemiology Program Office: Coordinates public health surveillance at CDC and provides domestic and international support through scientific communications and statistical and epidemiologic consultation. Trains experts in surveillance, epidemiology, and applied public health.

Public Health Practice Program Office: Trains the nation's force of public health workers in the latest disease prevention techniques. Develops community leadership and communicates information for public health action.

Alternative Employment Programs

CDC/ADSTR's student hiring programs are extensive and varied. They include the SCEP and STEP programs, summer hires, the PMI program, the Outstanding Scholar Program, and several undergraduate and postgraduate research opportunities. Some hiring programs are geared to minority students. See the CDC Web site for more information.

Physicians, engineers, scientists, nurses, pharmacists, or other health professionals may be eligible for the PHS Commissioned Corp. The Commissioned Corps is an all-officer organization that offers base salary; free medical and dental coverage; malpractice coverage; low-cost life insurance; 30 days paid vacation each year; a noncontributory retirement plan; and travel, housing, and subsistence allowances. For more information, contact U.S. Public Health Service Recruitment at (800) 279-1606 or via e-mail at recruit@psc.ssw.dhhs.gov.

Remarks

Hiring for the Agency for Toxic Substances and Disease Registry (ATSDR), a separate and smaller agency of the Public Health Service, is done through the CDC employment office.

Application Procedures

CDC lists current job openings on its Web site. Follow application directions on the vacancy announcement that interests you.

Toll Free: (888) CDC-HIRE (24-hour Job Hotline)
TDD: (770) 488-1821

Or, direct inquiries to:

Centers for Disease Control and Prevention
Human Resources Management Office
Mail Stop K-16
4770 Buford Highway
Atlanta, GA 30341-3724
(404) 639-3311

U.S. Food and Drug Administration (FDA)
www.fda.gov

Nature of Work: Consumer protection, health/health care, scientific research

Number of Employees: 9,300

Headquarters: Rockville, MD

Regional Locations: Locations in 167 U.S. cities, including Alameda, CA; Atlanta, GA; Baltimore, MD; Boston, MA; Buffalo, NY; Chicago, IL; Cincinnati, OH; Dallas, TX; Denver, CO; Detroit, MI; Houston, TX; Kansas City, MO; Lenexa, KS; Los Angeles, CA; Minneapolis, MN; Nashville, TN; New Orleans, LA; New York, NY; Maitland, FL; Philadelphia, PA; St. Louis, MO; San Francisco, CA; San Juan, PR; Seattle, WA; West Parsippany, NJ

Typical Background of New Hires: Biological sciences (entomology), biology, chemistry, food sciences (nutrition), medical sciences (toxicology, pharmacology), physical sciences

Mission

The FDA could be considered the principal consumer protection agency in the federal government. It is responsible for regulating products ranging from lipstick to X rays, from animal feed to paints, from canned peaches to penicillin. The FDA's goal is to see that all products are safe and effective.

Job Descriptions

Biologist/Microbiologist: Studies the distribution of microorganisms in natural and man-made environments, their reaction to physical and chemical factors, and their role as pathogenic and immunizing agents.

Chemist: Investigates, analyzes, and interprets the composition, molecular structure, and properties of substances and how they are affected by their environment. Analyzes the safety factors involved in the presence of certain chemicals.

Consumer Safety Officer: Enforces the laws and regulations protecting consumers from foods, drugs, cosmetics, fabrics, toys, and household products that are impure, improperly labeled, ineffective, or dangerous. Identifies substances and sources of adulteration and contamination and evaluates manufacturing practices. Requires a knowledge of various scientific fields such as chemistry, biology, pharmacology, and food technology.

Dietician: Conducts research into the use of diet in the cause and treatment of disease.

Entomologist: Conducts research into the role of insects as carriers of human disease. Inspects sanitary conditions of food, drug, and cosmetic establishments.

Food Technologist: Studies problems related to the development, improvement, and evaluation of food products; their production, use, processing, and preservation; and the utilization or disposal of by-products.

Mathematical Statistician: Reviews and evaluates scientific data and concepts involved with New Drug Applications (NDAs) submitted by regulated industry for approval of new drugs. May work in a research setting designing and analyzing complex biological experiments directed toward the determination of chronic, reproductive, and multigenerational effects of food additives and constituents on humans. Mathematical Statisticians, GS-11 to GS-15, are usually hired only at headquarters.

Pharmacologist: Works in laboratory and nonlaboratory settings to assess the action, absorption, distribution, metabolism, excretion, and use of drugs, toxic substances, and related chemicals. Analyzes effects in terms of safety and efficacy. Located in headquarters only.

Public Health Advisor/Analyst: Provides assistance to states and nongovernmental agencies in matters relating to the development, execution, and maintenance of public health programs. Conducts studies to identify current and future public health problems.

Major Activities and Divisions

The FDA has eighteen field locations, some with laboratories. It is also divided into several centers, each with a particular research focus.

The Center for Drug Evaluation and Research: Develops FDA policy with regard to the safety, effectiveness, and labeling of all drug products for human use.

The Center for Biologics Evaluation and Research: Administers regulation of biological products. It conducts AIDS-related research, inspects manufacturers' facilities for compliance with standards, and tests products submitted for release.

The Center for Food Safety and Applied Nutrition: Conducts research and develops standards on the composition, quality, nutrition, and safety of food and food additives, colors, and cosmetics.

The Center for Veterinary Medicine: Develops and conducts programs with respect to the safety and efficacy of veterinary devices and evaluates proposed use of veterinary preparations for animal safety.

The Center for Devices and Radiological Health: Carries out a national program designed to control unnecessary exposure of humans to potentially hazardous ionizing and nonionizing radiation.

The National Center for Toxicological Research: Conducts research programs to study the biological effects of potentially toxic chemical substances found in the environment.

Alternative Employment Programs

FDA offers the Student Temporary Employment Program (STEP) which targets graduate students to fill positions such as Engineering Aid, Lab Aid, or Computer Aid. Interested students must submit a resume or application to the headquarters address. For more information, call (301) 443-HIRE or (301) 443-8708.

Remarks

The most numerous entry-level positions at FDA are biologists, chemists, and consumer safety officers, primarily in the field locations. FDA has excellent informative recruitment literature available.

Application Procedures

The FDA Web site lists current positions. Follow the application directions on the vacancy announcement you have interest in.

Or, direct inquiries to the regional office that hires for the location in which you would like to work:

Headquarters:
FDA Personnel
Room 7B-43, Mail Code HFA-415
5600 Fishers Lane
Rockville, MD 20857
(301) 443-HIRE
Personnel: (301) 443-4473

Central Region (Philadelphia):
900 U.S. Customhouse
2nd and Chestnut Sts.
Philadelphia, PA 19106
(215) 597-8058

Southeast Region (Atlanta):
60 Eighth St. NE
Atlanta, GA 30309
(404) 253-1171

Pacific Region (San Francisco):
1301 Clay St., Suite 1180-N
Oakland, CA 94512-5217
(510) 637-3960

Southwest Region (Dallas):
7920 Elmbrook Rd., Suite 102
Dallas, TX 75247-4982
(214) 655-8100

Northeast Region (New York):
158-15 Liberty Ave.
Jamaica, NY 11433
(718) 340-7000

Centers for Medicare and Medicaid Services (CMS)
www.cms.gov

Nature of Work: Aged/children, funds/funding, health/health care, insurance, low-income people

Number of Employees: 4,300

Headquarters: Baltimore, MD, and Washington, DC

Regional Locations: Atlanta, GA; Boston, MA; Chicago, IL; Dallas, TX; Denver, CO; Kansas City, MO; New York, NY; Philadelphia, PA; San Francisco, CA; Seattle, WA

Typical Background of New Hires: Accounting, business economics, social sciences

Mission

CMS provides health insurance for more than 74 million Americans through Medicare, Medicaid, and SCHIP. CMS also performs a number of quality-focused activities, including regulation of laboratory testing (CLIA), development of coverage policies, and quality-of-care improvement. CMS maintains oversight of the survey and certification of nursing homes and continuing care providers, and makes available to beneficiaries, providers, researchers, and State surveyors information about these activities and nursing home quality.

Job Descriptions

Accountant: Works on the operating budget of CMS and monitors the work of contractors and other health-care providers. Classifies and evaluates financial data, records transactions, and analyzes financial reports. Accountants work in headquarters and regional offices.

Actuary: Uses statistical and mathematical skills to provide analysis and cost estimates concerning the financing of the Medicare and Medicaid programs and related legislative and regulatory modifications to these programs. Actuaries work in HQ offices.

Economist/Statistician: Conducts research and interprets economic and statistical data related to CMS programs. Prepares reports on the design, implementation, and evaluation of the Medicare and Medicaid program based on economic and statistical data and techniques. Economists work in HQ offices.

Health Insurance Specialist: Analyzes and evaluates programs and develops proposals for improvement. Studies the private health insurance industry, analyzes Medicare and Medicaid policies, and participates in inspection and evaluation activities. Program Analysts work in HQ and regional offices.

Managed Care Specialist: Coordinates, implements, and monitors overall operations of managed care health plans to ensure that the health care program delivers an appropriate level of medical service to Medicare enrollees.

Medicaid Program Specialist: Monitors and evaluates state Medicaid programs to ensure adherence to regulations. Medicaid Program Specialists work in regional offices.

Medical Technologist: Conducts reviews of laboratories for federal monitoring and laboratory certification purposes.

Medicare Contractor Operations Representative: Monitors and evaluates Medicare contractor operations to ensure adherence to the provisions of the contract as well as to the intent of the law and regulations. MCORs work in regional offices.

Nurse Consultant: Serves as a specialist in the review, analysis, and evaluation of Medicare contractors and state survey agencies and of the effectiveness and quality of services delivered by Medicare and Medicaid providers/suppliers. Nurse Consultants work in regional offices.

Policy Specialist: Provides advice and consultation regarding regulations and policy for complex or controversial issues such as eligibility or noninstitutional reimbursement for the Medicare and Medicaid programs. Policy Specialists work in regional offices.

Social Science Research Analyst (SSRA): Performs research and analysis and tests new policies and processes that are designed to improve Medicaid and Medicare program operation. SSRAs work in HQ offices.

Survey and Certification Program Operations Specialist: Monitors, evaluates, and provides technical assistance to state certification agencies involving Medicare and Medicaid activities which affect the delivery of health care. Reviews and assesses the quality of health care delivered by Medicare and Medicaid providers or suppliers. This specialty may include, but is not limited to, various health professionals such as nurses, medical technologists, dieticians, and pharmacists. Works in regional offices.

Note: CMS also hires many Budget Analysts, Management Analysts, and Computer Specialists. See Chapter 6 on common government positions for job descriptions.

Major Activities and Divisions

The Centers for Medicare & Medicaid Services (CMS) is organized around three centers to support the agency's key functions:

★ The Center for Medicare Management manages the traditional fee-for-service Medicare program. This includes development of payment policy and management of the Medicare fee-for-service contractors.

★ The Center for Beneficiary Choices provides beneficiaries with information on Medicare, Medicare Select, Medicare+Choice, and Medigap options. It also manages the Medicare+Choice plans, consumer research and demonstrations, and grievance and appeals functions.

★ The Center for Medicaid and State Operations focuses on programs administered by states, such as Medicaid, the State Children's Health Insurance Program (SCHIP), insurance regulation functions, survey and certification, and the Clinical Laboratory Improvements Act.

Alternative Employment Programs

CMS participates in many student hiring programs:

STEP, SCEP, and Student Volunteer Programs
(410) 786-1775

Outstanding Scholars Program
(410) 786-9245 or
Toll Free: (800) 735-2258

PMI Program
(410) 786-5563 or 0344

CMS also has a Diversity Summer Internship Program for students with majors relating to the health-care and/or management field. Send applications to:

Centers for Medicare & Medicaid Services
Mailstop C2-08-13
7500 Security Boulevard
Baltimore, MD 21244
Information: (410) 786-1775

Remarks

CMS actively recruits on college campuses throughout the country. The recruiting and job fair schedules are listed on their Web site.

Application Procedures

CMS's Web site lists current job openings. Follow application directions on the vacancy announcement you are interested in. Or, direct inquiries to:

Centers for Medicare and Medicaid Services
Division of Staffing and Employee Benefits
7500 Security Blvd.
Baltimore, MD 21244-1850
(410) 786-5505
Job Hotline: (410) 786-5587

For more information on economist, actuary, or statistician positions at CMS. Contact or send a resume to:

Center for Medicare & Medicaid Services
Mail Stop N3-01-21
7500 Security Boulevard
Baltimore, MD 21244-1850
(410) 786-6375
E-mail: bfreeburger@hcfa.gov

Health Resources and Services Administration (HRSA)
www.hrsa.gov

Nature of Work: Health/health care

Number of Employees: 2,000

Headquarters: Rockville, MD

Regional Locations: Atlanta, GA; Boston, MS; Chicago, IL; Dallas, TX; Denver, CO; Kansas City, MO; New York, NY; Philadelphia, PA; San Francisco, CA; Seattle, WA

Typical Background of New Hires: Health sciences, medical sciences, public health

Mission

HRSA provides leadership and direction to programs and activities designed to improve health services in the U.S. It develops health-care and maintenance systems that are adequately financed, comprehensive, interrelated, and responsive to the needs of individuals and families at all levels of society.

Job Descriptions

Public Health Program Administrator: Provides assistance to state, local, voluntary, public, and private entities, in matters relating to the planning and maintenance of health-related programs. Conducts studies to identify current and future public health problems and evaluates the effectiveness of public health programs and methods. May be involved in monitoring issues relating to rural health, acquired immune deficiency syndrome (AIDS); organ procurement, transplant, and donation; and other health-care issues.

Major Activities and Divisions

Bureau of Primary Health Care: Works to ensure the broad availability of health-care services to residents of medically underserved areas and to special groups.

Bureau of Health Professions: Coordinates, evaluates, and supports the development of the nation's health personnel.

Maternal and Child Health Bureau: Develops federal policy and programs pertaining to promotion of health care for mothers and children.

HIV/AIDS Bureau: Works to improve the quality and availability of care for people with HIV/AIDS and their families.

Alternative Employment Programs

HRSA participates in the Student Educational Employment Program, targeting both high school and college students. Several clerk-typist positions are filled annually at the GS-2 to GS-4 levels.

Remarks

HRSA does limited college recruiting and attends college fairs when the budget permits.

Application Procedures

Direct inquiries to:

Office of Personnel
HRSA
5600 Fishers Lane, Room 14A-46
Rockville, MD 20857
(301) 443-5460
TDD: (301) 443-3143
Fax: (301) 443-2682

Indian Health Service (IHS)
www.ihs.gov

Nature of Work: Health/health care, Native Americans

Number of Employees: 15,000

Headquarters: Albuquerque, NM (West HQ); Rockville, MD; Tucson, AZ (HQ: Office of Health Program Development)

Regional Locations: Aberdeen, SD; Albuquerque, NM; Anchorage, AK; Bemidji, MN; Billings, MT; Nashville, TN; Oklahoma City, OK; Phoenix, AZ; Portland, OR; Sacramento, CA; Tucson, AZ; Window Rock, AZ

Typical Background of New Hires: Engineering (biomedical, civil, electrical, environmental, mechanical), health sciences, medical sciences (dentistry, nursing, optometry, ophthalmology), psychology, social work/sociology

Mission

The Indian Health Service provides a comprehensive health services delivery system for American Indians and Alaska Natives with opportunity for maximum tribal involvement in developing and managing programs to meet their health needs. The goal of IHS is to raise the health level of the Indian and Alaska Native people to the highest possible level.

Job Descriptions

Community Health Nurse: Plans and coordinates community health programs and services. Assesses health status and determines nursing needs for the individual, the family, and the community. Implements and evaluates health planning and practices and provides primary health care. Works with expectant Indian mothers and their infants by promoting early care in pregnancy through home visits. Provides teenagers with counseling and guidance in health promotion and family living and immunizes infants and children against infectious diseases.

Community Injury Control Coordinator: Works with the Indian people on issues such as occupational safety and injury control programs. Identifies and recommends remedies for the causes of injury among the Indian people. Performs community and individual premises evaluations to determine and eliminate environmental health or safety deficiencies.

Dentist: Dental services are carried out in 243 locations, including IHS hospitals and health centers as well as 167 field offices and 26 mobile dental sites. In some locations, particularly in Alaska, itinerant IHS dental teams with portable equipment visit isolated villages—often by aircraft or boat. The dental program places priority on providing preventative and corrective dental care. Effective caries preventive measures, such as water fluoridation, that provide benefits at the community level are emphasized. Dental health staff members often work in coordination with environmental health workers, public health nurses, nutritionists, and pharmacists in carrying out the objectives of the dental health program.

Dietician/Public Health Nutritionist: Promotes nutritional health of Indians and Alaska Natives, especially infants, preschool children, adolescents, pregnant women, and the elderly. The dietician provides direct patient-care nutrition services, operates the dietetic department in an IHS hospital, and participates in training and career development for Indians in food service and community nutrition programs. The Public Health Nutritionist coordinates health promotion and community development activities with tribal and other federal programs.

Environmental Engineer: Works with the Indian people to improve home, community, and workplace environments. Sees that the availability and quality of water is adequate for domestic purposes and provides for safe and sanitary solid and liquid waste disposal facilities. Works with the Indian people in environmental planning; air, water, and solid-waste pollution control; and institutional environmental health in reservation areas. Assists tribes in the development and adoption of sanitary ordinances.

General Engineer: Provides for the construction, renovation, and plant operation of hospitals, health centers, personnel quarters, and other health-care facilities serving Indians and Alaskan Natives. Involved in site selection and development, facility planning, design and design review, construction and equipment installation, management and operation of healthcare facilities, etc. Opportunities are for disciplines in mechanical, biomedical, civil, and electrical engineering.

Health Educator: Assists Indians and Alaska Natives in assuming individual, family, and community responsibilities by increasing the understanding of how diseases can be reduced. Encourages the use of health services and addresses specific health and safety hazards faced by Indians and Alaska Natives.

Medical Social Worker: Working closely with physicians and nurses, professional social workers and paraprofessional associates deal with patient-related problems such as fear of treatment procedures, adjustment to limitations imposed by medical conditions, and worry about child care or loss of income while being hospitalized. If problems identified in the medical setting require outside assistance, medical social workers use community contacts to get supplemental services to patients and their families.

Optometrist/Ophthalmologist: Acts as part of a multidisciplinary health team. Examines eyes and related structures to diagnose the presence of vision problems, ocular diseases, and other abnormalities. Prescribes corrective lenses and medication to treat identified conditions. Conducts vision screening and vision safety programs for school-age children. Optometrists are located at health centers and hospitals. Ophthalmologists are employed in larger medical centers with optometrists.

Pharmacist: Works within a multidisciplinary health team. Acts as the primary source of drug information in all services. For ambulatory care, pharmacists are commonly involved in primary care programs for evaluating, treating, and monitoring patients. For inpatient services, pharmacists actively participate in the selection, dosing, and monitoring of drug therapy. May also become involved in the broader aspects of health-care management.

Physician: The IHS health program is a system of inpatient and ambulatory care facilities, which the IHS operates on Indian reservations and in Indian and Alaska Native communities. Physicians may work in one of 50 hospitals, 72 health centers, 12 school health centers, or 250 health stations or satellite field health clinics. Physicians provide a full range of preventive, primary medical, community health, and rehabilitative services, as well as alcoholism programs, to Indians and Alaska natives. IHS physicians may also engage in research through the Office of Health Program Development.

Psychologist: Provides counseling and guidance in the Indian and Native Alaskan communities. Focuses on helping the Indian person overcome cultural and linguistic barriers, to achieve self-sufficiency, and to maintain a cultural identity.

Major Activities and Divisions

IHS Health Programs: Health programs in IHS are designed specifically to meet the needs of the Indian and Alaska Native people. The programs are carried out in cooperation with Indian organizations at the national, regional, and local levels.

Research and Training: The Office of Health Program Development (OHPD) is responsible for developing new and improved methods of delivery of health services.

Alternative Employment Programs

Extern (Student) Employment Program (COSTEP): The IHS hires individuals enrolled in schools of medicine, osteopathy, dentistry, veterinary medicine, optometry, podiatry, pharmacy, public health, nursing, or allied health professions through the COSTEP program of the Public Health Service. The term of employment is during any nonacademic period of the year, not to exceed 120 days. In some cases, the student receives both a salary and payment of the school's tuition and fees.

IHS Scholarship Programs: Provides financial support for Indian students only to enroll in courses that will prepare them for acceptance into health professions schools or to enroll in courses leading to a baccalaureate degree in specific preprofessional areas such as premedicine or predentistry. The scholarship recipient must intend to serve the Indian people as a health-care provider upon completion of professional health-care education. A second scholarship program requires recipients to incur a one-year service obligation to the Indian Health Service for each year of scholarship support. Scholarship coordinator addresses and phone numbers are listed below. Approximately 50 students per year receive IHS scholarships.

Other IHS Programs: The Indian Health Service participates in a co-op program for high school and college students, typically beginning at the GS-3 level. These are usually support positions. IHS also participates in the Stay-in-School program. Contact IHS for more information.

Remarks

IHS hires mostly American Indians through its Indian Preference hiring procedures. Applicants of other ethnic backgrounds are encouraged to apply, but American Indian applicants will be given first preference. More than 50 percent of the IHS staff are of Indian or Alaska Native descent.

IHS offers a clinical clerkship program for medical students. Contact the area office in which you have interest.

Application Procedures

Direct inquiries to:

Headquarters:
Indian Health Service
Reyes Building
801 Thompson Avenue, Suite 400
Rockville, MD 20852-1627
(301) 443-6520

Nurse Recruitment: (800) 543-0387

Dentist Recruitment: (800) IHS-DENT

Job Vacancy Line: (301) 443-6520

Pharmacy Recruitment: (602) 364-7745 or (888) 366-4941 (toll free)

Scholarship Program: (301) 443-6197

IHS Area Offices:

Aberdeen Area
Federal Bldg.
115 4th Ave. SE
Aberdeen, SD 57401
(605) 226-7531
Fax: (605) 226-7321
Scholarship Coordinator:
(605) 226-7553

Alaska Area Native Health Services
4141 Ambassador Drive
Anchorage, AK 99508-5928
(907) 729-3686
Fax: (907) 729-3689

Albuquerque Area
5300 Homestead Rd, NE
Albuquerque, NM 87110
(505) 248-4102
Fax: (505) 248-4115

Bemidji Area
522 Minnesota Ave. NW, Room 119
Bemidji, MN 56601
(218) 444-0458
Fax: (218) 444-0461

Billings Area
2900 4th Avenue North
Billings, MT 59101
Health Professional Recruiter: (800)
277-5997

California Area
650 Capital Mall
Sacramento, CA 95814
(916) 930-3927
Fax: (916) 930-3952

Navajo Area
P.O. Box 9020
Window Rock, AZ 86515-9020
(928) 871-5811
Fax: (928) 871-1415

Oklahoma City Area
Five Corporate Plaza
3625 NW 56th Street
Oklahoma City, OK 73112
(405) 951-3768
Fax: (405) 951-3780

Phoenix Area
Two Renaissance Square
40 North Central Avenue
Phoenix, AZ 85004
(602) 364-5039
Fax: (602) 364-5042

Portland Area
1220 SW Third Ave. #476
Portland, OR 97204
(503) 326-4123
Fax: (503) 326-7280

Nashville Area
711 Stewarts Ferry Dr.
Nashville, TN 37214
(615) 467-1500
Fax: (615) 467-1501

Tucson Area
7900 S. J. Stock Road
Tucson, AZ 85746-7012
(520) 295-2405
Fax: (520) 295-2602

National Institutes of Health (NIH)
www.nih.gov

Nature of Work: Health/health care, libraries, scientific research

Number of Employees: 17,000

Headquarters: Bethesda, MD (75 buildings on more than 300 acres)

Regional Locations: None

Typical Background of New Hires: Biology, chemistry, library science, medical sciences, psychology

Mission

The mission of NIH is to improve the health of the American people. To carry out this mission, NIH conducts and supports biomedical research into the causes, prevention, and cure of diseases and communicates biomedical information to the public.

Job Descriptions

Biologist: Conducts research into the biological aspects and causes of certain diseases, depending upon the specialty of the Institute.

Chemist: Applies a professional knowledge of chemistry to conduct research into the composition, molecular structure, and properties of substances that may be linked to certain diseases.

Librarian: Provides medical library services and online bibliographic searching capabilities to private agencies and to the public. Acquires and makes available for distribution audiovisual instructional material for the health education community.

Medical Officer: Conducts research and research training on the causes, characteristics, prevention, control, and treatment of a wide variety of diseases.

Medical Technologist: Performs chemical, bacteriologic, hematologic, cytologic, and other tests and examinations of samples of fluids, tissues, and other substances.

Microbiologist: Conducts research on the characteristics and life processes of microorganisms involving the medical applications of work with protozoa, bacteria, viruses, rickettsiae, and other microscopic forms.

Nurse: Performs research in one or more phases of the field of nursing. Promotes better health practices and advises nurses who provide direct care to patients.

Psychologist: Conducts behavioral research into the processes and associated physical, psychological, and social factors of aging, human development, family structure, mental retardation, and reproduction.

Public Information Specialist: Disseminates biomedical information through informational media and public information techniques. Evaluates the public information potential of written material, illustrations, exhibits, and other materials.

Technical Information Specialist: Processes and transmits scientific biomedical information. Must possess a broad knowledge of biomedical scientific disciplines.

Major Activities and Divisions

National Cancer Institute: Conducts a National Cancer Program designed to expand existing scientific knowledge on cancer cause and prevention.

National Heart, Lung, and Blood Institute: Provides leadership for a national program in diseases of the heart, blood vessels, blood, and lungs.

National Human Genome Research Institute (NHGRI): Heads the Human Genome Project, an international research effort to characterize the genomes of human and selected model organisms through complete mapping and sequencing of their DNA.

National Library of Medicine: Serves as the nation's chief medical information source.

The National Institute on Alcohol Abuse and Alcoholism (NIAAA): Supports and conducts biomedical and behavioral research on the causes, consequences, treatment, and prevention of alcoholism and alcohol-related problems.

The National Institute on Deafness and Other Communication Disorders (NIDCD): Conducts and support biomedical and behavioral research and research training in the normal and disordered processes of hearing, balance, smell, taste, voice, speech, and language.

The National Institute of Dental and Craniofacial Research (NIDCR): Promotes the general health of American people by improving their oral, dental, and craniofacial health.

National Institute of Diabetes and Digestive and Kidney Diseases: Conducts and supports research into the causes and treatment of metabolic and digestive diseases.

The National Institute on Drug Abuse: Supports and conducts research across a broad range of disciplines, and ensures the effective use of the research results to improve drug abuse and addiction prevention, treatment, and policy.

National Institute of Allergy and Infectious Diseases: Conducts and supports research on the causes and treatment of diseases believed to be attributable to infectious agents and conducts research to help protect civilian populations from potential bioterrorism diseases such as smallpox, anthrax, and plague.

National Institute of Child Health and Human Development: Conducts and supports biomedical research on child health and maternal health.

National Institute of Environmental Health Sciences: Conducts research to measure the effects of chemical, biological, and physical factors in the environment on the health of man.

National Institute of General Medical Sciences: Conducts and supports research in basic biomedical science.

The National Institute of Mental Health: Conducts research in basic neuroscience, behavioral science, and genetics to gain an understanding of the fundamental mechanisms underlying thought, emotion, and behavior and the causes of mental illness.

National Institute of Neurological Disorders and Stroke: Conducts research on human neurological disorders such as epilepsy and muscular dystrophy.

National Eye Institute: Conducts and supports studies on the eye and visual system.

National Institute on Aging: Conducts research to increase the knowledge of the aging process and associated factors.

National Institute of Arthritis and Musculoskeletal and Skin Diseases: Conducts research in the major disease categories of arthritis and musculoskeletal and skin diseases.

National Institute for Biomedical Imaging and Bioengineering (NIBIB): Coordinates with biomedical imaging and bioengineering programs of other agencies and NIH institutes to support imaging and engineering research with potential medical applications.

The Center for Information Technology: Provides, coordinates, and manages information technology, and advances computational science as a vital partner in the discovery of biomedical knowledge.

The Center for Alternative Medicine: Studies a broad range of healing philosophies and therapies that conventional medicine does not commonly use, including the use of acupuncture, herbs, homeopathy, therapeutic massage, and traditional Oriental medicine.

The National Center for Research Resources: Supports the research community by providing access to diverse research technologies, instrumentation, specialized basic and clinical research facilities, animal models, genetic stocks, and biomaterials.

Clinical Center: NIH's center for clinical research, to which patients come from all over the world to participate in clinical studies.

Fogarty International Center: Promotes research on the development of science internationally as it relates to health.

National Center for Nursing Research: Conducts and supports research related to nursing and patient care.

The Center for Scientific Review: The central receipt point for most research grant and training applications submitted to the Department of Health and Human Services. Provides scientific merit review of most research grant and fellowship applications submitted to the NIH.

Alternative Employment Programs

PMI Program: NIH hires several outstanding graduates annually for this program. Go to www.jobs.nih.gov for specific NIH eligibility requirements.

The Summer Internship Program: A hiring program for high school, college and graduate-level students who are looking for opportunities in the administrative, management, clerical, and information technology (IT) career fields. See the NIH Web site for application instructions and deadlines.

Emerging Leaders Program: A two-year, full-time salaried program for academically outstanding graduates at the bachelor's and master's levels. See the NIH Web site for specific application instructions or e-mail questions to Emerging.Leaders@hhs.gov.

Research Training Opportunities: There are several other science, medical, and research-oriented programs available to students at all levels, from high school to postdoctoral. See the NIH Research Training page at http://grants1.nih.gov/training/ for available opportunities.

Application Procedures

Direct inquiries to:

NIH Jobs
National Institutes of Health
31 Center Drive, MSC 2207
Human Resources (OD): (301) 496-2400
Vacancy Hotline (OD): (301) 402-4111
NIH Summer Employment Job Hotline: (301) 496-2403
Fax: (301) 496-1209
E-mail: careers@box-c.nih.gov

Substance Abuse and Mental Health Services Administration (SAMHSA)
www.samhsa.gov

Nature of Work: Drugs/abuse, health/health care, scientific research

Number of Employees: 550

Headquarters: Rockville, MD

Regional Locations: Washington, DC

Typical Background of New Hires: Biology, chemistry, medical sciences (pharmacology), psychology, social work/sociology

Mission

SAMHSA provides national leadership in scientific research on drug and alcohol abuse, mental illness, and their related problems. Strategies are developed to cope with health problems and issues that arise with the use and abuse of alcohol and drugs and with mental illness and mental health.

Job Descriptions

Biologist: Performs scientific research in the field of biology, examining the physical and biological effects of drugs and toxic substances on the user and the biological aspects of mental health and illness.

Chemist: Investigates and interprets the composition and properties of drugs and related substances, the transformations that they undergo, and their physiological effects on the user.

Contract Specialist: Procures services, supplies, and collaborative agreements for SAMHSA using a variety of contractual arrangements. Most positions are filled at grades GS-9 through GS-12 and encompass all phases of contract management and administration.

Grants Management Specialist: Works with Project Officers to administer all phases of the grant programs, through monitoring the use of funds and termination or renewal of grant funding.

Medical Officer: Performs professional health-care work and research related to drug abuse and mental health disorders.

Nurse: Provides care to patients in hospitals and clinics. Promotes better health practices in the areas of drug and alcohol abuse.

Pharmacologist: Conducts research into the uses, qualities, and effects of drugs.

Psychologist: Provides psychological consultation to patients and families, especially in regard to drug and alcohol abuse and its effects. Systematically observes the relationship between behavior and physiological changes brought on by drugs or alcohol.

Public Health Advisor: Provides technical advice to state and local governments and to various public, private, and nonprofit organizations on matters related to obtaining financial support for projects on drug and alcohol abuse, alcohol patterns, and prevention and control activities. Assists organizations with the evaluation and improvement of their public health activities.

Social Worker: Provides direct services to individuals and families that are experiencing problems with drug and alcohol abuse. Provides consultation to members of related professions and community organizations on topics related to drug and alcohol abuse and other social work questions.

Sociologist: Conducts studies on behavioral patterns, social interaction, and social situations as they relate to drug or alcohol abuse populations, treatment outcome, or drug dependency. May examine residential areas in relationship to the incidence or prevalence of mental health disorders.

Statistician: Develops procedures and systems for the collection and analysis of statistical data depicting health-care needs and services.

Major Activities and Divisions

Center for Substance Abuse Prevention: Provides a focus for the federal effort to deal with issues associated with alcohol and drug abuse.

Center for Mental Health Services: Provides a focus for the federal effort to deal with mental health issues.

Center for Substance Abuse Treatment: Works to enhance programs dealing with the treatment of drug users as well as associated problems of alcoholism and mental illness.

Alternative Employment Programs

The Commissioned Officer Student Training and Extern Program (COSTEP): Assigns students in health professions to work with one of the seven Public Health Service (PHS) agencies. Opportunities provide students various responsibilities and duties that range from research to clinical services. Students are commissioned as Ensigns in the PHS and serve from 31 to 120 days per assignment. Salary is approximately $1700 per month and other benefits are provided. Contact the Commissioned Corps Director at (301) 443-9272.

SAMHSA also hires several co-op students per year for administrative, technical, and scientific positions. Typically, these students are undergraduates and begin at the GS-3 level. Contact the Co-op Program Director at (301) 443-5407 for more information.

SAMHSA also hires master's and Ph.D. students for internship positions, usually beginning at the GS-7 levels. For information on the Internship Programs, call the Intern Program Director at (301) 443-5407.

Other SAMHSA student hiring programs include the PMI program, a volunteer program, the Stay-in-School program for clerks and biological lab technicians, and a Staff Fellowship Program for Ph.D. students.

Application Procedures

Direct inquiries to:

Division of Personnel Management
Substance Abuse and Mental Health Services Administration
Parklawn Bldg., Room 14C-14
5600 Fishers Lane
Rockville, MD 20857
(301) 443-5407
Information: (301-443-4797)
Job Hotline: (301) 443-2282
E-mail: dhrm.samhsa.gov.

☆ Department of Housing and Urban Development
(www.hud.gov)

The Department of Housing and Urban Development (HUD)
www.hud.gov

Nature of Work: Housing

Number of Employees: 10,100

Headquarters: Washington, DC

Regional Locations: Atlanta, GA; Boston, MA; Chicago, IL; Denver, CO; Fort Worth, TX; Kansas City, MO; New York City, NY; Philadelphia, PA; San Francisco, CA; Seattle, WA. These ten regional offices oversee the field offices that implement HUD's programs.

Typical Background of New Hires: Accounting, business, computer science, economics, finance/banking, public administration, urban studies

Mission

Administers programs that help families become homeowners and facilitates the construction and rehabilitation of rental units. HUD also offers rental assistance to low-income families, ensures an adequate supply of mortgage credit, and combats housing discrimination.

Job Descriptions

Appraiser: Determines the market value of residential properties.

Attorney: Ensures HUD programs comply with legal, statutory, and regulatory requirements and represents the department in court when criminal and administrative cases are involved.

Community Development Representative: Administers forms of assistance that preserve and revitalize neighborhoods.

Economist: Assesses the impact of HUD policies and studies national labor, capital, mortgage, and housing markets.

Management Analyst: Improves the effectiveness of work methods, organizations, personnel utilization, and information and documentation systems.

Realty Specialist: Appraises, acquires, manages, and disposes of real estate in connection with HUD's various programs; services mortgages; and evaluates housing sites.

Urban Planner: Promotes the economic and social welfare of urban areas by analyzing economic trends, social problems, development costs, public finances, intergovernmental relationships, and urban design objectives.

Major Activities and Divisions

HUD is divided into several program offices:

Community Planning and Development Program: Administers Community Development Block Grants that provide decent housing and economic opportunities to low- and middle-income citizens.

Fair Housing and Equal Opportunity Program: Develops and implements housing and equal opportunity policies protecting people from discrimination.

Housing Program: Supervises programs supporting the production, financing, and management of new and rehabilitated housing.

Public and Indian Housing Program: Assists local public housing agencies manage programs for low-income families and for Native-American and Alaska Native communities.

The Office of Multifamily Housing Assistance Restructuring (OMHAR): Administers the Mark-to-Market program, which reduces rents on privately owned multifamily properties to market levels after housing subsidy contracts expire.

Government National Mortgage Association: Provides secondary-market financing for most FHA and VA home loans.

Alternative Employment Programs

HUD maintains a co-op program for professional, administrative, and technical occupations. The agency also runs a Volunteer Intern Program for college students. Most volunteer internships are in headquarters; however, openings are occasionally available at HUD field offices. HUD also participates in the PMI program.

Remarks

HUD's Incentive Awards Program offers bonuses to employees for outstanding job performance and for superior ideas. Child-care services and a fitness facility are available for a fee at HUD's headquarters.

Application Procedures

Direct inquiries to:

Chief, Staffing and Classification Branch
Office of Personnel
Department of Housing and Urban Development
451 7th St. SW, Room 2266
Washington, DC 20410
Personnel: (202) 708-0416
Information: (202) 708-1422
Vacancies: (202) 708-3203

☆ Independent Agencies

> ### U.S. Agency for International Development (USAID)
> ### www.usaid.gov
>
> **Nature of Work:** Agriculture, health, international affairs
>
> **Number of Employees:** 4,800
>
> **Headquarters:** Washington, DC
>
> **Regional Locations:** USAID has field missions in approximately 70 developing countries in Africa, Asia, Latin America and the Caribbean, and the Near East
>
> **Typical Background of New Hires:** Accounting, agriculture, anthropology, business, economics, education, finance, food sciences (nutrition), international affairs, marketing, political science, public health, social sciences, urban studies

Mission

USAID's purpose is to help people in the Third World acquire the knowledge and resources to build the economic, political, and social institutions needed for a more prosperous life. This assistance covers many diverse areas including agriculture, rural development, nutrition, family planning, health, education, energy, and technology.

Job Descriptions

Note: A graduate degree is required for some positions as noted below. The others require a bachelor's degree in an appropriate field. All positions require two years of experience beyond education.

Accountant: Maintains a comprehensive accounting system and provides financial and statistical data; develops systems of internal control for the disbursement and collection of funds; and provides advice on financial implications of existing grant loan agreements with host countries. Requires a CPA or an M.B.A.

Administrative Management Officer: Oversees a range of management and administrative support functions including personnel, contracting, and procurement. Plans for future support requirements at the assigned duty station.

Agriculture/Rural Development/Natural Resources Officer: Advises senior USAID and host government officials on agriculture, rural development, or natural resources–related project studies. Identifies problems and proposes solutions and participates in project development and program management. Duties include coordinating the flow of resources for agricultural projects, analyzing the effects on agriculture of proposed policies, and monitoring natural resources and environmental concerns. Requires a graduate degree in an agricultural, social, or environmental science.

Contract/Commodity Management Officer: Negotiates, awards, and administers contracts, grants and other agreements with individuals, firms, and institutions to carry out USAID-financed projects. Advises host country importers in the development of commodity procurement plans.

Education/Human Resources Development Officer: Assists with the development of host country educational systems. Designs strategies to improve existing educational programs as well as to promote organizational competencies related to institutional development. Participates in agency policy formulation, program design, and evaluation of activities. Requires a graduate degree in education, psychology, sociology, anthropology, or communications.

Health/Population/Nutrition Officer: Assists host country leaders in designing and managing health delivery systems, population and family planning projects, and nutrition and feeding programs. Works in conjunction with U.S. government personnel, contractors, grantees, and international agencies. Requires a Master of Public Health or Master of Science in Public Health degree.

Housing/Urban Development Officer: Assists, through the Office of Housing and Urban Programs, in planning, implementing, and monitoring USAID's shelter programs for below-median income families in developing countries and with USAID's broader urban programs.

International Training Specialist: Serves as a general development specialist in program design and implementation. Provides technical expertise in the area of training. Supports field training advisors.

Private Enterprise Officer: Designs and manages the overall private-sector strategy. Develops policies and mechanisms for financing the establishment, improvement, and expansion of productive private enterprise in a foreign country. Expands local, indigenous private sector activities and involves the U.S. private sector in the development process.

Program Economist: Conducts analyses of both the macroeconomic conditions of host countries and the microeconomic feasibility of individual projects. Examines balance of payments, government budgets, growth prospects, and income distribution. Conducts cost benefit analysis at the micro level. Requires a graduate degree in economics.

Program Officer: Advises the Mission Director and technical staff on USAID program policy. Ensures that proposed projects are feasible. Assists in designing USAID's country development strategy and in preparing USAID's budget.

Project Development Officer: Assists in the planning and implementation of USAID projects. Provides assistance to host government authorities and to private and public entities on nontechnical and financial aspects of project. Ensures that proposed projects are feasible and monitors projects to assure compliance with the provisions of project agreements.

Major Activities and Divisions

USAID is divided into several offices and bureaus, including:

Bureau for Democracy, Conflict and Humanitarian Assistance (DCHA): Coordinates disaster assistance, food aid, private and voluntary agency support and the American Schools and Hospitals Abroad program.

Bureau for Global Health (GH) and Bureau for Economic Growth, Agriculture and Trade (EGAT): The agency's repository of scientific and technical expertise. The Global Bureau designs and implements projects to address global problems, provides technical leadership and support to the agency, and sponsors research to understand, support and promote sustainable development.

Geographic Bureaus: Responsible for planning, formulating, and managing the implementation and evaluation of USAID development programs in their respective regions. All of the four geographic bureaus—Africa (AFR), Asia and the Near East (ANE), Europe and Eurasia (E&E), and Latin America and the Caribbean (LAC)— provide guidance and carry out project design and review, budget preparation, resource allocation and program coordination within their respective regions.

Alternative Employment Programs

The New Entry Professional (NEP) Program: This entry-level program trains qualified persons to become career Foreign Service Officers who will assume positions of increasing responsibility in managing USAID's foreign economic assistance programs. Training for the program begins in Washington, DC, and consists of orientation to the agency and subjects related to the foreign economic assistance program. Each intern then begins individual on-the-job training in Washington, which usually lasts about one year and includes language training. Interns also spend some time learning overseas. For more information on the

NEP program, visit http://www.usaid.gov/about/employment/nepbro.htm *or* http://www.usaid.gov/about/employment/cpfaqn.htm

Internships: USAID offers unpaid student internships. The basic qualifying factors are U.S. citizenship, a minimum age requirement of 16 years, current enrollment in school with a grade point average (GPA) of 3.0, and satisfactory completion of a USAID security clearance investigation. Applications are accepted from November 1 and must be received no later than January 31 of the year the internship is being requested.

Contact:

USAID
Summer Intern Program (M/HR/POD)
Ronald Reagan Building, Section 2.08-160 RRB
1300 Pennsylvania Avenue, NW
Washington, DC 20523

Overseas Internships: For an internship in a Mission overseas, apply directly to the Mission you have interest in. You can find a list of USAID missions at http://www.usaid.gov/procurement_bus_opp/osdbu/guide10a.htm. The deadline date does not apply to overseas internships. An expression of interest and resume should be sent to the overseas address and directed to the attention of the "Executive Officer."

Legal Internships: The Office of General Counsel recruits for year-round law school students for legal internships. Current law students should contact:

USAID/Office of General Counsel
1300 Pennsylvania Ave. NW, Room 6.06-074
Washington, DC 20523
(202) 712-4718

Remarks

Foreign language proficiency is required for tenure in the Foreign Service, but it is not a requirement for hiring. Foreign Service Officers will spend the majority of their careers overseas and must be willing to accept assignment anywhere in the world.

Application Procedures

USAID lists current vacancies for its NEP program, mid-level foreign service positions, and civil service positions on their Web site. Contact the staffing specialist listed on the vacancy announcement you have interest in. Or, direct inquiries to:

Agency for International Development
Recruitment Staff
320 21st St. NW, Room 658A, SA-36
Washington, DC 20523-3607
(202) 712-1143 or 0545

Central Intelligence Agency (CIA)
www.cia.gov

Nature of Work: Defense/national security, intelligence, international affairs

Number of Employees: 17,000

Headquarters: Langley, VA

Regional Locations: Worldwide—exact locations are classified

Typical Background of New Hires: Accounting, business, computer science, engineering, finance/banking, liberal arts, physical sciences, physics, public administration

---

Mission

Gathers and analyzes information on foreign adversaries; conducts counterintelligence operations abroad to frustrate foreign espionage; and undertakes covert action overseas at the President's direction.

Job Descriptions

Counterterrorism Analyst: Supports U.S. policy makers by monitoring and assessing the leadership, motivations, and plans of foreign terrorist groups and their sponsors.

Economic analyst: Supports U.S. policy makers by monitoring and assessing foreign economic policy and performance, trade and finance, and related trends that affect U.S. security.

Engineer/Scientist: Analyzes national security issues such as foreign weapons development, weapons proliferation, information warfare, and emerging technologies.

Intelligence Analyst: Collects, evaluates, and analyzes information from classified and unclassified sources to determine the information's implications for U.S. national security.

Missile Proliferation Analyst: Evaluates and analyzes information from classified and unclassified sources to assist in assessing the ballistic missile threat from countries of concern.

Political Analyst: Supports U.S. policy makers by evaluating the culture, goals, political processes, strengths, and motivations of foreign governments and entities.

Statistician: Applies quantitative skills to assess the threat from foreign weapon systems, analyze foreign political and economic developments, and support international treaty negotiations.

Clandestine Service Officer: Works to gather the intelligence and information needed by U.S. policy makers to make critical foreign policy decisions. Degrees in international business or international economics as well as the physical sciences are pluses. Some positions require extensive travel or relocation overseas. Specific titles within the Clandestine Service include Operations Officer, Staff Officer, and Collection Management Officer.

Electronic Specialist: Affects the configuration design, deployment, and maintenance of unique intrusion detection systems as well as locking hardware, security containers, and document destruction devices. Specialists are required to serve overseas assignments.

Information Systems Security Officer: Supports counterintelligence activities, information architecture development, and performs specialized technology analysis and integration.

Satellite Reconnaissance: Physicists and Program Managers develop system-level specifications and interface requirements. Position may involve hands-on testing, design, and fabrication. Opportunities for frequent travel.

Technicians/Engineers: Many other technical positions exist at CIA headquarters, including Web Developers, Telecom Info Systems Officers, Systems Engineers, and Software Developers. These positions support global CIA operations and may involve overseas assignments.

Open Source Officer: Researches unclassified (open source) foreign media and identifies information that is subsequently translated and distributed throughout the U.S. Intelligence community.

Foreign Language Instructors: Deliver programs that provide students with general and job-related foreign language communication skills and cross-cultural awareness needed to live and work abroad.

Foreign Language Specialist: Reads and translates communications and information into English. Must have native or near-native fluency in foreign language.

Polygraph Examiner: Screens and vets individuals in an ongoing effort for national security.

Major Activities and Divisions

Directorate of Operations: Conducts the agency's clandestine assignments, which include foreign intelligence collection and, in some instances, covert action.

Directorate of Science and Technology: Develops and applies advanced systems to collect, interpret, and disseminate information. Projects include video and image enhancement; chemical imagery; advanced antenna design; electrooptics; large systems modeling and simulation; and laser, analog, digital, and satellite communications. Also collects and processes intelligence information from broadcast and print media, telecommunications, and overhead photography.

Directorate of Intelligence: Evaluates and interprets information obtained from the Directorates of Operations and Science and Technology, assesses its implications, and passes the findings to government leaders.

Directorate of Administration: Provides services such as personnel and financial management, communications, computer programming, medicine, security, logistics, and training.

Alternative Employment Programs

The CIA divides its hiring programs into five areas: clandestine service; analytical positions; scientists, engineers, and technologist positions; language positions; and professional positions. Many of these offer co-ops, internships, and graduate studies programs. See www.cia.gov/cia/employment for information.

Remarks

The Clandestine Service has a special Professional Trainee (PT) Program for recent college graduates. Applicants accepted into this program will be assigned to Washington, DC for 18 months. During this time, PTs are evaluated for movement into the Clandestine Service Trainee (CST) Program, the traditional pipeline to serving overseas as an Operations Officer or Collection Management Officer. Contact: CST Division, P.O. Box 4605, Dept. Internet, Reston, VA 20195; Fax: (703) 613-7871

CIA personnel serving overseas receive special pay as well as allowances for housing, education for dependents, medical care, and other considerations.

Applicants must submit to strict background and medical evaluations as well as a polygraph test. Because the entire application process may take six or more months to complete, applicants should begin this process long before they are available for employment.

Application Procedures

The CIA strongly prefers that applications be submitted online. See the job postings on the CIA Web site for specific instructions. Or send your resume and cover letter to:

Recruitment Center
Attn: (fill in position applying for)
P.O. Box 4090, Dept: Internet
Reston, VA 20195

Or, direct inquiries to:

Central Intelligence Agency
Office of Personnel
Arlington, VA 22209-8727
Information: (703) 482-1100

Commodity Futures Trading Commission (CFTC)
www.cftc.gov

Nature of Work: Bonds/commodities, economic policy, law enforcement

Number of Employees: 550

Headquarters: Washington, DC

Regional Locations: Chicago, IL; Kansas City, MO; Los Angeles, CA; Minneapolis, MN; New York, NY

Typical Background of New Hires: Accounting, business, computer science, economics, law

---

Mission

Regulates trading on U.S. futures exchanges; monitors the activities of commodity exchange members, public brokerage houses, CFTC-registered futures industry salespeople, commodity pool operators, and commodity trading advisers.

Job Descriptions

Attorney: Advises the Commission on the legality of policies and regulations; works with U.S. attorneys in pursuing criminal violations of commodities regulations.

Auditor: Reviews transactions and activities of commodity exchange members ensuring compliance with Commission rules.

Computer Specialist: Develops, operates, and supports market surveillance and other automated systems.

Economist: Evaluates applications for new futures contracts submitted by exchanges to ensure that proposals adequately reflect cash market practices and meet the Commission's regulatory standards.

Research Economist: Studies the economic impact of Commission actions on manufacturers, farmers, exporters, wholesalers, and consumers; and uses econometric modeling to forecast economic and market trends.

Futures Trading Specialist/Investigator: Investigates illegal trading activity such as market manipulations, fraud, and trade abuses; assists state or federal law enforcement agencies conducting commodity violations.

Major Activities and Divisions

Division of Enforcement: Investigates and prosecutes Commodity Exchange Act violations.

Division of Trading and Markets: Drafts, implements, and enforces exchange regulations that prevent fraud, protect customer investments, and ensure the stability of commodity trading firms.

Office of the General Counsel: Provides legal advice to the Commission's operating divisions.

Division of Economic Analysis: Supervises daily futures market transactions, reviews new futures and options contract proposals, and conducts economic studies.

Alternative Employment Programs

The CTFC has a summer employment program, including summer opportunities for law students and other college students. The application deadline for summer employment is usually in February, so candidates should contact the CFTC regarding summer positions no later than the end of January.

The CFTC also employs students during the school year through the Student Educational Employment Program. Call the student employment coordinator at (202) 418-5003 for more information.

Application Procedures

The CTFC lists current job openings on its Web site. Follow application instructions for the position you are interested in. Or, direct inquiries to:

Commodity Futures Trading Commission
Office of Human Resources
Three Lafayette Center, 4th Floor
1155 21st St., NW
Washington, DC 20581
(202) 418-5003
CTFC Job Hotline: (202) 418-5009

Corporation for National and Community Service
www.nationalservice.org

Nature of Work: Social services, volunteers

Number of Employees: 600

Headquarters: Washington, DC

Regional Locations: 46 state offices nationwide

Typical Background of New Hires: Education, psychology, social sciences

Mission

The mission of the Corporation for National and Community Service is to promote the spirit and practice of voluntarism. This is carried out by more than 400,000 local volunteers in communities around the country. Whether the goal is to help adults learn to read, to help young people stay drug-free, or to provide companionship and services to the homebound elderly, the Corporation's programs and volunteers join citizens together to address the needs of a community and its people.

Job Descriptions

State Program Specialist: Develops, monitors, and evaluates a variety of community-based social service programs. Makes on-site visits to inspect and review conduct of assigned projects and programs. Provides technical assistance to project/program sponsors and maintains liaison with government and local officials. Assists in training events, workshops, and conferences.

Major Activities and Divisions

In partnership with state and local governments and nonprofit organizations, the Corporation for National and Community Service administers the AmeriCorps service program, VISTA and the National Civilian Community Corps, the National Senior Service Corps (Foster Grandparents, Senior Companions and the Retired, and Senior Volunteer Program) and Service-Learning.

Alternative Employment Programs

The Corporation for National Service maintains an active fellowship program. For information, call (202) 606-5000 Ext. 571 or e-mail fellowships@cns.gov.

There is also an internship program for support staff, technical, and general clerical positions. Applications for internships are accepted throughout the year. All internships at the Corporation for National Service are unpaid.

To apply for an internship, send a cover letter and resume to:

Corporation for National and Community Service
Internship Coordinator
1201 New York Ave. NW
Washington, DC 20525

Application Procedures

The Corporation for National and Community Service lists current job openings on its Web site. Follow the application instructions for the job in which you have interest, or, direct inquiries to:

The Corporation for National and Community Service
ATTN: Human Resources
1201 New York Ave.
Washington, DC 20525
(202) 606-5000
Toll Free: (800) 942-2677
E-mail: jobs@cns.gov

U.S. Equal Employment Opportunity Commission (EEOC)
www.eeoc.gov

Nature of Work: Business, discrimination, employment, insurance, minorities

Number of Employees: 2,700

Headquarters: Washington, DC

Regional Locations: Albuquerque, NM; Atlanta, GA; Baltimore, MD; Birmingham, AL; Charlotte, NC; Chicago, IL; Cleveland, OH; Dallas, TX; Denver, CO; Detroit, MI; Houston, TX; Indianapolis, IN; Los Angeles, CA; Memphis, TN; Miami, FL; Milwaukee, WI; New Orleans, LA; New York, NY; Philadelphia, PA; Phoenix, AZ; St. Louis, MO; San Antonio, TX; San Francisco, CA; Seattle, WA; Washington, DC; also many area/local offices

Typical Background of New Hires: Criminal justice, law, liberal arts, psychology

Mission

The EEOC enforces the laws against employment discrimination, including Title VII, the Age Discrimination in Employment Act, and the Equal Pay Act. EEOC coordinates all federal equal employment opportunity regulations and policies and is the appellate authority for federal sector complaints of employment discrimination.

Job Descriptions

Attorney: Conducts all of the agency's civil litigation except for Title VII cases against state and local governments and Supreme Court cases, which are litigated by the Solicitor General of the U.S. About one eighth of EEOC's staff are attorneys or law clerks, 60 percent of whom are located in field offices outside Washington, DC. Most work in the Office of General Counsel, the Office of Legal Counsel, or the Office of Review and Appeals.

Investigator: Receives and investigates employment discrimination charges. Meets with charging parties, employers, and other witnesses to secure information relative to a charge. Analyzes the data and writes recommendations on the findings. Visits employer facilities to investigate charges and helps resolve them by negotiating settlements between the complainants and employers.

Major Activities and Divisions

The Office of General Counsel: Employs attorneys at EEOC HQ and in 23 district offices. Conducts class, systematic, and individual discrimination lawsuits.

OUACHITA TECHNICAL COLLEGE

The Office of Legal Counsel: Located in Washington, DC only, is the principal advisor to the Commission on policy and nonenforcement litigation matters and represents EEOC and staff in defensive litigation and administrative hearings.

The Office of Review and Appeals: Located in Washington, DC, decides or recommends decisions on appeals from federal agency employees on equal opportunity complaints and petitions.

The Office of Program Operations: Manages, directs, and coordinates field office operations.

Alternative Employment Programs

Investigator positions are available through the student employment program for students at the sophomore level and above. Internships are also available. They are nonpaid, but can be used for course credit. Other, more specialized, programs include:

The Legal Intern Program: For ABA-approved law school students who have completed their first year. Hiring is conducted individually by each EEOC office. GS-5 or GS-9 level.

The Summer Legal Intern Program: For law students who have completed their first year or more at an ABA-approved law school. Term of employment is from May 13 to September 30; superior employees may be offered a permanent position effective upon graduation. Candidates must apply by March 15. GS-5 or GS-9.

The Summer Employment Program: Temporary administrative or professional jobs available from May 13 to September 30 and during other school breaks.

Remarks

EEOC conducts an Attorney Honor Program, which is designed to recruit outstanding third year law students, graduate law students, and judicial clerks. Interviewing is done on the college campus or at the EEOC office. All JD graduates must pass the bar exam within 14 months for entry on duty. Upon bar membership, the individual may be appointed to a permanent attorney position. GS-9, GS-11, GS-12. Call (202) 663-7175 for information.

Application Procedures

Each EEOC District Office is managing its own recruitment process. Contact each office for information on vacancies.

EEOC Headquarters
Employment Division
1801 L St., NW, Room 3050
Washington, DC 20507
(202) 663-4900

Note: District offices oversee hiring for local and area offices.

Albuquerque District Office
505 Marquette, NW, Suite 900
Albuquerque, NM 87102-2189
(505) 248-5201

Atlanta District Office
100 Alabama St., Suite 4R30
Atlanta, GA 30303
(404) 562-6800

Baltimore District Office
10 South Howard St., 3rd Floor
Baltimore, MD 21201
(410) 962-3932

Birmingham District Office
Ridge Park Place
1130 22nd St., Suite 2000
Birmingham, AL 32205
 (205) 731-0082/3

Boston Area Office
John F. Kennedy Federal Building
Government Center, 4th Floor, Room 475
Boston, MA 02203
(617) 565-3204

Buffalo Local Office
6 Fountain Plaza, Suite 350
Buffalo, NY 14202
(716) 551-4441

Charlotte District Office
129 West Trade St., Suite 400
Charlotte, NC 28202
(704) 344-6682

Chicago District Office
500 West Madison St., Suite 2800
Chicago, IL 60661
(312) 353-2713

Cincinnati Area Office
550 Main St., Suite 10019
Cincinnati, OH 45202
(513) 684-2851

Cleveland District Office
1660 W. Second St., Suite 850
Cleveland, OH 44113-1454
(216) 522-2001

Dallas District Office
207 S. Houston St., 3rd Floor
Dallas, TX 75202-4726
(214) 655-3355

Denver District Office
303 E. 17th Ave., Suite 510
Denver, CO 80203
(303) 866-1300

Detroit District Office
477 Michigan Ave., Room 865
Detroit, MI 48226
(313) 226-7636

El Paso Area Office
300 East Main Street
El Paso, TX 79901
(915) 534-6700

Fresno Local Office
1265 West Shaw Ave., Suite 103
Fresno, CA 93711
(559) 487-5793

Greensboro Local Office
2302 W. Meadowview Rd., Suite 201
Greensboro, NC 27405-7813
(336) 547-4188

Greenville Local Office
301 North Main St., Suite 1402
Greenville, SC 29601
(864) 241-4400

Honolulu Local Office
300 Ala Moana Blvd., Room 7123 A
P.O. Box 50082
Honolulu, HI 96850-0051
(808) 541-3120

Houston District Office
1919 Smith St., 7th Floor
Houston, TX 77002
(713) 209-3320

Indianapolis District Office
101 W. Ohio St., Suite 1900
Indianapolis, IN 46204
(317) 226-7212

Jacksonville Area Office
Dr. A.H. McCoy Federal Building
100 West Capitol St., Suite 207
Jackson. MI 39269
(601) 965-4537

Kansas City Area Office
400 State Ave., Suite 905
Kansas City, KS 66101
(913) 551-5655

Little Rock Area Office
820 Louisiana St., Suite 200
Little Rock, AR 72201
(501) 324-5060

Los Angeles District Office
255 E. Temple, 4th Floor
Los Angeles, CA 90012
(213) 894-1000

Louisville Area Office
600 Dr. Martin Luther King Jr. Place
Suite 268
Louisville, KY 40202
(502) 582-6082

Memphis District Office
1407 Union Ave., Suite 521
Memphis, TN 38104
(901) 544-0115

Miami District Office
1 Biscayne Tower, Suite 2700
Miami, FL 33131
(305) 536-4491

Milwaukee District Office
310 W. Wisconsin Ave, Suite 800
Milwaukee, WI 53203
(414) 297-1111

Minneapolis Area Office
330 South Second Avenue
Minneapolis, MN 55401-2224
(612) 335-4040

Nashville Area Office
50 Vantage Way, Suite 202
Nashville, TN 37228
(615) 736-5820

Newark Area Office
1 Newark Center, 21ˢᵗ Floor
Newark, NJ 07102-5233
(973) 645-6383

New Orleans District Office
701 Loyola Ave., Suite 600
New Orleans, LA 70113
(504) 589-2329

New York District Office
201 Varick St., Room 1009
New York, NY 10014
(212) 741-8815 or 2783

Norfolk Area Office
Federal Building, Suite 739
200 Granby Street
Norfolk, VA 23510
(757) 441-3470

Oakland Local Office
1301 Clay St., Suite 1170-N
Oakland, CA 94612-5217
(510) 637-3230

Oklahoma Area Office
210 Park Avenue
Oklahoma City, OK 73102
(405) 231-4911

Philadelphia District Office
21 South 5th St., 4th Floor
Philadephia, PA 19106
(215) 440-2600

Phoenix District Office
3300 N. Central Ave., Suite 690
Phoenix, AZ 85012-1848
(602) 640-5000

Pittsburgh Area Office
1001 Liberty Ave., Suite 300
Pittsburgh, PA 15222-4187
(412) 644-3444

Raleigh Area Office
1309 Annapolis Dr.
Raleigh, NC 27608-2129
(919) 856-4064

Richmond Area Office
3600 West Broad St., Room 229
Richmond, VA 23230
(808) 278-4651

San Antonio District Office
5410 Fredericksburg Rd., Suite 200
San Antonio, TX 78229-3555
(210) 281-7600

San Diego Area Office
401 B St., Suite 1550
San Diego, CA 92101
(619) 557-7235

San Francisco District Office
901 Market St., Suite 500
San Francisco, CA 94103
(415) 356-5100

San Jose Local Office
96 North 3ʳᵈ St., Suite 200
San Jose, CA 95112
(408) 291-7352

San Juan Area Office
525 F. D. Roosevelt Ave.
Plaza Las Americas
San Juan, PR 00918-8001
(787) 771-1464

Savannah Local Office
410 Mall Blvd., Suite G
Savannah, GA 31406-4821
(912) 652-4234

Seattle District Office
Federal Office Building
909 First Ave., Suite 400
Seattle, WA 98104-1061
(206) 220-6883

St. Louis District Office
Robert A.Young Building
1222 Spruce St., Room 8.100
St. Louis, MO 63103
(314) 539-7800

Tampa Area Office
501 East Polk St., 10th Floor
Tampa, FL 33602
(813) 228-2310

Washington Field Office
1400 L St., NW, Suite 200
Washington, DC 20005
(202) 275-7377

The Environmental Protection Agency (EPA)
www.epa.gov

Nature of Work: Environmental protection, scientific research

Number of Employees: 18,000

Headquarters: Washington, DC

Regional Locations: Atlanta, GA; Boston, MA; Chicago, IL; Dallas, TX; Denver, CO; Kansas City, MO; New York, NY; Philadelphia, PA; San Francisco, CA; Seattle, WA. Research and development laboratories are located in Research Triangle Park, NC; Cincinnati, OH; and Las Vegas, NV. EPA's National Enforcement Investigation Center is located in Denver, CO. Its Mobile Source Air Pollution Control facility is in Ann Arbor, MI.

Typical Background of New Hires: Biology, chemistry, computer science, engineering, geology, law, physical sciences

Mission

Prevents air, land, and water pollution by regulating the manufacture, use, and disposal of toxic substances. EPA also oversees the cleanup of polluted sites and supports research and antipollution activities.

Job Descriptions

Attorney: Drafts legislation and regulations; represents the agency in litigation; helps prosecute criminal violators of environmental regulations.

Biologist: Identifies biological hazards in the environment and develops remedies to stabilize or remove them.

Chemical Engineer: Studies methods of removing pollutants by chemical and biological means; designs, evaluates, and sets standards for waste treatment plants.

Criminal Investigator: Investigates alleged violations of environmental laws.

Environmental Engineer: Studies the impact of pollutants on the environment, develops remedial technologies, and evaluates pollution control techniques.

Environmental Protection Specialist: Develops environmental protection plans and programs and works on related grant proposals.

Environmental Scientist: Reviews, analyzes, and evaluates air and water quality and assesses pollution control regulations.

Geneticist: Evaluates the environmental hazards of bioengineered organisms.

Geologist: Examines geological formations and determines their capacity for containing toxic wastes.

Hydrologist: Studies and predicts hydrologic phenomena such as precipitation, evaporation, and stream flow.

Mechanical Engineer: Creates and evaluates pollution control technologies and monitoring systems.

Meteorologist: Compiles data on local and national weather patterns to help in the study and regulation of airborne pollutants.

Pathologist: Examines various pollution hazards and their relationship to the growth and transmission of diseases.

Pharmacologist: Reviews and evaluates pharmacological and toxicological data to determine whether a chemical meets approved standards for safety and labeling.

Radiation Engineer: Assesses and controls airborne radioactive emissions and measures radiation levels in the environment.

Toxicologist: Evaluates residue chemistry and toxicology data to ensure that levels of pesticides and other chemicals found in the environment will not harm public health.

Veterinary Officer (Veterinarian): Researches the toxicological and pathological effects of chemicals used in the control of livestock and plant pests.

Major Activities and Divisions

Office of Research and Development: Investigates the impact of pollutants on the environment and human health and studies the transport and control of pollutants.

Office of Air and Radiation: Regulates and monitors six principal air pollutants, as well as exceptionally hazardous substances such as beryllium and mercury. Also sets standards for the manufacture and sale of fuels or fuel additives and regulates airborne radioactive emissions.

American Indian Environmental Office: Coordinates the agency-wide effort to strengthen public health and environmental protection in Indian Country, with a special emphasis on building Tribal capacity to administer their own environmental programs.

Office of International Affairs Manages Agency: Involved in international policies and programs that cut across agency offices and regions. Provides leadership and coordination on behalf of the agency and acts as the focal point on international environmental matters.

Office of Solid Waste and Emergency Response: Issues permits for hazardous waste management facilities and removes or stabilizes hazardous waste sites.

Office of Water: Reduces water pollution by regulating municipalities and industries and by assisting states in developing effective control methods.

Office of Prevention, Pesticides and Toxic Substances: Registers new products; reviews hazards from existing products; and enforces pesticide use rules.

Office of Enforcement and Compliance: Enforces environmental laws; investigates the illegal discharge of toxic wastes into waterways and landfills and the deliberate destruction or falsification of environmental reports.

Alternative Employment Programs

National Network for Environmental Management Studies (NNEMS)
NNEMS is a comprehensive fellowship program managed by EPA's Office of Environmental Education. Research fellowships are available in many subjects and are open to both undergraduate- and graduate-level students.
Contact:

NNEMS Program
US EPA (1704A)
1200 Pennsylvania Ave. NW
Washington, DC 20460
(202) 564-0452
www.epa.gov/enviroed/students.html

The Student Environmental Associate Program and Diversity Initiative
EPA's Office of Environmental Justice sponsors this program, which draws students from a wide variety of communities and tribes across the country. Students complete a paid, full-time, on-site training opportunity of three to six months.
For information, contact:

The Environmental Careers Organization
179 South St.
Boston, MA 02111
(617) 426-4783
www.eco.org

EPA's National Center for Environmental Research (NCER) operates several programs that seek to improve educational opportunities for promising young people. Several graduate education fellowships for masters and doctoral level students in environmentally elated fields of study are available through these programs. Other opportunities include the visiting scientist programs (Resident Research Associates Program) for currently practicing environmental scientists and engineers.

For more information, call the toll-free help line at (800) 490-9194.

EPA maintains an internship program, and participates in the federal government's Outstanding Scholar Program. See the EPA Web site for more information. EPA also participates in the PMI program. For more information, contact the OPM at (202) 606-2525.

Application Procedures

The EPA has its own online job listings and application system called EZ HIRE, located at www.epa.gov/ezhire/.

Or, direct inquiries to:

Environmental Protection Agency
Recruitment and Employment Program
1200 Pennsylvania Ave.
Washington, DC 20460
(202) 260-2090 or 7690

For information on regional office vacancies, see www.epa.gov/epahome/locate2.htm. Or, contact one of the human resources offices below:

U.S. EPA Human Resources Offices

Andrew W. Breidenbach
Environmental Research Center
Human Resources Management
Division, Room 275
W. Martin Luther King Dr.
Cincinnati, OH 45268
(512) 569-7840

Ann Arbor
Human Resources Office
2000 Traberwood Dr.
Ann Arbor, MI 48105
(734) 214-4220

Research Triangle Park
79 TW Alexander Dr., MD-29
Research Triangle Park, NC 27711
Job Line: (919) 541-3014
Toll Free: (800) 433-9633

Human Resources Staff: Team Vegas
P.O. Box 98516
Las Vegas, NV 89193-8516
(702) 798-2401
Job Hotline: (702) 798-2418

Region 1
1 Congress St.
Suite 1100 (MHR)
Boston, MA 02114-2023
(617) 918-1980
Job Hotline: (617) 918-2079

Region 2
290 Broadway
New York, NY 10007
(212) 637-3550

Region 3
1650 Arch Street (3PM40)
Philadelphia, PA 19103-2029
(215) 814-5240

Region 4
Sam Nunn Federal Center
Human Resources Management
Branch
61 Forsyth St. SW, 9th Floor Tower
Atlanta, GA 30303
(404) 562-8182
Toll Free: (800) 241-1754

Region 5
77 West Jackson Boulevard
10th Floor, MP-10J
Chicago, IL 60604-3507
(312) 353-2026 or 2027

Region 6
Fountain Place
1445 Ross Avenue, Suite 1200
Dallas, TX 75202-2733
(214) 665-6544

Region 7
901 N. 5th Street
Kansas City, KS 66101
(913) 551-7041
Job Line: 913-551-7068

Region 8
999 18th St., Suite 500
Denver, CO 80202-2405
(303) 312-6190

Region 9
75 Hawthorne St.
San Francisco, CA 94105
(415) 744-1300
Job Hotline: (415) 744-1111

Region 10
1200 Sixth Ave., OMP162
Seattle, WA 98101
(206) 553-2959
Job Line: (206) 553-1240

Export Import Bank of the United States (EX-IM BANK)
www.exim.gov

Nature of Work: Banks, import/export, international affairs, marketing, trade

Number of Employees: 400

Headquarters: Washington, DC

Regional Locations: Chicago, IL; Houston, TX; Long Beach, CA; Miami, FL; New York, NY; Orange County, CA; San Francisco, CA

Typical Background of New Hires: Accounting, business, economics, finance/banking, law

Mission

Creates domestic jobs by helping U.S. exporters compete in overseas markets, provides guarantees of working capital loans for U.S. exporters, and guarantees the repayment of loans or makes loans to foreign purchasers of U.S. goods and services. Ex-IM Bank also provides U.S. exporters credit insurance, protecting them against the risks of nonpayment by foreign buyers.

Job Descriptions

Accountant: Records financial transactions resulting from loan repayments, service fees, and claims payments.

Computer Specialist: Designs and operates Ex-IM Bank's computer systems.

Economist: Monitors and evaluates economic trends in foreign countries, determines economic impact of particular transactions, and assesses the viability of loans.

Financial Analyst: Analyzes financing proposals and determines whether there is reasonable assurance of loan repayment.

Loan Specialist: Analyzes financial and credit risk factors and develops policies and procedures governing loan programs.

Major Activities and Divisions

Export Finance Group: Administers Ex-IM Bank's loan, guarantee, and insurance programs.

Working Capital Guarantee Program: Provides eligible exporters with access to working capital loans from commercial lenders.

Engineering Division: Evaluates the technical feasibility of proposed projects and monitors projects in progress.

Claims and Recoveries Division: Processes claims filed under Ex-IM Bank's guarantee and insurance programs and makes collections and recoveries.

Alternative Employment Programs

Ex-Im Bank offers paid summer Internships. Assignments are located primarily in Washington, DC with limited opportunities available in the regional offices. For information, call toll free (800) 565-3946, Option 3.

Application Procedures

Direct inquiries to:

Office of Human Resources
Export-Import Bank of the United States
811 Vermont Ave., NW
Washington, DC 20571
(202) 565-3300 or 3946
Toll Free: (800) 565-3946

Federal Communications Commission (FCC)
www.fcc.gov

Nature of Work: Communications/media

Number of Employees: 1,900

Headquarters: Washington, DC

Regional Locations: The FCC has 3 regional offices, 16 district offices, and 9 resident agent offices across the U.S. The regional and district offices are: Atlanta, GA: Boston, MA; Chicago, IL; Columbia, MD; Dallas, TX; Denver, CO; Detroit, MI; Kansas City, MO; Los Angeles, CA; New Orleans, LA; New York, NY; Philadelphia, PA; San Diego, CA; San Francisco, CA; Seattle, WA; and Tampa, FL.

Typical Background of New Hires: Engineering (electronic), law

Mission

Regulates interstate and international communications by radio, television, wire, satellite, and cable; assigns frequencies, power, and call signs; authorizes communications circuits; modifies and reviews licenses; inspects transmitting equipment; and controls interference.

Job Descriptions

Attorney: Reviews applications for radio licenses and represents the FCC before administrative law judges in formal adjudicatory hearings. Attorneys also perform appellate litigation and enforcement proceedings in the federal courts and review tariffs of telephone and telegraph companies.

Electronics Engineer: Investigates illegal or clandestine radio stations, inspects radio equipment on ships and land-based broadcast stations, determines the feasibility of directional antenna proposals, calculates horizontal and vertical plane radiation patterns for antenna systems, and develops methods of increasing spectrum usage.

Major Activities and Divisions

Consumer & Governmental Affairs Bureau: Communicates information to the public regarding Commission policies, programs, and activities. This Bureau is also charged with overseeing disability mandates.

Enforcement Bureau: Enforces the Communications Act, as well as the Commission's rules, orders, and authorizations.

International Bureau: Represents the Commission in satellite and international matters.

Media Bureau: Regulates AM and FM radio and television broadcast stations as well as Multipoint Distribution (i.e., cable and satellite) and Instructional Television Fixed Services.

Wireless Telecommunications: Oversees cellular and PCS phones, pagers, and two-way radios.

Wireline Competition Bureau: For rules and policies concerning telephone companies that provide interstate and intrastate telecommunications services to the public through the use of wire-based transmission facilities (i.e., corded/cordless telephones).

Alternative Employment Programs

The FCC has a Summer Law Intern Program, in which students can acquire firsthand knowledge of the Commission. Applications must be received by November 1.

The FCC also has a Work-Study program for law students. Although they are not compensated, students may obtain course credit.

Co-op opportunities are available for engineering students.

Application Procedures

Direct inquiries to:

Federal Communications Commission
Recruitment and Staffing
1919 M St., NW
Washington, DC 20554
Recruitment/Staffing: (202) 418-0130
Vacancies: (202) 418-0101
Job announcements (fax information line): (202) 418-2830
Toll Free: (888) 225-5322

Federal Deposit Insurance Corporation (FDIC)
www.fdic.gov

Nature of Work: Accounting/auditing, banks/banking, consumer protection, insurance/benefits

Number of Employees: 6,500

Headquarters: Washington, DC

Regional Locations: Atlanta, GA; Boston, MA; Chicago, IL; Dallas, TX; Kansas City, MO; Memphis, TN; New York, NY; San Francisco, CA There are also 90 field offices in the U.S.

Typical Background of New Hires: Accounting, business, economics, finance/banking

Mission

The Federal Deposit Insurance Corporation was established to promote and preserve public confidence in banks and to protect the money supply through provision of insurance coverage for bank deposits and periodic examinations of insured banks that are not members of the Federal Reserve System.

Job Descriptions

Bank Examiner: Performs an audit function at financial institutions to determine their safety and soundness and to ensure compliance with regulations. Assesses the adequacy of internal procedures, management functions, and financial conditions. Bank Examiners conduct on-site audits as a team effort. Travel takes place within an assigned region and can be as high as 90 percent. When not traveling, Bank Examiners work in an FDIC regional or HQ office. There are more than 1,800 examiners located in the FDIC field offices.

Compliance Examiner: Plans and conducts Community Reinvestment Act and fair lending compliance examinations at banking institutions, including assessing the quality of management. More than 380 Compliance Examiners, located in the field offices, conduct more than 1,900 examinations yearly.

Bank Liquidation Specialist: Liquidates accounts such as installment loans, charged-off assets, or small commercial loans. Advertises properties to be sold, checks current status of payments made by debtors, inspects collateral, and meets with debtors concerning repayment schedules.

Major Activities and Divisions

Division of Bank Supervision: Monitors banking practices at federally insured institutions to protect depositors and reduce risks

Division of Liquidation: Approves or disapproves a proposal to reduce or retire the capital of a bank. Terminates the insured status of a bank that engages in unsound practices.

Alternative Employment Programs

FDIC participates in the federal SCEP program as well as a summer internship program. For vacancy information, contact the FDIC personnel office serving the geographic area in which you have interest. Filing deadlines for summer jobs are generally mid-January through mid-March.

Remarks

FDIC has a continuing college recruitment program. Approximately 500–700 graduating college students per year are hired for the Bank Examiner position. Bank Examiners make up approximately 60 percent of FDIC's staff.

Application Procedures

FDIC hires Bank Examiners on a continuous basis. To apply, submit your resume, an SF-171, the OF-612 Optional Application for Federal Employment (try FDIC's interactive version at www2.fdic.gov/of612/), or a printable application package designed for Examiner positions at www.fdic.gov/about/jobs/supervision/apply.pdf.

For all positions, visit jobs@fdic.gov, or you may direct inquiries to the office in which you are interested:

Headquarters (Washington, DC):
Personnel Services Branch
550 17th St., NW
Room PA-1730-5007
Washington, DC 20429
(202) 942-3626
Toll Free: (800) 695-8052

Atlanta Region (AL, FL, GA, NC, SC, VA, WV)
Personnel Services Branch
1201 West Peachtree St., NE
One Atlantic Center, Suite 1800
Atlanta, GA 30309-3415
(404) 817-8906
Toll Free: (800) 765-3342

Boston Region (CT, ME, MA, NH, RI, VT)
Personnel Services Branch
15 Braintree Hill Park, Suite 100
Braintree, MA 02184
(781) 794-5500

Chicago Region (IL, IN, MI, OH, WI)
Personnel Services Branch
500 West Monroe St., Suite 3200
Chicago, IL 60661
(312) 382-6000

Dallas Region (CO, NM, OK, TX)
Personnel Services Branch
1910 Pacific Ave., Suite 400
Dallas, TX 75201
(972) 761-2199

Kansas City Region (IO, KS, MN, MO, NE)
Personnel Services Branch
2345 Grand Blvd., Suite 1200
Kansas City, MO 64108
(816) 234-8000

Memphis Region (AK, KY, LA, MS)
Personnel Services Branch
One Atlantic Center, Suite 1800
1201 West Peachtree St., NE
Atlanta, GA 30309-3415
(404) 817-8906
Toll Free: (800) 765-3342

New York Region (DE, MD, NJ, NY, PA, PR, VI)
Personnel Services Branch
15 Braintree Hill Park, Suite 100
Braintree, MA 02184
(781) 794-5500

San Francisco Region (AL, AZ, CA, GU, HI, ID, MT, NV, OR, UT, WA, WY)
Personnel Services Branch
25 Ecker St., 9th Floor
San Francisco, CA 94105
(415) 808-7932 or 8142

Federal Election Commission (FEC)
www.fec.gov

Nature of Work: Elections, politics
Number of Employees: 350
Headquarters: Washington, DC
Regional Locations: None
Typical Background of New Hires: Accounting, law, political science

Mission
Enforces the Federal Election Campaign Act of 1971, which provides for the public funding of presidential elections, requires public disclosure of the financial

activities of political committees, and regulates contributions made to influence federal elections.

Job Descriptions

Attorney: Analyzes complaints alleging violations of the Campaign Act and researches questions regarding FEC regulations and federal laws.

Auditor: Audits recipients of federal campaign funds and determines whether they comply with laws and regulations.

Public Affairs Specialist: Provides candidates, political committees, special interest groups, and the general public with information on the Campaign Act and FEC regulations.

Major Activities and Divisions

Audit Division: Certifies federal payments to primary candidates, general election nominees, and national nominating conventions.

Disclosure Division: Reveals the sources and expenditures of campaign funds from political committees supporting federal candidates.

Office of the General Counsel: Enforces campaign finance laws through reconciliation and court action.

Alternative Employment Programs

FEC maintains a summer intern program for law students. Interns perform legal research on specific topics and support FEC's litigation, enforcement, and regulatory functions.

Application Procedures

Direct inquiries to:

Federal Election Commission
Office of Personnel
999 E St., NW, Room 236
Washington, DC 20463
Personnel: (202) 694-1080
Information: (202) 694-1100
Toll Free: (800) 424-9530

The Federal Emergency Management Agency (FEMA)
www.fema.gov

Nature of Work: Disaster assistance, emergency preparedness, hazardous materials

Number of Employees: 2,500

Headquarters: Washington, DC

Regional Locations: Atlanta, GA; Boston, MA; Bothell, WA; Chicago, IL; Denton, TX; Denver, CO; Kansas City, MO; New York, NY; Philadelphia, PA; San Francisco, CA

Typical Background of New Hires: Business, engineering, public administration

Mission

FEMA was created to provide a single point of accountability for all federal emergency preparedness, mitigation, and response activities. The agency's goal is to enhance the use of emergency preparedness and response resources in preparing for and responding to the full range of emergencies, including natural, technological, and attack-related emergencies.

Job Descriptions

Emergency Management Specialist: Conducts research, supervises, and manages programs related to man-made, natural, and nuclear crises, including civil disaster response, recovery, and mitigation. Supports state and local governments in national security efforts, and disaster preparedness. Coordinates federal aid for Presidentially declared disasters, and plans civil emergency preparedness for peacetime nuclear or hazardous materials accidents.

Program Specialist: assists in the development of polices and procedures for the coordination and administration of disaster assistance programs for FEMA.

Insurance Examiner: Develops underwriting policy necessary to implement the provisions of various insurance programs related to FEMA.

Major Activities and Divisions

Readiness, Response, and Recovery Directorate: Provides leadership, training, readiness, and exercise support, and technical and financial assistance to strengthen citizens, communities, state, local and tribal governments, and professional emergency workers as they prepare for disasters.

Office of Preparedness: Develops national policy relating to national security emergencies.

The Federal Insurance Administration: Administers the National Flood Insurance Program and works to reduce future flood damage through flood plain management.

The Unites States Fire Administration: Coordinates the federal government's response to the nation's fire problem.

Alternative Employment Programs

FEMA hires approximately 15 students each year to work as volunteer interns in their headquarters office. For more information, call (202) 646-4081.

Remarks

For those interested in temporary intermittent employment, FEMA sponsors a Disaster Assistance Employee program, called CORE (Cadre of Response/Recovery Employees). This is on-call employment to perform temporary disaster work, and travel to disaster areas may be required with very short notice at any time of the year. Copies of the Disaster CORE vacancy announcements are available from:

Federal Emergency Management Agency
Disaster Workforce Services Branch
P.O. Box 129, Bldg. 729
Berryville, VA 22611
Toll Free: (800) 879-6076
(see the FEMA Web site for more information)

Application Procedures

FEMA maintains a list of open vacancy announcements on their Web site. See the specific announcement for information on how to apply. Or, mail applications to:

Federal Emergency Management Agency
Headquarters Personnel Operations Division
500 C St., SW, Room 816
Washington, DC 20472
Human Resources: (202) 646-4040
Job Hotline: (202) 646-3244

To apply for a regional position, mail application to:

FEMA
Resources Management
16825 South Seton Ave.
Emmitsburg, MD 21727

E-mailed applications should be sent to: Hire.Me@fema.gov. Or, fax your resume to the number listed on the vacancy announcement you are interested in.

Federal Labor Relations Authority (FLRA)
www.flra.gov

Nature of Work: Labor/management relations, law/justice

Number of Employees: 200

Headquarters: Washington, DC

Regional Locations: Atlanta, GA; Boston, MA; Chicago, IL; Dallas, TX; Denver, CO; San Francisco, CA; Washington, DC

Typical Background of New Hires: Industrial relations, law, political science, psychology, public administration

---

Mission
The FLRA oversees the Federal Service Labor Management Relations Program. It administers the law that protects the rights of employees of the federal government to organize, bargain collectively, and participate through labor organizations in decisions affecting them.

Job Descriptions
Attorney/Law Clerk: Analyzes assigned cases, including charges of unfair labor practices and representation petitions. Interviews witnesses and takes affidavits. Makes preliminary evaluation as to merits of the case and appropriate course of action. Under direction of the Regional Attorney, prepares for trial, including preparing notice of hearing, pleading, trial briefs, pretrial motions and opposition to pretrial motions of other parties, and other formal documents. Serves as a hearing officer in representation proceedings and conducts representation elections. Makes investigation of challenged ballots and/or objections to elections. This position often requires frequent travel. All applicants must have graduated from an accredited law school. Applicants for Law Clerk do not have to be members of the Bar. Applicants for Attorney must be admitted to a Bar.

Labor Relations Specialist: Conducts investigations into allegations of unfair labor practices raised by employees, agencies, or labor unions. Makes preliminary evaluation of the case's merits, recommends withdrawal of petition or charge when appropriate, and negotiates for informal/formal settlement agreement when litigation is not warranted. Serves as Hearing Officer in representation proceedings and prepares hearing officer's report and makes investigation of challenged ballots or objections to elections or the conduct of elections. Provides advice to labor and management on interpretation and application of the law and participates in programs to make the public more aware of the federal labor relations program. This position often requires frequent travel.

Major Activities and Divisions

The Authority: A quasi-judicial body of three members that resolves disputes over the negotiability of proposals made by federal employee unions in collective bargaining with federal agencies.

The Office of the General Counsel: Investigates alleged unfair labor practices and files and prosecutes unfair labor practice complaints before the Authority.

The Federal Service Impasses Panel: Provides assistance in resolving negotiation impasses between agencies and unions.

Alternative Employment Programs

FLRA hires degree-seeking students at the graduate and undergraduate levels for temporary or permanent positions in professional, administrative, and technical positions. See www.flra.gov/hrd/hrd_how.html for more information.

Remarks

FLRA lists its open vacancy announcements at www.flra.gov/29-jobs.html.

Application Procedures

Follow application instructions on the vacancy announcement in which you are interested. Or, contact:

Federal Labor Relations Authority
Human Resources Division
607 14th St., NW
Washington, DC 20424-0001
(202) 482-6660
Employment Line: (202) 482-6537 or
Toll Free: (877) 303-8945

Federal Maritime Commission (FMC)
www.fmc.gov

Nature of Work: Maritime activities, trade, wages/prices/rates, waterways

Number of Employees: 150

Headquarters: Washington, DC

Regional Locations: Hato Rey, PR; Houston, TX; Los Angeles, CA; Miami, FL; New York, NY; Seattle, WA

Typical Background of New Hires: Economics, law

Mission

Regulates U.S. and foreign-flag ocean carriers calling at American ports and freight forwarders and ocean terminal operators who participate in ocean commerce.

Job Descriptions

Attorney: Approves or denies tariff and license filings, drafts regulations, and participates in formal investigations and administrative hearings.

Economist: Studies competition in various trade areas, future commodity trends, and the economic impact of rates and tariffs.

Investigator: Ensures that common carriers, terminal operators, freight forwarders, and others involved in waterborne commerce comply with shipping statutes.

Transportation Specialist: Analyzes rates, tariffs, and subsidies for the purposes of improving waterborne commerce.

Major Activities and Divisions

The Bureau of Trade Analysis (BTA): Reviews agreements and monitors the concerted activities of common carriers by water under the standards of the Shipping Act of 1984.

The Bureau of Enforcement: Participates as trial counsel in formal adjudicatory proceedings, nonadjudicatory investigations, rulemaking proceedings (when designated by Commission order), and other proceedings initiated by the Commission.

The Bureau of Consumer Complaints and Licensing: Provides information and referrals in response to a wide range of informal inquiries, provides guidance with respect to licensing and bonding, and advises inquiring persons about various means available to resolve complaints

Alternative Employment Programs

FMC maintains a co-op program depending on the availability of funding.

Application Procedures

Direct inquiries to:

Director of Human Resources
Federal Maritime Commission
800 N. Capitol St., NW
Room 924
Washington, DC 20573-0001
(202) 523-5773

The Federal Mediation and Conciliation Service (FMCS)
www.fmcs.gov

Nature of Work: Labor/management relations

Number of Employees: 280

Headquarters: Washington, DC

Regional Locations: More than 70 offices in 36 states

Typical Background of New Hires: Industrial relations

Mission

The primary duty of FMCS is to promote labor-management peace. This responsibility is carried out by providing mediation assistance to labor and management in preventing and settling collective bargaining disputes. FMCS services are offered without charge to both private- and public-sector parties.

Job Descriptions

Federal Mediator: Performs duties in three main areas: dispute mediation; preventive mediation; and education, advocacy, and outreach. Applies knowledge of collective bargaining and labor-management problems in influencing bargainers to adjust their differences. Conducts meetings impartially and leads discussions to promote frank discussion and alleviate tension. Confers with representatives of labor and management, analyzes the issues in dispute, and measures their susceptibility to compromise. Formulates concrete suggestions for alternative solutions and suggests imaginative and practical arrangements to minimize crisis negotiations.

Most Federal Mediators begin at the GS-12 level and must have a minimum of several years' experience in collective bargaining negotiations. Well-qualified applicants who do not meet the experience requirement may be considered for a small number of developmental Mediator positions at a lower entry salary level.

Major Activities and Divisions

FMCS is involved in mediation services that include dispute resolution, consultation and liaison activities arbitration services, and preventive mediation. It also provides grant funds for labor-management committees that explore labor relations topics and offers training programs in such subjects as leadership training, labor history, and the handling of complaints and grievances.

Alternative Employment Programs

FMCS hires volunteer interns for various positions.

Remarks

FMCS is continuously recruiting for mediators. See their Web site for a copy of the recruitment bulletin.

Applicants for the Federal Mediator position must be willing to accept an assignment in any part of the U.S. The position requires the ability to travel and attend meetings on short notice, without regard to clock or calendar.

Application Procedures

FMCS has an online application form for its mediator positions. See www.fmcs.gov/vacancies/Med-Vacancy.PDF. Or, direct inquiries to:

Personnel Office
Recruitment Manager
Federal Mediation and Conciliation Service
2100 K St., NW
Washington, DC 20427
(202) 606-5460
Information: (202) 606-8100

Federal Trade Commission (FTC)
www.ftc.gov

Nature of Work: Consumer protection, law enforcement, marketing

Number of Employees: 1,000

Headquarters: Washington, DC

Regional Locations: Atlanta, GA; Chicago, IL; Cleveland, OH; Dallas, TX; Los Angeles, CA; New York, NY; San Francisco, CA; Seattle, WA

Typical Background of New Hires: Economics, law

Mission

Prevents unfair methods of competition in commerce and administers a wide variety of consumer protection laws.

Job Descriptions

Attorney: Enforces federal consumer protection statutes, such as truth-in-lending and fair credit reporting laws, as well as statutes prohibiting price fixing and anticompetitive corporate mergers. Applications are accepted on a year-round basis from experienced attorneys or in response to specific vacancy announcements.

Economist: Assesses the benefits and costs of potential FTC actions and studies the economic effects of regulations. The FTC recruits annually, usually in January, for Economists positions. Offers for employment for the fall are made by March of each year.

Major Activities and Divisions

Bureau of Consumer Protection: Ensures a free marketplace by suppressing unfair, deceptive, and fraudulent practices. This is accomplished through investigations, litigation, rule making, and consumer and business education.

Bureau of Competition: Regulates business practices that restrain competition.

Bureau of Economics: Advises on the economic merits of antitrust actions and formulates plans to improve competition.

Alternative Employment Programs

The FTC recruits annually for entry-level/law clerk positions. Third-year law students should submit a cover letter, a resume, a writing sample, and law school transcripts in order to be considered for positions available in October of the following calendar year. Positions are filled at the GS-11 and GS-12 levels and require completion of the J.D. degree. Individuals may be placed on fourteen-month appointments as Law Clerks pending admission to the Bar. Attorneys must be licensed and authorized to practice under the laws of a state, a territory, the District of Columbia, or the Commonwealth of Puerto Rico.

The FTC usually has a limited number of paid summer internships available to first- and second-year law school students. Law students may be hired at the GS-7 or GS-9 level, and most of these positions are located in the Bureau of Competition and the Bureau of Consumer Protection.

The FTC participates in the Outstanding Scholar Program, through which it hires Paralegal Specialists on a year-round basis. See www.ftc.gov/ftc/oed/hrmo/jobops.htm for more information.

The FTC has volunteer internships available primarily for students of law or economics. GS-1 through GS-4 student clerical positions are available as well, on an as-needed basis.

Application Procedures

FTC prefers to receive on-line resumes or applications such as those available online at USAJOBS. You may also mail a resume or application to the address below. The FTC does not accept resumes via e-mail or fax.

FTC Headquarters:
Federal Trade Commission
Human Resources Management Office
600 Pennsylvania Ave. NW, Room H-111
Washington, DC 20580
Human Resources: (202) 326-2021
Job Line: (202) 326-2020

Southeast Region
Federal Trade Commission
225 Peachtree St., NE, Suite 1500
Atlanta, GA 30303.
(404) 347-4836

Midwest Region
55 East Monroe St., Suite 1860
Chicago, IL 60603
(312) 353-4423

East Central Region
Federal Trade Commission
1111 Superior Avenue, Suite 200
Cleveland, OH 44114
(216) 522-4210

Southwestern Region
1999 Bryan St., Suite 2150
Dallas, TX 75201
(214) 767-5503

Northeast Region
Federal Trade Commission
1 Bowling Green
New York, NY 10004
(212) 264-1207

Western Region
901 Market St., Suite 570
San Francisco, CA 94103
(415) 995-5220
10877 Wiltshire Blvd., Suite 700
Los Angeles, CA 90024
(213) 209-7890

Northwest Region
2896 Federal Building
915 Second Ave.
Seattle, WA 98174
(206) 442-4656

General Services Administration (GSA)
www.gsa.gov

Nature of Work: Communications, historic preservation, inventory/supply, safety

Number of Employees: 14,000

Headquarters: Washington, DC

Regional Locations: Atlanta, GA; Auburn, WA; Boston, MA; Chicago, IL; Denver, CO; Ft. Worth, TX; Kansas City, KS; New York, NY; Philadelphia, PA; San Francisco, CA

Typical Background of New Hires: Accounting, architecture, business, communications, engineering (electronic, electrical, civil, mechanical)

Mission

GSA was established in 1949 to assume central responsibility throughout the government for procurement and management of property, supplies, and general services. As its role has evolved, GSA now provides its services only when a centralized approach will bring significant advantages.

Job Descriptions

Architect: Develops and coordinates architectural design and engineering functions necessary for new construction and repair or alteration projects. Ensures that all design work conforms to the requirements of GSA policy, regulations, design criteria, industry standings, and building codes.

Budget Analyst: Implements modern, effective, primary accounting systems through the use of off-the-shelf software and cross-servicing arrangements with client agencies. Counsels clients on how to achieve administrative savings.

Contract Specialist: Acquires services and supplies for the federal government. Conducts pre-award and post-award analyses, including industry analysis, market research, acquisition plans, and price and/or cost analysis, and contract administration.

Communications Management Specialist: Works to set in place and maintain a modern, cost-effective telecommunications system in the federal community. Works in cooperation with other agencies to reduce the time required to procure automated data processing equipment for federal agencies.

Communications Specialist: Provides help to other federal agencies in developing, promoting, and distributing information to the public. Cooperates with private-sector sponsors to provide the resources and funding needed to bring new consumer information to the public.

Computer Specialist: Provides technical expertise in the computer field. Advocates the modernization of the government's automated data processing operations to achieve the levels of efficiency present in the private sector. Works with client agencies to apply information technology that will improve operating effectiveness.

Engineer: Depending on area of expertise, may conduct professional engineering duties ranging from design and construction of building repair projects to developing specialty vehicles for agencies that have unique needs.

Federal Auditor: Works in a team environment on performance, financial, and information technology reviews of GSA operations. These positions are often located in The Office of Inspector General (OIG), Office of Audits

Management Analyst: Provides information, assistance, and counseling to business organizations on contracting opportunities with GSA and other federal agencies.

Realty Specialist: Acquires real estate interests across the country. Disposes of real estate at a fair value for the greatest benefit to the government and the public and transfers real estate to other federal agencies for continued federal use. Plans and manages real estate to attain its most efficient use. Requires a knowledge of real estate principles, practices, markets, and values.

Security Officer: Designs and enforces physical security programs to meet the needs of client agencies. Determines the security necessary for each building tenant, including the types of devices, systems, or services that would most effectively mitigate the risks identified. May regularly perform duties as a uniformed law enforcement official.

Major Activities and Divisions

The Public Buildings Service (PBS): Maintains more than 339 million square feet of workspace more than 1,600 communities. Designs and builds federal buildings and centers. Leases space, maintains existing facilities, and releases federal real estate assets. Promotes art in federal buildings, and restores historic structures.

The Federal Supply Service (FSS): Contracts with private companies to supply the products and services used by the federal government around the world.

The Federal Technology Service: Advises agencies on software development and procurement.

Office of Governmentwide Policy (OGP): Works with other federal agencies to develop policies and guidelines for establishing service contracts and for acquiring, managing, and disposing of the real estate, supplies, and equipment that federal employees need to do their jobs.

Alternative Employment Programs

GSA participates extensively in the federal student employment program and the PMI program. PMIs are hired through the Central Office; others are hired directly by the regional office.

Application Procedures

Direct inquiries to:

U.S. General Services Administration
Human Resources
1800 F St., NW
Washington, DC 20405
(202) 501-0370
Information: (202) 708-5082

International Trade Commission (ITC)
www.usitc.gov

Nature of Work: Import/export, international affairs, trade

Number of Employees: 400

Headquarters: Washington, DC

Regional Locations: None

Typical Background of New Hires: Agriculture, business, chemistry, economics, engineering, forestry, law, marketing

Mission

Studies all matters relating to U.S. foreign trade, including anticompetitive practices and their effects on domestic production, employment, consumption, and the global competitiveness of U.S. products.

Job Descriptions

Attorney: Investigates anticompetitive trading practices by foreign countries and executes cease and desist orders, tariff increases, and other ITC sanctions.

International Economist: Studies the effects of unfair trading practices on U.S. firms, assesses the international competitiveness of U.S. industries, and examines how particular trade developments affect domestic industries.

International Trade Analyst: Collects and analyzes data on the manufacture, distribution cost, import, and export of specific products. Data is obtained through contacts with trade associations, visits to factories, seminars, and conferences.

Statistician: Tracks U.S. imports and exports, collects and interprets data on specific U.S. industries, and designs procedures for gathering uniform statistical data.

Major Activities and Divisions

Import Relief for Domestic Industries: Determines whether an item is being imported into the U.S. in sufficient quantities to harm domestic industries.

Unfair Practices in Import Trade: Investigates allegations of unfair competition and, when such practices are found, issues cease and desist or exclusion orders.

Imports Sold at Less than Fair Value: Assists the Commerce Department in determining whether domestic industries are being injured through imports of subsidized merchandise.

Alternative Employment Programs

The ITC hires a small number of undergraduate and graduate students for a 12 week summer term. The most desirable backgrounds include business, economics, computers, international affairs, or law. Some clerical support positions are available for high school students. Submit a resume, OF-612, or SF171 to the USITC address below, attn: Summer Intern Coordinator. Or, fax to: (202) 205-2008.

Remarks

Each year, ITC furnishes dozens of studies on the competitive posture of specific U.S. industries to the President and to congressional committees.

Application Procedures

Employment applications are generally accepted only during open periods of vacancy announcements.

Direct inquiries to:

Office of Personnel
U.S. International Trade Commission
500 E St., SW
Washington, DC 20436
Personnel: (202) 205-2651
Information: (202) 205-2000

Merit Systems Protection Board (MSPB)
www.mspb.gov

Nature of Work: Labor/management relations

Number of Employees: 250

Headquarters: Washington, DC

Regional Locations: Atlanta, GA; Boston, MA; Chicago, IL; Dallas, TX; Denver, CO; New York, NY; Philadelphia, PA; San Francisco, CA; Seattle, WA

Typical Background of New Hires: Law, public administration

Mission

Ensures that federal employees are protected from abuses by agency management and that employment decisions are based on merit. Hears and adjudicates appeals by federal employees concerning adverse personnel actions such as removals, suspensions, and demotions.

Job Descriptions

Attorney: Litigates cases involving prohibited personnel practices, prohibited political activities, and other merit system violations.

Research Analyst: Conducts studies of the federal civil service to determine whether it is free of prohibited personnel practices. Also produces research reports on such topics as recruitment and retention practices, labor relations, and the Senior Executive Service.

Major Activities and Divisions

Office of the Administrative Law Judge: Conducts hearings and issues decisions in cases under the Board's original jurisdiction authority.

Office of Appeals Counsel: Conducts legal research and drafts opinions and orders for the Board.

Office of Policy and Evaluation: Conducts studies of the civil service and other federal merit systems.

Alternative Employment Programs

The Board offers summer internship and coop positions. See the career opportunities section of their Web site. The FRS offers Research Assistant positions to students with backgrounds in econometrics or mathematical statistics. Applications are accepted throughout the year, but interviewing and hiring usually takes place in early spring,

Application Procedures

Human Resources services are now being handled by APHIS. Contact them at 612-370-2088 or log on to www.aphis.usda.gov/mpls. Or, direct inquiries to:

Personnel Division
Merit Systems Protection Board
1120 Vermont Ave., NW
Washington, DC 20419
(202) 653-5916
Toll Free: (800) 209-8960
Vacancies: (202) 254-8013
TDD: (202) 653-8896

Federal Reserve System (FRS)
www.federalreserve.gov

Nature of Work: Banking

Number of Employees: 1,500

Headquarters: Washington, DC

Regional Locations: Federal Reserve Banks are located in Atlanta, GA; Boston, MA; Chicago, IL; Cleveland, OH; Dallas, TX; Kansas City, MO; Minneapolis, MN; New York, NY; Philadelphia, PA; Richmond, VA; San Francisco, CA; and St. Louis, MO. Branch banks are located in 25 other cities.

Typical Background of New Hires: Business, computer science, economics, finance/banking, law

Mission

Formulates and oversees policies affecting consumer credit and monetary issues. Also regulates banks, maintaining a stable industry.

Job Descriptions

Attorney: Counsels the Federal Reserve Board on matters relating to commercial, corporate, antitrust, administrative, and banking laws.

Bank Examiner: Audits Federal Reserve and branch banks ensuring that operations comply with established standards.

Information Technology Professional: Operates mainframe database systems, artificial intelligence systems, applications generators, local area networks, and distributed processing equipment.

Economist: Analyzes domestic financial markets and studies the competitive implications of bank mergers.

Financial Analyst: Monitors the health of state member banks and bank holding companies by reviewing financial data.

Major Activities and Divisions

The Board of Governors: Determines general monetary, credit, and operating policies for the Federal Reserve System.

Legal Division: Counsels the Board of Governors on matters such as bank mergers, bank holding companies, interest payments by member banks, reserve requirements, and foreign banking operations.

Division of Consumer and Community Affairs: Enforces consumer credit laws such as the Truth in Lending, Equal Credit Opportunity, and Electronic Fund Transfer Acts.

Division of Research and Statistics: Monitors and analyzes the impact of monetary policy on domestic financial markets.

Division of Monetary Affairs: Oversees open market operations and analyzes developments in money, credit, and Treasury markets.

Division of International Finance: Analyzes economic and financial developments in industrialized and developing countries.

Division of Banking Supervision and Regulations: Regulates the structure and conduct of the banking industry and approves bank mergers.

Division of Federal Reserve Bank Operations: Reviews the budgets of Federal Reserve Banks and oversees their financial transactions.

Alternative Employment Programs

The Board offers summer internship and co-op positions. The Board also hires Research Assistants who work in the Board's research divisions in Washington, DC. Applicants generally have training in econometrics or mathematical statistics. The Board accepts applications throughout the year, but it is best to submit your application by January 31 of the year in which you wish to start work.

Remarks

As audits are conducted on-site, Bank Examiners travel virtually 100 percent of the time. Frequent weekend trips home are paid for by the Federal Reserve. The Federal Reserve System has a separate grade and salary structure.

Application Procedures

Direct inquiries to:

Board of Governors of the Federal Reserve System
Division of Personnel
20th St. and Constitution Ave. NW
Washington, DC 20551
(202) 452-3880/3000
24-Hour Job Vacancy Line: (800) 448-4894

The National Aeronautics and Space Administration (NASA)
www.nasa.gov

Nature of Work: Aviation/space programs, defense and national security, energy, scientific research, transportation

Number of Employees: 18,850

Headquarters: Washington, DC

Locations: Cleveland, OH; Greenbelt, MD; Hampton, VA; Houston, TX; Huntsville, AL; Kennedy Space Center, FL; Las Cruces, NM; Moffett Field, CA; New Orleans, LA; New York, NY; Stennis Space Center, MS; Wallops Island, VA

Typical Background of New Hires: Computer science, engineering, mathematics, physical sciences, physics, space sciences

Mission

NASA was created in 1958 to pursue the peaceful exploration of the solar system. Until that time, space research was conducted by the military, which focused its work on ballistic missiles. NASA's focus is to research the civilian applications of space, such as communication and weather satellites, manned transportation, and astrophysics, but it is also involved in strategic defense systems.

Job Descriptions

Astronaut: NASA normally has about 130 to140 active members of the Astronaut Corps. About half are federal civil servants. The remaining are uniformed services members detailed to NASA. Members of the Astronaut Corps can be astronaut pilots, mission specialists, or payload specialists.

Engineer (Aerospace, Electrical, Mechanical), Computer Scientist, Mathematician, Scientist: Most engineers, scientists, and mathematicians engage in the research, development, design, testing, and evaluation of various projects relating to their areas of expertise. These Aerospace Technologist (AST) positions can be divided into more than seventy areas of expertise, including:

Applications Sciences: Involves the design and applications of remote sensing systems.

Data Systems: Involves the recording and mathematical computation of aerospace data and the numeric simulation of aerospace problems.

Facilities and Operations: Involves all phases of the aerospace research and development facilities and equipment including design, operation, and management.

Flight Systems: Works with aerospace flight systems.

Fluid and Flight Mechanics: Involves aerospace vehicle flight dynamics, including environmental interaction research.

Life Sciences and Systems: Examines the biological impact of the space environment and studies the nature and origin of life.

Materials and Structures: Works with aerospace flight vehicle structures and the evaluation of their behavior.

Measurement and Instrumentation Systems: Works with tracking systems, telemetry, and radio, optical, and mechanical systems to measure aerospace physical phenomena.

Propulsion Systems: Works with aerospace propulsion systems for the conversion of energy into power for transportation.

Space Science: Studies the atmospheres of earth and space, celestial mechanics, and astrophysics.

Technical Management: Involves a management perspective in the aerospace research and development programs.

Medical Doctor: NASA has a limited number of research and clinical positions for medical doctors. Most positions are located at the Johnson Space Center and involve research or support of programs associated with manned space flight.

Pilot: Conducts research, flight tests, training, safety, maintenance oversight, and operational airlift support. Most positions are located at either Dryden Flight Research Center at Edwards AFB or at Johnson Space Center in Houston, Texas. NASA pilots operate a variety of fixed- and rotary-wing aircraft in support of NASA research and development programs.

Major Activities and Divisions

Aeronautics and Space Technology: Develops technological advances in the areas of aeronautics and space for scientific, commercial, and military use.

Space Science and Applications: Conducts research on the origin and evolution of the universe and applies space systems and techniques to solve everyday problems on earth.

Space Flight: Works to improve the efficiency of all phases of the space shuttle system and to define the shuttle's role in such things as launching and rescuing communications satellites.

Space Tracking and Data Systems: Provides tracking, command, telemetry, and data acquisition support for earth-orbital science and other scientific missions.

Alternative Employment Programs

NASA participates in a number of hiring programs, including co-op, STEP, the PMI program, and many fellowship and grant programs. It also hosts the NASA Contracting Intern Program (NCIP) and the Summer High School Apprenticeship Research Program (SHARP). For more information, go to www.nasa.gov and click on job information, then student programs.

Remarks

NASA has an active campus recruitment program. Contact your college placement office for details. All Centers offer tuition reimbursement programs and many are located on campus-like settings with special amenities on premises.

Application Procedures

Address inquiries directly to the NASA Center in which you are interested. Many of the NASA centers have their own student employment programs, which are explained on their Web sites. To find the Web sites for the different NASA Centers, go to www.nasa.gov and click on the organizations index, or go directly to the Web sites listed below:

Ames Research Center
Personnel Office
Moffett Field, CA 94035
(650) 604-8000
www.arc.nasa.gov

(Aeronautical research laboratory: Focuses on astrobiology, aerodynamics, computational fluid dynamics, powered-lift and rotor craft technology, flight simulation, human factors, and airborne science. All Ames jobs are listed on the IFM Resume Management System—NASA Stars. The online Resume Builder is at: http://resume.nasa.gov.)

Dryden Flight Research Facility
Personnel Office
P.O. Box 273
Edwards, CA 93523-0273
(661) 276-3311
www.dfrc.nasa.gov

(NASA's primary installation for flight research.)

Glenn Research Center
Personnel Office
21000 Brookpark Rd.
Cleveland, OH 44135
(216) 433-4000
www.grc.nasa.gov

(Directs the U.S. aerospace propulsion and power programs. Devoted to the development of more efficient engine systems and is engaged in energy conservation research for communications satellites. Houses a supersonic propulsion wind tunnel.)

Goddard Space Flight Center
Personnel Office
Greenbelt, MD 20771
(301) 286-7918
Job Hotline: (301) 286-5326
www.gsfc.nasa.gov

(Conducts remotely controlled, earth-orbiting, and sounding rocket missions. Also works on the development and monitoring of a worldwide tracking and communications network. Acquires data relating to weather and climate research, earth resources, astronomy, and communications. GSFC includes several other properties, most significantly the Wallops Flight Facility near Chincoteague, Virginia.)

John F. Kennedy Space Center
Personnel Office
Kennedy Space Center, FL 32899
(407) 867-7110
www.ksc.nasa.gov

(The major launch facility for the Space Shuttle and unmanned space missions. Plans and directs preflight preparation of space vehicles and their cargoes.)

Langley Research Center
Personnel Office
Hampton, VA 23681
(757) 864-2558
www.larc.nasa.gov

(An extensive aeronautical research facility with more than 50 wind tunnels. Known for its airfoil research, the creation of spin avoidance and autocontrol techniques in high-performance military fighters, and the development of integrated software systems for aerospace engineering and design.)

Lyndon B. Johnson Space Center
Personnel Office
Houston, TX 77085
(281) 483-0123
www.jsc.nasa.gov

Marshall Space Flight Center

Personnel Office

Huntsville, AL 35812

(256) 544-2121

www.msfc.nasa.gov

(The primary center for the design and development of the space transportation system, such as the Lunar Roving Vehicle and Skylab. It is also the principal center for rocket propulsion systems.)

John C. Stennis Space Center
Personnel Office
Stennis Space Center, MS 39529-6000
(228) 688-2336
www.ssc.nasa.gov

(Supports the testing of the Space Shuttle's main engine and main orbiter propulsion systems.)

Headquarters Address
National Aeronautics and Space Administration
Personnel Division, Room 3J11
2 Independence Square
300 E St. SW
Washington, DC 20546
(202) 358-0100 (1543)
www.hq.nasa.gov

National Archives and Records Administration (NARA)
www.nara.gov

Nature of Work: Historic preservation, libraries, scholarly research

Number of Employees: 3,000

Headquarters: Washington, DC

Regional Locations: Anchorage, AK; Boston, MA; Chicago, IL; College Park, MD; Dayton, OH (RC only); Denver, CO; East Point, GA; Ft. Worth, TX; Kansas City, MO; Laguna Niguel, CA; New York, NY; Philadelphia, PA; St. Louis, MO (2 locations, RC only); San Francisco, CA; Seattle, WA; Suitland, MD

Typical Background of New Hires: Business, English, history, journalism

---

Mission

The National Archives and Records Administration is responsible for establishing procedures for managing the records of the U.S. government. The National Archives assists federal agencies in documenting their activities, administering their records management programs, and retiring their noncurrent records to Federal Records Centers. The agency also accessions, arranges, preserves, and makes available to the public the historically valuable records of the government and manages the Presidential Libraries System.

Job Descriptions

Archives Specialist: Appraises and arranges public records and historic documents. Provides reference service from record and manuscript depositories. Prepares inventories and guides to facilitate use of records. Conducts scholarly research using archival principles and techniques. Requires a comprehensive knowledge of the history of the U.S. and the institutions and organizations of the federal government. The majority of archivists work in the Office of National Archives or in the archives field branches.

Writer-Editor: Applies subject-matter knowledge and writing and editing skills to review written material and/or present pertinent facts in written form. Analyzes data for subject matter content and determines the type of presentation best suited to the audience being addressed. The majority of Writer-Editors work in the Office of Federal Register; some also work in the Office of Public Programs.

Major Activities and Divisions

Office of Federal Register: Prepares and publishes a variety of public documents, including the Federal Register, United States Statutes at Large, the Code of Federal Regulations, and the United States Government Manual.

Office of Records Services: Manages and categorizes records such as electronic records, military records, etc.

National Historical Publications and Records Commission (NHPRC): Cooperates with nonfederal agencies in gathering and publishing papers important to the study of American history.

Office of Presidential Libraries: Preserves and makes available for use the Presidential records and personal papers that document the actions of a particular President's administration.

Alternative Employment Programs

Many volunteer internships and other opportunities are available at NARA. Internships can be arranged any time during the year, and there are no application deadlines. Students interested in internships in the Washington, DC, area should contact: Student Intern Program, NARA, 8601 Adelphi Rd., Room 1200, College Park, MD 20740-6001. Call (301) 713-7390 or e-mail StudentInternProgram@nara.gov.

Remarks

Several grants, fellowships and educational programs exist at the NHPRC. See NARA's Web site for updated information.

Application Procedures

External hiring is coordinated through the personnel offices in St. Louis, Missouri, and in College Park, Maryland.

Direct inquiries to:

National Archives and Records Administration
Human Resources Operations Branch (NHHO)
9700 Page Blvd., Room 2002
St. Louis, MO 63132
Toll Free: (800) 827-4898

Washington area address:

National Archives and Records Administration
Human Resources Services Division (NHH)
8601 Adelphi Rd., Room 1200
College Park, MD 20740-6001
(301) 837-3710
Information: (301) 713-6800

National Credit Union Administration (NCUA)
www.ncua.gov

Nature of Work: Accounting/auditing, insurance/benefits

Number of Employees: 1,000

Headquarters: Alexandria, VA

Regional Locations: Albany, NY; Alexandria, VA; Atlanta, GA; Austin, TX; Chicago, IL; San Francisco, CA

Typical Background of New Hires: Accounting

Mission

The National Credit Union Administration is responsible for chartering, insuring, supervising, and examining federal credit unions.

Job Descriptions

Financial Institution Examiner: Maintains contact with the 20 to 30 credit unions in their assigned district, which may be approximately 200 square miles. Conducts on-site audits which, depending on the size of the credit union, may take from one day to three weeks. Determines solvency and compliance with regulations and assists credit unions in management and operations. Occasionally works in a team setting with other examiners at the audit site, but usually works independently. Advises groups interested in chartering federal credit unions.

On days when no on-site work is scheduled, examiners work out of their home. Examiners make their own audit and travel schedules. Requires self-motivation and independence.

Major Activities and Divisions

Office of Examination and Insurance (E&I): Provides national guidance for NCUA's efforts to assure the safety and soundness of federally insured credit unions.

Office of Credit Union Development: Fosters business development of credit unions by providing the guidance and education needed for the delivery of financial services. Facilitates the expansion of credit union services.

Alternative Employment Programs

NCUA has a small co-op program and offers summer clerical positions.

Remarks

It may be necessary for an examiner to travel 30 percent or more, including extensive overnight travel. The amount of travel depends on the geographic size and the dispersal of credit unions within the examiner's district.

Application Procedures

All hiring is coordinated through the headquarters office in Washington, DC. Applicants must apply in response to a specific job vacancy announcement (job postings can be found on the agency Web site). Contact the Office of Human Resources at ohrmail@ncua.gov for more information on employment at NCUA. Or, direct inquiries to:

National Credit Union Administration
Office of Human Resources
1775 Duke St.
Alexandria, VA 22314-3428
(703) 518-6510
Information: (202) 518-6300
Fax: (703) 518-6539

**National Endowment for the Arts
and the National Endowment for the Humanities
http://arts.endow.gov
www.neh.fed.us**

Nature of Work: Arts, education, funding, historic preservation

Number of Employees: 200 (each agency)

Headquarters: Washington, DC

Regional Locations: None

Typical Background of New Hires: Archaeology, arts, education, English, history, languages, religion, social sciences

Mission

The Endowment for the Arts fosters and sustains artistic excellence in America and creates a climate in which the arts may be experienced and enjoyed by the public.

The Endowment for the Humanities makes grants to individuals, groups, or institutions (schools, colleges, museums, public television stations, libraries, public agencies, and nonprofit groups) to increase understanding and appreciation of the humanities. According to the agency's authorizing legislation, the term "humanities" includes the study of art theory/history, language, linguistics, literature, history, jurisprudence, philosophy, archaeology, comparative religion, ethics, and some social sciences.

Job Descriptions

Humanities Administrator: Administers programs related to the grant-making divisions and offices of the Endowment for the Humanities. Typically requires significant experience or education in a particular humanities program area.

Program Specialist: Conducts grants research and analyzes educational proposals. Produces write-ups for the review of triannual arts council meeting. Ensures that incoming grants applications are correct and complete. Requires a bachelor's degree or equivalent experience in a particular arts or humanities program area.

Major Activities and Divisions

The Endowment for the Arts is divided into the following divisions: Dance/Design/ Media Arts/Museums/Visual Arts; AIE/Music/Opera/Presenting/Multidisciplinary;

and Folk and Traditional/Literature/Theater/Musical Theater/Planning and Stabilization.

The Endowment for the Humanities is divided into four divisions: Preservation and Access, Research, Education, and Public Programs; and three offices: Challenge Grants, Federal-State Partnership, and Enterprise.

Alternative Employment Programs

Internships are occasionally available.

Application Procedures

Direct inquiries to:

E-mail: jobapplications@arts.endow.gov, or mail to:

National Endowment for the Arts
1100 Pennsylvania Ave. NW, Room 627
Washington, DC 20506
(202) 682-5405
Job Hotline: (202) 682-5799
Fax: (202) 682-5666
E-mail: humanresources@neh.gov

National Endowment for the Humanities
1100 Pennsylvania Ave., NW, Room 418
Washington, DC 20506
(202) 606-8415 or 8281

The National Labor Relations Board (NLRB)
www.nlrb.gov

Nature of Work: Business, labor/management relations, law/justice

Number of Employees: 2,050

Headquarters: Washington, DC

Regional Locations: Albany, NY; Albuquerque, NM; Anchorage, AK; Atlanta, GA; Baltimore, MD; Birmingham, AL; Boston, MA; Brooklyn, NY; Buffalo, NY; Chicago, IL; Cincinnati, OH; Cleveland, OH; Denver, CO; Des Moines, IA; Detroit, MI; El Paso, TX; Ft. Worth, TX; San Juan, PR; Grand Rapids, MI; Hartford, CT; Honolulu, HI; Houston, TX; Indianapolis, IN; Jacksonville, FL; Las Vegas, NV; Los Angeles, CA (2); Memphis, TN; Miami, FL; Milwaukee, WI; Minneapolis, MN; Nashville, TN; Newark, NJ; New Orleans, LA; New York, NY; Oakland, CA; Overland Park, KS; Peoria, IL; Philadelphia, PA; Phoenix, AZ; Pittsburgh, PA; Portland, OR; St. Louis, MO; San Antonio, TX; San Diego, CA; San Francisco, CA; Seattle, WA; Tampa, FL; Tulsa, OK; Washington, DC; Winston-Salem, NC

Typical Background of New Hires: Accounting, business, economics, industrial relations, law, political science

Mission

The NLRB administers the law that governs relations between labor unions and employers whose operations affect interstate commerce. The NLRB determines the democratic choice by employees, through secret ballot elections, as to whether or not they wish to be represented by a union. The agency also acts to prevent unfair labor practices by either employers or unions.

Job Descriptions

Attorney (Board Member Offices, Washington): Reads and becomes familiar with the record and formal documents of the case assigned. Ascertains and discusses the issues and researches the law. Prepares legal memoranda for the Board's consideration and, after the case has been decided, prepares a draft of the final decision. Functions in much the same way as a law clerk does for a judge. Occasional travel.

Attorney (Office of the General Counsel, Washington): Analyzes, researches, and discusses issues pertaining to assigned cases. Drafts memoranda, briefs, and other documents. May be assigned to the Division of Advice, the Office of

Appeals, the Division of Enforcement Litigation, or the Legal Research and Policy Planning Branch. Occasional travel.

Field Attorney (Regional Offices): Begins by investigating cases and progresses into other functions. Drafts complaints, prepares cases for trial, and tries cases before Administrative Law Judges. In appropriate cases, field attorneys may seek injunctive relief in the federal district courts. Other duties may include serving as Hearing Officer in a contested representation election case, preparing drafts of decisions for the Regional Director, assisting in conducting representation elections, and advising members of the public. Frequent travel within the region.

Field Examiner: Conducts investigations into assigned cases. Gathers facts by meeting with employees and their foremen, shop stewards, business agents, personnel officers, and attorneys representing both labor and management. Recommends appropriate action on each case, including possible remedies or dismissal of the case. Arranges and conducts elections among groups of employees ranging in size from two to several thousand to determine whether or not they wish to be represented by a labor organization. Serves as a Hearing Officer in disputed representation cases.

Major Activities and Divisions

The NLRB is organized into two major parts: the five-member Board itself, which has its own staff, and the Office of the General Counsel. Agency authority is divided by law. The Board acts primarily as a quasi-judicial body in deciding cases upon formal records. The General Counsel is responsible for the investigation and processing of cases including their prosecution in the courts. The General Counsel also has general supervision over the agency's field offices.

Alternative Employment Programs

NLRB participates in the STEP and SCEP (co-op) student hiring programs. The NLRB also participates in the Student Volunteer Service Program that provides unpaid training to students in high school and college related to the student's academic program. For more information, call (202) 273-3980.

The NLRB sponsors a few law student internship positions through the Peggy Browning Fund. The Fund's mission is to provide law students with diverse, challenging work and educational experiences in the area of workers' rights. A salary stipend is paid by the Fund, not the NLRB. Contact the Fund's Web site by e-mail at www.peggybrowningfund.org, by mail at 1818 Market St., Suite 2300, Philadelphia, PA 19103, or by calling (215) 665-6815.

Remarks

The NLRB has more than 750 attorneys. About one third of them are assigned to the Washington office. Sixteen hundred of the 2,400 total employees of the NLRB are located in the regional, subregional, and resident offices listed above. Location preferences of prospective applicants are taken into account, and new hires may be given a choice of several office locations in which to begin employment.

Application Procedures

Direct inquiries to:

Personnel Branch
National Labor Relations Board
1099 14th St. NW
Washington, DC 20570-0001
(202) 273-3900
Information: (202) 273-1000

National Science Foundation (NSF)
www.nsf.gov

Nature of Work: Education, funding, scientific research

Number of Employees: 1,300

Headquarters: Arlington, VA

Regional Locations: None

Typical Background of New Hires: Accounting, business, computer science, economics, engineering, liberal arts, mathematics, physical sciences, social sciences

Mission

The Foundation is committed to expanding the nation's supply of scientists, engineers, and science educators. It does this by supporting a variety of programs and activities for education in science, mathematics, and engineering. NSF awards grants and contracts to academic research institutions, private research firms, industrial labs, and major research facilities. Experienced researchers and educators from around the country volunteer their time to help Foundation staff assess the merits of some 30,000 proposals a year.

Job Descriptions

Grants and Contracts Specialist: Examines grants and contracts to be awarded to scientific and educational institutions for accuracy, clarity, and compliance with NSF policy and federal regulations.

Public Affairs Specialist: Communicates the mission and accomplishments of NSF to the public. The format of this communication can be written or visual— portable exhibits, brochures, films, or videos.

Science Assistant: Provides scientific assistance in all phases of the proposal review process. Participates in volunteer reviewer selection by reading professional journals in the scientific field and doing library research to expand the volunteer reviewer base. Identifies reviewer conflicts of interests and makes recommendations regarding the proposal review process.

This position can be established for graduate-level students in any science area. NFS divisions typically cover engineering, biological and environmental sciences, social sciences and economics, behavioral and neural sciences, computer science, geosciences, math, physical sciences, and science/engineering education.

Program Director (Associate Program Director): Provides technical and scientific oversight to insure integrity and consistency in the proposal process. Administers review and award recommendations. Areas of expertise sought for these positions include geography, oceanography, astronomy, mathematics, engineering, computer science, and many others. These positions are typically filled on a one- or two-year visiting scientist, temporary, or intergovernmental personnel act (IPA) basis. Individuals eligible for these assignments include employees of state, local, or Indian tribal government, or institutions of higher education.

Major Activities and Divisions

The National Science Foundation is divided into several directorates and programs, which include: *Directorate for Biological Sciences; Directorate for Geosciences; Directorate for Engineering; Directorate for Social, Behavioral and*

Economic Sciences; Directorate for Computer and Information Sciences and Engineering; Directorate for Education and Human Resources; Environmental and Education Programs; Mathematical and Physical Sciences Directorate; International Programs; and *Office of Polar Programs.* See the NSF Web site for details on each area.

Alternative Employment Programs

NSF participates in a summer student hiring program, as well as the STEP and SCEP student employment programs. Typically, students work part-time while attending school and are eligible for full-time employment upon graduation. Student employment positions include Accountant, Grants Specialist, and Contracts Specialist.

NSF also hires students at the graduate levels for internship positions as Science Assistants. Contact the Internship Director for more information.

Other student programs: NSF participates in the PMI program (typical positions: Science Assistant, Public Affairs Specialist), an employment program for clerical positions, and an extensive summer program, in which college students are hired for office clerical positions.

Remarks

NSF does not conduct research itself and thus has no in-house laboratories or similar facilities.

Application Procedures

Direct inquiries to:

National Science Foundation
Division of Human Resource Management
4201 Wilson Blvd., Suite 315
Arlington, VA 22230
(703) 292-8180
Toll Free: (800) 628-1487 (Job Hotline)
Information: (703) 292-5111

National Transportation Safety Board (NTSB)
www.ntsb.gov

Nature of Work: Aviation/space programs, maritime activities, railroads, safety, transportation

Number of Employees: 420

Headquarters: Washington, DC

Regional Locations: Anchorage, AK; Atlanta, GA; Arlington, TX; Denver, CO; Gardena, CA; Parsippany, NJ; Seattle, WA; W. Chicago, IL

Typical Background of New Hires: Engineering, physical sciences, physics

Mission

Investigates the causes of accidents involving aircraft, railroads, highways, ships, and pipelines.

Job Descriptions

Metallurgist: Conducts postaccident analyses of wreckage ranging from aircraft parts to railroad tracks to determine whether failures resulted from inadequate design strength, excessive loading, or corrosion.

Transportation Safety Specialist: Performs on-site accident analyses. Assignments vary by expertise and can include specialists in air traffic control, aircraft operations, aircraft maintenance, locomotives and signals, and human factors.

Transportation Research Analyst: Writes reports and conducts safety studies and special statistical analyses relating to safety issues in all transportation modes, and develops safety recommendations for transportation agencies.

Major Activities and Divisions

Aviation: Investigates accidents involving all air carriers and general aviation accidents with fatalities. Recommends safety improvements to the Federal Aviation Administration in such areas as pilot training, aircraft maintenance and design, air traffic control procedures, and postaccident survival.

Railroad: Investigates all fatal rail accidents or any rail incident in which damage exceeds $150,000. Recommends safety improvements to such agencies as the Federal Railroad Administration, the Urban Mass Transportation Administration, Amtrak, state regulatory agencies, rapid transit agencies, trade associations, and common carriers.

Marine: Investigates all major accidents occurring on U.S. navigable waters, as well as major marine accidents in international waters involving U.S. merchant ships and public and nonpublic vessels. Makes safety recommendations to agencies such as the Coast Guard, the U.S. Army Corps of Engineers, shipping firms, and maritime trade organizations.

Highway: Investigates highway accidents with broad safety implications. These include bridge collapses, fatal accidents involving public transportation vehicles, and fatal collisions at grade crossings. Safety recommendations are directed to the U.S. Department of Transportation, state and local agencies, trade associations, and manufacturers.

Pipeline and Hazardous Materials: Investigates pipeline accidents and accidents resulting in the release of hazardous materials. NTSB concentrates on the effects of any materials released upon the public or emergency response teams, the handling of the emergency by local authorities, and the adequacy of federal standards for the transport of hazardous materials.

Alternative Employment Programs

None

Remarks

NTSB consists of five board members appointed by the President with the advice and consent of the Senate. Each member serves a five-year term.

Application Procedures

Direct inquiries to:

National Transportation Safety Board
Human Resources Division
490 L'Enfant Plaza East, SW
Washington, DC 20594
Vacancies: (202) 314-6239
Main Number: (202) 314-6000
Toll Free: (800) 573-0937 (Job Hotline)

Nuclear Regulatory Commission (NRC)
www.nrc.gov

Nature of Work: Environmental protection, hazardous materials, nuclear energy/issues

Number of Employees: 3,000

Headquarters: Rockville, MD

Regional Locations: Arlington, TX; Atlanta, GA; Chattanooga, TN; King of Prussia, PA; Las Vegas, NV; Lisle, IL

Typical Background of New Hires: Chemistry, engineering (electrical, environmental, materials, mechanical, nuclear), physical sciences (hydrology), physics (geophysics, health physics)

Mission

The NRC protects the public health and the environment in the civilian uses of nuclear materials in the United States. This is accomplished through the licensing of nuclear facilities and the possession, use, and disposal of nuclear materials; the development and implementation of requirements governing licensed activities; and inspection and enforcement activities to assure compliance with these requirements.

Job Descriptions

Effluents Radiation Specialist: Assesses the effectiveness of the various programs of power and research reactors and fuel facilities that deal with the management and control of radioactive waste. Assigned program review responsibility for a number of facilities and visits each facility several times a year. Interacts with state officials who have overview responsibilities with regard to the radiological programs of NRC facilities.

Emergency Preparedness Specialist: Assesses the quality and effectiveness of the Emergency Response programs of the facilities that use nuclear materials. Inspects the overall Emergency Response program and evaluates performance in drills. Verifies the operational readiness of the on-site facilities and personnel designated for emergency response.

Health Physicist: Develops policy, procedures, and criteria for regulating the use of radioactive materials. Evaluates environmental impact of facilities, sites, and activities involving uranium, thorium, and special nuclear materials. Performs radiological and environmental assessments using computer codes and technology. Headquarters locations only.

Material Health Physicist: Performs radiological and environmental protection inspections and investigations at various types of licensees' facilities that possess, use, and process by-product, source, and special nuclear materials. Verifies public health and safety and determines the status of compliance with NRC license conditions and federal regulations. Regulates activities involving nuclear medicine, isotope manufacturing, industrial uses of radioactive materials, research, and academic applications.

Radiation Specialist: Conducts specialized radiological inspections, including emergency preparedness, at all types of facilities licensed by the NRC. Inspections are conducted to assure protection of plant and facility workers and the public against any possibility of hazardous exposure to nuclear radiation.

Reactor Engineer: Develops regulations and provides guidance to ensure that licensed operators have the skills necessary to operate nuclear power plants safely. Formulates examiner training programs and reviews and evaluates the operator licensing examination area.

Reactor Inspector: Serves as a member of the technical staff in the regional offices with responsibility for the inspection of reactors and related investigations. Plans and conducts inspections in both construction and operation, including licensee quality assurance programs. Represents the NRC to the licensee and to state and local officials.

Regional Health Physicist: Conducts on-site inspections of facilities that are regulated and licensed by the NRC to possess and use radioactive materials. Documents inspections and findings, responds to emergencies, reviews license applications for the use of radioactive materials, and provides assessments of licensees' program effectiveness for NRC management.

Regional Radiation Specialist: Assesses the effectiveness of radiation protection programs of power and research reactors and fuel facilities by conducting on-site evaluation of the radiation safety program. Discusses radiation protection programs with all levels of the plant staff, evaluates the adequacy of procedures and policies, and directly observes personnel performance. Visits several power reactors two to four times a year. Develops periodic summary evaluation reports for the NRC management to use in characterizing the effectiveness of the licensee's program.

Resident Inspector: Serves on-site at nuclear power plants. Plans and conducts inspections at assigned plants during construction, preoperational testing, start-up, and operation to assure that plants are built and operated in accordance with NRC requirements.

Major Activities and Divisions

The Office of Nuclear Reactor Regulation: Evaluates all license applications, issues licenses, and regulates nuclear facilities.

The Office of Nuclear Materials Safety and Safeguards: Ensures public health and safety and protects the national security and environmental values in the licensing and regulation of nuclear materials.

The Office of Nuclear Regulatory Research: Conducts research relating to reactor safety and environmental protection.

Alternative Employment Programs

Nuclear Safety Intern Program: NRC hires recent graduates with bachelor's, master's, or doctoral degrees in health physics, earth sciences, or engineering to participate in on-the-job training, formal classroom training, and rotational assignments.

Honor Law Graduate Program: NRC hires graduating law students or judicial law clerks with strong academic records to work in the Office of the General Council. The two-year program is a prelude to a continuing permanent career as an attorney in OGC. Call (301) 415-1740 for information.

The NRC also maintains a co-op program and a summer intern program. For information, fax questions to (301) 415-3818 or mail inquiries to Mail Stop 0-3E17A at the address below.

Remarks

None

Application Procedures

The U.S. Nuclear Regulatory Commission
Office of Human Resources
Mail Stop T3-D29
Washington, DC 20555
(301) 415-1534 or 7400
Toll Free: (800) 368-5642
(Street Address: 11555 and 11545 Rockville Pike, Rockville, MD)

Region I
475 Allendale Rd.
King of Prussia, PA 19406
(610) 337-5000

Region II
Sam Nunn Atlanta Federal Center, 23
T85
61 Forsyth St. SW
Atlanta, GA 30303-8931
(404) 562-4400
Toll Free: (800) 577-8510

Region III
801 Warrenville Road
Lisle, Illinois 60532-4351
(630) 829-9500
Toll Free: (800) 522-3025

Region IV
Texas Health Resources Tower
611 Ryan Plaza, Suite 400
Arlington, TX 76011-8064
(817) 860-8100
Toll Free: (800) 952-9677

U.S. Nuclear Regulatory Commission
Technical Training Center
Osborne Office Center
5746 Marlin Road, Suite 200
Chattanooga, TN 37411-5677
(423) 855-6500

U.S. Nuclear Regulatory Commission
On-site Representatives Office
1551 Hillshire Dr., Suite A
Las Vegas, NV 89134
(702) 794-5047

Office of Personnel Management (OPM)
www.opm.gov

Nature of Work: Employment

Number of Employees: 3,150

Headquarters: Washington, DC

Regional Locations: Atlanta, GA; Aurora, CO; Boston, MA; Boyers, PA; Charlottesville, VA; Chicago, IL; Dallas, TX; Dayton, OH; Denver, CO; Detroit, MI; Honolulu, HI; Huntsville, AL; Kansas City, MO; Lancaster, PA; Macon, GA; Norfolk, VA; Philadelphia, PA; Raleigh, NC; San Antonio, TX; San Francisco, CA; San Juan, PR; Seattle, WA; Twin Cities, MN

Typical Background of New Hires: Business, education, labor relations, psychology, social sciences

Mission

OPM's role is to ensure that the federal government provides an array of human resources management services to applicants and employees. Through a range of programs designed to develop and encourage the effectiveness of the government employee, OPM supports government program managers in their human resources management responsibilities and provides benefits to retired employees.

Job Descriptions

Employee Development Specialist: Plans and administers programs designed to train and develop employees. Provides guidance to management concerning employee training and its relationship to management problems. Applies a knowledge of the techniques of education and training.

Insurance Benefits Claims Examiner: Determines the validity of insurance benefit claims and the correctness of the amount. Reviews all evidence previously developed and evaluates evidence for accuracy and validity.

Pay/Leave Specialist: Assists federal agencies by providing policy guidance and program implementation on pay and leave benefit administration.

Personnel Investigator: Determines the suitability of applicants under consideration for appointment in the federal government by checking on applicants for positions requiring national security or professional requirements.

Personnel Management Specialist: Directs or assists in directing a personnel management program. Provides technical assistance for work that involves specialized personnel functions.

Personnel Staffing Specialist: Performs work in recruitment, examination, selection, or placement of employees to staff government organizations.

Major Activities and Divisions

Employment Service: Manages programs associated with staffing federal positions and special programs for veterans, minorities, and women.

Federal Prevailing Rate Advisory Committee: Studies the Federal Wage System and other matters regarding the establishment of prevailing rates of pay.

Human Resources Systems Service: Provides policy direction in developing and evaluating personnel systems affecting management, pay, leave, and performance in the federal work force.

Investigations Service: Conducts investigations of applicants to support the selection and appointment process. Federal investigation divisions are located in DC, Atlanta, Chicago, Dallas, Philadelphia, and San Francisco.

Office of Executive Resources: Develops government-wide executive policy.

Office of Merit Systems Oversight and Effectiveness: Assesses agency effectiveness in personnel management at the government-wide, agency, and installation levels. Ensures compliance with personnel laws and regulations.

Retirement and Insurance Service: Administers the civil service retirement, health, and life insurance programs.

Alternative Employment Programs

OPM offers volunteer internships in numerous career fields, providing work assignments relevant to studies and career goals. The program is offered year-round and is generally six to eight weeks full or part time. Eligible applicants must be full- or part-time students currently enrolled in a college or university. Contact the program coordinator at (202) 632-7484 or TDD (202) 632-9345 or write to OPM, Division of Recruitment and Special Employment Programs, Attn.: Student Volunteer Program.

Application Prodecures

Direct inquiries to:

Office of Personnel Management
Office of Personnel and EEO
1900 E St. NW, Room 1447
Washington, DC 20415
(202) 606-2440 or 0832
Recorded Message: (202) 606-2400
E-mail: jobs4U@OPM.gov

Note: Make it clear that you are seeking positions within OPM itself rather than government-wide positions.

Peace Corps
www.peacecorps.gov

Nature of Work: Agriculture, education, foreign aid, volunteers

Number of Employees: 1,000

Headquarters: Washington, DC

Regional Locations: Atlanta, GA; Boston, MA; Chicago, IL; Dallas, TX; Denver, CO; Los Angeles, CA; Minneapolis, MN; New York, NY; San Francisco, CA; Seattle, WA; Washington, DC. Overseas offices in 70 countries.

Typical Background of New Hires: Agriculture, biological sciences, education, engineering, health science, languages, liberal arts, medical sciences

---

Mission

The activities of the Peace Corps are directed toward helping developing countries meet basic needs, fight disease and hunger, increase food production, and improve education levels so that eventually they are self-sufficient. Peace Corps volunteers and staff traditionally assist in agriculture, natural resources, health, rural development, education, science, business, and skilled trades projects.

Job Descriptions

Area Medical Officer (APCMO): Maintains the medical office at his or her assigned post. Conducts immunization and environmental health programs, provides treatment directly or arranges for other professional practitioners to provide treatment, and handles medical emergencies. Assists in program development for health, home economics, and agriculture projects. Works closely with the Country Director and the Office of Medical Services in Washington, DC. Qualifications: A medical degree and a current U.S. practitioner's license in medicine or osteopathy or a degree and license in nursing or certification as a physician's assistant.

Associate Peace Corps Director (APCD): Acts as the intermediary between volunteers and local officials, Peace Corps staff in Washington, the host country government, U.S. embassy personnel, and employees from other international agencies. Works with other agencies to generate funding for projects, improves and develops new programs, evaluates volunteer sites, trains volunteers, and monitors project progress.

The Peace Corps selects approximately 30 applicants for APCD positions each year. About half of the APCD positions require fluency in either French or Spanish. Most positions require strong communications and interpersonal skills, management expertise, and practical experience in program development. The following are specializations within the APCD position:

APCD/Agriculture: Assists volunteers involved in agricultural and natural resources projects designed to increase food production. These projects include agriculture education, animal husbandry, beekeeping, farm mechanics, soil science, forestry, and fisheries sciences. To qualify, a degree in agriculture, forestry, natural resources, or an agriculture-related discipline is often required.

APCD/Rural Development: Creates a physical infrastructure to expand development efforts throughout the country. Works with volunteers on road and bridge construction, irrigation and sanitation systems, urban and rural planning, buildings for education and health, and electrification networks. To qualify, a degree in rural sociology or a discipline related to rural development, such as civil engineering, architecture, construction, public works, or vocational education, is often required.

APCD/Health: Works with volunteers committed to expanding health care to rural areas of developing countries. The projects include disease control, nutrition extension, laboratory technology, nursing, occupational and physical therapy, and sanitation. To qualify, a degree and three to five years of experience in public health, medicine, or a related discipline is often required.

APCD/Education: Works with volunteers assigned to primary, secondary and vocational schools, and community education efforts. The subjects taught include math, science, business, English, physical education, library science, and industrial arts.

The Peace Corps also has a large international special education program. To qualify, a four-year degree in education or an advanced degree in a related discipline is often required.

APCD/Training: Directs the training staff, manages the training budget, and is responsible for ensuring that volunteers receive the highest-quality language instruction, cross-cultural sensitivity training, and technical preparation. To qualify, a degree in education or behavioral or managerial sciences is often required.

APCD/Programming and Training: Works closely with other staff members to ensure that programs are consistent with Peace Corps and host country development plans. Organizes and supervises training activities for incoming and current volunteers and hires training staff. To qualify, a degree in education, management, international affairs, social sciences, or a discipline related to planning is usually required.

APCD/Administration: Oversees the financial, administrative, and personnel operations. Manages the disbursement of funds, obligations, and liquidations; certifies travel and petty cash vouchers; purchases maintains and disposes of property and vehicles; maintains files and prepares reports as requested; and coordinates with the American Embassy administrative staff.

To qualify, a degree in management, business, or public administration and three to five years of experience in a related field are usually required.

Regional Recruiter: Screens qualified applicants for volunteer service in the Peace Corps and the United Nations Volunteer Program. Serves as point person for building awareness of all Peace Corps programs. Regional Recruiter positions are located in one of the 11 regional offices.

Major Activities and Divisions

The Peace Corps Operational Offices have several divisions: Volunteer Recruitment and Selection (includes University Programs and Minority Recruitment); Volunteer Support (includes Medical Services); Returned Volunteer Services, World Wise Schools, and Peace Corps Fellows; Office of Private Sector

Relations and International Volunteerism; Crisis Corps; and Center for Field Assistance & Applied Research.

The Peace Corps has a presence at many university campuses across the U.S. College students may wish to look into the Peace Corps' many university programs, such as the Peace Corps Preparatory Program and the Community College Model. Two programs, Master's International and Fellows/USA, combine service with a master's degree program.

Alternative Employment Programs

The Peace Corps participates in a paid summer intern program.

Remarks

The Peace Corps overseas staff is divided into paid staff (APCDs and APCMOs) and volunteer staff. Volunteers are needed with degrees and/or experience in agriculture, natural resources, education, liberal arts, fisheries, engineering, business, health professions, home economics, and the trade specialties.

Peace Corps employees receive time-limited appointments and most are limited to a maximum of five years (60 months) of employment with the agency. Training and orientation for new overseas staff lasts approximately 30 days and is offered four times a year, usually in Washington, DC. Salaries for APCDs and APCMOs depend on relevant experience and education. In most countries, Peace Corps also provides government leased housing, or in some cases provides a lodging allowance. Employees may receive education allowances for children aged 4 to 21 while enrolled in school.

Application Prodecures

APCDs and APCMOs are recruited by the Office of Personnel Policy and Operations, International Operations Divisions. For more information, direct inquiries to:

Peace Corps
Office of Human Resource Management
1111 20th St. NW, Room 2300
Washington, DC 20526
(202) 692-1200
Toll Free: (800) 424-8580 Ext. 1200
Fax: (202) 692-1201
E-mail: hrmjobs@peacecorps.gov

Postal Rate Commission
www.prc.gov

Nature of Work: Postal services, wages/prices/rates

Number of Employees: 50

Headquarters: Washington, DC

Regional Locations: None

Typical Background of New Hires: Accounting, economics, engineering, law, statistics

Mission

The Postal Rate Commission issues decisions to the U.S. Postal Service for postage rates and fees and mail classifications. It also proposes nationwide changes in postal services, initiates studies, and investigates complaints from the mailing public.

Job Descriptions

Accountant: Conducts cost analyses and cost accounting research to assess and evaluate postal operating costs.

Attorney: Works in one of two professional groups: the advisory group, which supports the efforts of the Commissioners in preparing their decisions or the litigation group, which represents the interests of the general public. Assignments are not rigidly structured; staff members will participate in a full range of projects.

Engineer: Applies a knowledge of industrial engineering and market analysis to a full range of projects concerning rate and classification design. Receives general guidance from senior personnel but a minimum of detailed supervision.

Statistician: Conducts market research related to postal systems, rates, and operating costs. Quantifies and evaluates gathered data.

Major Activities and Divisions

The Commission is a permanent professional federal agency. It is not part of the U.S. Postal Service. The Postal Rate Commission consists of the Offices of the Commissioners, the Office of the General Counsel, the Office of Rates, Analysis and Planning, the Office of the Consumer Advocate, and the Administrative Office.

Alternative Employment Programs
None

Application Prodecures
The Postal Rate Commission accepts resumes or OF-612's. The PRC Web site lists current vacancies.

Postal Rate Commission
Attn.: Administrative Office
1333 H St. NW, Room 300
Washington, DC 20268-0001
(202) 789-6840
E-mail: prc-admin@prc.gov

U.S. Postal Service
www.usps.gov

Nature of Work: Postal

Number of Employees: 856,550

Headquarters: Washington, DC

Regional Locations: The five Postal regions are headquartered at Chicago, IL; Memphis, TN; North Windsor, CT; Philadelphia, PA; and San Bruno, CA. These regions oversee 73 field division offices and over 40,000 post offices nationwide

Typical Background of New Hires: Business, computer science, criminal justice, engineering, labor relations (personnel), law, liberal arts, public administration

---

Mission
A fundamental commitment of the Postal Service is to provide swift and reliable mail delivery. To provide postal services responsive to public needs, the Postal Service operates its own planning, research, engineering, real estate, and procurement programs and maintains close ties with international postal organizations.

Job Descriptions
The Postal Service fills many of its major entry-level jobs on a designated "part-time flexible" (PTF) basis. The pay is on an hourly rate and the work is on a

flexible schedule. Many of these positions require the applicant to pass an exam, as indicated below. A sample test and primer for Postal Exam Battery 460 and 470 are located on the Postal Service Web site. Look for exam announcements on public bulletin boards in post offices and in local, federal, and state municipal buildings. These positions include:

City Carrier: Travels planned routes to deliver and collect mail, typically on foot or by vehicle, outdoors in all weather. Must have a current valid state driver's license and safe driving record. Must pass test 470.

Distribution Clerk: Sorts incoming and outgoing mail (including mail not handled by automated equipment) in plant or Post Office facilities. Must pass test 470.

Mail Processor: Operates mail processing equipment and acts as a troubleshooter. Collates, bundles, and transfers processed mail from one area to another, sometimes involving heavy lifting. Must pass test 470.

Mail Handler: Loads and unloads mail containers and transports mail and empty equipment throughout a building. Opens and empties sacks of mail. Involves heavy lifting. Must pass test 470.

Mark-up Clerk: Enters change-of-address data into a computer database, processes mail, and performs other clerical functions. Operates a keyboard to process changes. Must have passed a typing test and have good data entry skills. Must pass test 470.

Rural Carrier Associate: Sorts mail into delivery sequence for assigned route. Delivers and collects mail along a prescribed rural route by vehicle. Provides customers a variety of postal-related services. Must pass test 460.

Other common postal service positions include:

Engineer: Applies a knowledge of the physical and engineering sciences to develop and test electronic and automation equipment related to mail, mail sorting, address identification, and other postal needs.

Postal Inspector: Inspects post offices and related postal units to ensure compliance with postal laws and regulations. Investigates postal laws and surveys operating problems.

Real Estate Specialist: Appraises land and acquires real estate through negotiation of a contract or lease. Plans and manages real estate to attain its most efficient use.

Systems Analyst: Designs, develops, and tests automation equipment related to the efficient organization and management of the major post offices and postal services.

Major Activities and Divisions

Customer Cooperation: The Postal Service provides customer cooperation activities including the representation of interests of the individual mail customer through the Consumer Advocate.

Mail Delivery: The Postal Service maintains extensive processing and delivery systems and integrated bulk mail handling systems.

Postal Operations: The Postal Service maintains the postal rate structure and develops mail classification standards.

Law Enforcement: The Postal Inspection Service, the law enforcement arm of the Postal Service, protects the mail, postal funds, and property.

Alternative Employment Programs

There are two major employment programs for individuals wishing to enter a management position with the Postal Service:

★ *Management Intern Program:* The primary purpose of this program is to develop interns to meet future management and executive needs. The program is two to four years in length. It consists of two- to nine-month rotational assignments at all levels of the organization. All undergraduate degree requirements must be completed before entering the program. Interns are based at headquarters in Washington, DC, although some assignments are located in the regional and field division offices. Starting salaries are approximately $30,000 to $50,000 per year, based on education and experience. Management Interns are eligible for bonuses up to 12 percent of base salary annually.

To apply, submit a completed PS Form 991-MI (Application for Management Intern) and two letters of recommendation from an employer or professor to:

United States Postal Service
Employee Development and Education Division
Attn.: Management Intern Program
475 L'Enfant Plaza W, SW
Washington, DC 20260-4352

Applications are accepted only during an approximate six-week period in early spring. Interviews begin shortly after the closing date, and interns usually begin in mid-June.

✱ Management Associate Program: This program's purpose is to develop high-potential individuals to meet future management needs. The program normally runs three years and consists of on-the-job developmental assignments and related training at one of 73 Postal field divisions. The Associate gains a broad understanding of the Postal Service's mission through hands-on experience in various functions within the organization. An advanced degree or a bachelor's degree with two years of supervisory experience is required. Management Associates are based in any of the 73 field divisions. The salary range is approximately $30,000 to $40,000, depending on experience, education, and current salary.

To apply, submit a completed PS Form 991-M (Application for Management Associate Program) and an official transcript from the college from which you obtained the highest degree. Mail to the region where you wish to be considered:

Regional Director, Human Resources in

Eastern Region
Philadelphia, PA 29297-0840

Northeast Region
Windsor, CT 06006-0840

Southern Region
Memphis, TN 38166-0840

Western Region
San Bruno, CA 94044-0840

Student Hiring: During the summer months, college students may be hired as casual (temporary) employees. These positions do not require tests, and time on the job cannot apply toward career positions with the post office. Contact your local post office no later than January or February regarding summer employment opportunities.

Remarks

The Postal Service does not follow the GS pay schedule that the other federal agencies use. The largest pay system in the USPS is the PS scale, ranging from about $22,500 to about $47,000 per year for full-time career employees. U.S. Postal Service salaries remain competitive with those of other leading corporations. Benefits are similar to those offered in other government organizations, including 13 paid vacation days per year, 13 paid sick days per year, and 10 paid holidays.

Many postal service positions require a written test, such as the 470 battery examination. Test scores are strongly considered in hiring choices, and positions are highly competitive. To improve your chances of being hired, consult a test-preparation book before taking the exam.

Application Prodecures

You may apply for jobs or take exams for postal positions online at http://uspsapps.hr-services.org/.

Other job information can be found online at the postal service human resources site at www.usps.gov/hrisp.

Or, direct inquiries to:

United States Postal Service
Employment and Placement Division
475 L'Enfant Plaza SW
Washington, DC 20260-4352
Headquarters: 202-268-2000
Toll Free: (800) 276-5627 (Post Office Job Information Line)

Information about Inspection Service employment may be obtained from the Chief Postal Inspector at (202) 268-4267.

More information about jobs such as clerk, letter carrier, etc., including information about programs for veterans, may be obtained by contacting the nearest post office.

Railroad Retirement Board (RRB)
www.rrb.gov

Nature of Work: Insurance/benefits, railroads

Number of Employees: 1,500

Headquarters: Chicago, IL

Regional Locations: District offices in 35 states

Typical Background of New Hires: Accounting, criminal justice, liberal arts

Mission

The Railroad Retirement Board administers comprehensive retirement survivor and unemployment-sickness benefit programs for the nation's railroad workers and their families.

Job Descriptions

Actuary, Economist, and Statistician Positions: Assists the RRB in predicting the future income and outlays of the Railroad Retirement Account and provides vital data.

Auditor: Conducts audits at railroad industry sites to ensure that funds are intact and that monies due the Railroad Retirement Board are paid in a timely manner.

Claims Examiner (Unemployment): Examines claims for sickness benefits to ensure that eligibility requirements have been met. Also examines unemployment claims for eligibility. Positions located at HQ.

Claims Specialist (HIB): Handles Medicare claims from railroad workers. Coordinates with the Social Security Act on welfare coverage issues. Positions located at HQ.

Contact Representative: Takes initial applications for benefits, occasionally setting up itinerate services so as to handle claims in remote locations. Involves approximately 50 percent public contact and can involve extensive travel throughout the assigned district. No test is required for this position.

Criminal Investigator: Examines cases where fraud is suspected.

Field Office Claims Examiner: Handles unemployment claims that are submitted to a field office location. Examines records and documents for proof of eligibility. No test is required for this position.

Railroad Claims Examiner (Retirement): Examines claims for retirement annuities. Coordinates with the Social Security Act in the computation, payment, and financing of railroad retirement annuities.

Major Activities and Divisions

The Railroad Retirement Board's Office of Programs coordinates direct services to railroad retirement beneficiaries and all claims processing operations, including retirement and survivor programs, and unemployment and sickness benefits.

Alternative Employment Programs

None

Remarks

Most Claims Examiner positions require a written test that focuses on reading, writing, and basic math skills.

Application Prodecures

Direct inquiries to:

Bureau of Personnel
Railroad Retirement Board
844 North Rush St.
Chicago, IL 60611
(312) 751-4650 (4500 main line)

U.S. Securities and Exchange Commission (SEC)
www.sec.gov

Nature of Work: Bonds/commodities, business

Number of Employees: 2900

Headquarters: Washington, DC

Regional Locations: Atlanta, GA; Boston, MA; Chicago, IL; Denver, CO; Fort Worth, TX; Los Angeles, CA; Miami, FL; New York, NY; Philadelphia, PA; Salt Lake City, UT; San Francisco, CA

Typical Background of New Hires: Accounting, business economics, finance/banking, law (JD)

Mission

The SEC administers and enforces federal securities laws. The Commission regulates the nation's securities markets, stockbrokers, investment companies, and investment advisers and prescribes certain requirements for companies that issue stock or other securities.

Job Descriptions

Accountant: Drafts accounting and reporting regulations that apply to corporations whose securities are sold to the public. Examines financial statements filed with registration statements to determine if there is adequate disclosure of financial information. Reviews financial data to ascertain whether there have been violations of law or regulations in connection with the issue, purchase, and sale of securities.

The SEC hires accountants at the GS-12 and GS-13 levels. These positions require an undergraduate degree plus at least three years of professional experience. A CPA is preferred.

Attorney: Investigates violations of federal securities laws. Inspects self-regulatory systems, including the review of existing laws, and conducts hearings regarding the introduction of new rules. Examines registration and proxy statements, indentures, and applications.

Financial Analyst: Analyzes prospectuses, proxy statements, and reports of corporations to determine that full and fair disclosure has been made. Reviews reports and other data required to supervise and regulate transactions and trading on national securities exchanges and in the over-the-counter market. Reviews filings to ensure compliance with the financial standards of the Public Utility Holding Company Act of 1935. Works with attorneys and investigators in the surveillance of unusual trading activity. Typically works in the Divisions of Corporation Finance, Investment Management, Market Regulation, and Enforcement.

Applicants are considered at the GS-9, -11, and -12 levels. A GS-9 requires a master's degree in business, accounting, finance, or economics.

Financial Economist: Designs and conducts studies of the economic impact of existing and proposed rules promulgated by the SEC and self-regulatory agencies.

Investigator: Investigates and analyzes unusual market activity that may indicate possible violations of the law.

Securities Compliance Examiner: Examines the operational and financial practices and records of broker-dealers, investment advisers, mutual funds, and other classes of registrants. Investigates the registrants' procedures for safeguarding funds and securities of customers and assesses the financial liquidity of a broker-dealer to determine the adequacy of the firm's net capital and its overall financial health. Examines the distribution and selling of securities in over-the-counter and exchange trading.

Securities Compliance Examiners generally have financial or accounting training. They are principally employed in regional or branch offices. Applicants are considered at the GS-5 to GS-12 levels.

Major Activities and Divisions

The Division of Corporation Finance: Oversees public disclosure of financial and business information of companies that issue securities.

The Division of Enforcement: The chief investigative arm of the Commission. Investigations and trials are the day-to-day work of the staff of the Division of Enforcement.

The Division of Investment Management: Administers federal securities laws as they apply to regulation of and disclosure by investment companies and investment advisers. The Commission staff visits investment companies on a regular basis to review adherence to statutory requirements.

The Division of Market Regulation: Regulates the nation's securities markets and the activities of transfer agents, broker-dealers, and other market professionals.

The Office of the Chief Accountant: The principal adviser to the Commission on accounting, auditing, and financial reporting matters.

Alternative Employment Programs

☆ Summer Employment for High School, College, and Graduate Students

☆ 2003 Summer Honors Program for Law Students

☆ Law Student Observer Program

☆ SEC Student Temporary Employment Program (STEP)

Summer Honors Program for Law Students: A 10-week program available to first- and second-year law and J.D./M.B.A. students. Students assist staff members in daily duties or special projects that relate to their course of study.

Law Student Observer Program: First-, second-, and third-year law students or J.D./M.B.A.'s are eligible to work 15 to 20 (or sometimes 40) hours per week at the SEC. Participants are not paid for their time but are given course credit through the law school they attend.

Advanced Commitment Program: This program allows lawyers to begin work as law clerks before they pass the bar. It is designed for third-year law students, recent J.D. and J.D./M.B.A. graduates, graduating LL.M. students, and judicial law clerks.

Summer Employment Program: Open to undergraduate and graduate students (and some high school students.) Students perform administrative, research, and program-related duties. Most interviews for summer positions take place in April and May of each year, so applications should be sent in early.

The SEC also hires a number of students through the federal STEP program (described in chapter 00).

Remarks

The Commission operates a college and law school recruitment program, including on-campus visitations for interview purposes. Direct inquiries to (202) 942-4070.

Full addresses, phone numbers, and e-mail addresses for the district offices can be found at www.sec.gov/contact/addresses.htm.

Application Prodecures

Direct inquiries to:

Director of Human Resources
Securities and Exchange Commission
450 5th St., NW
Washington, DC 20549-0001
(202) 942-4144
SEC Hotline: 202-942-4150
TDD: (202) 942-4095.
E-mail: recruit@sec.gov.

Small Business Administration (SBA)
www.sba.gov

Nature of Work: Business, discrimination, minorities

Number of Employees: 4,000

Headquarters: Washington, DC

Regional Locations: Boston, MA; Chicago, IL; Dallas, TX; Denver, CO; Kansas City, MO; New York, NY; Philadelphia, PA; San Francisco, CA; Seattle, WA. District offices across the U.S.

Typical Background of New Hires: Accounting, business, economics, finance, marketing, public administration

---

Mission

The Small Business Administration concerns itself with the health of the nation's economy as seen in the growth of small businesses. It gives advice to new businesses, ensures opportunities for the socially and economically disadvantaged, and services small business loans.

Job Descriptions

Economic Development Specialist: Provides advice to small businesses through programs such as SCORE. Acts as a consultant and conducts management workshops for established as well as prospective business people in overcoming management problems.

Business Opportunity Specialist: Works to ensure that small business opportunities are available for the socially or economically disadvantaged. Most work in the Office of Minority Small Business and Capital Ownership Development.

Loan Specialist: Engages in the servicing of loans and is involved in small business liquidations. Most work in the Office of Finance and Investment or in the Disaster Offices.

Major Activities and Divisions

There are four operational divisions in the Small Business Administration: Capital Access, Entrepreneurial Development, Management and Administration, and Government Contracting and Business Development. There are nine regional offices, about seventy district offices, and four disaster area offices. The latter offices are in service only when there is a declared disaster. Their mission is to issue loans needed to repair or replace homes, businesses, and farms damaged or destroyed by disasters.

Alternative Employment Programs

The Small Business Administration participates in extensive student employment programs, including PMI, STEP, SCEP; Student Volunteer programs; College Work-Study programs; and Summer Employment Programs. The SEC also appoints students to law clerk positions who have earned their first law degree (LL.B. or J.D.) but have not yet been admitted to the bar. Appointments are made at the GS-9 and GS-11 levels and may not exceed 14 months.

Application Prodecures

Direct inquiries to:

U.S. Small Business Administration
Office of Human Resources
409 3rd St. SW, Suite 4200
Washington DC 20416
(202) 205-6190

For SBA positions outside the Washington, DC, area, call (303) 383-5627 or send correspondence to:

U.S. Small Business Administration
Office of Human Resources
633 17th St., 7th Floor
Denver, CO 80202

Smithsonian Institution
www.si.edu

Nature of Work: Arts/humanities, education, libraries, scholarly research, scientific research

Number of Employees: 5,100

Headquarters: Washington, DC

Regional Locations: Arizona, Florida, Maryland, Massachusetts, New York City, Virginia, and the Republic of Panama

Typical Background of New Hires: Accounting, anthropology, art history, biological sciences (entomology, ornithology, paleobiology, zoology), biology, botany, history, physical sciences (astrophysics, physiology)

Mission

In 1829, James Smithson, son of the Duke of Northumberland, bequeathed a sum of money to the United States to found an "establishment for the increase and diffusion of knowledge among men." Today, it is the world's largest museum complex and an important center for research. Its sixteen museums and the National Zoo hold more than 140 million objects and specimens. About one percent of the total collection is on public display, with the rest used for research.

Job Descriptions

Accountant: Classifies and evaluates financial data, including complex systems regarding Institution funding through federal appropriations, private gifts and grants, and income from endowments and business operations.

Conservator: Restores and preserves objects related to collections and exhibits in the various Smithsonian museums. Requires a background in studio art and chemistry. A master's degree in the field or equivalent experience is highly desirable.

Curator: Conducts specific scholarly work in a particular science, such as art history or American history. Requires a Ph.D.

Development Officer: Raises money from private sources to support the museum's programmatic activities or capital projects.

Editor/Writer: Oversees the production of printed material, including exhibit labels and brochures and catalogs, for the museums. Some editors and writers write for the museums' publications: *Smithsonian* magazine, *Smithsonian Air and Space,* or *Smithsonian Press.*

Education Specialist: Disseminates information through educational programs and materials relating to exhibits and museum collections. Designs, prepares, and schedules programs that enhance current exhibitions and develops independent activities to serve the needs of the school community.

Positions are located in each museum and research center. A degree in education or the subject of the museum is required. Informal (nonclassroom) education experience is highly desirable.

Exhibits Specialist: Designs, plans, constructs, and operates exhibits. Position requirements vary with the specific job, but include construction skills in various mediums, graphic arts, design, or interactive computer systems.

Historian: Conducts scholarly work related to a specific project. Collects and interprets specimens and data. A Ph.D. is often required.

Library Technician/Librarian: Collects, organizes, and preserves recorded knowledge in printed, written, audiovisual, or other media forms. Catalogs, classifies, and retrieves materials. Libraries are located in each museum and research center. Undergraduate degree in Library Science required for Library Technician; M.L.S. required for Librarian. A background in the subject of the museum is desirable. Positions also available at several archives located throughout the Institution.

Museum Specialist: Performs technical work in connection with the operation of public museums. Manages museum collections and monitors exhibit projects.

Museum Technician: Assists curators in research and mounting exhibits. An undergraduate degree in the subject of the museum is desirable. This is an entry-level museum position.

Photographer: Depending upon the nature of the assignment, this position may include the performance of still, motion picture, television, high-speed, aerial, or other camera work, and/or photographic processing work. May require a knowledge about the subject matter to be photographed.

Registrar: Organizes and maintains records of the objects or specimens in a collection. At the Smithsonian, the collections range from microscopic fleas at Natural History to a B-29 bomber at Air and Space. The records require the use of specialized software that includes digital images.

Scientist: Conducts technical and scholarly research on projects relating to museum collections and associated issues. Basic and applied research may span a wealth of scientific disciplines as varied as astronomy, anthropology, botany, ecology, mineral sciences, earth sciences, and veterinary medicine. A Ph.D. is often required.

Major Activities and Divisions

Museums and Centers:

Anacostia Museum: Exhibits, researches, and provides educational programs related to the African-American experience from the beginning of the slave trade to modern times.

Archives of American Art: Collects and preserves some 2,000 personal and professional papers of American painters, sculptors, critics, dealers, collectors, and records of museums and art societies.

Arthur M. Sackler Gallery: Devoted to the acquisition, study, interpretation, and exhibition of Asian art museums and art societies.

Conservation Analytical Laboratory: Provides a focus within the Smithsonian for conservation of the millions of artifacts in the museum collections.

Cooper-Hewitt Museum of Design and Decorative Arts: The more than 300,000 items in this collection include drawings, furniture, glass, woodwork, wall coverings, and other media. These serve as visual information for the study of design.

Freer Gallery of Art: Houses a collection of oriental art, which consists of more than 26,800 works.

Hirshhorn Museum and Sculpture Garden: Includes paintings by modern European and Latin masters and works representing 150 years of American and European sculpture.

John F. Kennedy Center for the Performing Arts: The Center presents a year-round program of the finest in music, dance, and drama from the U.S. and abroad.

National Air and Space Museum: The twenty-three exhibit halls trace the history of flight from the beginnings in balloon craft to the latest shuttle flight. The Paul E. Garber facility in Silver Hill, Maryland, houses the aircraft restoration operations for the museum.

National Gallery of Art: Houses one of the finest art collections in the world, illustrating Western man's achievements in painting, sculpture, and the graphic arts.

National Museum of African Art: NMAA is devoted to the acquisition, study, and exhibition of African paintings, sculpture, and graphic arts.

American Art Museum: Devoted to American painting, sculpture, and graphic art from the 18th century to the present. Houses a permanent collection of over 25,000 works.

National Museum of American History: NMAH is devoted to the exhibition, maintenance, and study of artifacts that reflect the experience of the American people. NMAH also offers the Dibner Library, a collection of rare books relating to the history of science and technology; the Eisenhower Institute for Historical Research, focusing on military history; and *Technology and Culture,* the international quarterly of the Society for the History of Technology.

National Museum of the American Indian: Headquartered in Washington, DC, with a gallery in the Alexander Hamilton Customs House in New York City, the museum houses a collection of one million objects of ethnographic material from native peoples of the western hemisphere. A new museum in the National Mall in DC is planned.

National Museum of Natural History: Through its collection of more than 84 million plants, animals, rocks and minerals, and cultural artifacts, NMNH provides a record of the natural and cultural history of the earth. The NMNH also operates the Smithsonian Marine Station at Link Port, Florida.

National Postal Museum: NPM presents stamps and postal artifacts in regard to the history and impact of the U.S. Postal Service.

National Portrait Gallery: NPG presents American history through the lives of men and women who have contributed significantly to its development, as depicted in a collection of portraiture in all media.

National Zoological Park: NZP maintains a collection of over 2,500 animals representing about 500 species. There is a conservation and research center for endangered species in Front Royal, Virginia.

Smithsonian Astrophysical Observatory: SAO is devoted to research into the basic physical processes that determine the nature and evolution of the universe. Data gathering facilities include the Fred Lawrence Whipple Observatory in Arizona, the Oak Ridge Observatory in Massachusetts, and the George R. Agassiz Station in Texas.

Research activities are organized into eight divisions: atomic and molecular physics, high-energy astrophysics, optical and molecular physics, high-energy astrophysics, planetary sciences, radio and geoastronomy, solar and stellar physics, and theoretical astrophysics. In addition to scientists, the observatory employs more than 250 support staff. Generally, an earned doctorate in astronomy, astrophysics, physics, or a related field is required for professional research positions.

Smithsonian Environmental Research Center: The SERC's research programs emphasize two major areas: regulatory and environmental biology and projects that include radiocarbon dating, education, and public information.

Smithsonian Tropical Research Institute: The STRI conducts research on basic biological processes, provides support of advanced training and tropical research by visiting scientists, and works on behalf of conservation in the tropics. Staff and students work throughout tropical regions of the Americas, Asia, and Africa, with headquarters in the Republic of Panama.

Alternative Employment Programs

Fellowships: The Office of Fellowships offers in-residence appointments for research and study using its facilities, with the advice and guidance of its staff members. Candidates are evaluated on their academic standing, experience, and the quality of the research project or study proposed and its suitability to Smithsonian programs. Application procedures and forms are provided by each sponsoring program or museum.

Internships: An internship at the Smithsonian Institution is a prearranged, structured learning experience scheduled within a specific time frame. The experience must be relevant to the intern's academic and professional goals and to research and museum activities of the Institution. Internships are arranged by contacting the appropriate internship coordinator at the museum, office, or research institute you are interested in or through the Internship Central Referral Service offered by the Smithsonian Center for Education and Museum Studies. Contact by e-mail: interninfo@scems.si.edu or visit the Web site at http://museumstudies.si.edu.

Some of the Smithsonian fellowship and internship programs include the Smithsonian Institution Fellowship Program, the Smithsonian Institution Latino Studies Fellowship Program, the Smithsonian Institution Molecular Evolution Fellowship Program, the Minority Internship Program, the James E. Webb Internship Program, and the Native American Awards Program.

The Smithsonian Institution conducts an extensive Volunteer Service program. Persons may serve as tour guides or information volunteers or may participate in an independent program, in which their educational and professional backgrounds are matched with curatorial or research requests from within the Smithsonian. Direct inquiries to the Visitor Information and Associates' Reception Center, 1000 Jefferson Drive SW, Washington, DC 20560. Call (202) 357-2700 or TDD (202) 381-4448 (for the hearing impaired).

Remarks

The Smithsonian offers predoctoral and postdoctoral grants through its Office of Fellowships and Grants. It also conducts a graduate program in the material aspects of American civilization for graduate students enrolled in cooperating universities through its Office of American Studies. Internship information is available through intern coordinators at each museum.

The Smithsonian is a trust instrumentality of the federal government. Most positions fall under the federal civil service.

Application Prodecures

Inquiries regarding employment in the Washington, DC, metropolitan area may
be directed to:

Main Office of Human Resources
750 9th Street NW, Suite 6100
Washington DC 20560-0912
(202) 275-1102

Business Ventures Human Resources Office
750 9th Street NW, Suite 7100
Washington DC 20560-0951
(202) 275-2062
Jobline: (202) 287-3102 (24-hour, automated phone)
TDD: 202-275-1110

Employment information for the following locations may be obtained by
contacting the organizations directly:

Cooper-Hewitt Museum
2 East 91st St.
New York, NY 10028
(212) 860-6868

National Gallery of Art
Fourth St. and Constitution Ave., NW
Washington, DC 20565
(202) 737-4215

Smithsonian Astrophysical Observatory
Personnel Department
160 Concord Ave.
Cambridge, MA 02138
(617) 495-7371

John F. Kennedy Center for the
Performing Arts
Washington, DC 20566
(202) 872-0466

Social Security Administration (SSA)

www.ssa.gov

Nature of Work: Health, insurance, social services

Number of Employees: 65,000

Headquarters: Baltimore, MD (also in Washington, DC, and Falls Church, VA)

Regional Locations: Atlanta, GA; Boston, MA; Chicago, IL; Dallas, TX; Denver, CO; Kansas City, MO; New York, NY; Philadelphia, PA; San Francisco, CA; Seattle, WA

Typical Background of New Hires: Business, liberal arts, mathematics, social sciences

Mission

The Social Security Administration conducts a national program of contributory social insurance whereby employees, employers, and the self-employed pay contributions that are pooled in special trust funds. When earnings stop or are reduced because the worker retires, dies, or becomes disabled, monthly cash benefits are paid to replace part of the earnings the family has lost.

Job Descriptions

Actuary: Makes actuarial appraisals of existing and proposed social insurance programs and analyzes actuarial data for benefit evaluations. Estimates future claims and program costs, evaluates demographic characteristics, and analyzes trust fund operations.

Attorney/Administrative Law Judge: Work nationwide to provide the public with a timely and judicious appeal for Social Security benefits. In the headquarters office, attorney-advisers and attorney-examiners review and act upon the decisions of administrative law judges.

Benefit Authorizer: Authorizes new types of entitlement for previously entitled beneficiaries and makes determinations to resume, reinstate, suspend, or terminate benefits. Makes determinations of benefit rates considering such factors of entitlement as type of benefit, age, family maximum, and changes in family composition.

Criminal Investigator: Plans and conducts surveillance of suspects; serves search warrants and subpoenas; conducts interviews with suspects, witnesses and informants; and testifies before grand juries or courts.

Economist: Collects, analyzes, and reports economic data relating to the retirement, survivors, disability, and supplemental security income programs. Measures the effects of Social Security benefit provisions on the individual, the family, and the economy. Conducts research in the area of general welfare and labor economics.

Foreign Claims Adjudicator: Examines Social Security benefits claims for claimants in foreign countries. Adjudicates all claims for retirement, survivors, and disability benefits

Hearings and Appeals Analyst: Reviews disability, retirement, survivors, or health insurance cases that are before the Appeals Council for review or have been appealed to the U.S. District Courts. Prepares an analysis of the case with a recommendation to the Appeals Council as to what action should be taken. Conducts postreview of hearing examiner decisions in order to identify problem areas or trends. Responds to inquiries from members of Congress, the legal or medical profession, and individual claimants.

Mathematical Statistician: Designs and adapts statistical methodology in the measurement of the impact of Social Security programs. Conducts statistical investigations in regard to the characteristics of beneficiaries, the demographic aspects of Social Security programs, and the economic effects of policy and programs.

Service Representative: Interviews beneficiaries or inquirers to determine the nature of their problem or interest and to resolve problems with payments or eligibility. Investigates case situations and questionable or incomplete reports and reconciles discrepancies. Provides beneficiaries with information or instruction. Identifies need for social services of people interviewed and refers them to appropriate organizations.

Social Insurance Claims Examiner: Determines the validity of Social Security benefit claims and the correctness of the benefit amount. Reviews and evaluates all evidence previously developed and approves, modifies or reverses the prior adjudication when necessary. Typically works in one of the six payment centers across the U.S.

Social Insurance Claims Representative: Takes and authorizes claims for Social Security benefits. Conducts personal and telephone interviews with claimants, employers, and others in order to obtain evidence for the development of claims and to obtain evidence for the resolution of cases involving discrepancies. Reviews files for completeness of information and assists claimants in obtaining evidence and in completing necessary forms. Typically works in the district offices across the U.S.

Social Insurance Program Analyst: Evaluates the effectiveness of the Social Security program. Formulates program objectives and makes recommendations concerning legislative proposals.

Social Science Research Analyst: Conducts research on the impact of Social Security programs on beneficiaries and the evaluation of alternative programs. Measures overall Social Security needs and program effectiveness. Conducts economic and social surveys to obtain information on the characteristics of beneficiaries or other population groups.

Statistician: Develops improved methods for obtaining data and plans forms and procedures for collecting and tabulating data. Uses statistical techniques to measure relationships pertaining to social insurance programs.

Major Activities and Divisions

The Social Security Administration (SSA) is headed by a Commissioner and has an organizational structure of eleven offices. The field organization, which is decentralized to provide services at the local level, includes ten regional offices, six processing centers, and approximately 1,300 field offices.

Alternative Employment Programs

SSA participates in the federal STEP, SCEP, and PMI student hiring programs, which are described in chapter—. Contact the regional office that hires for the geographic area in which you have interest.

SSA conducts campus recruiting and attends college career fairs across the country.

Remarks

SSA often hires bilingual individuals for its public contact career positions, such as Claims Representatives and Benefits Authorizers.

Application Prodecures

Direct inquiries to the office in which you are interested in working.

Headquarters:
Social Security Administration
Attn.: Recruitment and Placement
Branch
West High Rise Building, Room G-120
6401 Security Blvd.
Baltimore, MD 21235
(410) 965-4506
Toll Free: (800) 772-1213

Atlanta Region (AL, FL, GA, KY, MS, NC, SC, TN)
Social Security Administration
Personnel Operations
61 Forsyth St. SW, Suite 22T64
Atlanta, GA 30303
(404) 562-1201

Boston Region (CT, ME, MA, NH, RI, VT)
Social Security Administration
Center for Human Resources
J. F. Kennedy Federal Building,
Room 1900
Boston, MA 02203
(617) 565-9241

Chicago Region (IL, IN, MI, MN, OH, WI)
Social Security Administration
Center for Human Resources
P.O. Box 802105
Chicago, IL 60680-2105
(312) 575-6380

Dallas Region (AK, LA, NM, OK, TX)
Social Security Administration
Center for Human Resources
MOS-2, Room 550
1301 Young St., Suite 130
Dallas, TX 75202-5433
(214) 767-3120

Denver Region (CO, MT, ND, SD, UT, WY)
(same as Dallas Region above)

Kansas City Region (IA, KS, MO, NE)
Social Security Administration
Center for Human Resources
Personnel Administration Team
P.O. Box 15458
Kansas City, MO 64106
(816) 936-5820

New York Region (NJ, NY, PR, VI)
Social Security Administration
Center for Human Resources
Personnel Operations Team 3
P.O. Box 4700
Jamaica, NY 11431
(718) 557-5050

Philadelphia Region (DE, MD, PA, VA, WV, DC)
Social Security Administration
Center for Human Resources
MATSSC Building, 7th Floor
P.O. Box 8788
Philadelphia, PA 19101
(215) 597-9268

San Francisco Region (AZ, CA, HI, NV, GU, Trust Territory of Pacific Islands, American Samoa)
Social Security Administration
Center for Human Resources
Staffing/Classification Team
P.O. Box 4115
Richmond, CA 94804
(510) 970-8484

Seattle Region (AL, ID, OR, WA)
Social Security Administration
Center for Human Resources
Suite 2900, M/S 292B
701 Fifth Avenue
Seattle, WA 98104-7075
(206) 615-2036

Office of Central Operations (Nationwide)
Social Security Administration
Office of Central Operations
Center for Human Resources
Security West Building
1500 Woodlawn Dr., Room 1340
Baltimore, MD 21241
(410) 966-6300

Tennessee Valley Authority (TVA)
www.tva.gov

Nature of Work: Agriculture, energy, environmental protection, forestry/ wildlife, nuclear energy/issues, recreation, waterways

Number of Employees: 13,200

Headquarters: Knoxville, TN

Regional Locations: Chattanooga, TN; Nashville, TN; Muscle Shoals, AL

Typical Background of New Hires: Biology chemistry, engineering, physical sciences

Mission

The Tennessee Valley Authority is a federal corporation and the nation's largest public power company. As a regional development agency, TVA supplies low-cost, reliable power, supports a thriving river system, and stimulates sustainable economic development.

Job Descriptions

Archaeologist: Assesses historic properties and conducts field reconnaissance and surveys. Conducts archaeological surveys and stratifies areas into sampling units, both horizontally on ground surface and vertically in subterranean testing. Conducts laboratory analysis and evaluation of specimens recovered from investigations.

Atmospheric Analyst: Develops emissions and other input files required by air quality models. Evaluates results from emissions models for estimating air pollutant emissions from utility, industrial, mobile, commercial, other urban, and biogenic sources.

Chemist: Develops and improves fertilizers and investigates the use of organic materials as fuels.

Electrical Engineer: Designs and maintains electrical generating and distribution systems and develops electromechanical components and systems.

Mechanical Engineer: Assists in the planning and construction of generating facilities, oversees the installation of equipment, and supervises modifications.

Nuclear Engineer: Designs components of nuclear power facilities such as reactor cores and instrumentation. Supervises servicing, modifications, inspections, safety, and radiological control and prepares technical specifications.

Power Billing Analyst: Analyzes the validity of power usage demand and energy data for revenue bill purposes.

Many technician positions exist for recent graduates with two-year associate degrees or experienced workers, including: Telecommunications Technician, Design Technician (civil and electrical), Metering Technician, Transmission Systems Technician, Survey Technician, Combustion Turbine Plant Technician, and Project Control Specialist.

Major Activities and Divisions

Chief Administrative Office: Develops, directs, manages, and assesses the corporate-wide administrative functions, ensuring that they support the operating organizations and effectively promote TVA's missions and goals.

Chief Nuclear Office: Responsible for the nuclear generation of electricity in the Tennessee Valley region and operates three nuclear plants.

Chief Operating Office: Develops, manages, directs, and assesses TVA's non-nuclear operating units: Fossil and Hydro Power; Customer Group; Transmission and Power Supply; Resource Group; and Economic Development. These organizations ensure that the electric power generation, flood control, navigation, sale and interchange of electricity, economic development, natural resources, and research and technology development programs promote TVA's goals with sound policies and practices.

Alternative Employment Programs

TVA Co-op and Internship Programs: Interns and co-op students work alongside TVA professionals in the laboratories, customer service centers, corporate offices, and nuclear, fossil, and hydro plants that comprise the TVA system. Most interns and co-op students earn between $10 and $13.50 per hour, depending on their class standing and field of study. The typical internship entails a 40-hour workweek for two to four months during the fall, spring, or summer semesters. (co-op students work one semester). Interested students may apply online or by mail. Send application and the TVA Intern/Co-op Statement of Interest (available at www.tva.gov) to: TVA Intern/Co-op Program, 1101 Market St., EB 8B, Chattanooga, TN 37402-2801. Be sure to check application deadlines on the TVA Web site.

Remarks

TVA operates 11 fossil plants, three nuclear plants, 29 hydroelectric dams, five combustion-turbine installations, a pumped-storage plant, and an environmental research center. Its facilities are located throughout the seven-state TVA region, which includes almost all of Tennessee and parts of Mississippi, Kentucky, Alabama, Georgia, North Carolina, and Virginia.

Application Prodecures

Direct inquiries to:

Employee Service Center
400 West Summit Hill Dr., WT CP
Knoxville, TN 37902-1499
Fax: (865) 632-4452
E-mail: esc@tva.gov

Internship Program
Shared Resources
TVA Internship Program
1101 South Market St.
Chattanooga, TN 37402-2801
Fax: (423) 751-8707
E-mail: tvainfo@tva.gov

College Recruitment
Toll Free: (888) WRK-4TVA (975-4882) (Jobline)

U.S. Capitol Police
www.usajobs.opm.gov/EI51.htm

Nature of Work: Law enforcement
Number of Employees: Over 1,100
Headquarters: Washington, DC
Regional Locations: None
Typical Background of New Hires: Criminal justice

Mission

Created by Congress in 1828, the original duty of the United States Capitol Police was to provide security for the United States Capitol Building. Today, its mission has expanded to include providing police services for the entire Congressional community and its visitors. These services are provided through the use of specialty support units, a network of foot and vehicular patrols, and fixed posts.

Job Descriptions

United States Capitol Police Officer: Protects life and property. Prevents, detects, and investigates criminal acts, and enforces traffic regulations throughout a large complex of congressional buildings, parks, and thoroughfares. Protects members of Congress, officers of Congress, and their families throughout the entire United States and its territories.

Major Activities and Divisions

U.S. Capitol Police Officers can work special assignment areas, which include: Dignitary Protection, Criminal Investigations, Intelligence, Threats, Containment and Emergency Response Team, K-9, Communications, Motorized and Mountain Bicycle Patrol, Hazardous Devices, and Electronic Countermeasures.

Alternative Employment Programs

The U.S. Capitol Police may hire interns through the STEP program for temporary assignments, based upon funding.

Remarks

To sign up to take the entry-level examination for the position of Police Officer, visit www.usajobs.opm.gov/ei51.htm, where you will find a printable electronic application form that you may submit by fax at (202) 228-0437. Or, to register for an examination date and time, you may contact the Recruiting Section via telephone at (202) 224-9819 between the hours of 7:00 a.m. and 3:00 p.m.

Application Prodecures

An intensive selection process, which takes an average of five months to complete, involves a written examination, application review, personal interview, background investigation, polygraph examination, psychological evaluation, and medical examination.

For more information, contact:

United States Capitol Police
119 D St., N.E.
Washington, DC 20510-7218
Attn: Recruiting and Investigations Section
(202) 224-9820
Employment Information: (202) 224-9819
Fax: (202) 228-0437
E-mail: recruiting@cap-police.senate.gov

✮ Department of the Interior (www.doi.gov)

Bureau of Indian Affairs (BIA)
www.doi.gov/bureau-indian-affairs.html

Nature of Work: Education, Native Americans, forestry/wildlife, disaster assistance (fire fighting)

Number of Employees: 10,500

Headquarters: Washington, DC

Regional Locations: Aberdeen, SD; Albuquerque, NM; Anchorage, AK; Arlington, VA; Billings, MT; Gallup, NM; Juneau, AK; Minneapolis, MN; Muskogee, OK; Phoenix, AZ; Portland, OR; Sacramento CA

Typical Background of New Hires: Biology, education, engineering, forestry, land-use planning, minority studies (Native American studies), social work/sociology, soil science

Mission

The Bureau of Indian Affairs works with American Indians and Alaska natives in the management of their affairs under a trust relationship with the federal government and facilitates the development of their human and natural resource potential.

Job Descriptions

Elementary/Secondary Teacher: Teaches Native Americans and Alaska natives in classroom settings, both on and off reservations. Includes elementary, secondary, and postsecondary schools, boarding schools, contract schools, and adult education. Assists in the creation and management of educational systems for the benefit of the Native American and Alaskan people.

Engineer: Provides technical expertise in environmental engineering, mining, transportation systems, communication systems, and other fields.

Firefighter Positions: Work with the National Interagency Fire Center, Wildland Fire Programs, to provide organized, skilled crews for wildland and prescribed fire operations. Specific titles include Emergency Firefighter, Hotshot, and Prevention Technician.

Forester: Assists in managing forest resources, including wildlife, timber, and minerals, and recommends techniques which ensure the conservation of these resources.

Range Conservationist: Assists Native Americans and Alaska Natives in overcoming difficulties such as shortages of water supplies, pastures overgrazed by livestock, or dense brush interfering with forage growth. Plans grazing systems, offers advice on water management, and recommends conservation techniques.

Realty Specialist: Offers real estate expertise on contractual documents and the buying, selling, or management of property.

Social Worker: Provides assistance and services relating to medical care referrals, vocational guidance, and counseling for individual and family cases. Obtains information on problems through interviews and home visits.

Soil Conservationist: Suggests conservation tactics and pollution control methods and offers technical help in the construction of ponds, terraces, and contour strip-cropping systems. Often works directly in the field.

Major Activities and Divisions

Tribal Government Services Division: Provides needed social and community development programs.

Education Division: Assists in the creation and management of educational systems.

Trust Services Division: Acts as trustee for the lands and moneys of Native Americans and Alaska Natives.

Through the National Interagency Fire Center, the Branch of Wildland Fire Management provides for wildland fire protection, fire use and hazardous fuels management, and emergency rehabilitation of Indian forest and range lands held in trust by the U.S. You may reach the Fire Center, located in Boise, Idaho, at (208) 387-5447.

Alternative Employment Programs

BIA offers summer jobs at the field installations, giving strong preference to Indian applicants to fill these positions. It does not currently have a co-op or internship program.

Remarks

The BIA gives preference to American Indian applicants, but it does not exclusively hire American Indians. Some recruitment is conducted at colleges and universities with large Native American populations.

Application Prodecures

Direct inquiries to the office that handles the hiring for the area in which you would like to work.

Headquarters
Bureau of Indian Affairs
Branch of Personnel Services
1951 Constitution Ave., NW
Washington, DC 20245
Information: (202) 208-3710
Personnel: (202) 343-2539

Regional Offices

115 4th Ave., SE
Aberdeen, SD 57401
(605) 226-7343

615 N. 1st St.
P.O. Box 26567
Albuquerque, NM 87125-6567
(505) 346-7590

P.O. Box 368
Anadarko, OK 73005
(405) 247-6673

316 N. 26th St.
Billings, MT 59101
(406) 247-7943

Box 25520
Juneau, AK 99802
(907) 586-7177

5th and W. Okmulgee
Muskogee, OK 74401
(918) 687-2296

1 N. 1st St.
P.O. Box 10
Phoenix, AZ 85001
(602) 379-6600

911 NE 11th Ave.
Portland, OR 97232-4169
(503) 231-6702

2800 Cottage Way
Sacramento, CA 95825
(916) 978-6000

Navajo Area Office

P.O. Box 1060
Gallup, NM 87305-1060
(505) 863-8314

Eastern Office

3701 N. Fairfax Dr., Suite 260
Arlington, VA 22203
(703) 235-2571

Bureau of Land Management (BLM)
www.blm.gov

Nature of Work: Energy, environmental protection, forestry/wildlife, land management, mining, recreation, waterways, disaster assistance (fire fighting)

Number of Employees: 10,800

Headquarters: Washington, DC

Regional Locations: Anchorage, AK; Billings, MT; Boise, ID; Cheyenne, WY; Denver, CO; Lakewood, CO; Phoenix, AZ; Portland, OR; Reno, NV; Sacramento, CA; Salt Lake City, UT; Santa Fe, NM; Springfield, VA

Typical Background of New Hires: Archaeology, biology, cartography, earth sciences (surveying hydrology), engineering, forestry, geology, land-use planning, law, physical sciences, recreation

Mission

The Bureau of Land Management oversees 260 million acres of public lands primarily located in the far West and Alaska. Resources managed by the Bureau include timber, minerals, fish and wildlife, geothermal energy, wildlife habitat, endangered plant and animal species, rangeland vegetation, and rivers.

Job Descriptions

Archaeologist: Conducts scientific studies into the anthropological and archaeological history of public land areas. Involves field research at dig sites. Makes recommendations as to the use and development of historical properties.

Cartographer: Graphically represents geographic information through the use of cartographic methods. Evaluates conflicting evidence concerning the character or physical features of the earth. Constructs maps and charts through mathematical, geodetic, and geographic methods.

Engineer: Provides technical expertise in efficient natural resource management, including the building of bridges and waste-treatment systems, the use of mechanical equipment for fire control or brush cutting, and communications systems such as remote telephone and microwave systems. BLM hires civil, electrical, communications, and mining engineers.

Environmental Protection Specialist: Monitors management practices and techniques to ensure that environmental impact is considered in land usage.

Fire Program Positions: The Bureau of Land Management employs more than 1,500 people in the fire program. These employees are hired both as permanent and temporary employees. Entry-level Fire Program Positions include Fire Lookout and Fire Crew positions. Experienced firefighters can become members of the Hotshot Crew or the Fuels Module Crew. Other positions requiring experience include Dispatcher, Engine Operator, Helitack Crew, Smokejumper, and Fire Prevention Officer. Permanent employees in the Bureau's fire program have opportunities to progress even further as Fire Management Officers and Fuels Program Managers.

Forester: Develops and conserves natural forest resources such as timber, forage, watersheds, land, and wildlife. Conducts research in the development of scientific instruments used in forest management.

Geologist: Conducts field research on rock types, rock structure, geologic history, and groundwater conditions. May use aerial photos and seismic and electrical resistivity geophysical methods. Solves problems and makes recommendations regarding road construction, timber harvesting, soil stability, and other issues.

Hydrologist: Determines and analyzes watershed conditions and climatic variables in terms of land-management potentials and hazards. Studies the influence of grazing, timber harvest, minerals management, recreation use, and other management activities on water resources.

Land Law Examiner: Researches laws, contracts, and regulations governing the acquisition, management, usage, and leasing of public lands. Makes recommendations regarding resource extraction, the issuance of rights-of-way, payment programs, and other realty and land-use issues.

Outdoor Recreation Planner: Communicates knowledge of natural resources and wildlife management through the design and implementation of interpretive and educational programs.

Physical Scientist: Positions involve work in either an advanced specialized area of the physical sciences or a blend of many physical science areas such as geology, hydrology, and cartography.

Range Conservationist: Analyzes range resources, fitting the number of livestock and game animals to the available forage supply. Measures how forage plants respond to use by animals and examines how to convert forage to animal products more efficiently.

Soil Scientist: Determines the significance of basic differences of soil capability to resource management. Conducts soil inventories, maps soil area boundaries, and makes recommendations regarding soil conservation tactics.

Wildlife Biologist: Coordinates wildlife needs with other land management activities such as timber harvest, livestock grazing, public use, or road construction. Plans habitat adjustments and suggests courses of action to decrease the detrimental effects on wildlife habitats.

Major Activities and Divisions

The BLM operates its many and diverse programs through its Renewable Resource and Planning Office; Minerals, Realty, and Resource Protection Office; and its Landscape Conservation System. It operates its Fire Program through the National Interagency Fire Center in Boise, Idaho, (208) 387-5447.

Alternative Employment Programs

The BLM participates in the federal STEP and SCEP programs. It targets engineering and physical science majors at the bachelor's and master's levels.

Application Prodecures

BLM has current vacancies listed on the Internet at www.usajobs.opm.gov/a9blm.htm and www.nc.blm.gov/jobs/.

Or, direct inquiries to:

National Human Resources Management Center
Denver Federal Center, Building 50
P.O. Box 25047
Denver, CO 80225-0047
(303) 236-6503

Headquarters Address
Bureau of Land Management
Department of the Interior
Washington, DC 20240
(202) 501-5125
Fax: (202) 452-5124

Bureau of Reclamation
www.usbr.gov

Nature of Work: Agriculture, energy, environmental protection, forestry/ wildlife, recreation, waterways

Number of Employees: 5,700

Headquarters: Denver, CO

Regional Locations: Billings, MT; Boise, ID; Boulder City, NV; Denver, CO; Sacramento, CA; Salt Lake City, UT; Washington, DC

Typical Background of New Hires: Agriculture, agronomy, biology, earth sciences (hydrology), economics, education, engineering, environmental science, geology, land-use planning, meteorology, soil science

Mission

The Bureau of Reclamation is responsible for the development and conservation of the Nation's water resources in the western U.S. It provides municipal and industrial water supplies, hydroelectric power generation, irrigation water for agriculture, flood control, river navigation, river regulation and control, water-quality regulation, fish and wildlife enhancement, and outdoor recreation.

Job Descriptions

Agronomist: Conducts research into such issues as waterweed control and the identification of crop problems.

Biologist: Studies and assesses the biological impact of Bureau projects and prepares environmental statements for proposed federal water resource projects.

Civil Engineer: Plans, constructs, and operates multiple-purpose water development projects involving structures such as storage dams, hydroelectric power plants and pumping plants, canals, tunnels, and pipelines. Specialization is possible in structures, hydraulics, hydrology, geotechnical, construction management, research, project development, or sanitary work.

Electrical Engineer: Designs, installs, operates, and maintains electrical equipment in dams, hydroelectric power plants, pumping plants, and switchyards. Specialization is possible in the applications of computers, microprocessors, electrical equipment, analysis of power systems, power and water control systems, and design of high-voltage transmission systems.

Environmental Engineer: Evaluates the effects of reclamation projects on the environment. Manages air, land, and water resources by developing controls to minimize environmental consequences and to protect and enhance ecosystems. Specialization is possible in water and wastewater treatment, environmental modeling, environmental health, water resources, and hazardous water disposal.

Geologist: Collects and studies samples of minerals, sediments, rocks, and natural liquids and gases. Investigates the influence of climate, topography, plants and animals, and water bodies on specific geological processes.

Hydrologist: Participates in water-related projects such as salinity control, groundwater recharge, and the development of plans for the conservation of water resources.

Natural Resource Specialist: Assesses the impact of water development projects on indigenous wildlife, fishes, and plants of the West. Works to rehabilitate or maintain natural ecosystems that existed before the impact of construction projects and recommends programs to protect species and natural lands from harm.

Mechanical Engineer: Designs, installs, operates, and maintains mechanical equipment associated with power plants, pumping plants, and irrigation systems. Specialization is possible in low-head hydrosolar applications and energy conservation systems, water measurement controls and automation, structural analysis, fabrication and welding, nondestructive testing, and desalinization.

Meteorologist: Conducts research into such weather-related projects as weather modification and cloud seeding.

Realty Specialist: Makes recommendations as to the protection, orderly development, and use of public lands. Involved in the buying, selling, and leasing of federal lands and maintaining public land records.

Soil Scientist: Studies soil capabilities in regard to effective output and resource management. Conducts soil inventories, maps soil area boundaries, and recommends strategies for soil conservation and efficient usage.

Major Activities and Divisions

The projects of the Bureau of Reclamation are numerous and diverse. It serves as the fifth-largest electric utility in the 17 Western states and the nation's largest wholesale water supplier, administering 348 reservoirs. It provides 140,000

Western farmers with irrigation water for 10 million farmland acres and operates 58 hydroelectric power plants.

Alternative Employment Programs

The Bureau participates in the federal SCEP and STEP hiring programs. It also sponsors several job corps centers, which are part of a residential education and job training program for at-risk youth. At Reclamation's training centers in Colorado, Idaho, Utah, and Washington, disadvantaged young people are provided academic, vocational, and social skills. The Bureau hires teachers or training technicians to assist students in gaining the skills they need. See www.usbr.gov and click on Employment for more information.

Application Prodecures

To learn more, contact the regional office directly that handles the geographical area in which you'd like to work:

Human Resources Operations (Denver-Lakewood, CO and Washington, DC)
Denver Federal Center
Building 67, Attn: D-4320
P.O. Box 25007
Denver, CO 80225
(303) 445-2684

Pacific Northwest Region (ID, WA, OR, MT, Northwestern WY)
1150 N. Curtis Rd, Suite 100
Boise, ID 83706-1234
(208) 378-5114

Mid-Pacific Region (OR, Northern NV, Northern CA)
2800 Cottage Way
Sacramento CA 95825-1898
(916) 978-5471

Lower Colorado Region (AZ, Southern NV, Southern CA)
Attn: LC-5000
P.O. Box 61470
Boulder City, NV 89006-1470
(702) 293-8000

Upper Colorado Region (NM, Northeastern AZ, TX, CO, UT, Southwestern WY)
Attn: UC-502, Room 6107
125 South State St.
Salt Lake City, UT 84138-1102
(801) 524-3686

Great Plains Region (CO, NE, KS, OK, MT, WY, ND, SD, TX)
Attn: GP-3500
P.O. Box 36900
316 North 26th St.
Billings, MT 59101-1362
(406) 247-7696

U.S. Fish and Wildlife Service (FWS)
www.fws.gov

Nature of Work: Environmental protection, forestry/wildlife, law enforcement, recreation

Number of Employees: 8,850

Headquarters: Washington, DC

Regional Locations: Anchorage, AK; Albuquerque, NM; Atlanta, GA; Denver, CO; Ft. Snelling, MN; Hadley, MA; Portland, OR

Typical Background of New Hires: Biological sciences (zoology), environmental sciences (natural resource management), natural sciences, recreation

Mission

FWS conserves, protects, and enhances fish and wildlife and their habitats for the continuing benefit of the American people. The Service promulgates an environmental stewardship ethic based on ecological principles, scientific knowledge of wildlife, and a sense of moral responsibility.

Job Descriptions

Fishery Biologist: Studies the life history, habitats, classification, and economic relations of aquatic organisms. Manages fish hatcheries and fishery resources. Gathers scientific data on fish species and the effects of natural and human changes in the environment on the survival and growth of fish. Monitors fish hatchery operations and regulates fishing practices.

General Biologist: Conducts wildlife management field studies and collects samples for assessment. Designs subject field surveys to ensure that results are scientifically valid and conducts independent literature surveys in support of field studies.

Outdoor Recreation Planner: Designs and conducts a variety of interpretive and educational programs that integrate wildlife areas and programs with public usage. Communicates knowledge of fish and wildlife management. May involve some use of graphic arts, interpretive display techniques, or media production.

Refuge Manager: Manages national wildlife refuges to protect and preserve migratory and native bird species, mammals, endangered species, and other wildlife. Devises wildlife management programs and public use policies at the refuge.

Special Agent: Investigates violations of federal laws for the protection and conservation of wildlife. Performs surveillance, raids, and contraband seizures and makes arrests. May also pilot aircraft in connection with enforcement duties.

Wildlife Biologist: Studies the distribution, abundance, habitats, mortality factors, and economic values of mammals, birds, and other wildlife. Plans wildlife management programs, restores or develops wildlife habitats, regulates wildlife populations, and controls wildlife diseases.

Major Activities and Divisions

Migratory Birds and State Programs Directorate: Works to conserve migratory bird populations and their habitats in sufficient quantities to prevent them from being considered as threatened or endangered. Includes the Division of Migratory Bird Management and the Division of Bird Habitat Conservation.

Fisheries and Habitat Conservation Directorate: Works to restore and maintain the health of the nation's fish and wildlife resources. Includes the Division of Fish and Wildlife Management Assistance and Habitat Restoration, and the Division of the National Fish Hatchery System.

Endangered Species Directorate: Shares responsibility for the Endangered Species Act with the National Marine Fisheries Service in the Department of Commerce.

International Affairs Directorate: Seeks to strengthen the interest and ability of local conservation and natural resources institutions and communities in regions around the world to conserve wildlife.

National Wildlife Refuge System: A system of lands set aside to protect wildlife species; this system encompasses more than 93 million acres and more than 570 national wildlife refuges and wetland management districts across the U.S.

Law Enforcement Directorate: Assists wildlife conservation and protection efforts by focusing on potentially devastating threats to wildlife resources such as illegal trade, unlawful commercial exploitation, habitat destruction, and environmental contaminants. The Division investigates wildlife crimes, regulates wildlife trade, helps Americans understand and obey wildlife protections laws, and works in partnership with international, state, and tribal counterparts to conserve wildlife resources.

Remarks

The above list of regional locations does not include the many national wildlife refuges, fish and wildlife laboratories and centers, cooperative research units, and national fish hatcheries in which many employees of the Service work across the United States.

Alternative Employment Programs

The U.S. Fish and Wildlife Service has annual summer positions available at grades 1 through 4. These jobs are posted on the FWS Web site. While the FWS does participate in the federal SCEP student hiring program, it currently does not have an internship program for students interested in the biological sciences. It is working to devise a Biological Sciences Intern Program, so check the FWS Web site for information as this program develops.

For volunteer opportunities with the FWS, call toll free (800) 344-WILD.

Application Prodecures

The FWS lists vacancies on its Web site (link to USAJOBS). Follow the application instructions on the vacancy announcement of interest. Or, contact:

U.S. Fish and Wildlife Service
Department of the Interior
18th and C Streets, NW
Personnel Management Division
Washington, DC 20240
(202) 208-6104
Information: (202) 208-5634 or (703) 358-1743
Fax: (202) 219-2071

U.S. Geological Survey (USGS)
www.usgs.gov

Nature of Work: Earth science, research

Number of Employees: 10,000

Headquarters: Reston, VA

Regional Locations: Major regional research centers are in Lakewood, CO; Menlo Park, CA; Reston, VA. More than 200 field offices exist throughout the U.S.

Typical Background of New Hires: Cartography, earth sciences (hydrology, geophysics), environmental sciences, geology

Mission

The mission of the USGS is to provide geologic, topographic, and hydrologic information that contributes to the wise management of the nation's natural resources and that promotes the health, safety, and well-being of the people. This information consists of maps, databases, and descriptions and analyses of the water, energy, and mineral resources; land surface; underlying geologic structure; and dynamic processes of the earth.

Job Descriptions

Cartographer: Works in various aspects of cartographic production, including both manual cartography and digital cartographic production. Some positions require security clearances and drug testing. Second- or third-shift work may be involved.

Chemist: Analyzes and tests various geologic substances to determine their composition, quality, purity, and other characteristics.

Geologist: Maps geological surface deposits, bedrock, subsurface phenomena, and mineral deposits. Makes and records geological field observations and collects samples for laboratory analysis.

Geophysicist: Conducts research concerning the electric, magnetic, and gravitational field of the earth; the motion and constitution of the earth; and cosmic physics in its relation to the earth and its atmosphere.

Hydrologist: Studies the interactions within the hydrologic cycle with relation to precipitation, stream flow, and subsurface water. Investigates the transport of sediment and dissolved materials in natural waters and assesses the biological changes that result.

Physical Scientist: Conducts research, analysis, and testing that relate to a combination of several physical science fields, with no one science predominant.

Wildlife Biologist: Conducts ecological investigations of complex land, water, and habitat problems and issues. Develops reports and recommendations for resource protection, mitigation, and enhancement.

Major Activities and Divisions

There are four program divisions within the USGS. Each division conducts research in its scientific issue area and has a presence at each of the three major regional offices. These scientific issue areas are biology, geology, geography (mapping), and water. The Biological Resources Division is detailed in the next profile.

Alternative Employment Programs

USGS participates in the STEP and SCEP programs. You may browse USGS vacancies and apply for student jobs online at http://interactive.usgs.gov/Student/Apply/index.asp.

Remarks

USGS has a vacancy notification system that allows you to fill out a form specifying the types of jobs and locations that interest you, and the system will automatically e-mail you whenever a vacancy meeting your criteria opens up on OPM's USAJOBS Web site.

The USGS provides technical assistance and participates in cooperative scientific studies in many countries. Upper-level positions may often involve overseas travel.

Application Prodecures

There are three major regional USGS offices.

Headquarters Personnel Office (and Eastern Region)
Chief, Recruitment and Placement
12201 Sunrise Valley Dr., MS-601
Reston, VA 20192
(703) 648-4000
Personnel: (703) 648-6131
Toll Free: (888) ASK-USGS
Fax: (703) 648-4113

Central Region
U.S. Geological Survey
Box 25046, Denver Federal Center
Denver, CO 80225
(303) 236-5900
Job Hotline: (303) 236-5846

Western Region Personnel Office
Staffing Chief
345 Middlefield Rd., MS 213
Menlo Park, CA 94025
(650) 853-8300
Toll Free: (800) 223-8081 (Option 1, Job Hotline)

Biological Resources Division/USGS
www.biology.usgs.gov

Nature of Work: Biology, research, wildlife

Number of Employees: 1,900

Headquarters: Washington, DC, metro area (Reston, VA)

Regional Locations: Denver, CO; Leetown, WV; Seattle, WA

Typical Background of New Hires: Biological science, botany, computer science, ecology, forestry, microbiology, zoology

---

Mission
To assist in providing the scientific understanding and technologies needed to support the sound management and conservation of our nation's biological resources. The NBS has no regulatory mandate, management responsibility, or advocacy role. It is dedicated to independent science.

Job Descriptions

Biological Sciences Technician: Performs habitat management and development. Maintains and operates biological equipment and facilities. Conducts biological surveys.

Research Biologist: Conducts field studies and biological research to determine the effect, influence, and status of living organisms in various biota.

Wildlife Biologist: Conducts ecological investigations of complex land, water, and habitat problems and issues. Develops reports and recommendations for resource protection, mitigation, and enhancement.

Major Activities and Divisions

Research: Conducts research on contaminants and fish and wildlife disease. Tests for commercial and recreational fishing potential and registers chemicals affecting wildlife habitats.

Inventory and Monitoring: Work includes population monitoring, rare and exotic species surveys, and information sharing with federal, state, and other agencies.

Information Technology Services: Plans and implements technology systems for the objective collection, storage, retrieval, analysis, and dissemination of comprehensive biological data for use by researchers, planners, and others.

Remarks

The Biological Resources Division has Science Centers located throughout the U.S. See http://biology.usgs.gov/pub_aff/centers.html for exact locations.

Application Prodecures

Direct inquiries to:

Biological Resources Division/USGS
12201 Sunrise Valley Dr., MS601
Reston, VA 20192
(703) 648-7471

Minerals Management Service (MMS)
www.mms.gov

Nature of Work: Energy, environmental protection, mining, scientific research, taxes/revenues

Number of Employees: 1,700

Headquarters: Washington, DC

Regional Locations: Anchorage, AK; Lakewood, CO; Camarillo, CA; New Orleans, LA

Typical Background of New Hires: Accounting, biology, engineering, environmental sciences, geology, mathematics, meteorology, oceanography, physics

Mission

The Minerals Management Service conducts all leasing and resource management functions for the nation's Outer Continental Shelf (OCS), which has the potential to supply a significant portion of this nation's future oil and gas needs. The MMS leases offshore areas for exploration and production and monitors drilling and production activities to protect the coastal environments and ensure proper royalty collection.

Job Descriptions

Environmental Protection Specialist: Assists state and local governments on matters relating to environmental protection programs and proposals. Writes environmental impact statements in regard to OCS projects.

Geologist: Maps superficial deposits, bedrock, subsurface phenomena, and mineral deposits. Makes and records geological field observations and collects samples for laboratory analyses.

Geophysicist: Conducts scientific research in exploration geophysics, including gravimetric, magnetic, electrical, and seismic methods; and laboratory and field studies of the physical properties of rocks and minerals. Prepares reports for reference or publication.

Oceanographer: Researches ocean phenomena such as tides, sea ice, currents, waves, and sediments in their relation to temperatures, densities, circulation, etc., including their effect on animal and plant life.

Petroleum Engineer: Performs engineering studies of oil fields. Works on improving primary and secondary recovery methods, including radioactive tracer experiments in water flooding. Conducts research on subjects such as porous reservoir rock, "bottom hole" samples, and underground storage of natural gas. Also supervises development of departmental oil and gas leases.

Physical Scientist: Performs work in the field of physical sciences that includes a combination of disciplines and fields. May specialize in one discipline or conduct work involving several areas of physical science.

Major Activities and Divisions

The MMS is divided into two major programs: Offshore Minerals Management and Minerals Revenue Management. The Offshore program, which manages the mineral resources on the OCS, comprises three regions: Alaska, the Gulf of Mexico, and the Pacific. The Minerals Revenue program is headquartered in Washington, DC, but operationally based in Denver, Colorado. The Gulf of Mexico regional office employs more than 500 people and has district offices in Houma, Lafayette, Lake Charles, and New Orleans, Louisiana, and Lake Jackson, Texas, with a subdistrict office in Corpus Christi, Texas. The Pacific Outer Continental Shelf Region manages 79 federal oil and gas leases offshore near southern California.

Alternative Employment Programs

The Alaska Regional Office provides opportunities for Alaska Native and American Indian students through its INSTEP internships. The program combines a ten-week work experience with a 6-credit course taught at University of Alaska Anchorage.

The Pacific Regional Office in Camarillo, California, hosts a Stay-in-School Internship program. It also hires several students each year to participate in the Department of the Interior's Minority Summer Internship Program. Student interns work with an assigned mentor to learn about the many facets of managing the Pacific Outer Continental Shelf.

For more information, contact:

Minerals Management Service, Pacific Region
770 Paseo Camarillo, 4th Floor
Camarillo, CA 93010

Remarks

The Offshore Mineral's Management program has an informative Web page for the Gulf of Mexico region. It highlights positions within their local area and gives an overview of typical MMS careers. OMM also has intern program pages for the Pacific and Alaska OCS regions.

Application Prodecures

All MMS jobs are listed on OPM's Web site, www.usajobs.opm.gov, which can be reached through the MMS Web site. Or, direct inquiries to:

Headquarters
Minerals Management Service
1849 C Street, NW
Washington, DC 20240
(202) 208-3985

Washington, DC Metropolitan Area
Department of the Interior
Minerals Management Service
Staffing and Classification Branch
Atrium Building
381 Eden St.
Herndon, VA 22070-4817
(703) 787-1410

Minerals Revenue Management

Minerals Management Service
P.O. Box 25165
Denver, CO 80225
(303) 231-3162

Alaska OCS Region

Minerals Management Service
949 East 36th Ave., Room 300
Anchorage, AK 99508-4363
(907) 271-6070
Toll Free: (800)764-2627

Pacific OCS Region

Minerals Management Service
770 Paseo Camarillo
Camarillo, CA 93010
(805) 389-7520
Toll Free: (800) 6PAC-OCS

Gulf of Mexico OCS Region

Minerals Management Service
1201 Elmwood Park Blvd.
New Orleans, LA 70123-2394
(504) 736-2595
Toll Free: (800) 200-GULF

National Park Service
www.nps.gov

Nature of Work: Environmental protection, forestry/wildlife, historic preservation, law enforcement, recreation

Number of Employees: 7,500 permanent full-time; 22,000 including seasonal employees

Headquarters: Washington, DC

Regional Locations: Anchorage, AK; Atlanta, GA; Denver, CO; Omaha, NE; Philadelphia, PA; Oakland, CA. Interpretive Design Centers: Denver, CO; Harpers Ferry, WV

Typical Background of New Hires: Anthropology, archaeology, engineering, geography, history, hotel/restaurant management, landscape architecture, land-use planning, natural sciences, recreation

Mission

The National Park Service has been preserving, protecting, and managing the natural, cultural, historical, and recreational areas of the National Park System since its creation in 1916. Its mission is to conserve natural and cultural resources and to provide the public with recreational and educational experiences.

Job Descriptions

Archaeologist, Historian, Anthropologist, Geographer: Concerned with the Park System's cultural resources. Most of these staff positions are located in the Denver Service Center or the Regional Offices.

Concessions Specialist: Evaluates and monitors restaurants and other concessions operated by private contractors in the National Park Service.

Engineer, Architect, Landscape Architect, Recreational Planner: Mostly work in the Planning and Design Facility in Denver, Colorado. Work on the design of National Park Service sites in terms of environmental impact, educational and inspirational quality, and accessibility.

Fire Program Positions: Fire jobs involve performing field and laboratory work in support of a park or group of parks' vegetation and fire-monitoring programs. Job titles include Dispatcher, Ecologist, Fire Management Officer, Meteorologist, and Forestry Technician. Some positions require prior fire fighting experience.

Others may involve travel. For more information, log on to www.nps.gov/fire/ jobs/descrip.htm.

Geologist, Biologist, Physical Scientist: Research-oriented positions, limited in number and usually requiring advanced degrees or specialized experience.

Museum Specialist: Designs exhibits, manages museum collections, and participates in museum education. Most design work is conducted at Harpers Ferry Center. Other curatorial positions are located in parks and involve management of the site collections or technical conservation work.

Park Police: Preserve the peace, investigate and prevent accidents and crimes, arrest violators, and provide crowd control. Includes horse-mounted, motorcycle, helicopter, and canine units. Usually work in a large urban area such as Washington, DC, New York City, or San Francisco.

Park Ranger: Performs work in the conservation of resources and fire control. Disseminates scientific, natural, or historical information; enforces laws; and performs search and rescue missions. Manages wildlife, forests, lakeshores, historic properties, and recreation areas.

Writer-Editor/Public Information Specialist: Develops Park Service publications and informational programs. Mostly works in Washington, DC, or the regional offices.

Major Activities and Divisions

Although the Park System is not divided into specific program areas, it has a vast array of sites and services. The System comprises 321 units and 83 million acres of land in 49 states, Puerto Rico, Guam, and the Virgin Islands. It contains national preserves, parks, historic sites, battlefields, parkways, and national monuments.

A national Interagency Fire Center is located in Boise, Idaho. Besides the NPS, there are several federal agencies with program areas involving wildfire management, including the Fish and Wildlife Service, the Bureau of Indian Affairs, the Forest Service, NOAA's National Weather Service, and the Bureau of Land Management. For more information, go to www.nifc.gov/.

Alternative Employment Programs

Internships are available, but are administered at the park level or in various NPS centers and offices. Therefore, there is no centralized list of available internships. Contact parks directly by telephone or mail.

Many volunteer opportunities are available through the Student Conservation Association, which operates three volunteer programs: the Resource Assistant Program for young adults, the High School Program, and the Conservation Career Development Program. For information, contact: Student Conservation Association, 1800 N. Kent St., Arlington, VA 22209; telephone: (703) 524-2441.

The National Park Service hires employees on a seasonal basis or as volunteers through the Volunteers in Parks (VIP) program. For more information, contact any regional office or log on to www.nps.gov/volunteer/.

The National Park Service employs a large number of seasonal/temporary employees to fill positions ranging from Park Ranger to Biological Technician. Applicants may apply for employment year round. For more information, call the Seasonal Employment Program at (202) 208-5074 or log on to www.sep.nps.gov/.

Application Prodecures

Direct inquiries to the regional office that handles the hiring for the location in which you would like to work:

Washington Office
National Park Service
Interior Building
1849 C St., NW
Washington, DC 20240
Human Resources: (202) 619-7256

Harpers Ferry Center
National Park Service
Harpers Ferry, WV 25425
(304) 535-6371

Applications for temporary employment should be sent to National Park Service, 1849 C Street NW, Washington, DC 20240; telephone: (202) 208-5074.

Alaska Area Region
Regional Director
National Park Service
2525 Gambell St. Room 107
Anchorage, AK 99503
(907) 257-2687

Northeast Region
Regional Director
National Park Service
U.S. Custom House
200 Chestnut St., Fifth Floor
Philadelphia, PA 19106
(215) 597-7013

Midwest Region
Regional Director
National Park Service
1709 Jackson St.
Omaha, NE 68102
(402) 221-3471

National Capital Region
Regional Director
National Park Service
1100 Ohio Dr., SW
Washington D.C. 20242
(202) 619-7256

Intermountain Region
Regional Director
National Park Service
12795 Alameda Pkwy.
Denver, CO 80225
(303) 969-2500

Southeast Region
Regional Director
National Park Service
1924 Building
100 Alabama St., SW
Atlanta, GA 30303
(404) 562-3100

Pacific West Region
Regional Director
National Park Service
One Jackson Center, Suite 700
1111 Jackson Street
Oakland, CA 94607
(510) 817-1300

Office of Surface Mining, Reclamation, and Enforcement (OSM)
www.osm.gov

Nature of Work: Environmental protection, funds/funding, mining, safety

Number of Employees: 650

Headquarters: Washington, DC

Regional Locations: Albuquerque, NM; Alton, IL; Big Stone Gap, VA; Birmingham, AL; Casper, WY; Charleston, WV; Columbus, OH; Denver, CO; Harrisburg, PA; Indianapolis, IN; Knoxville, TN; Lexington, KY; Morgantown, WV; Olympia, WA; Pittsburgh, PA; Tulsa, OK; Wilkes-Barre, PA

Typical Background of New Hires: Accounting, engineering (mining), environmental science, physical science

Mission

As both a regulatory and funding agency, the OSM works with and through the states to assure a balance between coal production and environmental protection. It also works to ensure that lands affected by mining are restored for other uses and to eliminate dangers to citizens and damage to the environment.

Job Descriptions

Engineer (Civil/General/Mining): Helps establish technical standards for OSM reclamation and enforcement efforts. Interprets and implements the Surface Mining Control and Reclamation Act, studying performance standards and technical requirements. Technical recommendations may include measures necessary to stabilize landslides, correct erosion and sedimentation problems, abate or treat acid mine drainage, control mine subsidence, and extinguish mine fires. Involves on-site research and investigation. Positions are mainly located in the Appalachian, Mid-Continent, and Western Regional Coordinating Centers in Pittsburgh, Pennsylvania; Alton, Illinois; and Denver, Colorado.

Environmental Scientist: Assesses the environmental impact of surface mining techniques in terms of habitat destruction, soil erosion, effect on the hydrologic cycle, and other factors.

Fee Compliance Specialist (Accountant/Auditor): Collects civil penalties and abandoned mine land fee payments. Assists in auditing mine land fee payments.

Geologist: Reviews technical programs designed to meet the Surface Mining Control and Reclamation Act (SMCRA) requirements and provides technical support to Federal and State inspectors. Positions are usually located in Pittsburgh, Pennsylvania; Alton, Illinois; and Denver, Colorado.

Hydrologist: Studies and evaluates the effects of surface mining on the quantity, rates of movement, and quality of water in the various phases of the hydrologic cycle. Reviews technical programs designed to meet the Surface Mining Control and Reclamation Act (SMRCA) requirements. Positions are usually located in Denver, Pittsburgh, and Alton, Illinois.

Realty Specialist: Makes recommendations as to the protection, orderly development, and use of public lands. Conducts sensitive negotiations with landowners, corporate representatives, state and federal officials, and representatives of other political subdivisions. Works with businesses and Indian tribes involving complex special-client relationships. Prepares various realty instruments associated with voluntary consent to enter, use of police power, or acquisition of realty interests. Positions are located in Washington, DC, Denver, Pittsburgh, and Alton, Illinois.

Surface Mining Reclamation Specialist: Conducts and oversees survey, reclamation, and enforcement work to ensure that surface mining operations are conducted in a manner that protects the environment and that affected lands are returned to a stable condition compatible with the value and uses of surrounding lands. Plans and conducts entire survey process, investigates mining operations for violations of federal and state plans, and conducts surveys due to public complaints about damage from blasting and possible pollution from mine sites. Positions are located in all field offices. These positions usually require some travel.

Wildlife Biologist: Studies the effects of surface mining on the habitats of various wildlife species and proposes reclamation strategies to restore those habitats.

Major Activities and Divisions

OSM operates through four program support directorates. These are Regulatory Support, Reclamation Support, Technical Support, and Environmental Operations.

Alternative Employment Programs

Office of Surface Mining sponsors a Summer Watershed Intern Program for students committed to restoring abandoned coal mine lands that have acid mine drainage and/or other environmental concerns. Internships are available for college students who are currently studying in the fields of environmental and civil engineering, biological studies or other environmental-related fields and reclamation activities. For more information, call (202) 208-2937.

OSM also typically hires one to four PMI students annually, and participates in a student employment program for clerical positions. Contact the student employment director at (202) 208-2953.

OSM maintains an employment program for students at the bachelor's or master's level working toward a degree in the physical sciences. Students usually work as Reclamation Specialists or Engineers. Typically, one to ten students are hired per year. Contact the student employment director at (202) 208-2953. OSM also typically hires one to four PMI students annually and participates in a student employment program for clerical positions.

Remarks

The Office of Surface Mining actively recruits on college campuses. Check with your campus placement office for interview dates.

Application Procedures

The Office of Surface Mining does not accept printed resumes or applications for jobs. All applications and resumes must be submitted using the online employment server. For more information, go to www.osm.gov/jobs.htm.

Direct inquiries to the regional office that handles hiring for the location in which you would like to work:

Western Regional Coordinating Center
Office of Surface Mining
1999 Broadway, Suite 3320
Denver, CO 80202
(303) 844-1400
(Oversees the NM, WA, and WY field offices)

Appalachian Region and Washington Headquarters
Office of Surface Mining
Human Resources Division
1951 Constitution Ave., NW
Washington, DC 20240
(202) 208-2719
Human Resources: (202) 208-2773
(Oversees OH, KY, TN, PA, WV, VA field offices.)

Mid-Continent Region
Office of Surface Mining
501 Belle St.
Alton, IL 62002
(618) 463-6460
(Oversees the AL, OK, IN, IL field offices)

✬ Judicial Branch
(www.loc.gov/global/judiciary.html)

Administrative Office of the United States Courts
www.uscourts.gov

Nature of Work: Administrative, justice, law

Number of Employees: 950

Headquarters: Washington, DC

Regional Locations: None

Typical Background of New Hires: Business, computer science, criminal justice, law, mathematics, social sciences

Mission

Provides program management and administrative support to the federal courts throughout the nation. Supports judges, circuit executives, clerks of court, probation and pretrial services officers, court reporters and interpreters, court librarians, and federal defenders in such areas as legislative public affairs, program and policy analysis, budget and finance, human resources, contracting and procurement, automation, and statistics.

Job Descriptions

Attorney: Advises judges and other court officials on administrative matters such as case management, court governance, and local rules of court.

Computer Programmer/Programmer Analyst / Systems Analyst: Programs computer systems. Works closely with user groups to develop programming specifications. Defines user requirements and prepares feasibility studies.

Management Analyst: Reviews and evaluates the management and operations of the federal courts.

Probation Programs Specialist: Develops policies on probation and pretrial work in such areas as drug and alcohol treatment, witness protection, and sentencing.

Major Activities and Divisions

Bankruptcy Division: Determines the duty stations and staff needs of bankruptcy judges and clerks.

Court Administration: Examines the accounts of court officers; allocates money for court operations; prepares statistical reports; and oversees court travel.

Magistrates Division: Administers the offices of U.S. magistrates and prepares legal and administrative manuals.

Probation and Pretrial Services Division: Manages the financial accounts and procedures of the federal probation offices.

Statistics Division: Compiles and analyzes data on financial and programmatic operations.

Alternative Employment Programs

Internships are often available. Call the telephone number below.

Application Procedures

Direct inquiries to:

Administrative Office of the U.S. Courts
AO Personnel, G-200
1 Columbus Circle, NE
Washington, DC 20544
(202) 502-2100
Human Resources: (202) 502-3100

The Supreme Court of the United States
(and the U.S. Court System)
www.supremecourtus.gov/

Nature of Work: Law/justice, libraries

Number of Employees: 325

Headquarters: Washington, DC

Regional Locations: U.S. District Courts across the country

Typical Background of New Hires: Criminal justice, law (J.D.), library science (academic backgrounds vary widely)

Mission

The Supreme Court comprises the Chief Justice of the United States and eight Associate Justices. Power to nominate the Justices is vested in the President of the United States, and appointments are made with the advice of the Senate. The officers of the Supreme Court are the Clerk, the Reporter of Decisions, the Librarian, and the Marshal. The term of the court begins, by law, the first Monday in October of each year and continues as long as the business before the Court requires, usually until about the end of June. Approximately 5,000 cases are passed upon in the course of a term.

Job Descriptions

Law Clerk: Assists justices in background research of cases. Assigned one-year appointments. Hired by individual justices. Should be in the top 5 percent of graduating class of law school. These positions begin at the GS-12 equivalent level. Interested students must either write or telephone an individual justice for consideration.

Assistant Librarian: Selects, catalogs, and classifies materials in the Supreme Court library, which is open to members of the bar of the Court, attorneys for the various federal departments and agencies, and members of Congress. May involve searching services and/or the development of information retrieval systems. Some positions require a broad knowledge of law.

Police Officer: Polices the courts and ensures the safety of court personnel and litigants. Police Officers are paid on the Capitol Hill police scale (approximately a GS-7 level entry equivalent).

Probation Officer: Conducts investigations and prepares reports for the court that may include recommendations for sentencing of individuals convicted of federal offenses. Enforces conditions imposed by the court on offenders/defendants to reduce risk to the community and to provide correctional treatment.

Major Activities and Divisions

Lower Courts: Known as constitutional courts, the lower courts share in the exercise of judicial power. These courts have judges who hold office for life during good behavior. They include the U.S. Court of Appeals, the U.S. Court of Appeals for the Federal Circuit, the United States District Courts, the Territorial Courts, and the Judicial Panel on Multi-District Litigation.

Special Courts: Known as legislative courts, the special courts are created by Congress, and their judges hold office for such term as Congress prescribes, whether it be for a fixed period of years or during good behavior. These include the United States Claims Court, the United States Court of International Trade, the United States Court of Military Appeals, the United States Tax Court, and the Temporary Emergency Court of Appeals.

Alternative Employment Programs

The Supreme Court Fellows program allows outstanding students from diverse backgrounds such as diverse professions and academic backgrounds, including law, the social and behavioral sciences, public and business administration, systems research and analysis, communications, and the humanities to learn firsthand about the federal judiciary. For more information, call (202) 479-3415.

Although the Supreme Court does not offer co-op or internship positions, it does hire high school or college graduates to be Messengers. These are temporary positions (90-day appointments) with the possibility of permanent placement. Other courts within the U.S. courts system may have internship programs. Go to www.uscourts.gov/employment/opportunity.html for more information.

Application Procedures

Direct inquiries to:

Supreme Court of the United States
One 1st St., NE
Personnel Office, Room 3
Washington, DC 20543
(202) 479-3404
Information: (202) 479-3000

☆ Department of Justice (www.usdoj.gov)

Department of Justice / Attorney Employment
www.usdoj.gov

Nature of Work: Legal

Number of Employees: 9,000 (attorneys)

Headquarters: Washington, DC

Regional Locations: Nationwide

Typical Background of New Hires: Law

Mission

As the federal government's law firm, the Department of Justice provides legal advice to the President, and represents the federal government in legal matters.

Job Descriptions

Attorney: The primary responsibility of the Department is to represent the United States in court. The Department's legal practice includes many substantive areas, and therefore an attorney's specific duties will vary from organization to organization.

Major Activities and Divisions

Antitrust Division: Enforces civil and criminal federal antitrust laws; this may include prosecuting criminal bid-rigging and price-fixing cases and reviewing mergers and acquisitions.

Civil Division: Represents the federal government in matters involving claims for and against the government, including commercial litigation, challenges to the constitutionality or legality of federal programs, torts, claims arising under immigration laws, and consumer protection.

Civil Rights Division: Primarily enforces federal laws and executive orders that prohibit unlawful discrimination.

Criminal Division: Prosecutes cases involving public corruption, computer fraud and white-collar crime, organized crime, illegal drugs, child exploitation and obscenity, and internal security.

Environment and Natural Resources Division: Litigates and develops enforcement policy in pollution, public lands and natural resources, and Native American issues.

Tax Division: Handles civil and criminal litigation arising from the internal revenue laws, including tax refund suits, tax claims in bankruptcy, collection actions, administrative summonses, tort actions against Internal Revenue Service officials, and financial institution and health care fraud.

Alternative Employment Programs

Each year, the Justice Department's Legal Intern Program hires students who have finished their first year of law school. Typically, these are volunteer positions and are located in Washington, DC, in field offices, and in U.S. Attorneys' Offices nationwide. For more information, contact the Office of Attorney Recruitment and Management, Volunteer Summer Legal Intern Positions, U.S. Department of Justice, Room 7254–Main Building, 950 Pennsylvania Ave., NW, Washington, DC 20530-0001, or go to www.usdoj.gov/oarm/ and click on intern Volunteer Opportunities.

Application Procedures

All Justice Department organizations accept unsolicited attorney applications; therefore, applicants may send their resume directly to the organization in which they have interest. The Justice Department's Web site has excellent information for employment seekers, including a directory of organizational addresses and contacts for job seekers. You can find this at www.usdoj.gov/oarm/attvacancies.html.

For more information, contact:

The U.S. Department of Justice
Office of Attorney Personnel Management
Main Building, Room 6150
10th St. and Pennsylvania Ave., NW
Washington, DC 20530
(202) 514-1432
24-hour Information and Voice-mail: (202) 514-3396
TDD: (202) 516-2113

Bureau of Prisons
www.bop.gov

Nature of Work: Law enforcement

Number of Employees: 33,250

Headquarters: Washington, DC

Regional Locations: Annapolis Junction, MD; Atlanta, GA; Dublin, CA; Dallas, TX; Kansas City, MO; Philadelphia, PA

Typical Background of New Hires: Criminal justice, law, social sciences

Mission

Operates the federal penal system's prisons and community treatment centers.

Job Descriptions

Attorney: Represents the Bureau in matters such as tort claims, conditions-of-confinement, mental competency, personal liability, contract protests, and injunctive actions.

Chaplain: Provides for the spiritual and religious welfare of inmates.

Correctional Officer: Enforces the rules and regulations governing penal institutions, supervises inmate work assignments, and counsels inmates.

Correctional Treatment Specialist: Recommends educational, work, vocational training, and counseling programs to inmates. Works with inmates, their families, probation officers, social agencies, and others in developing release plans for inmates.

Drug Treatment Specialist: Conducts interviews to determine inmate treatment eligibility; conducts drug education classes for groups of inmates; provides group and individual counseling to inmates with substance use disorders.

Food Service Specialist: Supervises the operation of food supply services at federal prisons, including storerooms, kitchens, dining rooms, meat shops, and bakeries.

Human Resources Specialist: Supports the organization in recruiting, labor relations, compensation, benefits, employee relations, and security.

Medical Officer: Provides medical and dental care to inmates and oversees health care programs at prisons.

Nurse Practitioner: Provides care to sick or injured inmates and promotes better health practices.

Pharmacist: Compounds prescriptions and dispenses and preserves drugs, medicines, and chemicals.

Psychologist: Provides consultative services to inmates, helping them adjust to prison life and post-release.

Recreation Specialist: Evaluates, plans, and organizes recreational programs for inmates.

Safety Specialist: Administers the safety and occupational health laws and regulations at correctional institutions.

Teacher: Teaches inmates, including those having environmental, cultural, and economic disadvantages.

Training Instructor: Administers vocational training programs for inmates.

Major Activities and Divisions

Central Office: Located in Washington, DC, this office issues standards and policy guidelines and coordinates all Bureau activities on a nationwide basis.

Correctional Programs Division: Oversees correctional services, drug abuse treatment, chaplaincy service, and personnel management.

Health Services Division: Provides medical, psychiatric, and dental support services and promotes health and safety at each institution.

Industries, Education and Vocational Training (IE&VT) Division: Oversees the education, vocational training, and Inmate Placement Program for the Federal Bureau of Prisons (BOP). In addition, the IE&VT Division manages Federal Prison Industries (FPI).

Alternative Employment Programs

The Bureau of Prisons participates in the SCEP and STEP federal student hiring programs and offers summer internships from mid-May until the end of September. It also participates in a junior COSTEP program for students who have completed at least one year of study in medical, dental, or veterinary school or have completed at least two years of study in a health-related field. For more information about student employment opportunities, call (202) 307-3177 or e-mail BOP-HRM/ Recruitment@bop.gov.

Remarks

Correctional Officers must successfully complete the Correctional Officer training program at the Federal Law Enforcement Training Center in Glynco, Georgia.

Application Procedures

Direct inquiries to:

Chief of Recruiting
Federal Bureau of Prisons
Room 460, HOLC
320 1st St., NW
Washington, DC 20534
(202) 307-3204

Drug Enforcement Administration (DEA)
www.DEA.gov

Nature of Work: Drugs/abuse, law enforcement

Number of Employees: 9,500

Headquarters: Washington, DC

Regional Locations: Atlanta, GA; Boston, MA; Caribbean; Chicago, IL; Dallas, TX; Denver, CO; El Paso, TX; Detroit, MI; Houston, TX; Los Angeles, CA; Miami, FL; Newark, NJ; New Orleans, LA; New York, NY; Philadelphia, PA; Phoenix, AZ; San Diego, CA; San Francisco, CA; Seattle, WA; St. Louis, MO. DEA also has offices in 56 foreign countries.

Typical Background of New Hires: Chemistry, criminal justice

Mission

Enforces drug laws and regulations by suppressing major trafficking organizations, apprehending their leaders, and seizing their assets. DEA also enforces regulations concerning the legal manufacture and distribution of controlled substances.

Job Descriptions

Many DEA positions involve overseas travel or extensive overseas assignments. DEA employs several hundred workers overseas in its foreign offices.

Diversion Investigator: Audits companies legally producing controlled substances ensuring compliance with applicable laws.

Forensic Chemist: Works with state-of-the-art instruments that analyze many different types of evidence, and conducts research in the development of new methods of analysis. Provides expert testimony in federal and state courts to support the DEA enforcement mission

Intelligence Research Specialist: Researches complex projects in such areas as drug cultivation and production, methods of transportation, trafficking routes, and analysis of trafficking organizations. Develops and presents information to case agents, supervisory personnel, U.S. Attorneys, and grand juries for use in seizure and forfeiture of assets and prosecution purposes.

Special Agent: Investigates the criminal production and distribution of drugs, gathers evidence, testifies in criminal court proceedings, and gives public presentations on DEA's responsibilities.

Major Activities and Divisions

Office of Aviation Operations (OA): Provides aviation support to domestic offices and program initiatives throughout the U.S. These operations consist of air-to-ground, air-to-water, air-to-air, electronic surveillance, and photographic reconnaissance. Based at Ft. Worth, Texas, Alliance Airport, OA consist of 95 aircraft and 117 special agents/pilots.

The Computer Forensics Program (CFP): Applies computer technology and specialized seizure and evidence handling techniques to retrieve information from computer systems for investigative or intelligence purposes.

Demand Reduction Program: Works to educate the public about the dangers of drugs and the effects of drug abuse on the nation.

High Intensity Drug Trafficking Areas Program: Works to reduce drug trafficking in the most critical areas of the country, thereby reducing its impact in other areas.

Intelligence Program: Initiates new investigations of major drug organizations, strengthens ongoing ones and subsequent prosecutions, develops information that leads to seizures and arrests, and provides policy makers with drug trend information

Mobile Enforcement Teams Program: Helps local law enforcement entities attack the violent drug organizations in their neighborhoods.

Diversion Control Program: Works to eradicate the problems associated with the diversion of legitimately manufactured controlled substances into the illicit drug market.

Alternative Employment Programs

Student hiring programs are available, depending on funding availability.

Remarks

DEA basic Agents attend a 16-week training course held at the Justice Training Center in Quantico, Virginia. In addition to undergoing a grueling physical training program, basic Agents receive extensive training in all facets of drug law enforcement operations.

Diversion Investigators, Intelligence Research Specialists, and Forensic Chemists must also complete extensive training courses.

Application Procedures

Direct basic inquiries to:

Drug Enforcement Administration
Office of Personnel
2401 Jefferson Davis Highway
Alexandria, VA 22301
 (202) 307-1000

Special Agent Recruitment
Drug Enforcement Administration
700 Army Navy Dr.
Arlington, VA 22202
Toll Free: (800) DEA-4288

Diversion Investigator Applicants
DEA Headquarters
Attn: Diversion Investigator Hiring
(ODAP)
2401 Jefferson Davis Highway
Alexandria, VA 22301
(202) 307-8846

Intelligence Research Specialist Applicants
DEA Headquarters
Attn: NPMS
2401 Jefferson Davis Highway
Alexandria, VA 22301

Forensic Chemist applicants should log on to www.usdoj.gov/dea/job/chemist/application.htm for a list of DEA laboratories, including addresses and phone numbers to contact.

Federal Bureau of Investigation (FBI)
www.fbi.gov

Nature of Work: Intelligence, law enforcement

Number of Employees: 22,300

Headquarters: Washington, DC

Regional Locations: 56 field offices across the U.S. and 30 foreign liaison offices

Typical Background of New Hires: Accounting, computer science, engineering, language, law, liberal arts

Mission

Investigates violations of most federal laws. Emphasis is placed on fighting organized crime, drugs, terrorism, white-collar crime, and foreign counter-intelligence.

Job Descriptions

Special Agent: Conducts sensitive national security investigations into such matters as organized crime, white-collar crime, public corruption, financial crime, fraud against the government, bribery, copyright matters, civil rights violations, bank robbery, extortion, kidnapping, air piracy, terrorism, foreign counterintelligence, interstate criminal activity, fugitive and drug-trafficking matters. Gathers and reports facts; locates witnesses; compiles evidence in cases involving federal jurisdiction; and testifies in court.

Professional Support Positions: The FBI hires many people with diverse academic and career experience to fill support positions. These include crime scene specialists, linguists, intelligence research specialists, laboratory technicians, fingerprint experts, biologists, chemists, language specialists, information technology specialists, and many others. All are working to improve the safety and security of the nation. Log on to www.fbijobs.com/ for more information and current vacancy listings.

Major Activities and Divisions

Counter-Terrorism Division: Consolidates all FBI counter-terrorism initiatives. The National Infrastructure Protection Center (NIPC) and the National Domestic Preparedness Office (NDPO) are assigned to this division.

Criminal Investigative Division: Counters various types of criminal activity, including terrorism, violent crime, organized crime, discrimination, and white-collar crime.

Criminal Justice Information Services Division: Operates the Bureau's automated fingerprint service.

Investigative Services Division: Extracts information from case files and other sources to identify future trends and means of preventing crime and threats to national security.

National Security Division: Gathers and analyzes data on the composition and movement of terrorist, subversive, and organized criminal organizations.

Laboratory Division: Conducts the FBI's forensic science research.

Alternative Employment Programs

The FBI Academy, located on the Marine Corps Base at Quantico, Virginia, offers a full-time, unpaid internship. Interns typically are majoring in accounting, adult education, behavioral sciences, hotel management, human resource management, communications, interviewing and interrogations, and media and television production.

FBI Honors Internship Program: Located in Washington, DC, the Honors program offers FBI internships to academically outstanding college juniors or graduate students. Contact the FBI field office nearest your campus for applications and additional information.

The FBI's National Center for the Analysis of Violent Crime (NCAVC) offers full-time unpaid internships to students who are at least a college junior with a minimum GPA of 3.0. Duties are related to the violent crime research of the NCAVC. Direct questions to: FBI Academy–NCAVC, Quantico, Virginia 22135; telephone: (703) 632-4358.

The FBI also participates in the PMI hiring program and recruits extensively on college campuses across the U.S.

Remarks

Special Agents must successfully complete a 16-week training program at the FBI Academy in Quantico, Virginia. The program includes academic study, physical fitness training, and instruction in firearms and self-defense.

Application Procedures

See vacancy listings at www.fbijobs.com. Or, direct inquiries to:

Federal Bureau of Investigation
National Recruitment Program
9th St. and Pennsylvania Ave., NW
Washington, DC 20535
(202) 324-3000

Or, contact the Applicant Coordinator at the nearest FBI office. Find addresses and phone numbers for field office locations at www.fbi.gov/contact/fo/info.htm.

Immigration and Naturalization Service (INS)
www.ins.gov

Nature of Work: Immigration, law enforcement

Number of Employees: 32,787

Headquarters: Washington, DC

Regional Locations: Burlington, VT; Dallas, TX, Laguna Niguel, CA (regional offices). INS also has district offices and centers across the U.S. and overseas offices in Bangkok, Mexico City, and Rome.

Typical Background of New Hires: Criminal justice

Mission

Controls the entry of aliens into the U.S. by denying admission to unqualified aliens; maintains information on alien status; deports aliens not legally entitled to reside in the U.S.; and facilitates the certification and citizenship process.

Job Descriptions

Asylum Officer: Determines if an applicant for asylum satisfies the requirements of the Immigration and Nationality Act.

Adjudications Officer: Reviews applications to become a U.S. citizen, to import foreign workers, and other requests.

Border Patrol Agent: Prevents the illegal entry of aliens into the U.S. by patrolling border crossings. Position requires a five-month training program (including Spanish language classes) at one of the Border Patrol Academies. First duty stations are often along the Southwest Border.

Deportation Officer: Tracks the deportation proceedings of illegal aliens and facilitates their removal by working with foreign embassies to arrange travel documents and transportation.

Detention Enforcement Officers: Apprehend, arrest, transport, and process aliens being detained and/or deported for violations of immigration laws.

Immigration Agent (Enforcement): Performs law enforcement and administrative tasks involving employer sanctions, criminal aliens, and the apprehension of absconders from deportation proceedings.

Immigration Information Officer (IIO): Provides information about immigration and nationality law and regulations for people applying for benefits.

Immigration Inspector: Inspects the immigration status of persons arriving at all U.S. ports of entry.

Special Agent: Investigates violations of the Immigration and Naturalization Act and other statutes.

Major Activities and Divisions

The INS has four major mission areas:

* ✶ Conducts immigration inspections of travelers entering (or seeking entry) to the United States as they arrive at officially designated ports of entry.

* ✶ Regulates permanent and temporary immigration to the United States.

* ✶ Maintains control of U.S. borders. The Border Patrol is responsible for securing the 8,000 miles of international boundaries in vehicles, aircraft, or boats, as well as on horseback or on foot.

* ✶ Identifies and removes people who have no lawful immigration status in the United States.

Alternative Employment Programs

INS maintains a co-op program for various occupations, depending on the availability of funding.

Remarks

All applicants for Border Patrol positions must take a written exam. To register for the exam through the Internet, go to http://staffing.opm.gov/BPA. Or, to register for the exam by telephone through the Telephone Application Processing System (TAPS), call toll free (888) 300-5500. Immigration Inspectors must also take a written exam.

More information on Border Patrol positions can be found at www.ins.usdoj.gov/graphics/lawenfor/bpatrol/index.htm.

Application Procedures

The INS does not have a complete list of its current vacancies on its Web site. Try OPM's USAJOBS for a current vacancy listing, or contact:

INS Headquarters
Headquarters Personnel Support Section
425 I St.
Washington, DC 20536
Attn.: Human Resources
Human Resources: (202) 514-2530
Information: (202) 514-4316, 4330, or 4354

U.S. Marshals Service
www.usdoj.gov/marshals

Nature of Work: Law enforcement

Number of Employees: 4,100

Headquarters: Washington, DC

Regional Locations: Regional offices and suboffices are located nationwide as well as in Guam and Puerto Rico.

Typical Background of New Hires: Criminal justice

Mission

Protects federal courts, judges, attorneys, and jurors; apprehends most federal fugitives; operates the witness security program; transports federal prisoners; executes court orders and arrest warrants; administers the National Asset Seizure and Forfeiture Program; and prevents civil disturbances.

Job Descriptions

Deputy U.S. Marshal: Apprehends fugitives who have escaped prison, violated parole, or failed to appear before courts as ordered. Protects federal courts, judges, attorneys, and witnesses. Serves processes and warrants, guards endangered witnesses, transports prisoners, and seizes and manages assets acquired from criminal activities.

Major Activities and Divisions

Office of the Associate Director for Operations: Administers the Service's enforcement, court security, witness protection, prisoner transportation, and asset seizure and forfeiture programs.

Special Operations Group: Quells mob violence in situations requiring federal intervention.

Office of the Assistant Director for Inspections: Investigates and evaluates alleged violations of misconduct by employees of the U.S. Marshals Service.

Alternative Employment Programs

The U.S. Marshals Service maintains a co-op program for students from various disciplines.

Remarks

Applicants for Deputy U.S. Marshal positions must pass the Deputy U.S. Marshal exam before being considered for a position. There are also several other aspects to the application process, including a psychological suitability screening, a medical examination, and a fitness assessment.

Application Procedures

Direct inquiries to the district recruiting officer for the geographic area in which you'd like to work. Names, addresses, and phone numbers of district recruiting officers can be found at www.usdoj.gov/marshals/careers/recrdir.html. Or, contact:

U.S. Marshals Service
Human Resources Division
Law Enforcement Division
Washington, DC 20530-1000
(202) 307-9000

☆ Department of Labor

The job site for all DOL agencies is at www.jobs2.quickhire.com/dol/.

Bureau of Labor Statistics (BLS)
www.bls.gov

Nature of Work: Economic policy, statistics

Number of Employees: 2,500

Headquarters: Washington, DC

Regional Locations: Atlanta, GA; Boston, MA; Chicago, IL; Dallas, TX; Kansas City, MO; New York, NY; Philadelphia, PA; San Francisco, CA

Typical Background of New Hires: Computer science, economics, mathematics, statistics

Mission

The BLS gathers and publishes information about the U.S. economy that is relevant to current issues. This impartial and sometimes sensitive statistical data has become the basis for setting national economic policy affecting employment, unemployment, prices, wages, productivity, industrial relations, and occupational safety and health. The Bureau publishes such statistical collections as the *Monthly Labor Review, Employment and Earnings*, and *Occupational Outlook Quarterly*, as well as surveys such as the *Consumer Price Index*, and the *Producer Price Index*.

Job Descriptions

Computer Specialist: Designs and implements data processing systems to support the Bureau's statistical surveys. In all stages of planning, designing, and implementation of computer systems, programmers work as a team with economists and statisticians. The standard programming language at the Bureau is PL/1, although COBOL is used for some applications. The data base management system standard for the Bureau is TOTAL.

Economist: Gathers economic data by planning and conducting surveys and through other techniques. Prepares statistical tables and charts that present economic data and prepares reports for BLS publications.

Mathematical Statistician: Gathers statistical data and applies statistical methods to draw inferences from this data as to magnitudes, differences, and relationships. Assists in the development of statistical techniques and surveys and prepares charts, tables, and reports for BLS publications.

Major Activities and Divisions

BLS headquarters and regional offices are organized along Program lines. Each regional location has a Regional Commissioner who reports to the Associate Commissioner for Field Operations located in Washington, DC. Under the Regional Commissioner are three Assistant Regional Commissioners, one each for Price, Compensation, and Federal/State Cooperative Programs. Each region also has a public information unit, staffed primarily with economists.

Remarks

BLS requires applicants for Economist positions to take a test. Information on test dates and sites and other recruitment information can be found on the BLS Web site at www.BLS.gov. A test-prep guide for the economist test can be found at http://stats.bls.gov/bls/econprepguide.htm.

BLS regional offices also have opportunities for part-time employment for qualified candidates collecting data used to develop the Consumer Price Index. See the BLS Web site for more information.

Alternative Employment Programs

BLS offers several student hiring programs:

* ✶ Co-op Program: Offers a chance for a noncompetitive appointment after graduation. For information, call (202) 691-6606 or (800) 827-5334 toll free.

* ✶ Summer Employment Program: A summer employment position in BLS is a temporary job that begins after May 12 and ends before October 1 of the same year. Applications must normally be submitted to BLS between March 15 and April 1. For information, call (202) 691-6615.

* ✶ PMI Program: As described in Chapter 5. For specific BLS information, call (202) 691-6612.

Application Procedures

Entry-level Economist positions (GS-5 or GS-7) in BLS Regional Office cities may be applied for through a single announcement open for an "indefinite" time period. This means that a job seeker may apply for an Economist position in eight cities where the BLS has offices without a specific vacancy being available.

Direct inquiries to the Regional Office in which you would like to work:

Region 1: Boston, MA (includes New York City)
JFK Federal Building, Room E-310
Boston, MA 02203
(617) 565-2358 or 2337

Region 2: New York, NY
(limited openings - use Region 1 contacts for more employment opportunities in NY city and state)
Regional Economic Analysis and Information
201 Varick St., Suite 800
New York, NY 10014-4811
(212) 337-2425

Region 3: Philadelphia, PA
The Curtis Center - BLS Suite 610-East
170 South Independence Mall
Philadelphia, PA 19104
(215) 861-5656

Region 4: Atlanta, GA
Atlanta Federal Center
61 Forsyth St., SW, Room 7T50
Atlanta, GA 30303
(404) 562-2499

Region 5: Chicago, IL
Federal Office Building, Ninth Floor
230 S. Dearborn St.
Chicago, IL 60604
(312) 353-7200 Ext 503

Region 6: Dallas, TX
Federal Bldg., Room 221
525 Griffin St.
Dallas, TX 75202-5028
(214) 767-6951
or

Kansas City, MO
1100 Main Street
Kansas City, MO 64105

Regions 9 and 10: San Francisco, CA
71 Stevenson St., Suite 600
San Francisco, CA 94119-3766
(415) 975-4375

Or, direct inquiries to:

U.S. Bureau of Labor Statistics
Division of Human Resources
2 Massachusetts Avenue, NE, Suite 4230
Washington, DC 20212-0001
(202) 691-5200
Toll Free: (800) 827-5334
Jobs Questions: AskRecruit@bls.gov

Employment and Training Administration (ETA)
www.eta.gov

Nature of Work: Employment, low-income people

Number of Employees: 1,400

Headquarters: Washington, DC

Regional Locations: Atlanta, GA; Boston, MA; Chicago, IL; Dallas, TX; Denver, CO; Kansas City, MO; New York, NY; Philadelphia, PA; San Francisco, CA; Seattle, WA

Typical Background of New Hires: Economics, industrial relations, psychology, social sciences

Mission

The ETA administers programs to provide work experience and training for groups having difficulty entering or returning to the workforce and monitors state employment offices and employment insurance programs.

Job Descriptions

Manpower Development Specialist: Designs and administers programs regarding employment resources, job requirements, employee development, and utilization of the labor force.

Unemployment Insurance Program Specialist: Develops and evaluates federal and state unemployment insurance programs. Sets minimum standards and relays new information regarding state employment security agencies and the administration of their social insurance programs.

Major Activities and Divisions

Office of Employment Security: Manages programs operated by the state employment agencies.

Office of Job Training: Develops and issues federal policies pertaining to the operation of the Job Training Partnership Act. The goal of the act is to train or retrain and place eligible (usually economically disadvantaged) individuals in permanent, unsubsidized employment.

Alternative Employment Programs

ETA offers summer internships that are related to a student's major. It also offers other student employment positions.

Application Procedures

Direct inquiries to:

Employment and Training Administration
200 Constitution Ave., NW, Room S5214
Washington, DC 20210
(202) 219-6871

Employment Standards Administration
www.dol.gov/dol/esa

Nature of Work: Employment, wages/prices/rates

Number of Employees: 4,000

Headquarters: Washington, DC

Regional Locations: Atlanta, GA; Boston, MA; Chicago, IL; Dallas, TX; Denver, CO; Kansas City, MO; New York, NY; Philadelphia, PA; San Francisco, CA; Seattle, WA

Typical Background of New Hires: Economics, law, liberal arts, social sciences

Mission

The Employment Standards Administration oversees programs dealing with minimum wage and overtime standards, registration of farm labor contractors, determining prevailing wage rates to be paid on government contracts, nondiscrimination on government contracts, and workers' compensation programs.

Job Descriptions

Equal Opportunity Specialist: Evaluates and investigates compliance programs and problems. Participates in research projects that identify patterns of minority and female underutilization or discrimination. Analyzes employment data from compliance reports to determine employment patterns affecting minority group persons in the workforce.

Salary and Wage Specialist: Collects information from selected occupational samples regarding current pay rates and wage benefits. Analyzes pay data and constructs or verifies pay schedules or rates.

Wage and Hour Compliance Specialist: Investigates commercial, industrial, and agricultural organizations to determine compliance with labor laws. Conducts negotiations to correct violations and to secure future compliance. Makes recommendations concerning compliance, advises state employment staff on the rights of employees, and supplies information regarding federal labor laws.

Workers' Compensation Claims Examiner: Performs quasi-legal work in developing, adjusting, or authorizing the settlement of claims that pertain to unemployment, disability, and death compensation.

Major Activities and Divisions

Wage and Hour Division: Administers programs designed to protect low-wage workers.

Federal Contract Compliance Program: Establishes policies to ensure nondiscrimination in employment by government contractors.

Office of Workers' Compensation Programs: Administers the three basic federal workers' compensation laws.

Office of Labor Management Standards: Ensures basic standards of democracy and fiscal responsibility in labor organizations representing employees in private industry.

Alternative Employment Programs

The Employment Standards Administration: Hires co-op students to fill entry-level professional positions and offers a limited summer hiring program as the budget allows.

Application Procedures

Direct inquiries to:

Employment Standards Administration
200 Constitution Ave., NW, Room S3316
Washington, DC 20210
(202) 693-0001

Mine Safety and Health Administration (MSHA)
www.msha.gov

Nature of Work: Mining, safety

Number of Employees: 2,300

Headquarters: Arlington, VA

Regional Locations: There are 16 district offices, 23 subdistrict offices, and 109 field offices throughout the U.S.

Typical Background of New Hires: Engineering, health sciences

Mission

MSHA develops safety and health programs and standards aimed at preventing and reducing mine accidents and occupational diseases in the mining industry.

Job Descriptions

Mine Safety and Health Inspector/Specialist: Works to prevent conditions that are potentially hazardous to the safety and health of mine workers. Reviews and cites violations in underground and/or surface mines. Usually involves travel.

Mining Engineer: Relates the search for, efficient removal of, and transportation of ore to the health and safety of mine workers. Requires general knowledge of construction and excavation methods, materials handling, and the processes involved in preparing mined materials for use.

Major Activities and Divisions

Coal Mine Safety and Health: Enforces the Mine Act at all U.S. coal mines. Conducts inspections of underground and surface coal mines, investigates fatal and serious nonfatal accidents, and issues citations and orders for any observed violations.

Metal and Nonmetal Mine Safety and Health: Enforces the Mine Act at all metal and nonmetal mining operations in the United States. Conducts inspections and issues citations when violations are observed. Investigates mine accidents and complaints of hazardous conditions reported by miners.

Alternative Employment Programs

MSHA offers a limited student employment program and hires a small number of students to work during the summer.

Application Procedures

Direct inquiries to:

Mine Safety and Health Administration
Ballston Towers #3, Room 500
4015 Wilson Blvd.
Arlington, VA 22203
(703) 235-1452

Occupational Safety and Health Administration (OSHA)
www.osha.gov

Nature of Work: Safety

Number of Employees: 2,300

Headquarters: Washington, DC

Regional Locations: Atlanta, GA; Boston, MA; Chicago, IL; Dallas, TX; Denver, CO; Kansas City, MO; New York, NY; Philadelphia, PA; San Francisco, CA; Seattle, WA

Typical Background of New Hires: Biology, engineering, physical sciences, psychology, public health, social sciences

---

Mission

OSHA develops occupational safety and health standards and issues safety regulations. It conducts investigations and inspections to determine the status of compliance with safety and health standards and issues citations for noncompliance.

Job Descriptions

Industrial Hygienist: Conducts inspections to enforce federal health and safety standards. Studies occupational health hazards affecting employees, and develops federal safety and health standards. Provides technical assistance in the development of industrial hygiene programs in both the public and private sectors. Usually involves field travel.

Safety Engineer: Develops safety standards designed to prevent occupational accidents by reducing potential hazards. Evaluates proposed designs to ensure conformance with engineering standards.

Safety and Occupational Health Specialist: Identifies occupational hazards and assesses potential accident risk. Conducts on-site investigations into occupational accidents and prescribes accident preventive techniques. Requires knowledge of engineering and scientific principles.

Major Activities and Divisions

OSHA is divided into several directorates that work to develop safety and health standards and ensure their compliance in workplace settings across the U.S. These include: the Directorate of Construction, the Directorate of Compliance Programs, the Directorate of Health Standards Programs, and the Directorate of Safety Standards Programs.

Alternative Employment Programs

OSHA hires approximately one to ten students annually to fill positions as Computer Specialists, Engineers, and Industrial Hygienists. These typically begin at the GS-4 level and are filled by college students in their sophomore and junior years. Contact the student employment director at (202) 523-8013 for more information.

Application Procedures

Direct inquiries to:

Occupational Safety and Health Administration
Frances Perkins Building
200 Constitution Ave., NW
Washington, DC 20210
(202) 693-1999

Pension and Welfare Benefits Administration (PWBA)
www.dol.gov/pwba/welcome.html

Nature of Work: Insurance/benefits

Number of Employees: 500

Headquarters: Washington, DC

Regional Locations: Atlanta, GA; Boston, MA; Chicago, IL; Dallas, TX; Fort Wright, KY; Kansas City, MO; Los Angeles, CA; New York, NY; Philadelphia, PA; San Francisco, CA

Typical Background of New Hires: Accounting, business, economics, finance/banking, law

Mission

PWBA enforces the standards designed to protect more than $1 trillion in pension and other benefits.

Job Descriptions

Employee Benefit Plan Specialist: Works to protect the interests of employees who participate in private pension and welfare plans and the beneficiaries of those employees.

Investigator (Pension): Conducts investigations into complaints of violations of labor legislation relating to pension administration. Develops violations cases for referral to the Department of Justice and negotiates compliance. Provides technical assistance on pension laws and legislation.

Major Activities and Divisions

PWBA is divided into several program offices that carry out its mission. These include the Office of Exemption Determinations, the Office of Regulations and Interpretation, the Office of Health Plan Standards and Compliance Assistance, and the Office of Enforcement.

Alternative Employment Programs

PWBA may offer student employment positions, depending upon budget constraints.

Application Procedures

Direct inquiries to:

National Capital Service Center
Pension and Welfare Benefits Administration
200 Constitution Ave., NW
Washington, DC 20210
(202) 693-8664

> ### Pension Benefit Guaranty Corporation (PBGC)
> ### www.pbgc.gov
> **Nature of Work:** Business, insurance/benefits
> **Number of Employees:** 750
> **Headquarters:** Washington, DC
> **Regional Locations:** None
> **Typical Background of New Hires:** Accounting, business, mathematics

Mission

PBGC insures more than 66,000 defined-benefit pension plans in the private sector. It is a self-financing, wholly owned government corporation governed by a Board of Directors consisting of the Secretaries of Labor, Commerce, and Treasury.

Job Descriptions

Accountant: Performs a variety of functions, including overseeing premium collections, transferring assets into the trust fund, tracking employer liability, administering the revolving fund, developing manual and automated systems, and administering revolving funds used in the Corporation's daily operations.

Actuary: Reviews and identifies data needed for actuarial purposes. Analyzes plan documents of terminated pension plans in order to determine benefit entitlement and calculates the Title IV benefits for each plan participant. Calculates the present value of guaranteed benefits and allocates pension plan assets by priority categories according to Tide IV of ERISA and PBGC regulations. Develops instructions for benefit determinations.

Attorney: Works in the Office of the General Council. The Office oversees all of the litigation of PBGC, most of it in the federal courts. Unlike most federal agencies, PBGC has independent litigating authority, and a PBGC attorney can expect to retain responsibility for a case in litigation. PBGC has a staff of about 80 attorneys, and cases are diverse, ranging over bankruptcy, pensions, labor law, procurement and tax — all in the context of substantial federal court litigation.

Auditor: Works on range-specified audit assignments that facilitate the efforts of higher-level auditors. Assists with field audits of plans terminated under distress procedures. Audits small- to mid-size defined pension plans that have no obvious complicating features and prepares correspondence and management reports.

Financial Analyst: Works in several parts of the Corporation, projecting long-range trends, overseeing investments, developing contingency plans, valuing assets, and assisting the legal and executive staffs in conducting settlement negotiations.

Pension Law Specialist: Reviews, verifies, calculates, and authorizes benefit payments to the participants and beneficiaries covered by the benefit plans that are or will be trusteed by the PBGC. Determines legal and policy issues requiring resolution prior to the determination of level of benefits and provides assistance in processing "missing" participants.

Major Activities and Divisions

Besides its internal administrative offices, PBGC is broken down into four program-related departments: the Insurance Operations Department, the Corporate Finance and Negotiations Department, the Financial Operations Department, and the Participant and Employer Appeals Department.

Alternative Employment Programs

PBGC hosts an intern program for students typically in their freshman and sophomore years in college. Common positions include Legal Intern and International Foundation Intern.

PBGC also participates in the federal Student Educational Employment Program that includes students in both high school and college.

Summer law clerks (second-year law students) are hired under the General Counsel's Program for Honor Law Graduates (Honors Program). Recent Law School graduates can also be hired under the Honors program. See www.pbgc.gov/about/jobopps.htm for more information.

Application Procedures

Direct inquiries to:

Pension Benefit Guaranty Corporation
Attn.: Human Resources Department
1200 K St., NW, Suite 120
Washington, DC 20005
(202) 326-4110

Veterans Employment and Training Service (VETS)
www.dol.gov/dol/vets/

Nature of Work: Employment, veterans programs

Number of Employees: 260

Headquarters: Washington, DC

Regional Locations: There are VETS offices in every Department of Labor region as well as in every state. The regions are Atlanta, GA; Boston, MA; Chicago, IL; Dallas, TX; Denver, CO; Kansas City, MO; New York, NY; Philadelphia, PA; San Francisco, CA; and Seattle, WA.

Typical Background of New Hires: Business, psychology, public administration, social sciences

Mission

VETS works closely with and provides grants and technical assistance to state employment services to ensure that veterans are provided the priority employment and training services required by law. VETS also administers Job Training Partnership Act grants for training of eligible veterans.

Job Descriptions

Veterans Employment Specialist: Works with State Employment Security Agencies and Job Training Partnership Act recipients to see that veterans are given preferential employment and training services. Coordinates with employers, labor unions, veterans' service organizations, and community organizations through public information and outreach activities. Provides federal contractors with management assistance in complying with their veterans' affirmative action and reporting obligations.

Veterans Program Specialist: Administers the Veterans' Reemployment Rights Program. Provides assistance to help restore job, seniority, and pension rights to veterans following absences from work for active military service. Protects employment and retention rights of members of the Reserve or National Guard.

Major Activities and Divisions

VETS directs the Department of Labor's veterans employment and training programs through a nationwide network that includes regional administrators, directors (in each state), and assistant directors (one for each 250,000 veterans in each state).

Alternative Employment Programs

No student hiring programs available at this time.

Remarks

Most Veterans Employment Specialist positions are restricted to veterans.

Due to its small size, the Veterans Employment and Training Service has minimal recruitment activity and does not have its own personnel office.

Application Procedures

Direct inquiries to:

Veterans Employment and Training Service
U.S. Department of Labor
200 Constitution Ave., NW, Room S-1316
Washington, DC 20210
(202) 693-4700

To contact a regional office, see the VETS Web site at www.dol.gov/dol/vets/public/aboutvets/contacts/main.htm.

☆ Legislative Branch

Congressional Research Service (CRS)
www.loc.gov/crsinfo/

Nature of Work: Scholarly research

Number of Employees: 900

Headquarters: Washington, DC

Regional Locations: None

Typical Background of New Hires: Economics, engineering, international affairs, law, political science, statistics

Mission

CRS provides nonpartisan analytical research and reference assistance to Congress, including policy analyses, legal information, and legislative histories. CRS is part of the Library of Congress.

Job Descriptions

Audiovisual Specialist: Produces audiovisual representations of CRS research products.

Bill Digester: Indexes and digests bills introduced in Congress.

Issue Brief Editor: Edits and manages the publication of Issue Briefs that summarize public policy issues.

Legislative Attorney: Analyzes the legal implications of legislation and public policy.

Librarian: Provides reference and bibliographic support.

Paralegal Assistant: Provides research and reference assistance to attorneys as well as to members and committees of Congress.

Policy Analyst: Conducts policy research in the social sciences, economics, foreign affairs, biology, general engineering, physical sciences, and operations research.

Public Affairs Specialist: Arranges and coordinates seminars, conferences, orientations, and briefings for members of Congress and their staffs.

Research Assistant: Supports policy analysts by providing research and reference assistance.

Translator: Translates documents and technical materials into and from a variety of foreign languages.

Major Activities and Divisions

CRS is organized into six interdisciplinary research divisions:

American Law Division: Conducts research in all areas of U.S. public law.

The Domestic Social Policy Division (DSP): Supports the Congress with research, analysis, and information on domestic policy and social program issues.

Foreign Affairs, Defense, and Trade Division: Covers a comprehensive range of U.S. foreign, defense, and trade policy issues and provides translations for Members and Committees.

The Government and Finance Division (G&F): Responsible for researching a broad range of policy areas and issues related to American government and politics, the structure and administration of Congress, the economy, public finance, and financial services.

The Information Research Division (INF): Provides a wide range of services, including reference, information, and research.

The Resources, Science, and Industry Division (RSI): Covers an array of legislative issues involving natural resources and environmental management, science and technology, and industry and infrastructure.

Alternative Employment Programs

The CRS Law Recruit Program offers law students the opportunity for permanent employment as legislative attorneys with the CRS American Law Division. The program is open to law students in their final year of law school.

The CRS Volunteer Internship Program is open to college undergraduates, graduate students, postgraduate students, faculty members, and other professionals who are seeking work experience in a public policy research organization. Volunteers assist professional CRS staff members in performing research and reference in response to public policy–related inquiries.

CRS also participates in the PMI program, described in chapter 00.

Application Procedures

Direct inquiries to: employment@crs.loc.gov. Or, by mail to:

Congressional Research Service
Administration Office
Library of Congress
101 Independence Ave., SE
Washington, DC 20540
(202) 707-8803

Congressional Budget Office (CBO)
www.cbo.gov

Nature of Work: Economic policy

Number of Employees: 250

Headquarters: Washington, DC

Regional Locations: None

Typical Background of New Hires: Economics, public administration

---

Mission

Provides the Congress with nonpartisan information relating to the U.S. economy, the federal budget, and federal programs. Because of its nonpolitical mandate, CBO makes no policy recommendations but instead presents options and alternatives for Congress to consider.

Job Descriptions

Program Analyst: Examines specific issues affecting the federal budget by analyzing current policies, developing alternative approaches, and projecting their impacts. May specialize in one of the division areas listed below.

Research Assistant: Supports the work of Program Analysts by tracking legislation, drafting testimony, collecting and manipulating data, and conducting policy research.

Major Activities and Divisions

Macroeconomics Division: Prepares CBO's economic projections, analyzes the effects of fiscal policy on the economy, and advises the Congress on general macroeconomic issues such as employment, production, income, saving, investment, trade, interest rates, and inflation.

Budget Analysis Division: Develops cost estimates of specific pieces of legislation, studies budget reform proposals, and develops automated budgetary information systems.

Tax Analysis Division: Estimates tax revenue and analyzes expenditures.

Microeconomics and Financial Studies Division: Analyzes policies relating to agriculture, energy, the environment, industry, public works, technology, transportation, and the federal budget process.

Health and Human Resources Division: Studies the costs and effectiveness of policies dealing with income assistance, Social Security, health education, employment and training, social services, housing, and community development.

National Security Division: Analyzes budgetary issues relating to manpower and strategic and conventional forces.

Alternative Employment Programs

CBO maintains a summer intern program. Typically, applications for the program must be submitted by March 1. Details can be found at www.cbo.gov/jobs.shtml

Application Procedures

CBO lists current job announcements on its Web site. If you wish to apply, submit applications electronically with attachments in MS Word, WordPerfect, PDF, or text formats to jobs@CBO.gov.

Or, direct inquiries to:

Congressional Budget Office
410 Ford House Office Building
Second and D Streets, SW
Washington, DC 20515
(202) 226-2628

General Accounting Office (GAO)
www.gao.gov

Nature of Work: Auditing

Number of Employees: 3,300

Headquarters: Washington, DC

Regional Locations: Atlanta, GA; Boston, MA; Chicago, IL; Dallas, TX; Dayton, OH; Denver, CO; Huntsville, AL; Kansas City, MO; Los Angeles, CA; Norfolk, VA; San Francisco, CA; Seattle, WA

Typical Background of New Hires: Accounting, business, computer science, public administration

Mission

Investigates whether government programs comply with applicable laws and regulations and determines whether they are achieving desired results.

Job Descriptions

Accountant: Audits agency financial statements and accounting systems; develops and interprets accounting and auditing policy.

Computer Scientist: Reviews the government's acquisition and use of computer and telecommunications systems.

Evaluator: Designs and implements reviews of federal programs and policies using a variety of analytical techniques.

Major Activities and Divisions

GAO is organized into the following teams and offices: Acquisition and Sourcing Management Team; Applied Research and Methods Team; Defense Capabilities and Management Team; Education, Workforce, and Income Security Team; Financial Management and Assurance Team; Financial Markets and Community Investments Team; Health Team; Information Technology Team; International Affairs and Trade Team; Natural Resources and Environment Team; Office of Special Investigations; Physical Infrastructure Team; Strategic Issues Team; and the Tax Administration and Justice Team.

Alternative Employment Programs

GAO maintains a co-op program for graduate and undergraduate students majoring in public administration, accounting, computer science, and related programs. GAO participates in the PMI program, and volunteer student internship positions are available at the headquarters location throughout the year.

Remarks

GAO's Training Institute offers classes in computers, statistics, and management. The agency's headquarters has modern fitness and day-care facilities.

Application Procedures

GAO lists current vacancies online, and encourages those interested in vacancies to submit applications electronically to recruit@gao.gov (MS Word format preferable) or fax to (202) 512-2539. Each job announcement contains an online application link.

Call (202) 512-4900 or 1-800-WORKGAO for more information. Mailing address:

U.S. General Accounting Office
Office of Recruitment
441 G St., NW
Washington, DC 20548

United States Government Printing Office (GPO)
www.gpo.gov

Nature of Work: Information, printing

Number of Employees: 3,500

Headquarters: Washington, DC (the Central Office)

Regional Locations: Atlanta, GA; Boston, MA; Chicago, IL; Columbus, OH; Dallas, TX; Denver, CO; Hampton, VA; Los Angeles, CA; New York, NY; Philadelphia, PA; St. Louis, MO; San Francisco, CA; Seattle, WA (Regional printing procurement offices). Satellite offices in Charleston, SC; Juneau, AK; New Orleans, LA; Oklahoma City, OK; Pittsburgh, PA; San Antonio, TX; San Diego, CA.

Typical Background of New Hires: Graphic arts (printing sciences, printing management, or printing technology)

Mission

Created primarily to satisfy the printing needs of Congress, GPO is today the focal point for printing, binding, and information dissemination for the federal community. Approximately 35 customer agencies and departments, in addition to the Congress, rely on the printing and procurement services of GPO. Probably the best-known ongoing effort of GPO is production of the Congressional Record, the printed compilation of each daily session of Congress. The office also distributes and sells millions of books, pamphlets, and other publications each year.

Job Descriptions

Librarian: Catalogues and classifies reports, documents, books, pamphlets, and other publications printed by the GPO. Supports the acquisition, format conversion, and classification functions of the Library Programs Service.

Printing Specialist (Customer Services division): Coordinates printing and binding requests from Congress and federal agencies. Acts as liaison with agencies, determines whether work should be produced in-house or procured, schedules work, prepares estimates, and maintains an inventory of paper products.

Printing Specialist (Office of Financial Management): Analyzes production charges on the jacket cost summaries, develops set rates for Congressional work, computes complicated billing of rider requisitions, and resolves disputes relating to customer billings. Examines and certifies vouchers, processes contractual and tort claims, and contacts contractors relative to disputes.

Printing Specialist (Printing Procurement Department): Develops contracts for printing and binding services with printing plants in the private sector. Prepares pre-award surveys, develops and writes specifications for advertised contracts, monitors contract compliance of commercial contractors, prepares bid lists, issues invitations for bids, recommends awards for contracts, and administers contracts. Works in the Central Office or at one of 20 field establishments.

Printing Specialist (Production Department): Coordinates and controls printing functions within five major production areas: the electronic systems development, graphic systems development, electronic photocomposition, press, and binding divisions. Studies and makes recommendations on printing operations, procedures, equipment, and workflow. Involved in the development and use of automated microcomputer-based composition systems.

Major Activities and Divisions

The Central Office in Washington, DC, is divided into the Printing Procurement Department, the Production Department, and the Quality Control and Technical Department. The Customer Services divisions include the Congressional Printing Management Division, the Typography and Design Division, and the Institute for Federal Printing and Electronic publishing. Besides the Central Office, GPO has a printing plant in Denver, Colorado, 20 regional procurement offices with several satellite facilities, a major distribution facility, and 18 bookstores across the country.

Alternative Employment Programs

GPO participates in the federal Outstanding Scholar Program and the Student Educational Employment Program.

GPO hires a small number of printing science or computer science majors for co-op positions in its central office. The Student Employment program typically targets juniors in an undergraduate program, to begin at the GS-4 level.

GPO also offers an internship program, typically filling Printing Assistant, Accountant, Computer Scientist, and other professional positions. These are usually filled by undergraduate-level students.

The agency also offers a Volunteer Program for students interested in clerical positions.

Remarks

GPO has a nationwide recruitment program that targets college campuses with strong printing sciences or graphic arts programs. Printing Specialist positions have traditionally been continuously open.

Printing Specialists enter into a two-year training program. Trainees are provided rotational assignments within their department and take part in special classroom courses and technical on-the-job training.

Application Procedures

The GPO Web site lists current vacancies at www.access.gpo.gov/employment/job1.html. Or, direct inquires to:

U.S. Government Printing Office
Employment Branch (Stop: PSE)
North Capitol and H Streets, NW
Washington, DC 20401
(202) 512-1200
E-mail: recruitment @gpo.gov

Library of Congress
www.loc.gov

Nature of Work: Libraries, scholarly research

Number of Employees: 4,800

Headquarters: Washington, DC

Regional Locations: None

Typical Background of New Hires: Computer science, languages, library science

---

Mission

As the national library of the U.S., the Library of Congress possesses books and pamphlets on every subject in a variety of languages, the world's largest collection of aeronautical literature, the personal papers of presidents, maps, movies, photographs, recordings, government documents, and newspapers and periodicals from around the world.

Job Descriptions

Computer Specialist: Operates the Library of Congress's database, which contains bibliographic and cataloging information on the Library's vast holdings. Also designs software and networks that facilitate distribution of these data to users across the country.

Copyright Specialist: Analyzes claims and determines whether they meet the legal and procedural requirements for registration. Conducts research to determine registrability of a claim.

Librarian/Library Technician: Selects, catalogs, and classifies publications, other printed works, and audiovisual material and provides reference services.

Research Analyst: Assists in classifying and cataloging the Library's holdings.

Major Activities and Divisions

Copyright Office: Reviews and grants copyrights to literary works, musical compositions, and other types of intellectual property.

Law Library: Maintains the Library's collection of legal material that comprises the following divisions: American-British Law, European Law, Far Eastern Law, Hispanic Law, and Near Eastern and African Law.

National Programs: Operates the Library's various extension services, such as the American Folklore Center, Children's Literature Center, and Education Liaison Office.

Area Studies: Maintains the Library's African, Middle Eastern, Asian, European, and Hispanic literature.

General Reference: Provides reference services relating to federal research and science and technology.

Special Collections: Acquires and preserves the Library's holdings of maps, manuscripts, motion pictures, music, prints, photographs, and rare books.

Alternative Employment Programs

The Library of Congress has a co-op program for graduate students enrolled in programs related to the following occupations: Librarian, Social Analyst, Economist, Foreign Affairs Analyst, Legislative Attorney, Administrative Officer, and Computer Science Analyst.

The Library's Foreign Area Associates program gives students experience in fields related to foreign area studies and foreign language.

The Library also hosts a junior fellows program for undergraduates in their junior or senior years, graduate students, or recent college graduates. Fellowships last 2–3 months during the summer. For more information, contact:

Junior Fellows Program Coordinator
Library Services, Room LM-642
Library of Congress
Washington, DC 20540-4600
(202) 707-5330
Fax: (202) 707-6269
E-mail: jrfell@loc.gov

Application Procedures

The library of congress lists current vacancies on their Web site at www.loc.gov/hr/employment/.

Or, direct inquiries to:

The Library of Congress
Recruitment and Placement Office
101 Independence Ave., SE
Washington, DC 20540
(202) 707-5620
Information: (202) 707-2905

☆ Department of the Navy
(www.donhr.navy.mil/jobs/)

Secretary of the Navy (SECNAV)
www.chinfo.navy.mil/

Nature of Work: Auditing, budget analysis

Number of Employees: 10,000

Headquarters: Washington, DC

Regional Locations: Nationwide

Typical Background of New Hires: Accounting, business, liberal arts, social sciences

Mission

The Secretary of the Navy (SECNAV) is responsible for setting policies and conducting the affairs of the Department of the Navy, including: recruiting, organizing, supplying, equipping, training, mobilizing, and demobilizing. The Secretary also oversees the construction, outfitting, and repair of naval ships, equipment, and facilities.

Job Descriptions

Auditor: Evaluates the effectiveness and efficiency of management policies, systems, procedures, and controls. Ensures financial integrity and effective use of resources by the Navy and Marine Corps.

Budget Analyst: Determines financial needs, outlines spending programs, drafts and defends budget documents.

Major Activities and Divisions

Financial Management and Comptroller: Manages the Navy's budget process and sophisticated accounting systems and produces statistical and financial reports.

Research, Development, and Acquisition: Develops, acquires and supports affordable technology systems for Navy, Marine Corps, Joint, and Allied Forces.

Installations and Environment: Works to ensure efficient, publicly responsive, and technologically advanced pollution prevention, conservation, compliance, cleanup, safety and occupational health programs. Learn more at www.enviro.navy.mil.

Manpower and Reserve Affairs: Provides civilian oversight through developing integrated military and civilian human resources policies and programs.

Alternative Employment Programs

The organization maintains a trainee program. Known as the Centralized Financial Management Trainee Program, it consists of two years of on-the-job training, formal classroom studies, and rotational assignments.

Application Procedures

The Department of the Navy has a Web site designed to assist civilian job seekers in navigating the many job opportunity announcements and application procedures. See www.donhr.navy.mil/jobs/ for simple guidelines to the application process. Navy civilian vacancy announcements are listed at www.resume.hroc.navy.mil/JobOpportunities/jobs_employment_opportunites.htm.

The Department of the Navy has seven Human Resources Service Centers located worldwide. Each Center recruits individuals to fill Navy and Marine Corps civilian positions occurring in its serviced area. The Centers are listed below.

East
HRSC–EAST
Norfolk Naval Shipyard, Bldg. 17
Portsmouth, VA 23709-5000
E-mail: wantajob@east.hroc.navy.mil

Europe
HRSC–EUROPE
PSC 821, Box 121
FPO AE 09421-5000
E-mail: wantajob@esc.hroc.navy.mil

Northeast
HRSC–NE
RESUMIX UNIT
111 S. Independence Mall, East
(Bourse Bldg.)
Philadelphia, PA 19106-2598
E-mail: wantajob@ne.hroc.navy.mil

Northwest
HRSC–NW
3230 NW Randall Way
Silverdale, WA 98383
E-mail: wantajob@nw.hroc.navy.mil

Pacific
HRSC–PAC
178 Main St., Bldg. 499
Honolulu, HI 96818-4048
E-mail: wantajob@pac.hroc.navy.mil

Southeast
HRSC–SE
9110 Leonard Kimble Rd.
Stennis Space Center, MS 39522-0002
E-mail: wantajob@se.hroc.navy.mil

Southwest
HRSC–SW
525 B St., Suite 600
Attn: Code 53–Resume Intake Unit
San Diego, CA 92101-4418
E-mail: wantajob@sw.hroc.navy.mil

Naval Air Systems Command (NAVAIR)
www.navair.navy.mil

Nature of Work: Aviation/space programs, military affairs, scientific research, weapons

Number of Employees: 30,000

Headquarters: Crystal City, VA

Regional Locations: Nationwide

Typical Background of New Hires: Computer science, engineering

Mission

Develops advanced aircraft, combat systems, avionics, and related equipment for the Navy and Marines.

Job Descriptions

Aerospace Engineer: Improves the performance of aircraft and missiles by obtaining aerodynamic and moment data from wind tunnels.

Electrical/Electronics Engineer: Develops advanced avionics and control systems, sensors, navigation equipment, integrated computer systems, radars, and fire control systems.

Mechanical Engineer: Plans the construction of experimental models and test techniques for engines, armaments, and other equipment and components. Develops and modifies mechanical drive systems for helicopters and works on various components of reciprocating and turbine engines.

Metallurgical Engineer: Develops special purpose alloys for aircraft, missiles, engines, guns, and armor.

Major Activities and Divisions

Research and Technology: Conducts research leading to improved combat systems, aircraft, weapons, surveillance systems, and avionics.

Electronic Warfare and Mission Support Programs: Administers programs designed to improve logistics, airborne strategic communications, air traffic control equipment, and jet training programs.

Anti-Submarine Warfare and Assault Programs: Oversees research, development, and modifications of airborne antisubmarine warfare.

Cruise Missile Projects: Manages programs related to remotely piloted vehicles and cruise missiles.

Weapon Programs: Administers research and logistics for the Harpoon missile and other weapon systems.

Systems and Engineering: Responsible for flight systems, crew systems, propulsion and power, reconnaissance and imaging systems.

Tactical Aircraft Programs: Designs and modifies tactical aircraft and crew ejection systems.

Alternative Employment Programs

Summer employment may be available for engineering students with two or more years of education. Co-op opportunities may be available for engineering students as well.

Application Procedures

Naval Air Systems Team

Human Resources Office
Attn: Professional Recruiting
22095 Fortin Circle, Bldg. 1489
Patuxent River, MD 20670
Toll Free: (800) 787-9804 (Professional Recruitment Office)

Naval Air Warfare Center Aircraft Division (NAWCAD)
www.nawcad.navy.mil

Nature of Work: Aviation/space programs, military affairs, scientific research, weapons

Number of Employees: 11,300

Headquarters: Patuxent River, MD

Regional Locations: Lakehurst, NJ; Orlando, FL

Typical Background of New Hires: Engineering (aerospace, electronics, electrical, mechanical, materials, industrial, computer)

Mission

As part of the Naval Air Systems Command, NAWCAD's mission is to be the Navy's principal research, development, test and evaluation, engineering, and fleet support activity for naval aircraft, engines, avionics, aircraft support systems, and ship/shore/air operation.

Job Descriptions

Aerospace Engineer: Works on airframes and structures, automatic control and stabilization, flight control, high- and low-speed aerodynamics, and flight simulators.

Electrical and Electronic Engineer: Develops and evaluates electrical systems and subsystems, including antisubmarine avionics, electronic countermeasures, early warning systems, navigation instruments, and digital computers.

Logistics Management Specialist: Supports a full range of weapons systems through applying theory and practices of logistics management. Works in design interface and maintenance planning as part of the systems engineering processes and provides analyses and technical studies showing the impact on operational readiness.

Mechanical Engineer: Designs sonobuoys, helicopter hoists, cooling systems, release mechanisms, and weapons delivery systems.

Major Activities and Divisions

Antenna Test Range: Investigates aircraft radar transmissions and signatures.

Dynamic Flight Simulator: Simulates the maneuvers of high performance Naval aircraft.

Inertial Navigation Laboratory: Develops and tests new instruments allowing for greater navigational precision.

Naval Air Facility: Determines the flight characteristics of prototypes.

Sonar Development Facility: Tests sonobuoys and other types of submarine detection equipment.

Alternative Employment Programs

None

Application Procedures

Direct inquiries to:

Naval Air Warfare Center
Aircraft Division, Human Resources Office
Building 2189, M553
Attn.: Professional Recruiting
Patuxent River, MD 20670-5304
Job Information Office: (301) 757-4128/4129
www.hro.navair.navy.mil

Naval Facilities Engineering Command (NAVFAC)
www.navfac.navy.mil

Nature of Work: Environmental protection, military affairs

Number of Employees: 24,000

Headquarters: Alexandria, VA

Regional Locations: Norfolk, VA; Charleston, SC; San Diego, CA; Pearl Harbor, HI; Great Lakes, IL; Jacksonville, FL; Pensacola, FL; Port Hueneme, CA; and other locations worldwide

Typical Background of New Hires: Architecture, business, engineering

---

Mission

Designs, builds, maintains, and repairs all Navy and Marine Corps shore facilities. Also manages energy supply and usage and provides technical support for environmental protection.

Job Descriptions

Architect: Designs naval shore installations such as housing, schools, hospitals, and aviation facilities.

Civil Engineer: Designs military housing, roads, drainage systems, waste-treatment plants, floating structures, cargo-handling systems, and other naval structures.

Contract and Procurement Specialist: Administers contracts ensuring that goods and services are delivered on time and at the agreed-upon cost.

Electrical Engineer: Designs, installs, and maintains large shore-based electrical generating and distribution systems.

Environmental Engineer: Develops methods for controlling and eliminating pollutants.

Fire Protection Engineer: Develops procedures, equipment, and systems for preventing and extinguishing fires.

Industrial Engineer: Prepares broad engineering programs for plant layouts, buildings, and facilities.

Mechanical Engineer: Designs or modifies building structures, utilities, and support systems.

Realty Specialist: Appraises, purchases, manages, and disposes of real property. Also manages buildings and assists in the design of building layouts.

Structural Engineer: Assists in the construction of housing, river channels, missile sites, airbases, and other naval facilities.

Major Activities and Divisions

Specific NAVFAC programs include contracting, acquisition, military and ocean facility construction, test and evaluation, and environmental safety and health.

Alternative Employment Programs

Summer employment opportunities are available for students with one year of college or more. Co-op positions are available for engineering students.

Remarks

Two-year overseas assignments are available to employees with between one and five years of experience.

Application Procedures

Direct inquiries to:

Headquarters: Naval Facilities Engineering Command
Washington Navy Yard
1322 Patterson Ave., SE, Suite 1000
Washington, DC 20374-5065
Administration: (202) 685-9078 / DSN 325-9078

Naval Sea Systems Command (NAVSEA)
www.navsea.navy.mil

Nature of Work: Maritime activities, military affairs, scientific research, weapons

Number of Employees: 50,000

Headquarters: Washington, DC, and Arlington, VA

Regional Locations: Naval shipyards are located in Bremerton, WA; Charleston, SC; Long Beach, CA; Pearl Harbor, HI; Philadelphia, PA; Portsmouth, NH; Portsmouth, VA; Vallejo, CA. There are also more than 50 shore installations nationwide and over 70 worldwide detachments.

Typical Background of New Hires: Engineering

Mission

Designs, develops, modernizes, and repairs the Navy's ships and shipborne weapons and combat systems.

Job Descriptions

Civil Engineer: Designs shipyard facilities for repairing and overhauling naval vessels.

Computer Engineer: Develops computer programs for integrating diverse combat systems and uses computer-aided design to determine optimum systems for new ships.

Electrical/Electronics Engineer: Develops advanced radar and sonar concepts and provides life-time engineering management for internal communications, guidance systems, electro-optic fire control systems, and weapons.

Mechanical Engineer: Designs mechanical systems for shipboard propulsion, auxiliary, and material handling systems.

Naval Architect: Conceptualizes new ship designs, analyzes ship area and space allocations, and conducts research in such fields as ship structures, habitability, weight, stability, and manning.

Nuclear Engineer: Works in all aspects of nuclear propulsion, including reactor core design, instrumentation, and physics.

Major Activities and Divisions

Ship Design and Integration: Conceives, develops, and integrates naval ships and shipboard systems.

Ship Systems: Oversees the design and installation of all ship hull, mechanical, propulsion, auxiliary, and electrical systems and equipment.

Combat Systems: Provides engineering services for all ship combat systems and related conventional and nuclear ordnance.

Alternative Employment Programs

NAVSEA maintains a student internship program.
See www.people.navsea.navy.mil/jobs/looking.htm for more information.

Remarks

Entry-level engineers are placed in a two-year Engineers-in-Training (EIT) program. During this period, EITs rotate through various offices to gain a broader understanding of the Command.

Application Procedures

For more information on NAVSEA Career Opportunities, contact:

Naval Sea Systems Command
Washington Navy Yard
1333 Issac Hull Ave., SE, Stop 9913
Washington, DC 20376-9913
Fax: (202) 781-4625
E-mail: Recruiternssc@navsea.navy.mil

Naval Surface Warfare Center, Dahlgren Division (NSWCDD)
www.nswc.navy.mil

Nature of Work: Maritime activities, military affairs, scientific research, weapons

Number of Employees: 4,300

Headquarters: Dahlgren, VA

Regional Locations: Dam Neck, VA; Panama City, FL

Typical Background of New Hires: Computer science, engineering, mathematics, operations research analysis, physics

Mission

Provides research, development, test and evaluation, engineering, and fleet support for Surface Warfare, Surface Ship Combat Systems, Ordnance, Strategic Systems, Mines, Amphibious Warfare Systems, Mine Countermeasures, and Special Warfare Systems.

Job Descriptions

Aerospace Engineer: Solves problems related to aerodynamics and aeroballistics and applies that knowledge toward developing surface to air missiles and reentry vehicles.

Computer Scientist: Designs hardware and software for operating weapons systems, develops artificial intelligence systems, and constructs computer networks and protocols.

Electrical/Electronics Engineer: Designs and installs navigation systems, electronic countermeasures, fire control and phased-array radars, and equipment for real-time digital signal and image processing.

Mathematician: Develops mathematical models for simulating different combat and aeronautical conditions, designs and evaluates computer software and artificial intelligence systems.

Mechanical Engineer: Analyzes stress in shipboard structures such as radar and gun mounts and missile launchers and develops structures and weapons components able to survive harsh environments.

Operations Research Analyst: Conducts research and development in areas such as surface ship combat systems, surface ship defense systems, Navy strategic systems targeting, strategic systems fire control and strike warfare.

Physicist: Develops efficient rocket motors and uses advanced techniques for creating new materials.

Systems Engineer: Provides systems engineering, including requirements definition, simulation, modeling, analysis, and evaluation relative to the development and operation of tactical computer programs including firmware for surface weapon systems.

Major Activities and Divisions

As a part of the Naval Sea Systems Command (NAVSEA) family, the Naval Surface Warfare Center, Dahlgren Division (NSWCDD) consists of three organizations: The NSWC Dahlgren Lab in Dahlgren, Virginia, the Coastal Systems Station in Panama City, Florida, and the Combat Direction Systems Activity in Virginia.

Alternative Employment Programs

NSWCDD maintains a co-op program for engineering and computer science students at the undergraduate and graduate levels. There are also a limited number of positions for students studying Aerospace Engineering, Mechanical Engineering, Physics, Operations Research Analysis and Mathematics. For more information about these positions, call (540) 653-8701 or e-mail: recruit@nswc.navy.mil.

NSWCDD also participates in the Science and Engineering Apprentice Program (SEAP), which offers apprenticeships for high school students who are interested in science and engineering. The students are assigned to a participating laboratory to pursue scientific experiences with a scientist or engineer who serves as a mentor to the apprentice for eight continuous summer weeks. Call (202) 994-2234 for more information.

Remarks

NSWCDD develops its engineers by placing them in various rotational assignments. These assignments expose new employees to different areas of NSWCDD and are tailored to the individual's personal development goals.

Application Procedures

NSWC prefers that you mail or e-mail your resume. Direct inquiries to the facility where you seek employment, or e-mail: recruit@nswc.navy.mil. Or, call toll free (800) 352-7967.

Recruiting Coordinator
Human Resources Department, Code PD
Dahlgren Division
Naval Surface Warfare Center
17320 Dahlgren Road
Dahlgren, VA 22448-5100

Commanding Officer
Naval Surface Warfare Center, Dahlgren Division
Coastal Systems Station
Attn: Recruiting
6703 West Highway 98
Panama City, FL 32407-7001
(904) 234-5839 or (202) 394-2506

Commanding Officer
Attn: Management Assistance Office
Combat Direction Systems Activity, Dam Neck
Naval Surface Warfare Center
1922 Regulus Avenue
Virginia Beach, VA 23461-2097

Naval Undersea Warfare Center Division
www.nuwc.navy.mil

Nature of Work: Maritime activities, military affairs, scientific research, weapons

Number of Employees: 3,800

Headquarters: Newport, RI

Regional Locations: Keyport, WA; Oahu and Kauai, Hawaii; San Diego, CA

Typical Background of New Hires: Computer science, engineering

Mission

As part of the Naval Sea Systems Command, the Center concentrates on antisubmarine warfare technology.

Job Descriptions

Computer Engineer: Develops systems for tracking targets and firing weapons as well as computers that detect and track submarines and simulate combat situations.

Electronics Engineer: Conducts research in such fields as sonar systems, using transducers and array geometry, signal processing, reconnaissance systems, and communications.

Mechanical Engineer: Designs systems for storing, handling, loading, and launching weapons.

Major Activities and Divisions

NUWC Division Newport: Responsible for the full life cycle of submarine and undersea warfare systems, including research and development, prototyping, systems development, and fleet support.

Division Keyport: Provides test and evaluation; in-service engineering, maintenance, and repair; fleet readiness; and industrial-base support for undersea warfare systems, countermeasures, and sonar systems. The main facility is located at Keyport, Washington, in the Puget Sound. Detachments are located in Lualualei and Pearl Harbor, Hawaii and San Diego, California. Fleet testing and logistics sites are located at Nanoose, British Columbia, and Hawthorne, Nevada.

Alternative Employment Programs

The Naval Undersea Warfare Center Division Newport offers student internships through the College of Engineering at the University of Rhode Island. Send resume to:

Placement Officer, Code 5822
1176 Howell St.
Newport, RI 02841
Fax: (401) 832-4106
E-mail: recruit@npt.nuwc.navy.mil

Remarks

The Center's proximity to a large number of major universities provides opportunities for postgraduate studies. Educational plans are available for professional development including tuition and salary grants.

Application Procedures

All current job openings at NUWC Division Newport are listed on the Internet at www.fedworld.gov/jobs/jobsearch.html.
    Or, direct inquiries to:

Human Resources Office
NAVUNSEAWARCENDIV Newport
1176 Howell St.
Newport, RI 02841-1708
(401) 841-2311

Naval Weapons Center (NWC)
www.nawcwpns.navy.mil/

Nature of Work: Military affairs, scientific research, weapons

Number of Employees: 5,000

Headquarters: China Lake, CA; Point Mugu, CA

Regional Locations: None

Typical Background of New Hires: Computer science, engineering, mathematics, physics

Mission

As part of the Navy's Space and Naval Warfare Systems Command, the Naval Weapons Center develops and evaluates missile systems for air warfare and operates a test range for parachutes.

Job Descriptions

Aeronautical Engineer: Studies the aerodynamic heating of missiles; designs rocket and ramjet motors; and performs stability analyses.

Computer Scientist: Writes and documents microprocessor applications and systems software and develops simulation and integration software for avionics systems.

Electrical/Electronics Engineer: Designs guidance system hardware and software, performs analog and digital simulations, develops radar and antenna systems, designs and integrates receivers of logic processing circuits, creates microprocessors for fuzes, and develops inertial systems and sensors.

Mathematician: Analyzes aircraft/weapon performance and performs feasibility and target vulnerability studies.

Mechanical Engineer: Designs and tests airframes, rocket motor nozzles, valves, and control system actuators and conducts stress analyses of structural components of rocket propellant grains.

Physicist: Applies electro-optic and laser technologies to guidance systems; conducts research and development involving low-power laser systems, pattern recognition technologies, and holographic computer design codes.

Software Engineer: Designs, tests, evaluates, and documents software for real-time, highly constrained, embedded computer systems.

Major Activities and Divisions

NWC engineers work on more than 1,500 programs. The areas of major involvement include air-to-air and air-to-surface weapons; antiradiation weapons; parachute systems; avionics hardware and software for the A-6, A-7, AV-8B, F/A-18, and AH-1 aircraft; tactical electronic warfare and countermeasures systems; and propulsion, explosives, warhead, guidance, and fuze technology.

Alternative Employment Programs

The Naval Weapons Center maintains a summer employment program for students with more than one year of college and a co-op program for engineering and computer science students.

Remarks

All employees with bachelor's and master's degrees are assigned to the Junior Professional Development Program during their first year of employment. The program allows new employees to explore career options through mentored rotations lasting two to three months.

Graduate-level courses in a variety of disciplines are taught on-site. Off-site graduate and undergraduate programs are taught by California State University faculty members.

Application Procedures

Direct inquiries to:

Naval Air Warfare Center
Professional Recruitment—CRS
China Lake, CA 93555-6001
(619) 939-6033

Space and Naval Warfare Systems Command (SPAWAR)
www.spawar.navy.mil

Nature of Work: Aviation/space programs, maritime activities, military affairs, scientific research, weapons

Number of Employees: 28,000

Headquarters: Washington, DC

Regional Locations: Charleston, SC; Norfolk, VA; San Diego, CA; New Orleans, LA; Chantilly, VA; other sites across the U.S.

Typical Background of New Hires: Engineering (electronics/electrical); computer science

Mission

Develops, purchases, repairs, and modifies Naval warfare systems such as space systems. SPAWAR also coordinates all advanced antisubmarine warfare development programs and manages seven research and development centers and eight engineering centers.

Job Descriptions

Electronics Engineer/Computer Scientist: Develops diverse naval warfare systems including satellite communications, space and ocean surveillance platforms, computer systems, navigation aids, electronic warfare devices, and communications equipment.

Major Activities and Divisions

SPAWAR Systems Center, Charleston: Designs, builds, tests, fields, and supports many of the front-line command, control, communications, computers, and intelligence systems in use today or planned for the future. Information can be found at www.chas.spawar.navy.mil/ or via e-mail: recruit@spawar.navy.mil.

SPAWAR Systems Center, Norfolk: Designs, develops, delivers, and supports integrated information systems for the U.S. Navy and the U.S. Marine Corps. Call 757-443-0700 for information.

Space and Naval Warfare Systems Center, San Diego: The U.S. Navy's research, development, test and evaluation, engineering and fleet support center for command, control, and communication systems and ocean surveillance. Log on to www.spawar.navy.mil/sandiego/html/jobs.html for employment information.

SPAWAR Information Technology Center, New Orleans: Delivers enterprise-wide integrated information management/information technology solutions and life-cycle support.

SPAWAR SPACE Field Activity, Chantilly: Provides line management staffing of the National Reconnaissance Office and coordinates naval space research, development, and acquisition activities between NRO and other space programs. For job information, contact: Chief, Human Resource Management Group, at (703) 808-5181 for military assignments or (703) 808-1728 for civilian assignments.

Activities:

Command and Control: Develops electronic data processing and display systems that allow a commander at sea or on shore to see in real time both his forces and those of the enemy.

Marine Corps Systems: Develops communications systems, surveillance radars, and air traffic control systems.

Shipboard Communications: Conducts research in such fields as fiber optics, electromagnetic wave theory, high-speed circuit switching, and integrated voice/data transmission.

Submarine Communications: Develops systems allowing submarines to transmit, receive, and process communication signals using extremely low and extremely high frequencies.

Shore Communications: Develops shore-based communications systems, allowing shore installations to transmit and receive command and control information to and from ships and submarines.

Antisubmarine Warfare: Designs advanced electronic and computer-based signal processing systems to detect and track enemy submarines.

Space Systems: Works with satellites, space systems, and their instrumentation for the purposes of oceanography and meteorology, microwave imagery, navigation, cryptology, surveillance, and directed-energy weapons.

Systems Effectiveness: Ensures that equipment continues to operate in severe environments such as temperature, humidity, vibration, shock, and electromagnetic fields.

Alternative Employment Programs

SPAWAR maintains a summer employment program for students with more than one year of college and a co-op program for engineering students.

Application Procedures

Information on Navy civilian employment opportunities may be found at the Department of the Navy Civilian Human Resources Online Web site at www.donhr.navy.mil/.

Or, contact specific regional locations for job information:

SPAWAR San Diego, CA, locations

Information on employment opportunities in San Diego may be found directly at:

www.resume.hroc.navy.mil/vacancy/vac_list.cfm?REGION=SOUTHWEST

Human Resource Service Center Southwest

www.donhr.navy.mil/HRSC/hrsc.asp?ItemArea=8
525 B St., Suite 600
San Diego, CA 92101-4418
(619) 615-5500

SPAWAR Charleston, South Carolina locations

SPAWAR Norfolk - Chesapeake, Virginia locations

Information on employment opportunities in the South Carolina low country and tidewater Virginia areas may be found directly at:

www.resume.hroc.navy.mil/vacancy/vac_list.cfm?REGION=SOUTHEAST

Human Resource Service Center Southeast

www.donhr.navy.mil/HRSC/hrsc.asp?ItemArea=7
9110 Leonard Kimble Rd.
Stennis Space Center, MS 39522-0002

Military Sealift Command (MSC)
www.msc.navy.mil

Nature of Work: Military, transportation, defense

Number of Employees: 7,500 (4,700 federal civil service)

Headquarters: Washington, DC

Regional Locations: Norfolk, VA.; San Diego, CA; locations around the world include Naples, Italy; Yokohama, Japan; and Manama, Bahrain.

Typical Background of New Hires: Various

Mission

Provides ocean transportation of equipment, fuel, supplies, and ammunition to sustain U.S. forces worldwide during peacetime and in war for as long as operational requirements dictate.

Job Descriptions

Acquisition Trainee: Performs "cradle to grave" management of highly technical systems, equipment, facilities, supplies, and services. A degree in business or public administration is preferred. Qualifications include a GPA of at least 3.45 (on a 4.0 scale).

Marine Transportation Specialist Intern: An entry-level hiring program for recent college graduates with a GPA of 3.45 or higher. Specialists begin at the GS-7 level and are promoted to GS-12 after three years. A degree in marine transportation or transportation/logistics and a third mates license is particularly desired. May require a secret-level clearance.

Port Engineer/Marine Systems Engineer/Marine Engineer/Naval Architect: Assists in the oversight of the maintenance, repair, and design of government-owned ships operated by the U.S. Navy. May work at key U.S. ports, various U.S. shipyards, and offices in Washington, DC; Japan; and Italy. Applies knowledge of commercial ship operations, standards, and regulations. Draws upon experience or schooling in mechanical, electronic, or electrical areas; corrosion control and coatings; naval architecture; power plant systems; or ship construction projects.

At-Sea Employment Opportunities (Afloat Positions): Afloat positions include such skilled-trade work as Able Bodied Seaman, Engine Utilityman, Deck Engineer Machinist, Unlicensed Junior Engineer, Second Electrician,

Refrigeration Engineer, Electronics Technician, Assistant Engineer, Radio Electronics Technician, and Medical Services Officer. These positions are described on the MSC Web site at www.msc.navy.mil/apmc/opening.asp.

Activities and Divisions

The command is organized around four key programs:

The Naval Fleet Auxiliary Force: Composed of 34 ships, NFAF provides direct support for Navy combatant ships, allowing them to remain at sea for extended periods of time. NFAF ships perform underway replenishment services for Navy battle groups and deliver food, fuel, spare parts, and ammunition.

The Special Mission Program: Composed of 29 ships that carry out specialized missions, including oceanographic surveys, missile tracking, coastal surveys, cable laying and repair, submarine escort, and deep submergence rescue support.

The Prepositioning Program: Oversees 35 strategically located ships laden with military equipment and supplies for the U.S. Army, Air Force, Navy, and Marine Corps.

The Sealift Program: Responsible for a fleet of chartered tankers and dry cargo ships that move Department of Defense cargo during peacetime and war.

Remarks

MSC is one of three component commands reporting to the joint service U.S. Transportation Command, known as USTRANSCOM. In addition to MSC, two other Department of Defense transportation component commands, the U.S. Army's Military Traffic Management Command and the U.S. Air Force's Air Mobility Command, fall under the command of USTRANSCOM.

Alternative Employment Programs

See the "fast track" intern and trainee hiring programs above.

Application Procedures

For more information on afloat positions, contact the marine personnel employment office at the MSC Afloat Personnel Management Center in Virginia Beach, Virginia, at (800) 793-4628; 757-417-4260/59/42/43/46/40; or via e-mail at apmc124.mscmarineemp@msc.navy.mil.

Applicants for Acquisition Trainee positions should mail or fax a resume to:

Military Sealift Command, Code N101
914 Charles Morris Court, SE
Washington Navy Yard
Washington, DC 20398-5540
Fax: (202) 685-5942

For information on engineering and architecture positions, call: (202) 685-5771.

Headquarters Address
Military Sealift Command
914 Charles Morris Court SE
Washington Navy Yard
Washington, DC 20398-5540
Toll Free: (888) SEALIFT (General Information)
         (800) 793-4628 (Marine Employment Opportunities)

☆ State Department
(www.state.gov)

State Department

www.state.gov

Nature of Work: Immigration, international affairs

Number of Employees: 24,800 (about 5,000 civil service employees in the U.S.)

Headquarters: Washington, DC

Regional Locations: Over 250 embassies and consulates in more than 180 countries

Typical Background of New Hires: Economics, history, international affairs, languages, law, political science

Mission

Advises the President on foreign policy by monitoring events in foreign countries. The Department also represents the U.S. government overseas, negotiates treaties with other nations, and protects U.S. citizens and their property abroad.

Job Descriptions

Civil Service positions:

Attorney: Prepares cases for trial or quasi-judicial hearings, interprets and drafts regulations and procedures, and examines contracts and other legal documents.

Computer Specialist: Designs software and implements systems that meet the State Department's automated data processing requirements.

Passport Examiner: Processes applications for U.S. passports and related services.

Public Information Specialist: Disseminates information concerning the State Department's activities through such media as newspapers, magazines, radio, and television.

Technical Information Specialist: Analyzes and transmits scientific, technological, and other specialized information.

Visa Examiner: Determines whether an applicant who has applied for a U.S. visa is suitable for entry into the U.S.

Foreign Service Officer positions:

Foreign Service Officer–Administrative Affairs: Supports the operations of U.S. embassies and consulates overseas through activities such as identifying budget priorities, operating telecommunications and pouch/mail facilities procuring supplies and arranging leases, managing personnel, and maintaining the security of embassies and consulates.

Foreign Service Officer–Consulate Affairs: Issues visas and assists Americans overseas involved in serious accidents or emergencies.

Foreign Service Officer–Economic Affairs: Analyzes and reports on key economic indicators affecting U.S. interests.

Foreign Service Officer–Political Affairs: Monitors and interprets political matters affecting U.S. interests.

Foreign Service Specialist Positions:

Facilities Maintenance Specialist: Manages the upkeep of buildings, grounds, fixtures, and utilities overseas.

Financial Management Officer: Manages the financial activities of diplomatic and consular posts.

General Services Officer: Manages the physical resources and logistical functions at diplomatic and consular posts.

Human Resources Officer: Recruits, conducts employee training and development, oversees employee relations, administers salary and benefits, develops employee policies and procedures and writes position classifications.

Construction Engineer: Monitors and reports on contract work overseas to ensure that the construction of new properties and renovation of existing properties are completed properly.

Information Management Specialist: Manages and operates worldwide information technology infrastructure, including PC local and wide area networks, telecommunications systems, telephone and UHF/VHF programs, and diplomatic pouch and mail services.

Information Management Technical Specialist: Surveys, installs, and maintains associated hardware and software of PC local and wide area networks, UHF/VHF land mobile programs, and/or telephone PBX systems. Three separate technical divisions are PC LAN/WAN, telephone, and radio.

Regional English Language Officer: ELOs overseas are responsible for all Department of State–sponsored English teaching activities in that country. Regional ELOs are responsible for English language program activities in several countries, necessitating extensive travel. ELOs working in Washington, DC, provide administrative support to overseas programs, work on research and development materials, conduct seminars, and provide consultative services to overseas posts or host-country institutions.

Information Resource Officer: IROs provide professional guidance to 170 Information Resource Centers (IRCs) located at U.S. embassies abroad. Through extensive travel within an assigned region, IROs counsel Mission Officials on effective information program resources and services, assess staff needs, carry out regional training programs, promote U.S. electronic information resources, and establish contacts with host country information and library institutions.

Printing Specialist: Coordinates worldwide publishing, printing management programs, printing information technology, and related systems.

Health Practitioner: Acts as primary care provider and administers a full range of community health-care services, including preventive health education for the official mission community.

Regional Medical Technologist: Performs visitations to regional area Health Units to evaluate and monitor performance of local laboratory technologists. Maintains own laboratory and x-ray equipment at post of assignment.

Regional Medical Officer: Serves in support of U.S. government employees and their families. Provides primary medical care and appropriate health information and disease prevention program at each post of responsibility.

Regional Medical Officer/Psychiatrist: Serves in support of U.S. government employees and their family members. The RMO/P's duties include providing primary psychiatric care for each post in the supported geographical region.

Office Management Specialist: Performs general office management and administrative support duties at diplomatic and consular posts.

Diplomatic Courier: Safeguards and escorts diplomatic pouches containing classified and sensitive material between U.S. diplomatic missions overseas and the Department of State.

Security Engineering Officer: Provides technical security support and engineering expertise to protect U.S. Foreign Service posts. Work may be in Washington, DC, Fort Lauderdale, Florida, or overseas.

Security Technical Specialist: Provides support, program management, and maintenance duties in worldwide technical security programs, which protect Department of State facilities and personnel from technical espionage, acts of terrorism, and crime.

Diplomatic Security Special Agent: Specially trained Foreign Service security professionals and sworn law enforcement officers. Overseas, advises ambassadors on all security matters and manages security programs designed to protect personnel, facilities, and information. In the U.S., Special Agents protect the Secretary of State and visiting foreign dignitaries, investigate passport and visa fraud, and conduct personnel security investigations.

Major Activities and Divisions

Regional Bureaus: The State Department's six geographic bureaus (the Bureaus of African Affairs, European and Eurasian Affairs, East Asian and Pacific Affairs, Western Hemisphere Affairs, Near Eastern Affairs, and South Asian Affairs) conduct U.S. foreign policy throughout the world.

Functional Bureaus

The Bureau of Arms Control: Leads U.S. negotiations for arms control agreements for nuclear, conventional, and chemical and biological weapons and their delivery systems.

The Nonproliferation Bureau: Leads U.S. efforts to prevent the spread of weapons of mass destruction (nuclear, chemical, and biological weapons) and their missile delivery systems.

The Bureau for Verification and Compliance: Is responsible for the supervision of all matters relating to verification of and compliance with international arms control, non-proliferation, and disarmament agreements.

The Bureau of Diplomatic Security: Employs regional security officers and engineers to protect U.S. personnel and missions overseas, advises U.S. ambassadors on all security matters, and provides an effective security program against terrorist, espionage, and criminal threats at U.S. diplomatic facilities.

The Bureau of Economic and Business Affairs: Formulates policies relating to food, energy, trade, finance, development, and aviation and maritime issues.

The Bureau of Intelligence and Research: Produces intelligence studies and coordinates intelligence and research programs with other federal agencies.

The Bureau of International Organization Affairs: Develops policies relating to U.S. participation in international organizations such as the United Nations.

The Bureau of Public Affairs: Provides news organizations and the general public with information on foreign policy.

The Bureau of Consular Affairs: Administers and enforces immigration and nationality laws.

The Bureau of Politico-Military Affairs: Provides policy guidance on military assistance, nuclear issues, and arms control.

The Bureau of Oceans and International Environmental and Scientific Affairs: Oversees foreign policy as it relates to oceans, fisheries, environment, population, nuclear technology, energy, outer space, and technology transfer.

The Bureau of Democracy, Human Rights, and Labor (DRL): Oversees initiatives and policies to promote and strengthen democratic institutions, civil society, and respect for human and worker rights.

The Bureau for International Narcotics and Law Enforcement Affairs (INL): Is charged with reducing illicit drug flows to the U.S.

The Bureau of population, Refugees, and Migration (PRM): Coordinates the Department's policy on global population, refugees, and migration issues and manages migration and refugee assistance appropriations.

The Bureau of Educational and Cultural Affairs (ECA): Fosters mutual understanding between the people of the United States and other countries.

The Office of International Information Programs (IIP): Is the principal international communications service for the U.S. foreign affairs community.

The Office of Protocol: Advises the President, Vice President, and the Secretary of State on diplomatic procedures and international customs.

The Office of the Coordinator for Counterterrorism (S/CT): Heads U.S. Government efforts to improve counterterrorism cooperation with foreign governments.

The Legal Adviser: Counsels the Secretary of State on matters of international law arising from the conduct of U.S. foreign relations.

Alternative Employment Programs

The State Department offers paid summer internships and year-round, unpaid work-study internships. Most positions are located in Washington, DC; however, a limited number of openings are overseas. Since most intern positions require a security clearance (a six-month process), the application deadline is usually November 1 of the preceding year. Students interested in spring or fall internships should apply at least six months prior to that date.

In addition to these internships, the State Department participates in several government-wide student programs, including Stay-in-School, Presidential Management Intern (PMI), and the Co-op program. The State Department also hires entry-level clerical workers through their Summer Clerical Employment and Student Worker Trainee programs. For more information on internships, call (202) 619-4360.

Remarks

Applicants interested in Foreign Service positions must pass the Foreign Service examination, which consists of rigorous oral and written assessments. Contact the State Department's Foreign Service recruitment division at the telephone number below. A year or more can pass between taking the exam and placement.

Application Procedures

For information on civil service careers, direct inquiries to:

Office of Recruitment, Examination and Employment
United States Department of State
HR/REE, SA-1
2401 E St., NW, 5H
Washington, DC 20522
(202) 261-8888
Fax: (202) 261-8841
E-mail: careers@state.gov

For information on Foreign Service careers, direct inquiries to:

Foreign Service
U.S. Department of State
P.O. Box 9317
Arlington, VA 22219
(703) 875-7490 (also includes information on other state department careers
and internships)

For information on student programs, direct inquiries to:

Attn: Student Programs
U. S. Department of State
Recruitment Division, SA-1
2401 E Street, NW, 5th Floor
Washington, DC 20522-0151
(202) 619-4360 (internships)

For more information on careers with the Bureau for Diplomatic Security, log
on to their Web site at www.ds.state.gov/. Other State Department career
information can be found at www.careers.state.gov.

☆ Department of Transportation (www.dot.gov)

U.S. Coast Guard
www.uscg.mil

Nature of Work: Defense and national security, disaster assistance, law enforcement, maritime activities, military affairs, transportation, waterways

Number of Employees: 6,000 (as well as 38,000 active duty and 35,000 auxiliarists)

Headquarters: Washington, DC

Regional Locations: Alameda, CA; Baltimore, MD; New York, NY; Portsmouth, VA

Typical Background of New Hires: Communications, engineering, environmental science

Mission

The Coast Guard is a branch of the Armed Forces of the United States at all times and is a service within the Department of Transportation except when operating as part of the Navy in time of war or when the President directs. The Coast Guard's responsibilities are diverse; they include maritime law enforcement, search and rescue, and waterways management.

Job Descriptions

Engineer (Aerospace): Performs maintenance engineering and design engineering on aircraft being modified or procured for use in U.S. Coast Guard air interdiction operations. Investigates and resolves technical problems concerning the modification of structures, discrepancies, and malfunctions.

Engineer (Chemical): Recommends, monitors, and evaluates research and development projects related to materials safety in the transportation and containment of bulk liquids, liquified gases, and other transported elements.

Engineer (Civil): Evaluates civil engineering projects in terms of their effect on Coast Guard missions, compliance with applicable laws, and engineering adequacy.

Engineer (Electrical): Develops regulations related to commercial vessel electrical systems. Evaluates proposals submitted by shipbuilders and others.

Engineer (Electronics): Plans, acquires, installs, and maintains Coast Guard Loran-C equipment, racons, radio beacons, and Vessel Traffic Service (VTS) systems, among other Coast Guard electronic devices.

Engineer (Environmental): Ensures that compliance and restoration projects meet the requirements of federal environmental regulations.

Engineer (Fire Prevention): Ensures that specifications are met for the design, construction, and general fire safety features of vessels.

Engineer (Mechanical): Designs, evaluates, and produces various Coast Guard Aids to Navigation (AtoN) and other marine equipment.

Engineer (Structural): Applies a knowledge of engineering and construction practices to bridge structures and construction specifications and procedures.

Environmental Protection Specialist: Assesses the environmental impact of projects pending Coast Guard approval. Identifies, evaluates, and documents environmental impact prior to final Coast Guard decision on the project.

Marine Information Specialist: Evaluates incoming navigational data and prepares usable information for Notice to Mariners, Light Lists, and miscellaneous chart and publication corrective information. Consults with personnel from each Coast Guard district, the Defense Mapping Agency, and the National Ocean Service to exchange information and resolve conflicting data.

Marine Insurance Examiner: Examines applications for Certificates of Financial responsibility submitted by all types of vessel owners and operators including shipyards, scrappers, and politically sensitive vessel owners.

Marine Safety Specialist: Reviews marine casualty boards and casualty investigations of vessel collisions to determine the extent of violation of rules of the road. Assesses Coast Guard programs for navigation safety and considers the need for revision.

Marine Transportation Specialist: Develops written merchant marine engineering examinations and associated publications.

Marine Vessel Operations Specialist: Develops merchant marine deck officer and operator examinations and associated publications.

Merchant Marine Licensing Specialist: Evaluates merchant marine license applications. Prepares authoritative replies to correspondence concerning the regulatory, policy, and interpretive aspects of licensing.

Naval Architect: Develops policy for the regulation of merchant vessels in the areas of vessel maneuverability, dynamically supported craft, and naval vessel design.

Vessel Traffic Specialist: Provides technical marine traffic management expertise in planning the establishment of vessel traffic services.

Major Activities and Divisions

The U.S. Coast Guard has five strategic goals:

Defense Readiness: The Coast Guard works in coordination with all the U.S. Armed Forces in all phases of operations on land, sea, or air in the U.S. Maritime Defense Zones.

Maritime Safety: The Coast Guard conducts search and rescue efforts, maintains aids to navigation, and acts to reduce the probability of mishaps.

Maritime Law Enforcement: The Coast Guard enforces all applicable federal laws on the high seas and waters subject to U.S. jurisdiction, including the interdiction of illegal drugs and migrants.

Protection of Natural Resources: The Coast Guard's prevention, enforcement, and response tasks in marine environmental protection help to reduce the amount of pollution entering America's and the world's waterways.

Maritime Mobility: Charged with ensuring a safe, efficient, and effective marine transportation system, the Coast Guard regulates and inspects commercial and private vessels, licenses merchant mariners, manages waterways, and protects the security of America's ports.

Alternative Employment Programs

The Coast Guard participates in a summer employment program in locations across the U.S., as well as an intern program for legal students. The Coast Guard also participates in the federal PMI program, as well as the SCEP co-op hiring program.

Remarks

Some recruitment is conducted for students with a marine/environmental-related engineering degree.

The Coast Guard has a new Civilian Career Entry-Level Opportunity Program designed to attract entry-level, high-quality college graduates into its workforce.

Application Procedures

Civilian vacancy announcements can be found at www.uscg.mil/jobs/Jobs.html. Other DOT Vacancy Announcements are available through the TASC DOT Connection Fax-On-Demand system at (202) 366-9397 or outside the Washington, DC, area, call (800) 525-2878.

For civilian positions, direct inquiries to the appropriate office:

U.S. Coast Guard Jobs
CGPC-CPM
2100 Second St., SW
Washington, DC 20593-0001
(202) 267-2229
Job Information: (202) 267-2331

Commander (PC)
U.S. Coast Guard MLC-PAC
Coast Guard Island
Alameda, CA 94501-5100
(510) 437-3196
DOT Job Hotline: (202) 366-9397

U.S. Coast Guard Yard
Civilian Personnel Office
Curtis Bay
Baltimore, MD 21226-1797
(410) 636 7274
Job Information: (410) 636-7777

Commander (PC)
U.S. Coast Guard
MLC-ATL-Portsmouth
Federal Building
431 Crawford St.
Portsmouth, VA 23704-5004
(757) 398-6287

Mission

The Federal Aviation Administration regulates air commerce in ways that best promote its development and safety and fulfill the requirements of national defense. It controls the use of navigable airspace of the U.S. and regulates both civil and military operations. The FAA oversees the air traffic control and navigation systems for civil and military aircraft and works to control aircraft noise, sonic boom, and other environmental effects of aviation.

Job Descriptions

Air Traffic Control Specialist (En Route Centers): Gives aircraft instructions, air traffic clearances, and advice regarding flight conditions during the en route portions of the flight. Provides separations between aircraft flying along the federal airways or operating into or out of airports not served by a terminal facility. Uses radar and manual procedures to keep track of the progress of all instrument flights within the center's airspace. Transfers control of aircraft to other controllers when the aircraft enters another facility's airspace.

Air Traffic Control Specialist (Flight Service Stations): Relays air traffic control instructions, assists pilots in emergency situations, provides airport advisory services, and initiates and participates in searches for missing or overdue aircraft. Provides information on the station's particular area, including terrain, weather peculiarities, preflight and inflight weather information, suggested routes, icing, and any other information important to the safety of a flight. Often meets pilots face to face.

Air Traffic Control Specialist (Towers): Directs air traffic so it flows smoothly and efficiently. Gives pilots taxiing and takeoff instructions, air traffic clearances, and advice based on personal observations and information received from the National Weather Service. Provides separation between landing and departing aircraft, transfers control of aircraft on instrument flights to the en route controllers when the aircraft leaves tower airspace, and receives control of aircraft coming into tower airspace from controllers at adjacent facilities.

Aviation Safety Inspector (Avionics): Conducts surveillance of the avionics portion of air carrier and air taxi programs. Evaluates avionics technicians and repair facilities and inspects aircraft for airworthiness. Investigates and reports on accidents and violations. Requires related work experience.

Aviation Safety Inspector (Maintenance): Evaluates mechanics and repair facilities for initial and continuing certification. Inspects aircraft and related equipment for airworthiness and evaluates the overall maintenance programs of air carriers and similar commercial operators. Investigates and reports on accidents and violations. Requires related work experience.

Aviation Safety Inspector (Manufacturing): Inspects prototype or modified aircraft, aircraft parts, and avionics equipment for conformity with design specifications and safety standards. Assumes FAA certificate responsibility for assigned manufacturing facilities and makes original airworthiness determinations. Requires related work experience.

Aviation Safety Inspector (Operations): Examines airmen for initial and continuing certification and qualification. Evaluates the operations of air carriers and similar commercial aviation operations for adequacy of facilities, equipment, procedures, and overall management to ensure safe operation of the aircraft. Investigates and reports on accidents and violations. Requires related work experience and an airline transport pilot certificate or commercial pilot certificate with instrument airplane rating.

Cabin Safety Inspector: Provides technical support regarding cabin safety for assigned air carriers and air operators. Applicants must have three years experience.

Airway Transportation Systems Specialist (ATSS)/Electronics Technicians (ET): Installs and maintains electronic equipment and lighting aids associated with facilities and services required for aviation navigation to assure a reliable, safe, and smooth flow of air traffic. This involves work with radar, communications, computers, navigational aids, airport lighting aids, and electrical/mechanical support for facilities on and off airports within the network of the National Airspace System (NAS).

Civil Aviation Security Specialist (Special Agent): Coordinates and performs assessments, inspections, and advisory work regarding compliance with Federal Aviation Regulations to ensure the security of the aviation traveling public.

Civil Aviation Security Specialist (Dangerous Goods and Cargo): Conducts surveillance and inspections of all U.S. air carriers and foreign air carriers serving the United States to ensure that regulations regarding the transportation of dangerous goods and cargo are being followed.

Civil Aviation Security Specialist (Federal Air Marshal): Federal Air Marshals are special agents who fly on selected high-risk routes to deter hijacking attempts and ensure the safety of passenger and crewmembers. They receive intensive, highly specialized law enforcement training at the William J. Hughes Technical Center in Atlantic City, New Jersey. These positions were formerly called "Sky Marshals." See www.faa.gov/apa/FACTSHEET/2000/fact4Aug.htm for more information on Federal Air Marshals.

Major Activities and Divisions

Safety Regulation: The FAA issues and enforces regulations and minimum standards relating to the manufacture, operation, and maintenance of aircraft.

Airspace and Air Traffic Management: The safe and efficient utilization of the navigable airspace is a primary objective of the FAA. The agency operates a network of airport towers, air route traffic control centers, and flight service stations. It develops air traffic rules, allocates the use of airspace, and provides for the security control of air traffic to meet national defense requirements.

Air Navigation Facilities: The FAA is responsible for the construction or installation of visual and electronic aids to air navigation, and for the maintenance, operation, and quality assurance of these facilities.

Civil Aviation Abroad: To promote aviation safety and encourage civil aviation abroad, the agency exchanges aeronautical information with foreign authorities.

Commercial Space Transportation: The agency regulates and encourages the U.S. commercial space transportation industry. It licenses commercial space launch facilities and private sector launching of space payloads on expendable launch vehicles.

Research, Engineering, and Development: The FAA engages in research, engineering, and development aimed at providing the systems and procedures needed for a safe and efficient system of air navigation and air traffic control.

Other Programs: The FAA provides a system for registering aircraft and recording documents affecting title or interest in aircraft and their components.

Alternative Employment Programs

The FAA participates in the Outstanding Scholar program and an FAA Student Intern Program. It also uses the Airway Facilities Collegiate Training Initiative (AF-CTI) Program and the Air Traffic Collegiate Training Initiative Program to provide a source for hiring students from colleges and trade schools with Federal Aviation Administration (FAA) approved curriculum for entry-level positions. See more information on special hiring programs at www.faa.gov/careers/employment/SH.htm.

Remarks

To qualify for Air Traffic Control Specialist positions, a person must not be over 30 years of age, unless he or she has experience in air traffic control. Currently, the FAA is only hiring graduates of FAA approved postsecondary educational programs, current or former federal employees with prior air traffic control specialist experience, or retired military air traffic controllers for positions in the En Route Center or Terminal Options. See www.faa.gov/careers/employment/atc.htm for more information on air traffic control positions.

Airway Transportation Systems Specialists and Electronics Technicians are hired primarily from a national register or pool of qualified applicants called AFCAPS (Airway Facilities Centralized Applicant pools). Individuals must submit an application through AFCAPS to be considered for employment. See www.faa.gov/careers/employment/atss-et.htm for more information.

Avionics, maintenance, and operations inspectors are hired primarily from a pool of qualified applicants. To be considered, individuals must complete the application process as outlined in the nationwide vacancy announcement: FAA-

ASI-99-001-27152. For manufacturing inspectors, see the FAA Nationwide Vacancy Announcement, FAA-AIR-99-MFG-37247. Cabin Safety Inspector positions are listed individually on the FAA Web site. For more information on all Safety Inspector position qualifications and application procedures, see www.faa.gov/careers/employment/asi.htm

Civil Aviation Safety Specialist positions are posted on the FAA Web site when vacancies occur.

The FAA also hires many civil, electrical, mechanical, aerospace, environmental, and industrial engineers. Some FAA careers may involve overseas employment. These positions are posted on the FAA Web site.

Application Procedures

Information on FAA careers can be found at www.faa.gov/careers/employment/jobinfo.htm.

Application forms can be found at http://jobs.faa.gov/ApplicationForms.asp.

Or, direct inquiries to the appropriate FAA regional office:

Mike Monroney Aeronautical Center
(Oklahoma City)
Personnel Operations Division,
AMH-200
P.O. Box 25082
Oklahoma City, OK 73125
(405) 954-4508

Aviation Careers, AMH-300
P.O. Box 26650
Oklahoma City, OK 73126-4934
(405) 954-4657

Alaskan Region (Alaska)
Human Resource Management
Division, Attn: AAL-14
222 West 7th Ave., #14
Anchorage, AK 99513-7587
(907) 271-5747

Central Region (MO, KS, IA, NE)
Human Resource Management
Division, ACE-10
901 Locust St., Room 402
Kansas City, MO 64106
(816) 329-2650

Eastern Region (NY, PA, WV, MD, NJ, DE, VA)
Human Resource Division, Attn:
AEA-10
Federal Aviation Administration
One Aviation Plaza
Jamaica, NY 11434
Air Traffic Jobs: (718) 553-3157
Other Jobs: (718) 553-3137

Great Lakes Region (ND, SD, MN, WI, MI, IL, IN, OH)
Human Resource Management
Division, Attn: AGL-18
2300 E. Devon Ave.
Des Plaines, IL 60018
(847) 294-7731

New England Region (ME, NH, VT, MA, CT, RI)
Human Resource Management
Division, Attn: ANE-14
12 New England Executive Park
Burlington, MA 01803
(781) 238-7280 or 7254

Northwest Mountain Region (WA, OR, ID, WY, CO, UT, MT)
Human Resource Division, Attn:
ANM-14
1601 Lind Ave., SW
Renton, WA 98055-4056
(425) 227-2014

Southern Region (KY, TN, NC, SC, MS, AL, GA, FL)
Human Resource Division, Attn:
ASO-14
P.O. Box 20636
Atlanta, GA 30320
(404) 305-5330

Southwest Region (TX, AR, LA, NM, OK)
Human Resource Management
Division, ASW-10
Ft. Worth, TX 76193
(817) 222-5850
Recorded Job Information: (817) 222-5855

FAA Technical Center (in Atlantic City, NJ)
Human Resource Management
Branch, Attn: ACT-110
Atlantic City International Airport, NJ 08405
(609) 485-6620

Western Pacific Region (CA, NV, AZ, the Pacific)
Human Resource Management
Division, Attn: AWP-10
P.O. Box 92007
Los Angeles, CA 90009
(310) 725-7801
TDD: (310) 725-7848

Washington, DC Area
Human Resource Management
Division, Attn: AHR-19
800 Independence Ave., SW
Washington, DC 20591
Job Information Line: (202) 267-8007
Personnel: (202) 267-8012

Transportation Security Administration
www.tsa.dot.gov
Nature of Work: Transportation, national security
Number of Employees: Approx. 60,000 (approx. 51,000 screeners)
Headquarters: Washington, DC
Regional Locations: Stationed at one of 429 airports across the U.S.
Typical Background of New Hires: Transportation, criminal justice, intelligence

Mission

Established in November 2001 in the aftermath of the World Trade Center tragedy, the Transportation Security Administration is designed to protect the nation's transportation systems to ensure freedom of movement for people and commerce. The bulk of the new agency's authority is centered on the air transportation system, particularly protecting against terrorist threats, sabotage, and other acts of violence.

Job Descriptions

Transportation Security Screener: Provides frontline security and protection of air travelers, airports, and airplanes. Identifies dangerous or deadly objects in baggage and cargo and on passengers and prevents those objects from being transported onto aircraft. (Complete qualifications standards for this position can be found on the TSA Web site.)

Law Enforcement Officer: Performs law enforcement duties primarily concerned with alleged or suspected offenses against the security of our national airports and criminal laws. Works to prevent, detect, and enforce airport transportation security and criminal laws, executes arrest warrants, and responds to real or potential security violations through searches, seizures, and arrests.

Major Activities and Divisions

The current TSA organizational model includes four major program divisions: Aviation Operations, Maritime and Land Security, Security Regulations and policy, and Intelligence.

Remarks

At the time of this writing, TSA is a young agency, and many programs are still being formulated. TSA plans to hire and deploy security screeners and supervisors at 429 airports across the U.S. The screener workforce is anticipated to exceed 30,000 people. In addition, TSA will employ thousands of Federal Law Enforcement Officers (LEOs), as well as intelligence and support personnel.

Alternative Employment Programs

Temporary summer jobs are available in some program offices. See the TSA Web site for current information.

Application Procedures

Security Screeners can apply online when a vacancy announcement is open. Or, you may complete an application by phone at (877) 631-5627 (877-631-JOBS). The TSA does not accept resumes by mail.

Security Screener and Law Enforcement Employment:
Toll Free: (888) 328-6172

Transportation Security Administration:
400 Seventh St., SW
Washington, DC 20590
(866) 289-9673

Federal Highway Administration (FHWA)
www.fhwa.dot.gov

Nature of Work: Highways/roads, safety, transportation

Number of Employees: 3,000

Headquarters: Washington, DC

Regional Locations Atlanta, GA; Baltimore, MD; Lakewood, CO; Olympia Fields, IL; San Francisco, CA. There are also 52 Division Offices, generally in the capital of each state.

Typical Background of New Hires: Business, economics, engineering (civil), marketing, mathematics, urban studies

---

Mission

The FHWA encompasses highway transportation in its broadest scope, seeking to coordinate highways with other modes of transportation to achieve the most effective balance of transportation systems.

Job Descriptions

Civil Engineer: Develops policy and standards for testing in the quality control of construction material. Evaluates highway project proposals and environmental impact statements. Participates in the planning, design, construction, and maintenance aspects of highways. Coordinates the design and preparation of state highway plans, including preliminary specifications and estimates for construction contracts.

Community Planner: Provides policy direction and technical assistance to other elements of the FHA, state highway agencies, and local planning agencies in establishing highway planning programs that are consistent with state and national goals. Conducts or assists in technical reviews, evaluations, and coordination of statewide and urban transportation planning programs.

Contract Specialist: Procures supplies, construction, research, and other services related to highway projects using formal advertising and negotiating methods. Evaluates contract price/cost proposals.

Economist: Forecasts future highway travel demand, analyzes future highway system requirements, and projects future highway funding options. Involves the development and application of statistical and economic analysis packages.

Motor Carrier Safety Specialist: Conducts on-site safety and hazardous materials compliance reviews and enforcement investigations of motor carriers. Performs periodic roadside vehicle inspections and on-site compliance reviews of carriers' business records and operating practices for evidence of safety violations. Often requires experience in the safety field.

Operations Research Analyst: Develops transportation policy analysis models and highway-related databases. Prepares travel forecasts and studies of cost allocation issues.

Realty Specialist: Participates in the development and implementation of policies and procedures relating to right-of-way appraising, acquisition, relocation assistance payments and service on federal and federal-aid projects. Communicates with state highway department officials concerning federal policy and procedures.

Major Activities and Divisions

The FHWA is divided into several core business units:

The Infrastructure Core Business Unit provides leadership, technical expertise, and program assistance in federal-aid highway programs, asset management, pavements, and bridges to help sustain America's mobility.

Planning, Environment and Real Estate: Serves as FHWA's advocate for environment protection, comprehensive intermodal and multimodal transportation planning, and for fair acquisition and management of real property.

Highway Safety Programs: Administers highway-related safety guidelines providing for the identification and surveillance of accident locations; highway design, construction, and maintenance; traffic engineering services; and highway-related aspects of pedestrian safety.

Operations: Maintains a national network for trucks, reviews state truck size and weight enforcement programs, and assists in obtaining uniformity among the states in the area of commercial motor carrier registration and taxation reporting.

Federal Lands Highway Program: Funds more than 80,000 miles of federally owned roads that are open to the public and serve federal lands, such as forest highways, park roads, and Indian reservation roads.

Research, Development and Technology Program: Searches for ways to improve the quality and durability of highways and streets, reduce construction costs, and reduce the negative impacts of highway transportation.

Alternative Employment Programs

Summer Transportation Internship Program for Diverse Groups (STIPDG): The STIPDG is part of the Garrett A. Morgan Technology and Transportation Futures Program (GAMTTFP). The STIPDG offers transportation research opportunities, work experience, and on-site visits to introduce students to many aspects of the complex field of transportation. Open to graduate and undergraduate students.

Summer Employment Program: FHWA offers summer employment to graduate and undergraduate students. Call the Human Resource office that hires for the region in which you have interest.

The FHWA Professional Development Program: Provides approximately two years of entry-level career development for college graduates with a bachelor's or master's degree to serve in a variety of disciplines such as engineering, planning, or intelligent transportation systems. Contact a Human Resources Office listed below or log on to www.fhwa.dot.gov/aaa/pdp/index.htm.

Application Procedures

Vacancy announcements are listed on the USAJOBS Web site, and are available by fax through the DOT Connection Fax-On-Demand system at (202) 366-9397 or (800) 525-2878.

Direct inquiries to the office that covers your region of interest. (See www.fhwa.dot.gov/field.html.)

FHWA Office of Human Resources
HAHR-22, Room 4334
400 Seventh St., SW
Washington, DC 20590
(202) 366-0541
Job Line: (202) 366-9397
Fax Number: (202) 366-3749
E-mail: Vacancy.System@fhwa.dot.gov

FHWA Lakewood Human Resources Office (Covers northern and western U.S.)
555 Zang St., Room 400
Lakewood, CO 80228
(303) 969-5772
Fax Number: (303) 969-5790
E-mail: LHRC.LHRC@fhwa.dot.gov

FHWA Atlanta Human Resources Office (covers eastern and southern U.S.)
60 Forsyth St., Suite 8M20
Atlanta, GA 30303
(404) 562-3585
Fax: (404) 562-3705
E-mail: AHRC@ga.fhwa.dot.gov

Federal Railroad Administration (FRA)
www.fra.dot.gov

Nature of Work: Railroads, safety, transportation

Number of Employees: 700

Headquarters: Washington, DC

Regional Locations: Atlanta, GA; Chicago, IL; Cambridge, MA; Kansas City, MO; Hurst, TX; Philadelphia, PA; Sacramento, CA; Vancouver, WA

Typical Background of New Hires: Accounting, business, computer science, economics, engineering, physical science

Mission

The FRA's mission is to enforce rail safety regulations, to administer railroad financial assistance programs, to conduct research in railroad safety, and to set national rail policy.

Job Descriptions

Economist: Tracks the economic health of the railroad industry, assesses the economic impact of nonsafety regulations, identifies economic trends, and monitors labor issues. Conducts economic modeling to monitor industry conditions and to establish an analytical base from which the agency formulates its positions on mergers and acquisitions.

General Engineer: Conducts research and development related to improving railroad safety and enhancing intercity ground transportation through advances in railroad technology.

Financial Analyst: Assists in the administration of financial assistance to shortline and regional railroads. Audits Amtrak's financial performance and monitors the financial trends of the railroad industry.

Railroad Safety Inspector: Inspects for compliance with federal laws, regulations, and standards. Conducts and reports on accident investigations, ensuring the maintenance of safe operating conditions throughout the nation's network of rail lines. Often requires experience in rail safety practices. There are five occupational disciplines: Hazardous Materials, Operating Practices, Motive Power and Equipment, Track, and Signals and Train Control. Occasionally, trainee-level opportunities are available for this position.

Major Activities and Divisions

The Office of Safety: Oversees 54 nationwide field offices. Ensures that U.S. safety standards are met in regard to all aspects of railroad industry. Consists mostly of Safety Inspectors and Engineers.

The Office of Policy and Program Development: Establishes policy on rail issues such as rail mergers, regulation and deregulation, carrier issues, and rail-line shutdowns.

The Office of Railroad Development: Administers programs for railroad passenger and freight services, high-speed ground transportation, railroad research and development, the Northeast Corridor Improvement Program, and the Transportation Test Center.

The Transportation Test Center: A 50-square-mile facility in Pueblo, Colorado, which provides testing for advanced and conventional rail systems and techniques designed to improve ground transportation.

Alternative Employment Programs

The FRA participates in the federal STEP and SCEP programs, as well as a volunteer hiring program. There are also two summer employment programs at FRA: the Summer Employment Program and the Summer Transportation Internship Program for Diverse Groups. Call (202) 366-1168 for more information.

Application Procedures

Visit the FRA employment Web site at www.fra.dot.gov/o/hr for current vacancy announcements and application procedures.

Or, direct inquiries to:

Federal Railroad Administration
Office of Human Resources, RAD-11
1120 Vermont Avenue, NW, Mail Stop 30
Washington, DC 20590
(202) 493-6116
Job Hotline: (202) 366-0584
Fax Back System, Toll Free: (800) 821-0471

Federal Transit Administration (FTA)
www.fta.dot.gov

Nature of Work: Funds/funding, safety, transportation

Number of Employees: 500

Headquarters: Washington, DC

Regional Locations: Atlanta, GA; Cambridge, MA; Chicago, IL; Denver, CO; Fort Worth, TX; Kansas City, MO; New York, NY; Philadelphia, PA; San Francisco, CA; Seattle, WA

Typical Background of New Hires: Accounting, engineering, public administration, urban studies

Mission

FTA assists in the funding, planning, and development of urban mass transportation systems with the cooperation of public and private mass transportation companies.

Job Descriptions

Community Planner: Provides policy direction and technical assistance to other elements of FTA and to local planning agencies in establishing mass transit systems that are consistent with area and national goals.

General Engineer: Serves as a resource to staff members on engineering issues and funded transit projects. Projects vary from the design and construction of small maintenance and storage facilities to the complex design and construction of rail facilities.

Grants Management Specialist: Administers grants and loans that assist communities in acquiring or improving equipment and facilities needed for urban mass transit systems.

Transportation Program Specialist: Acts as liaison between FTA and transit authorities. Plans and establishes improved mass transportation facilities, equipment, and techniques. Typically employed in a regional office.

Program and Divisions

Grant Programs: FTA has several grant programs, divided according to recipient and purpose.

Research and Technology: FTA supports technological innovation regarding such issues as transportation security and safety, personal mobility, fuel consumption and air pollution, and ridership trends.

Alternative Employment Programs

FTA participates in the federal STEP and SCEP student employment programs.

Application Procedures

Direct inquiries to:

Office of Human Resources
Federal Transit Administration
400 7th St., SW
Room 9113, TAD-30
Washington, DC 20590
(202) 366-2513
Fax: (202) 366-7890
E-mail: FTAJOBS2@fta.dot.gov

Maritime Administration (MARAD)
www.marad.dot.gov

Nature of Work: Emergency preparedness, maritime activities, trade, transportation, waterways

Number of Employees: 1,000

Headquarters: Washington, DC

Regional Locations: Des Plaines, IL; Kings Point, NY (Merchant Marine Academy); New Orleans, LA; New York, NY; Norfolk, VA; San Francisco, CA

Typical Background of New Hires: Architecture, engineering, transportation

---

Mission

MARAD administers programs to aid in the development and operation of the U.S. Merchant Marine. It supervises the construction of merchant-type ships for the government and directs emergency merchant ship operations.

Job Descriptions

Engineer: Works with Naval Architects in designing and maintaining merchant marine ships and in examining and evaluating National Defense Reserve Fleet (NDRF) vessels. Applies a professional knowledge of engineering technology, including strength and strain analysis, elastic limits, maximum unit stresses, coefficients of expansion, and resistance to corrosion.

Naval Architect: Performs engineering and architectural work concerning the form, strength, performance, and operational characteristics of ships. Makes stability and buoyancy calculations and develops data for launching, loading, operations, and drydocking of ships in an efficient manner. Examines NDRF vessels for seaworthiness.

Ship Operations Analyst: Conducts analyses on water transportation systems and services, including commercial trade systems, ship-building or acquisition vessel plans, and domestic waterborne shipping systems.

Subsidy Rate Analyst: Analyzes the differential in foreign and domestic vessel operating costs. Determines a direct subsidy amount to be paid to U.S. shipping companies to offset the higher cost of operating vessels in foreign trade under the American flag, compared to operating costs under foreign flags.

Trade Specialist: Examines domestic fleet and U.S. flag vessel services in terms of trade markets, commodities moves, and modal competition.

Transportation Industry Analyst: Conducts research and makes recommendations as to current maritime development and future trends in trade, markets, intermodal transportation, emerging technologies, economic developments, fuels and materials, and national defense requirements.

Transportation Specialist: Compiles information on domestic fleet and U.S. flag vessel services as they relate to industry regulatory controls, customs and competitive practices of vessels, and industry operations and services.

Major Activities and Divisions

Policy and International Trade: Works to achieve equitable access to foreign markets for U.S. shipping firms.

Port, Intermodal, and Environmental Activities: Seeks to improve the use of U.S. ports, port facilities, and domestic shipping. Works to decrease ship-generated pollution and helps to eliminate environmental problems at U.S. ports and MARAD-operated facilities.

National Security: Administers programs to provide commercial and government-owned shipping capability in times of national emergency and to meet Department of Defense strategic sealift requirements.

Financial Approvals and Cargo Preference: Manages the cargo preference program and conducts financial analysis activities in support of several MARAD programs, including the shipbuilding and shipyard modernization loan guarantee program.

Shipbuilding and Ship Operations: Supervises the construction of merchant-type ships for the government.

Alternative Employment Programs

None

Remarks

MARAD operates the U.S. Merchant Marine Academy at Kings Point, New York, which trains men and women to be officers in the American Merchant Marine. Applicants to the Academy must be nominated by a member of Congress. All academy graduates receive U.S. Coast Guard licenses and Bachelor of Science degrees.

Application Procedures

Direct inquiries to:

DOT, Maritime Administration
Office of Personnel
400 7th St., SW
Washington, DC 20590
(202) 366-4149
Toll Free: (800) 99-MARAD

National Highway Traffic Safety Administration (NHTSA)
www.nhtsa.dot.gov

Nature of Work: Highways/roads, safety, scientific research, transportation

Number of Employees: 700

Headquarters: Washington, DC

Regional Locations: Atlanta, GA; Cambridge, MA; Denver, CO; East Liberty, OH (test facility); Fort Worth, TX; Olympia Fields, IL; Kansas City, MO; Baltimore, MD; San Francisco, CA; Seattle, WA; White Plains, NY

Typical Background of New Hires: Engineering, mathematics, psychology, public relations

Mission

NHTSA was established to carry out a congressional mandate to reduce the mounting number of deaths, injuries, and economic losses resulting from traffic accidents on the nation's highways. The administration also establishes safeguards to protect purchasers of motor vehicles and to prescribe safety features and levels of safety-related performance for vehicles.

Job Descriptions

Engineer (Electrical): Studies the design of motor vehicles from an electrical safety standpoint. Examines vehicles for defects and ensures that detected problems are properly handled by the manufacturer of the vehicle. Provides guidance and leadership in the regulation and planning aspect of the automobile industry. Some engineers work in the Vehicle Research and Testing facility in East Liberty, Ohio. Most are stationed at headquarters in Washington.

Engineer (Mechanical): Studies vehicle safety issues, such as seatbelt and air bag effectiveness, defects investigation, and crashworthiness. Provides guidance and leadership in the regulation and planning aspect of the automobile industry. Some engineers work in the Vehicle Research and Testing facility. Most are stationed at headquarters in Washington.

Engineering Research Psychologist: Conducts research in the interdisciplinary areas of driver behavior and driver-vehicle interaction. Studies human and vehicle factors in accident avoidance, pedestrian safety, standards enforcement, and occupant protection. Must have a B.A. with at least 24 semester hours in psychology.

Highway Safety Specialist: Provides technical and administrative leadership to state and local governments in the development of highway safety programs. Works with private organizations and community groups in promoting NHTSA programs in such areas as bicycle safety, seat belt usage, school bus safety, and drunk driving awareness.

Mathematical Statistician: Works with analysts and engineers to compile statistics based on NHTSA research. Prepares statistical information for use in enforcement, safety, and public education programs.

Operations Research Analyst: Conducts scientific and technical analyses to develop a system to evaluate the effectiveness of NHTSA programs and standards. Requires a technical background in a math or research related major.

Major Activities and Divisions

Safety Performance Standards: Works to reduce the occurrence of highway crashes and to decrease the severity of injuries in motor vehicle accidents.

Safety Assurance: Consists of the Office of Defects Investigation and the Office of Vehicle Safety Compliance.

Traffic Safety Programs: Provides federal matching funds to assist states with their driver, pedestrian, and motor vehicle safety programs.

Research and Development: NHTSA administers a broad program of research, development, testing, demonstration, and evaluation of motor vehicles, operator and pedestrian safety, and accident data collection and analysis.

Alternative Employment Programs

NHTSA hires students for positions related to their majors.

Application Procedures

Direct inquiries to:

Director of Personnel
U.S. Department of Transportation
National Highway Traffic Safety Administration
400 7th St., SW, Room 5306
Washington, DC 20590
Human Resources: (202) 366-1784
Information: (202) 366-9550

Research and Special Programs Administration (RSPA)
www.rspa.dot.gov

Nature of Work: Emergency preparedness, hazardous materials, safety, scientific research, transportation

Number of Employees: 795

Headquarters Location: Washington, DC

Regional Locations: Atlanta, GA; Cambridge, MA; Denver, CO; Houston, TX; Kansas City, MO; Oklahoma City, OK

Typical Background of New Hires: Computer science, engineering (materials, mechanical, petroleum, structural), transportation

Mission

RSPA is responsible for a number of transmodal programs involving safety regulation, emergency preparedness, and research and development. Emphasis is given to hazardous material transportation and pipeline safety, transportation emergency preparedness, safety training, technology sharing, multimodal transportation research activities, and the collection and dissemination of air carrier economic data.

Job Descriptions

General Engineer/Petroleum Engineer: Serves as part of a nationwide team that applies engineering and enforcement techniques to investigate gas operators and liquid carriers for compliance with federal pipeline safety standards. Investigates pipeline accidents by examining pipeline components involved, assessing the impact of the accident on the area, interviewing witnesses, and evaluating other data to determine if there are violations of regulations. All types of pipeline facilities are inspected for construction, design, operation, and maintenance. Pipelines may be located offshore or in deepwater ports and may involve the transport of hazardous liquids, natural gas, or liquified natural gas. Travel is regional within an approximate ten-state area and is typically 50 percent.

Transportation Specialist: Conducts research activities involving one or more specialized transportation functions. Reviews and interprets safety regulations and collects data on issues of safety, hazardous materials transportation, economy, environmental impact, and operation.

Major Activities and Divisions

Office of Hazardous Materials Safety: Enforces regulations for the safe transportation of hazardous materials.

Office of Pipeline Safety: Enforces safety standards for the transportation of gas and hazardous liquids by pipeline.

Transportation Systems Center: Focuses on air and marine transportation systems; the social, economic, and environmental effects of transportation; and the maintenance of national transportation statistics.

Office of Emergency Transportation: Develops plans for maintaining a high state of federal transportation emergency preparedness, including national defense and emergencies caused by natural disasters.

Office of Innovation, Research and Education: Coordinates the Department's research and development program.

Volpe Center: Addresses national and international transportation issues related to safety, security, environment, mobility, and economic growth and trade.

Alternative Employment Programs

The Volpe Internship: Offers tuition assistance and paid work opportunities at the Volpe Center in Cambridge, Massachusetts for outstanding graduate students in engineering, scientific, and social science disciplines who wish to work in the field of transportation. E-mail at recruiting@volpe.dot.gov or call (617) 494-2500.

RSPA maintains a student employment program, typically filling engineer positions at the GS-3, -4, and -5 levels. The agency also hires several interns each year to fill varied positions. Each program typically fills one to ten positions annually. Call (202) 366-5608 for more information.

RSPA also participates in employment programs for clerical support positions and sponsors a volunteer internship program.

Application Procedures

Direct inquiries to:

Research and Special Programs Administration
Office of Personnel
400 7th St., SW
Washington, DC 20590
(202) 366-5608
Job Hotline: (202) 366-9397

☆ Treasury Department (www.ustreas.gov)

Bureau of Alcohol, Tobacco, and Firearms (ATF)
www.atf.treas.gov

Nature of Work: Law enforcement, taxes/revenue

Number of Employees: 4,700

Headquarters: Washington, DC

Regional Locations: Atlanta, GA; Chicago, IL; Columbus, OH; Dallas, TX; New York, NY; San Francisco, CA; Baltimore, MD; Boston, MA; Charlotte, NC; Detroit, MI; Kansas City, MO; Los Angeles, CA; Louisville, KY; Nashville, TN; New Orleans, LA; Philadelphia, PA; Seattle, WA; St. Paul, MN; Tampa, FL; Washington, DC. Future sites proposed for Houston, TX; Miami, FL; and Phoenix, AZ.

Typical Background of New Hires: Accounting, business, criminal justice, law

Mission

Regulates the alcohol, tobacco, firearms, and explosives industries and enforces federal firearms and explosives laws.

Job Descriptions

Auditor: Conducts arson investigations and ensures the collection of excise taxes through audits of businesses selling alcoholic beverages, tobacco products, firearms, and explosives.

Document Analyst: Performs document examinations using sequential morphological, chemical, microscopic, photographic, and computer imaging techniques and prepares reports of findings and expert opinions developed from the examination and analysis of evidence.

Firearm/Toolmarks Examiner: Examines, using chemical, physical, and instrumental techniques, a wide variety of physical evidence associated with firearms and toolmark cases. Responds to major scenes to assist in the proper collection, preservation, and packaging of physical evidence. Provides court testimony.

Inspector: Examines and analyzes records, reports, and operations. Also evaluates compliance with the laws applicable to business activities and examines products manufactured or sold by businesses regulated by ATF. Refer to the "ATF Inspector" section on the ATF Web page for more information.

Special Agent: Investigates violations of federal laws involving explosives, arson, firearms, illicit liquor, and tobacco. These investigations involve surveillance, participation in raids, interviewing suspects and witnesses, making arrests, obtaining search warrants and searching for physical evidence. E-mail: agentinfo@atf.treas.gov. or refer to the "ATF Special Agent" section on the agency Web page for more information.

Major Activities and Divisions

Firearms: ATF Firearms program pursues an integrated regulatory and enforcement strategy. Investigative priorities focus on armed violent offenders and career criminals, narcotics traffickers, narco-terrorists, violent gangs, and domestic and international arms traffickers. Regulatory operations involve issuing firearms licenses and conducting firearms licensee qualification and compliance inspections.

Arson and Explosives: Regulates explosives and investigates explosives incidents and arsons, using National Response Teams, International Response Teams, and Arson Task Forces. These teams consist of ATF Special Agents, Auditors, Technicians, Laboratory Personnel, and canines.

Alcohol/Tobacco: Regulates the qualification and operations of distilleries, wineries, and breweries as well as importers and wholesalers in the industry. Collects alcohol beverage and tobacco excise taxes, and issues permits to manufacture tobacco products or operate tobacco export warehouses.

Alternative Employment Programs

ATF participates in many federal student hiring programs, including the Outstanding Scholar program, STEP, SCEP, PMI, and a student volunteer program.

Remarks

Special Agents must undergo specialized instruction at the Federal Law Enforcement Training Center at Glynco, Georgia. This consists of written and physical tests, as well as graded practical exercises and a firearms proficiency test. Inspectors undergo formal classroom instruction supplemented by on-the-job training. Formal classroom instruction consists of two basic training classes totaling nine weeks.

Upcoming ATF job fair events are listed on the Virtual Job Fair Web site: www.usajobs.opm.gov/ncsc.htm

Application Procedures

Direct inquiries to:

Bureau of Alcohol, Tobacco and Firearms
Personnel Division
650 Massachusetts Ave., NW, Room 4100
Washington, DC 20226
(202) 927-8610
Agent Applicants Only: (202) 927-5690

Bureau of Engraving and Printing (BEP)
www.bep.treas.gov

Nature of Work: Arts

Number of Employees: 2,600

Headquarters: Washington, DC

Regional Locations: Fort Worth, TX

Typical Background of New Hires: Chemistry, engineering, graphic arts (printing sciences), physical sciences, statistics

---

Mission

Designs and prints currency, postage stamps, Treasury obligations, and customs and revenue stamps.

Job Descriptions

Chemist: Formulates inks and papers resulting in durable documents that resist counterfeiting.

Electrical Engineer: Designs, installs, and maintains electrical networks.

Industrial Engineer: Evaluates the interplay of employees and machines to improve productivity.

Mechanical Engineer: Designs and integrates electromechanical printing processes and equipment.

Police Officer: Patrols designated areas in order to detect and prevent violations. Maintains law and order, preserves the peace, protects the life, property and civil rights of the employees and visitors of the BEP. Requires certification by the Bureau's Medical Officer as physically qualified to perform arduous duties, with emphasis on eyesight, color distinction, hearing, and mobility.

Printing Management Specialist: Establishes printing standards and determines production runs.

Statistician: Applies statistical techniques that improve quality.

Major Activities and Divisions

Office of Applied Research and Technical Services: Solves various printing problems, such as counterfeit-resistant currency and securities.

Office of Engineering: Oversees the installation and operation of the Bureau's presses and other equipment.

Office of Quality Assurance: Ensures that printed documents are produced according to standards of acceptable quality.

Alternative Employment Programs

BEP participates in the STEP program and the Outstanding Scholar program.

Application Procedures

Direct inquiries to:

Bureau of Engraving and Printing
Staffing and Classification Division
14th and C Streets, SW
Washington, DC 20228
(202) 874-3019
Human Resources: (202) 874-2633

Bureau of the Public Debt
www.publicdebt.treas.gov

Nature of Work: Accounting/auditing

Number of Employees: 2,000

Headquarters: Washington, DC

Regional Locations: Parkersburg, WV

Typical Background of New Hires: Accounting, business, computer science

Mission

Borrows money needed to operate the federal government. Accounts for the resulting public debt by selling government securities.

Job Descriptions

Accountant: Classifies and evaluates financial data, records transactions in financial records, develops and installs new accounting systems, prepares and analyzes financial statements.

Information Technology Specialist: Provides specialized and technical IT services within the areas of systems analysis, systems development, and computer programming.

Pension Payroll Specialist: Assists in administering the District of Columbia (DC) pension benefits system for approximately 16,000 annuitants, including DC teachers, police and firefighters, judges, park police, and Uniformed Secret Service annuitants.

Major Activities and Divisions

Public Debt borrows about $2 trillion each year by conducting some 140 auctions, as well as through the continuous sale of savings bonds at 40,000 locations throughout the country.

Alternative Employment Programs

The Bureau occasionally uses student programs to hire accountants, budget analysts, management analysts, program analysts, and information technology specialists.

Application Procedures

Direct inquiries via e-mail to: PersOffice@bpd.treas.gov

Bureau of the Public Debt
Employment and Classification Branch
200 Third St., P.O. Box 1328
Parkersburg, WV 26106-1328
Recorded Job Information: (304) 480-6144
General Employment Information: (304) 480-6650

Washington Address
999 E St., NW
Washington, DC 20239
(202) 480-7799

U.S. Customs Service
www.customs.ustreas.gov

Nature of Work: Drugs/abuse, import/export, international affairs, law enforcement, taxes/revenue

Number of Employees: 20,200

Headquarters: Washington, DC

Regional Locations: Customs Management Centers are located in Atlanta, GA; Baltimore, MD; Boston, MA; Buffalo, NY; Chicago, IL; Detroit, MI; El Paso, TX; Houston, TX; Laredo, TX; Long Beach, CA; Miami, FL; New Orleans, LA; New York, NY; Portland, OR; San Diego, CA; San Francisco, CA; San Juan, PR; Seattle, WA; Tampa, FL; Tucson, AZ. These Customs Management Centers oversee the operation of more than 300 ports of entry. The Customs Service also operates a Canine Enforcement Training Center at Front Royal, VA. Science Laboratory locations include: Chicago, New York, New Orleans, Los Angeles, San Francisco, and Savannah.

Typical Background of New Hires: Business, criminal justice

Mission

The United States Customs Service is the primary enforcement agency protecting the nation's borders. It is the only border agency with an extensive air, land, and marine interdiction force and with an investigative component supported by its own intelligence branch. Also guards against the infringement of American copyrights, patents, trademarks, and intellectual property.

Job Descriptions

Canine Enforcement Officer: Trains and uses dogs to prevent drug smuggling.

Customs Inspector: Prevents smuggling, fraud, and other criminal acts by inspecting baggage, cargo, and mail arriving in the U.S. Assesses and collects duties, excise taxes, fees, and penalties levied on imported merchandise.

Criminal Investigator: Prevents smuggling and other crimes by apprehending suspects at U.S. ports of entry. Gathers evidence by interviewing witnesses, conducting searches, speaking to informants, and undercover surveillance. Investigates violations of U.S. Customs laws, such as the illegal shipment of arms and high-technology goods to foreign countries and conspiracies to defraud the U.S. government of revenue.

Customs Scientist: Analyzes and identifies materials such as chemicals and metals; textiles and wearing apparel; rubber and plastics; food products; pharmaceuticals and biologicals; items associated with criminal investigations, such as narcotics, other dangerous drugs, and trace evidence; and products in violation of U.S. patent, copyright, and trademark laws. May be required to testify in court.

Import Specialist: Assesses duties and taxes on commercial cargo arriving at international airports, border crossings, and other locations. Enforces fair trade laws, copyright and trademark laws, health and safety laws, as well as quota and visa restrictions.

Pilot/Aviation Enforcement Officer (AEO): From one of many aviation branches across the U.S. and Puerto Rico, pilots are part of a team of aviators responsible for detecting and pursuing aircraft illegally intruding into U.S. airspace. The Customs fleet includes C-550 Citations, Piper Cheyennes, AS350s, UH-60 Blackhawks, C206/210s, and B-200/C-12s. AEOs serve as primary law enforcement officers on Customs interdiction aircraft and must be able to perform warrant and arrest, surveillance, intelligence, and communications duties.

Major Activities and Divisions

The Office of Border Coordination: The point of coordination for Customs activities along the U.S./Canada border and the Southwest border of the United States. Coordinates drug interdiction policy with other federal agencies.

Office of Investigations: Responsible for U.S. Customs investigations and intelligence subprocesses, oversight of the foreign and domestic investigative offices, and the air and marine interdiction programs.

Office of International Affairs: Manages international activities and programs and conducts Customs bilateral and multilateral relations with other countries. Oversees the negotiation and implementation of all international agreements.

Office of Strategic Trade: Identifies and confronts major trade issues facing the United States by innovative research and analysis and by the creation of coordinated interventions.

The Research Laboratory: A centralized research facility that provides scientific support to Customs Headquarters and the Field Laboratories.

Office of Information Technology Laboratories and Scientific Services: Consists of the field laboratories that conduct analysis and identification of materials and products.

Alternative Employment Programs

The U.S. Customs Service Law Enforcement Explorer Program: Provides opportunities for students to participate in federal enforcement-related activities within the Customs Service. Law Enforcement Explorer positions offer programs in law enforcement and criminal justice, which provide Explorers with practical training and hands-on experience. Qualified candidates must be between the ages of 14 and 21, and attending high school or enrolled in college.

Remarks

The U.S. Customs Service includes 20 Customs Management Centers (CMC's) and 304 air, sea, and land ports in the United States, including preclearance offices in Puerto Rico, the Virgin Islands, the Bahamas, and Canada. It also includes many investigations field offices and scientific laboratories.

Application Procedures

Direct inquiries to:

Customs Headquarters
1300 Pennsylvania Ave., NW
Washington, DC 20229
Toll Free: (800) 944-7725

For more information about aviation careers with the U.S. Customs Service, contact an aviation recruiter at (361) 698-6700 or (904) 777-8919.

For information regarding Science Officer positions, contact the laboratory in which you would like to work. Complete descriptions of the science laboratory specialization areas and contact information can be found at www.customs.ustreas.gov/about/about.htm. Or, contact:

Laboratories and Scientific Services
U.S. Customs Service
1300 Pennsylvania Ave., Suite 1500 N
Washington, DC 20229
(202) 927-1060
Fax: (202) 927-2060
E-mail: LAB-HQ@customs.treas.gov

Inquiries regarding the Research Laboratory should be directed to:

Research Laboratory
U.S. Customs Service
7501 Boston Blvd., Suite 113
Springfield, VA 22153
(703) 921-7200
Fax: (703) 921-7155
E-mail: LAB-RESEARCH@customs.treas.gov

Financial Management Service (FMS)
www.fms.treas.gov

Nature of Work: Taxes/revenue

Number of Employees: 2,100

Headquarters: Washington, DC

Regional Locations: Austin, TX; Kansas City, MO; Philadelphia, PA; San Francisco, CA

Typical Background of New Hires: Accounting, business, computer science, finance/banking

Mission

Receives tax collections, duties, and other public monies; manages the government's central accounting and financial system; settles claims for lost or forged government checks and mutilated currency; and invests Social Security and other trust funds.

Job Descriptions

Accountant: Reviews agency financial data, develops and installs new accounting systems, and prepares and analyzes financial statements and reports.

Computer Specialist: Designs and operates automated accounting and other types of information systems.

Financial Management Specialist: Coordinates budget, accounting, and managerial financial reporting; evaluates and reports on program accomplishments.

Management Analyst: Determines whether management controls are consistent with desirable business methods and creates organizations capable of achieving diverse objectives.

Program Analyst: Determines whether a program is successfully accomplishing its objectives and recommends improvements.

Major Activities and Divisions

Working Capital Management: Oversees programs for improving government-wide cash management, credit management, debt collection, and financial management systems.

Payments: Pays all Treasury checks issued for federal salaries, goods and services, and income tax refunds as well as social security, veterans, and other major federal benefit programs.

Collections: Supervises the collection of government receipts.

Central Accounting and Reporting: Maintains the central system that accounts for the monetary assets and liabilities of the Treasury.

Alternative Employment Programs

FMS participates in student hiring programs depending on funding.

Application Procedures

Direct inquiries to:

Department of the Treasury
Financial Management Service
Human Resources Division
3700 East-West Hwy., Room 170A
Hyattsville, Maryland 20782
(202) 874-8090

Internal Revenue Service (IRS)
www.irs.gov

Nature of Work: Accounting/auditing, law enforcement, taxes/revenue

Number of Employees: 112,000

Headquarters: Washington, DC

Regional Locations: Atlanta, GA; Chicago, IL; Cincinnati, OH; Dallas, TX; New York, NY; Philadelphia, PA; San Francisco, CA. There is also a Data Center in Detroit, MI; at least one District office in each state; and ten Tax Service Centers.

Typical Background of New Hires: Accounting, business, computer science, criminal justice, economics, finance/banking, law, liberal arts, political science

---

Mission

Collects the revenue that finances the federal government and investigates instances of tax abuse and fraud.

Job Descriptions

Attorney: Attorneys at the IRS become involved in arbitration, corporate law, criminal law, disclosure, employee benefits, international taxation and labor law among other tax-related legal areas. Chief Counsel attorneys draft regulations and rulings, provide legal guidance to taxpayers, and litigate in tax court. Divisions that employ the majority of Chief Counsel's attorneys include Corporate, Criminal Tax, International, and several others. See www.jobs.irs.gov/ for more information.

Computer Specialist: Designs and operates automated data processing systems that maintain and update individual and business tax accounts. Also produces data used for refund checks, bills, and notices.

Computer Investigator (Special Agent): Applies investigative skills and knowledge of specialized equipment to recover data that may have been encrypted, password protected, or hidden by other means, helping to provide evidence that can lead to the conviction of individuals guilty of money laundering or tax law violations.

Internal Auditor: Audits and evaluates all levels of the IRS's internal operations.

Internal Security Inspector: Investigates prospective employees ensuring they meet integrity standards and, when warranted, investigates criminal allegations against current employees.

Internal Revenue Agent: Reviews individual and business tax returns to determine correct tax liability and determines the tax treatment of employee benefit plans and exempt organizations.

Internal Revenue Officer: Collects delinquent tax accounts and secures delinquent tax returns. Analyzes financial statements and conducts research, interviews, and investigations.

Criminal Investigation Special Agent: Conducts financial investigations of tax evasion and tax fraud. Investigations may include tracking criminal transactions through cyberspace and international work. Agents may assume special assignments that involve multiagency task forces with other federal agencies (e.g., DEA, FBI, and ATF); Presidential campaign protective assignments; or undercover assignments.

Tax Compliance Officer: Interacts with customers who are served by the Small Business/Self Employed Division to resolve both general and technical customer issues.

Tax Specialist: Provides technical tax guidance, tax-related accounting consultation and other services related to prefiling and filing processes. Conducts surveys, studies, and focus groups to determine the effectiveness of existing agency tax-specific services and customizes communication materials to assist voluntary compliance.

Taxpayer Resolution Representative: Provides face-to-face assistance to taxpayers, including resolving examination, collection and account issues related to prefiling, filing, and postfiling processes.

Major Activities and Divisions

The IRS is divided into four major operating divisions, aligned by types of taxpayers.

Wage and Investment: This division serves approximately 116 million taxpayers who file individual and joint tax returns.

Small Business and Self-Employed: This division serves the approximately 45 million small businesses and self-employed taxpayers.

Large and Mid-Size Business: Serves corporations with assets of more than $10 million.

Tax Exempt and Government Entities: Serves employee benefit plans and tax-exempt organizations, such as nonprofit charities and governmental entities.

Other major offices include:

Chief Counsel (Counsel): Provides legal interpretation and represents the IRS with impartiality, so that taxpayers will know the law is being applied with integrity.

Appeals: Resolves tax controversies without litigation on an impartial basis.

Taxpayer Advocate Service: Helps taxpayers resolve problems with the IRS and recommend changes to prevent the problems.

Criminal Investigation Division (CID): Serves the American public by investigating potential criminal violations and financial crimes.

Communications & Liaison (C&L): Provides a communications capability that promotes understanding of the IRS mission and goals.

Alternative Employment Programs

At this writing, the IRS is reorganizing their internship programs. See www.jobs.irs.gov for an update on current programs for high school and college students.

The Office of Chief Counsel does maintain a summer legal intern program and an honors program for law students. Click on "opportunities for attorneys" at www.jobs.irs.gov for information.

Remarks

The IRS conducts extensive college campus recruiting. See their Web site for an up-to-date schedule.

Application Procedures

IRS job openings are listed on OPM's USAJOBS Web site. See individual vacancy announcements for application procedures. Or, for further information:
  For attorney positions, direct applications to:

Office of Chief Counsel/Internal Revenue Service
Attorney Recruitment and Retention Programs, Room 4032
Personnel Policy and Operations Division [CC:FM:Ppo:A]
1111 Constitution Ave., NW
Washington, DC 20224

Or, direct general inquiries to:

Personnel Office
Internal Revenue Service
1111 Constitution Ave., NW
Washington, DC 20224
(202) 622-6300

United States Mint
www.usmint.gov

Nature of Work: Banking, marketing

Number of Employees: 2,800

Headquarters: Washington, DC

Regional Locations: Denver, CO; Fort Knox, KY; Philadelphia, PA; San Francisco, CA; West Point, NY

Typical Background of New Hires: Business, engineering, finance/banking, marketing

Mission

Produces bullion and domestic and foreign coins and manufactures and sells national commemorative medals.

Job Descriptions

Marketing Specialist: Promotes the sale of commemorative coins such as the American Eagle Gold Coin, as well as other types of uncirculated coin sets.

Mechanical Engineer: Designs and integrates fabrication machinery into the Mint's production processes.

Metallurgist: Develops new techniques for fabricating numismatic items out of bullion.

Major Activities and Divisions

Marketing: Advertises and sells bullion coins and other numismatic products.

Operations: Oversees the production of coins and other products, conducts research and development, and ensures final products conform to specified quality standards.

Alternative Employment Programs

The Mint maintains a student hiring program for certain occupations.

Application Procedures

The U.S. Mint Web site at www.usmint.gov has a Job Finder that will search for job opportunities that match your interests and capabilities. Provide an e-mail address and information about job preferences. Instant e-mail notification allows you to respond to a job match at your convenience. Current job openings are listed at "job finder" on the main Web site.

Or, direct inquiries to:

United States Mint
Chief, Employment and Classification Division
633 3rd St., NW
Washington, DC 20220
(202) 354-7227

Office of Thrift Supervision (OTS)
www.ots.treas.gov

Nature of Work: Finance

Number of Employees: 1,500

Headquarters: Washington, DC

Regional Locations: Atlanta, GA; Dallas, TX; Jersey City, NJ; and San Francisco, CA.

Typical Background of New Hires: Accounting, business administration, computer science, economics, finance, law

Mission

Charters and regulates federal savings associations and savings banks and regulates state-chartered savings associations.

Job Descriptions

Accountant: Designs accounting policies and procedures.

Attorney: Represents the Office in litigation, administrative proceedings, enforcement, general law development, and interpretation of regulations and legislation.

Computer Systems Analyst: Conducts management and feasibility studies and develops and maintains current application systems.

Economist: Models savings and mortgage markets and the operations of thrift institutions.

Examiner: Assesses the financial condition, management practices, and accounting procedures at thrift institutions and determines whether they are operated in accordance with applicable laws and regulations.

Major Activities and Divisions

Regulates thrift institutions so as to ensure that they are financially stable and are operated using safe and sound management and accounting procedures and according to rules and regulations.

Alternative Employment Programs

None currently available.

Application Procedures

Current job openings are listed on the OTS Web site. Or, direct inquiries to:

Human Resources Division
Office of Thrift Supervision
1700 G St., NW, Second Floor
Washington, DC 20552
Main line: (202) 906-6000 Ext.5 for Human Resources

U.S. Secret Service

www.secretservice.gov or www.ustreas.gov/usss/

Nature of Work: Law enforcement

Number of Employees: 4,500

Headquarters: Washington, DC

Regional Locations: Over 125 field installations in the United States and abroad

Typical Background of New Hires: Business, criminal justice, liberal arts, social sciences

Mission

Protects the President and Vice President and their families, Presidential candidates, and foreign leaders visiting the United States. The Secret Service also investigates violations of counterfeiting laws and fraud or forgery involving government securities, credit cards, computers, and electronic fund transfers.

Job Descriptions

Forensic Examiner: Provides analysis for questioned documents, fingerprints, false identification, credit cards, and other related forensic science areas. Uses both instrumental and chemical analysis when reviewing evidence.

Physical Security Specialist: Conducts physical security surveys to identify hazards and implement countermeasures. May include installing and maintaining intrusion detection, video assessment, and access control systems, as well as technical surveillance equipment in support of criminal investigations. May conduct fire and life safety surveys, develop countermeasures to explosive threats, and/or develop countermeasures to chemical/biological/radiological threats against protected persons or facilities.

Uniformed Division Officer: Guards the White House and the official residence of the Vice President, the Main Treasury Building and Annex, and foreign diplomatic missions and embassies in the Washington, DC, area. Also provides protection for the U.S. President, Vice President, President-elect, Vice President–elect, and other political figures and their families.

Special Agent: Special agents are charged with two missions: protection and investigation. They provide personal security to the President and Vice President and their families as well as candidates to those offices. They also protect foreign leaders visiting the United States and enforce counterfeiting, financial, fraud, and forgery laws. Newly appointed special agents may be assigned to duty stations anywhere in the United States. Throughout their careers, agents may experience frequent travel and reassignments to Secret Service offices throughout the United States or liaison assignments in foreign countries.

Major Activities and Divisions

Forensic Services Division: Coordinates forensic analysis, including photographic, graphic, video, and audio and image enhancement services, the Voice Identification Program, and the Forensic Hypnosis Program.

Financial Crimes Division: Conducts criminal investigations involving Financial Systems Crimes, including bank fraud; access device fraud; telemarketing; telecommunications fraud (cellular and hard wire); computer fraud; automated payment systems and teller machines; and other financial crimes.

Counterfeit Division: Protects against counterfeiting by constantly reviewing the latest reprographic/lithographic technologies and maintaining a relationship with the Bureau of Engraving and Printing and the Federal Reserve System.

Technical Security Division: Establishes a secure environment for all protectees at both permanent and temporary locations and provides technical assistance to Special Agents on investigative assignments.

Alternative Employment Programs

The Secret Service maintains a two-year work-study program for numerous professional positions. These are available to undergraduate students in accounting, business management, information technology, telecommunications, and others.

The Secret Service also has a two-year Special Agent work-study program for graduate or law students. Students work closely with special agents to gain practical experience in criminal investigation techniques. Positions are limited to the DC area.

The Secret Service also participates in the federal Stay-in-School program.

Remarks

The Secret Service participates in career fairs and campus recruitment. See their Web site for a current schedule.

Application Procedures

For further information, visit the Secret Service Web site and click on Contact the Personnel Division to send an electronic message. Or, contact the personnel office at a Secret Service field office (field offices can be found on the Web site. Click on U.S. Secret Service field offices.) Or, direct inquiries to:

U.S. Secret Service
Personnel Division
950 H St., NW, Suite 912
Washington, DC 20223
 (202) 406-5271 or 5800
Toll Free: (888) 813-8777

Office of the Comptroller of the Currency (OCC)
www.occ treas.gov

Nature of Work: Banks

Number of Employees: 3,400

Headquarters: Washington, DC

Regional Locations: Atlanta, GA; Chicago, IL; Dallas, TX; Kansas City, MO; New York, NY; San Francisco, CA. These regional offices oversee numerous field offices nationwide.

Typical Background of New Hires: Accounting, business, economics, finance/banking

Mission

Supervises the operations of national banks, including their overseas operations.

Job Descriptions

Asset Management Specialist: Evaluates how well a bank controls and manages the risks inherent in its fiduciary and asset management activities.

Bank Information Systems Specialist (BIS): Evaluates technology and bank information systems related functions at national banks.

Capital Markets Specialist: Assesses risk associated with asset liability management and trading activities.

Consumer Compliance Specialist: Ensures that national banks comply with consumer protection laws and regulations.

Credit Specialist: Evaluates the level of credit risk and how well that risk is managed in bank asset portfolios.

Bank Examiner: Working as part of a team, bank examiners supervise domestic and international activities of national banks. This is accomplished by off- and on-site analyses of loan and investment portfolios, capital, earnings, liquidity, funds management, and internal controls. The majority of OCC's employees are Bank Examiners.

Economist/Research Analyst: Conducts policy analysis and monitors the financial health of the banking system to identify sources of risk.

Mortgage Banking Specialist: Applies knowledge of the risk, controls, and management of mortgage bank activities; interest rate risk; hedging; mortgage servicing; asset securitization; liquidity; and funding.

Major Activities and Divisions

Bank Supervision Operations (BSOP): Conducts examinations of national banks.

Economics Department: Made up of the Economic Analysis Division, Policy Analysis Division, and Risk Analysis Division.

International Affairs: Oversees the OCC's international activities, including formulating policies for the examination of federal branches and agencies of foreign banks.

Alternative Employment Programs

OCC Bank Examiner Intern Program: Available nationwide for students in their junior or senior year or graduate students. Bank Examiner interns are given exposure to all phases of the financial services industry.

Application Procedures

Current OCC job vacancies are listed on the OCC Web site. Or, direct inquiries to:

OCC Headquarters (for jobs in
Washington, DC, and cities
nationwide)
Attn: Human Resources
250 E St., SW
Washington, DC 20219
(202) 874-4590

Northeastern District (for jobs in MA,
NJ, NY, PA, and Washington, DC)
OCC
Attn: Human Resources
1114 Avenue of the Americas, Suite
3900
New York, NY 10036
(212) 790-4090

Southeastern District (for jobs in AL,
FL, GA, MS, NC, SC, TN, VA, and WV)
OCC
Attn: Human Resources
Marquis One Tower, Suite 600
245 Peachtree Center Ave., NE
Atlanta, Georgia 30303
(404) 588-4590

Central District (for jobs in IL, IN, KY,
MI, OH, and WI)
OCC
Attn: Human Resources
One Financial Place, Suite 2700
440 South LaSalle St.
Chicago, IL 60605
(312) 360-8921

Midwestern District (for jobs in IA, KS,
MN, MO, NE, ND, and SD)
OCC
Attn: Human Resources
2345 Grand Blvd., Suite 700
Kansas City, MO 64108
(816) 556-1812

Southwestern District (for jobs located
in AK, LA, OK, and TX)
OCC
Attn: Human Resources
500 North Akard St., Suite 1600
Dallas, TX 75201
(214) 720-7032

Western District (for jobs in AZ, CA,
CO, MT, NM, UT, and WA)
Attn: Human Resources
50 Fremont St., Suite 3900
San Francisco, CA 94105
(415) 545-5933

☆ Department of Veterans Affairs (www.va.gov)

Department of Veterans Affairs (VA)
www.va.gov

Nature of Work: Employment, handicapped, health/health care, insurance/ benefits, veterans programs
Number of Employees: 223,000
Headquarters: Washington, DC
Regional Locations: VA has 58 regional offices across the U.S. as well as hundreds of medical centers and facilities.
Typical Background of New Hires: Dental sciences, medical sciences, pharmacy, psychology, recreation, religious studies, social work, therapy sciences

Mission

The Department of Veterans Affairs operates diverse programs to benefit veterans and their families. These benefits include compensation payments for disabilities or death related to military service, pensions, education and rehabilitation, home loan guaranty, burial, and a medical care program.

Job Descriptions

Cemetery Administrator: Manages the operations of cemeteries. Requires ability to meet and deal with diverse people and to budget, schedule, and supervise.

Chaplain: Performs professional work involved in a program of spiritual welfare and religious guidance for patients in the VA health-care system.

Corrective Therapist: Applies practices of physical education and rehabilitation therapy, using physical exercise to maintain the health or to achieve physical or mental rehabilitation of patients.

Dental Officer: Performs professional work in the prevention, diagnosis, and treatment of diseases, injuries, and deformities of the teeth, jaws, organs of the mouth, and other structures associated with the oral cavity.

Dietitian: Plans and directs the preparation and service of regular and modified diets to patients. Instructs patients in the requirements of prescribed diets.

Educational Therapist: Evaluates the learning ability or educational level of patients by use of educational tests and measurements. Some work to rehabilitate the blind or to diminish emotional stress and channel energies into acceptable forms of behavior.

Health System Administrator: Coordinates resources and programs to achieve the critical balance between the administrative and clinical functions in the VA health-care system. May manage a health-care delivery system involving several institutions or may be responsible for the administrative management of a division of an individual health care system.

Hospital Housekeeping Manager: Supervises hospital housekeeping programs, ensuring sanitation with acceptable levels of bacteriological cleanliness.

Manual Arts Therapist: Evaluates vocational potential of patients and devises projects and equipment to maintain or improve skills of patients.

Medical Officer: Performs professional work in one or more fields of medicine. Requires a Doctor of Medicine or Doctor of Osteopathy degree and a license to practice medicine.

Medical Radiologist: Applies the use of radiant energy equipment and instruments for radiographic, observational, or therapeutic purposes.

Medical Technician: Performs or directs chemical, bacteriologic, hematologic, cytologic, and other tests of samples of fluids, tissues, and other substances.

Nurse: Provides care to patients in the VA health-care system. Promotes better health practices.

Occupational Therapist: Treats patients using remedial activities, such as handicrafts to promote recovery or achieve rehabilitation of patients. Performs disability evaluations, such as manual dexterity, attention span, and work tolerance.

Optometrist: Examines the eye for diseases and defects and prescribes correctional lenses or exercises. Requires a license to practice optometry.

Pathologist: Makes the final diagnostic examinations of specimens of human tissues and/or cell preparations. Conducts work in histopathology and cytology.

Pharmacist: Prepares, selects, compounds, and dispenses drugs, medicines, and chemicals. Conducts research in developing special variations of standard formulas to meet the needs of individual patients.

Physical Therapist: Treats patients using therapeutic exercise, massage, and physical agents such as air, water, electricity, sound, and radiant energy.

Prosthetic Representative: Renders prosthetic and sensory aids services to disabled patients. Serves as an adviser to physicians with regard to selection, prescription, and acquisition of prosthetic devices.

Psychologist: Performs professional work in human behavior, applying knowledge of psychological principles, theories, and methods to practical situations and problems.

Recreation/Creative Arts Therapy: Evaluates the history, interests, aptitudes, and skills of patients by interviews and tests. Devises therapy activities involving dance, art, music, and/or psychodrama.

Recreation Specialist: Evaluates the recreation needs of patients. Administers recreation activities and programs that promote the physical, creative, and social development of patients.

Social Services Representative: Provides assistance to individuals and families served by social welfare programs. Obtains background information through interviews and home visits, establishes eligibility to make use of agency resources, and explains and encourages the use of agency and community resources.

Social Worker: Provides direct services to individuals and families in need of social resources or support.

Speech Pathologist/Audiologist: Studies and provides therapeutic treatment for communications disorders as reflected in impaired hearing, voice, language, or speech.

Veterans Claims Examiner: Performs quasi-legal work involved in examining the settlement of claims filed by veterans and their dependents or beneficiaries.

Vocational Rehabilitation Specialist: Works on the vocational rehabilitation problems of the physically or mentally disabled. Plans training programs for those whose employability is impaired and places them in gainful employment. Counsels, supervises, and motivates during the adjustment to training or the work situation.

Major Activities and Divisions

Veterans Health Administration: Provides hospital, nursing home, and domiciliary care to eligible veterans. It operates 163 medical centers, as well as many domiciliaries, clinics, and nursing home care units in the U.S.

Veterans Benefits Administration: Administers vocational rehabilitation and education programs to eligible veterans. Provides credit assistance to satisfy the housing credit needs of eligible veterans. Provides VA life insurance for the benefit of service members, veterans, and their beneficiaries.

National Cemetery System: Provides cemeterial services to veterans and other eligibles.

Alternative Employment Programs

The VA has an extensive student employment program, hiring more than 40 students per year to fill administrative and semiprofessional positions. Students typically begin at the GS-4 or GS-5 levels and are usually in their junior year in college. Contact your school placement office for more information.

The VA also participates in the PMI program and conducts a volunteer program for students to fill administrative positions.

Remarks

Many of the positions requiring medical expertise are under the VA's excepted merit system and therefore do not require typical civil service application procedures.

Application Procedures

Job information can be found on the main VA Web site at www.va.gov/jobs/. Or, see these job-specific sites:

* Information on VHA executive headquarters positions is available at the VHA Executive Recruitment Web site at www.vhaexecrecruit.cio.med.va.gov/.

* Licensed health-care professionals interested in VA employment may visit the VHA Placement Service Web Site to find vacancy information and apply for positions with the Veterans Health Administration. For additional information, call the Health Care Staff Development and Retention Office (HCSDRO) at (504) 589-5267.

* For information on careers in audit, investigations, healthcare inspections, and other areas, see the OIG Web page at www.va.gov/oig/53/vacancies.htm.

For many positions, hiring decisions are made locally. Direct inquiries to the personnel officer at the VA facility in which you wish to work. For more information, you may contact the VA headquarters:

Department of Veterans Affairs
Human Resources Division
Tech World Plaza
810 Vermont Ave., NW
Washington, DC 20420
Personnel: (202) 273-4901
Main Number: (202) 273-5400

PART III

CAREER SEARCH INDEX

This Career Search Index lists the many federal agencies that may fit your needs in terms of types of positions offered, the mission of the agency, and the location of the agency. You as a job seeker can then lead a targeted search for agencies and job possibilities that interest you most, rather than reading through all of the agency listings.

Note that certain common federal positions are not detailed in the Career Search Index, since they can be found in nearly every federal agency. See Chapter 8, "Positions in Demand," for descriptions of these positions.

AGENCY NAME

OCCUPATIONAL INTEREST

Federal Dept. → Page No. →	Agriculture																	Air Force	Army					
	99	101	111	105	109	107	141	116	117	120	122	124	137	130	139	142	135	145	153	148	151	149	157	155
	AMS	ARS	FSA	APHIS	ERS	CSREES	RHS	GIPSA	FNS	FSIS	FAS	FOREST	RMA	NASS	RBS	RUS	NRCS	LOGISTICS	TRADOC	AUDIT	CECOM	CORPS	TANKAUTO	TRAFFIC
Accounting		●					●								●	●		●	●					●
Aerospace Science																								
Agriculture	●	●	●		●	●		●			●		●	●			●							
Agronomy	●	●	●			●									●	●								
Anthropology																								
Archaeology												●												
Architecture																						●		
Arts																								
Biological Science		●		●		●						●					●							
Business	●		●				●	●	●				●	●					●				●	●
Cartography																	●							
Chemistry		●																						
Computer Technology																			●	●				
Criminal Justice																								
Earth Science												●												
Economics		●			●		●	●			●		●	●	●									●
Education						●						●							●					
Engineering		●										●			●	●	●	●			●	●	●	
English/Journalism																								
Environmental Science				●								●					●					●		
Finance							●								●		●							●
Forestry												●					●							
Geography						●																		
Geology													●											
Health Science									●															
History						●																		
Home Economics						●			●															
Intelligence																								
International Affairs																			●					
Labor Relations																								
Languages																			●					
Law						●																		
Liberal Arts																								
Library Science																								
Management		●													●	●								
Marketing	●		●								●				●									
Mathematics		●		●										●										
Media Communications																								
Medical Science																								
Meteorology																								
Minority Studies																								
Oceanography																								
Physical Science		●															●							
Physics																								
Political Science						●																		
Psychology																								
Public Administration									●															
Public Relations																								
Real Estate						●																		
Recreation																	●							
Religion																								
Social Science						●																		
Statistics		●				●								●										●
Transportation		●																						
Urban Studies																								
Veterinary Medicine	●		●							●														

AGENCY NAME

OCCUPATIONAL INTEREST

Federal Dept. groups (with page numbers):
- **Commerce** — CENSUS (160), BEA (159), EDA (162), ITA (164), NIST (167), NOAA (169), BIS (176), NTIS (172), MBDA (166), PTO (179), NTIA (173), CS (180)
- **Defense** — DCAA (182), DTRA (194), DIA (184), DSS (186), DLA (188), DODEA (190), NIMA (196), NSA (198)
- **Education** — EDUCATION (201)
- **Energy** — DOE (204), FERC (210)
- **Executive Office** — USTR (213), OMB (215)
- **HHS** — ACF (220), CMS (233), AHRQ (217), SAMHSA (248)

Occupational Interest	CENSUS	BEA	EDA	ITA	NIST	NOAA	BIS	NTIS	MBDA	PTO	NTIA	CS	DCAA	DTRA	DIA	DSS	DLA	DODEA	NIMA	NSA	EDUCATION	DOE	FERC	USTR	OMB	ACF	CMS	AHRQ	SAMHSA
Accounting	•	•											•								•	•	•		•		•		
Aerospace Science																													
Agriculture																							•						
Agronomy																													
Anthropology																													
Archaeology																													
Architecture																						•							
Arts																													
Biological Science						•				•					•	•						•	•						•
Business		•	•					•				•					•					•	•	•		•			
Cartography	•				•														•										
Chemistry					•					•					•	•						•							
Computer Technology	•	•			•	•	•		•	•	•				•		•			•									
Criminal Justice								•								•													
Earth Science					•																	•							
Economics	•	•	•	•				•				•			•							•		•	•			•	•
Education																		•			•								
Engineering		•	•		•		•		•						•	•	•		•		•	•							
English/Journalism																						•							
Environmental Science																						•	•						
Finance	•		•					•	•												•	•	•	•					
Forestry																													
Geography	•														•				•										
Geology															•														
Health Science																												•	
History																													
Home Economics																													
Intelligence														•															
International Affairs			•									•	•		•														
Labor Relations																													
Languages															•				•										
Law			•							•	•										•			•					
Liberal Arts																		•											
Library Science																													
Management		•							•			•					•									•			
Marketing			•						•	•		•																	
Mathematics	•				•	•														•									
Media Communications																													
Medical Science																												•	•
Meteorology						•																							
Minority Studies									•																				
Oceanography						•																							
Physical Science					•	•	•								•							•	•						
Physics						•				•					•	•													
Political Science												•			•														
Psychology																												•	
Public Administration									•			•										•			•				
Public Relations																													
Real Estate																													
Recreation																													
Religion																													
Social Science																						•				•	•	•	•
Statistics	•	•																										•	
Transportation																													
Urban Studies																													•
Veterinary Medicine																													

AGENCY NAME

OCCUPATIONAL INTEREST

Federal Dept. / Page No. by agency:

- **HHS:** FDA (230), HRSA (237), CDC-ATSDR (226), NIH (244), IHS (238)
- **Housing:** HUD (251)
- **Interior:** BIA (358), BLM (361), NBS (372), RECLAIM (364), FWS (367), USGS (370), MMS (374), NPS (377), OSM (381)
- **Justice:** DEA (392), FBI (395), INS (397), MARSHAL (399), PRISONS (390), ATTNY (388)
- **Labor:** BLS (401), ESA (405), ETA (404), MSHA (407), PWBA (410), OSHA (408)

Occupational Interest	FDA	HRSA	CDC-ATSDR	NIH	IHS	HUD	BIA	BLM	NBS	RECLAIM	FWS	USGS	MMS	NPS	OSM	DEA	FBI	INS	MARSHAL	PRISONS	ATTNY	BLS	ESA	ETA	MSHA	PWBA	OSHA
Accounting						•							•		•		•									•	
Aerospace Science																											
Agriculture										•																	
Agronomy										•																	
Anthropology														•													
Archaeology								•						•													
Architecture																											
Arts																											
Biological Science	•		•	•			•	•	•	•	•	•	•														•
Business						•																				•	
Cartography								•				•															
Chemistry	•		•	•												•											
Computer Technology						•			•								•					•					
Criminal Justice														•		•	•		•	•	•						
Earth Science								•	•	•		•															
Economics						•				•												•	•	•	•		
Education		•					•																				
Engineering				•			•	•		•			•	•	•		•								•		•
English/Journalism																											
Environmental Science		•							•	•	•	•		•	•												
Finance						•																				•	
Forestry							•	•	•																		
Geography													•														
Geology								•	•	•		•	•		•												
Health Science		•	•		•																				•		•
History														•													
Home Economics																											
Intelligence																	•										
International Affairs																	•										
Labor Relations																							•				
Languages																	•	•									
Law								•									•		•	•		•			•		
Liberal Arts																	•							•			
Library Science				•																							
Management						•																				•	
Marketing																											
Mathematics													•									•					
Media Communications																											
Medical Science	•	•	•	•	•																						
Meteorology										•			•														
Minority Studies							•																				
Oceanography													•														
Physical Science	•							•	•	•	•	•	•	•	•												•
Physics													•														
Political Science																											
Psychology			•	•	•																				•		•
Public Administration		•				•																					
Public Relations																											
Real Estate																											
Recreation														•													
Religion																											
Social Science			•		•		•													•				•	•		•
Statistics		•																						•			
Transportation																											
Urban Studies						•																					
Veterinary Medicine																											

AGENCY NAME

Department groupings — **Labor** (PBGC, VETS); **Navy** (SECNAV, NAVAIR, NAVFAC, NAVSEA, NSWCDD, NUWCD, NAWCAD, NWC, MILSEA, SPAWAR); **State** (STATE); **Transportation** (TSA, FAA, FHWA, FRA, MARAD, NHTSA, RSPA, COAST, TRANSIT); **Treasury** (BATF, PRINT, DEBT, FMS, IRS, OTS)

OCCUPATIONAL INTEREST

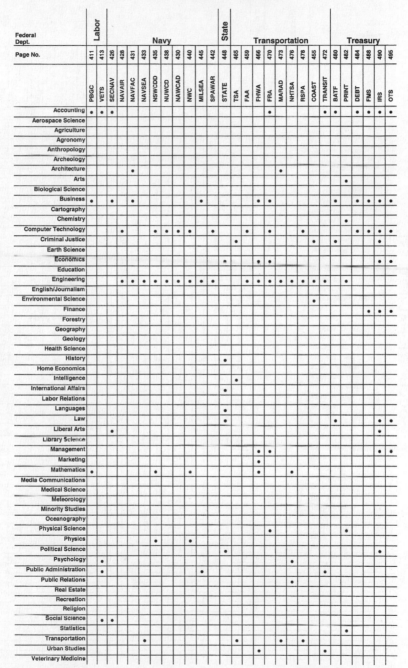

Occupational Interest	PBGC	VETS	SECNAV	NAVAIR	NAVFAC	NAVSEA	NSWCDD	NUWCD	NAWCAD	NWC	MILSEA	SPAWAR	STATE	TSA	FAA	FHWA	FRA	MARAD	NHTSA	RSPA	COAST	TRANSIT	BATF	PRINT	DEBT	FMS	IRS	OTS
Page No.	411	413	426	428	431	433	435	438	430	440	445	442	448	465	459	466	470	473	476	478	455	472	480	482	484	488	490	495
Accounting	•	•	•														•					•	•		•	•	•	•
Aerospace Science																												
Agriculture																												
Agronomy																												
Anthropology																												
Archeology																												
Architecture					•														•									
Arts																								•				
Biological Science																												
Business	•		•		•						•					•	•						•		•	•	•	•
Cartography																												
Chemistry																								•				
Computer Technology				•			•	•	•	•		•			•		•		•						•	•	•	•
Criminal Justice														•						•	•		•				•	
Earth Science																												
Economics													•			•	•										•	•
Education																												
Engineering			•	•	•	•	•	•	•	•	•	•				•	•	•	•	•	•		•	•				
English/Journalism																												
Environmental Science																					•							
Finance																										•	•	•
Forestry																												
Geography																												
Geology																												
Health Science																												
History													•															
Home Economics																												
Intelligence														•														
International Affairs													•															
Labor Relations																												
Languages													•															
Law													•										•				•	•
Liberal Arts			•																								•	
Library Science																												
Management																•	•										•	•
Marketing																•												
Mathematics	•						•			•						•		•										
Media Communications																												
Medical Science																												
Meteorology																												
Minority Studies																												
Oceanography																												
Physical Science																		•							•			
Physics						•			•																			
Political Science													•														•	
Psychology		•																	•									
Public Administration		•									•											•						
Public Relations																			•									
Real Estate																												
Recreation																												
Religion																												
Social Science		•	•																									
Statistics																									•			
Transportation					•										•			•		•								
Urban Studies																•						•						
Veterinary Medicine																												

AGENCY NAME

OCCUPATIONAL INTEREST (rows) × Agency Name (columns)

Column groups: **Treasury** = OCC, CUSTOMS, MINT, SECRET · **Veterans** = VETERANS · **Independent** = all remaining columns.

Occupational Interest	OCC	CUSTOMS	MINT	SECRET	VETERANS	NATSERV	AID	CIA	CFTC	EPA	EXIMBANK	FCC	FDIC	FEC	FEMA	FLRA	ART/HMN	FMC	FMCS	FRS	FTC	GSA	ITC	SSA	MSPB	NASA	NARA	NCUA
Page No.	498	485	493	496	401	263	254	258	261	271	276	278	280	282	284	286	310	288	289	299	291	293	296	349	297	301	306	308
Accounting	•						•	•	•		•		•	•								•						•
Aerospace Science																												
Agriculture							•																•					
Agronomy																												
Anthropology							•																					
Archaeology																	•											
Architecture																	•					•						
Arts																												
Biological Science										•																		
Business	•	•	•	•			•	•	•	•	•		•		•							•	•	•	•		•	
Cartography																												
Chemistry									•																			
Computer Technology								•	•	•												•				•		
Criminal Justice		•		•																								
Earth Science																												
Economics	•						•	•	•	•	•		•							•	•	•	•					
Education						•	•										•											
Engineering			•				•	•		•		•			•							•	•			•		
English/Journalism																	•										•	
Environmental Science																												
Finance	•		•				•	•			•		•							•								
Forestry																							•					
Geography																												
Geology									•																			
Health Science								•																				
History																	•										•	
Home Economics																												
Intelligence								•																				
International Affairs							•	•																				
Labor Relations																		•	•									
Languages																	•											
Law								•	•	•	•	•		•	•		•			•	•	•	•		•			
Liberal Arts			•				•																•					
Library Science																												
Management						•		•		•					•							•	•				•	
Marketing		•					•																•					
Mathematics																								•		•		
Media Communications												•										•						
Medical Science					•																							
Meteorology																												
Minority Studies																												
Oceanography																												
Physical Science								•		•																	•	
Physics								•																			•	
Political Science							•							•		•												
Psychology					•	•										•												
Public Administration							•									•		•								•		
Public Relations																												
Real Estate																												
Recreation					•																							
Religion					•												•											
Social Science			•	•	•	•											•						•					
Statistics																												
Transportation																												
Urban Studies							•																					
Veterinary Medicine																												

AGENCY NAME

OCCUPATIONAL INTEREST

Federal Dept. Page No. / Occupational Interest	NLRB 312	NSF 314	NTSB 317	NRC 319	OPM 323	PEACE 325	POST RAT 329	RRB 335	SBA 340	SMITH 342	TVA 353	POLICE 356	EEOC 365	POSTAL 330	SEC 337	COURTS 384	CBO 417	CRS 415	GAO 419	LIBRARY 423	SUPREME 385	GPO 421
Independent spans NLRB–SEC; **Legislative & Judicial** spans COURTS–GPO																						
Accounting	●	●					●	●	●						●				●			
Aerospace Science																						
Agriculture						●																
Agronomy																						
Anthropology										●												
Archeology																						
Architecture																						
Arts										●												●
Biological Science						●				●	●											
Business	●	●		●									●	●	●	●			●			
Cartography																						
Chemistry			●								●											
Computer Technology		●												●		●			●	●		
Criminal Justice								●				●	●	●		●					●	
Earth Science																						
Economics	●	●					●		●						●		●	●	●			
Education					●	●																
Engineering		●	●	●	●	●					●				●				●			
English/Journalism																						
Environmental Science																						
Finance								●						●								
Forestry																						
Geography																						
Geology																						
Health Science							●															
History											●											
Home Economics																						
Intelligence																						
International Affairs																			●			
Labor Relations					●								●									
Languages						●														●		
Law	●						●					●	●	●	●	●			●		●	
Liberal Arts		●			●	●						●	●									
Library Science																				●	●	
Management	●			●					●													
Marketing									●													
Mathematics		●																	●			
Media Communications																						
Medical Science							●															
Meteorology																						
Minority Studies																						
Oceanography																						
Physical Science		●	●	●						●	●											
Physics			●	●																		
Political Science	●																		●			
Psychology				●									●									
Public Administration									●					●		●		●	●			
Public Relations																						
Real Estate																						
Recreation																						
Religion																						
Social Science		●		●												●						
Statistics							●											●				
Transportation																						
Urban Studies																						
Veterinary Medicine																						

AGENCY NAME

AGENCY MISSION

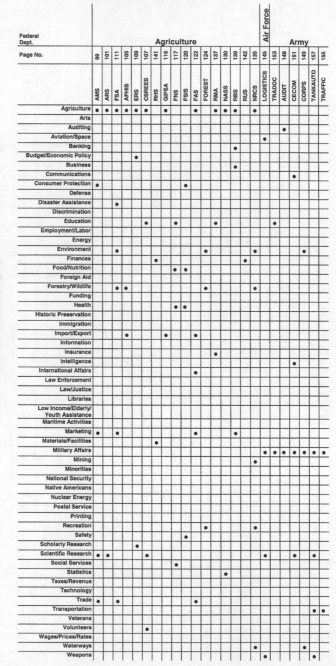

Federal Dept.	Agriculture																	Air Force	Army					
Page No.	99	101	111	105	109	107	141	116	117	120	122	124	137	130	139	142	135	145	153	148	151	149	157	155
	AMS	ARS	FSA	APHIS	ERS	CSREES	RHS	GIPSA	FNS	FSIS	FAS	FOREST	RMA	NASS	RBS	RUS	NRCS	LOGISTICS	TRADOC	AUDIT	CECOM	CORPS	TANKAUTO	TRAFFIC
Agriculture	●	●	●	●	●	●		●			●	●	●	●			●							
Arts																								
Auditing																				●				
Aviation/Space																			●					
Banking															●									
Budget/Economic Policy					●																			
Business															●									
Communications																					●			
Consumer Protection	●									●														
Defense																								
Disaster Assistance			●																					
Discrimination																								
Education						●			●			●										●		
Employment/Labor																								
Energy																								
Environment		●										●					●					●		
Finances							●									●								
Food/Nutrition									●	●														
Foreign Aid																								
Forestry/Wildlife		●	●									●					●							
Funding																								
Health									●	●														
Historic Preservation																								
Immigration																								
Import/Export			●						●		●													
Information																								
Insurance													●											
Intelligence																					●			
International Affairs										●														
Law Enforcement																								
Law/Justice																								
Libraries																								
Low Income/Elderly/ Youth Assistance																								
Maritime Activities																								
Marketing	●		●								●			●										
Materials/Facilities								●																
Military Affairs																		●	●	●	●	●	●	●
Mining																●								
Minorities																								
National Security																								
Native Americans																								
Nuclear Energy																								
Postal Service																								
Printing																								
Recreation												●					●							
Safety										●														
Scholarly Research					●																			
Scientific Research	●	●		●																	●	●	●	
Social Services									●															
Statistics														●										
Taxes/Revenue																								
Technology																								
Trade	●	●									●													
Transportation																							●	●
Veterans																								
Volunteers						●																		
Wages/Prices/Rates																								
Waterways																		●				●		
Weapons																		●					●	

AGENCY NAME

AGENCY MISSION

Departments / Page numbers:
- **Commerce** — CENSUS (160), BEA (159), EDA (162), ITA (164), NIST (167), NOAA (169), BIS (176), NTIS (172), MBDA (166), PTO (179), NTIA (173), CS (180)
- **Defense** — DCAA (182), DTRA (194), DIA (184), DSS (186), DLA (188), DODEA (190), NIMA (196), NSA (198)
- **Education** — EDUCATION (201)
- **Energy** — DOE (204), FERC (210)
- **Executive Office** — USTR (213), OMB (215)
- **HHS** — ACF (220), CMS (233), AHRQ (217)

Agency Mission	CENSUS	BEA	EDA	ITA	NIST	NOAA	BIS	NTIS	MBDA	PTO	NTIA	CS	DCAA	DTRA	DIA	DSS	DLA	DODEA	NIMA	NSA	EDUCATION	DOE	FERC	USTR	OMB	ACF	CMS	AHRQ
Agriculture																												
Arts																												
Auditing													•															
Aviation/Space																												
Banking																												
Budget/Economic Policy		•	•																						•			
Business	•					•			•	•	•	•													•			
Communications																												
Consumer Protection																												
Defense						•							•	•	•	•	•	•	•	•				•				
Disaster Assistance																								•				
Discrimination																												
Education																					•			•				
Employment/Labor			•																									
Energy																						•	•					
Environment				•																		•						
Finances																												
Food/Nutrition																												
Foreign Aid																												
Forestry/Wildlife																												
Funding																										•	•	
Health																										•	•	•
Historic Preservation																												
Immigration																												
Import/Export												•																
Information								•			•																	
Insurance																											•	
Intelligence															•	•			•									
International Affairs			•				•			•	•		•											•				
Law Enforcement							•										•											
Law/Justice									•																			
Libraries								•																				
Low Income/Elderly/Youth Assistance							•																			•	•	
Maritime Activities																		•										
Marketing												•																
Materials/Facilities																	•											
Military Affairs																		•										
Mining																												
Minorities																												
National Security						•							•		•	•			•	•				•				
Native Americans																												•
Nuclear Energy																						•						
Postal Service																												
Printing																												
Recreation																												
Safety																												
Scholarly Research																												
Scientific Research					•	•						•						•	•		•							•
Social Services																												
Statistics	•	•																										
Taxes/Revenue																												
Technology						•						•																
Trade			•																					•				
Transportation																												
Veterans																												
Volunteers																												
Wages/Prices/Rates																												
Waterways				•																								
Weapons																		•										

AGENCY NAME

AGENCY MISSION

Federal Dept.	HHS					Housing	Interior									Justice						Labor				
Page No.	230	237	226	244	238	251	358	361	372	364	367	370	374	377	381	392	395	397	399	390	388	401	405	404	407	410
	FDA	HRSA	CDC-ATSR	NIH	IHS	HUD	BIA	BLM	NBS	RECLAIM	FWS	USGS	MMS	NPS	OSM	DEA	FBI	INS	MARSHAL	PRISONS	ATTNY	BLS	ESA	ETA	MSHA	PWBA
Agriculture										•																
Arts																										
Auditing																										
Aviation/Space																										
Banking																										
Budget/Economic Policy																						•				
Business																										
Communications																										
Consumer Protection	•																									
Defense																										
Disaster Assistance							•	•																		
Discrimination																										
Education			•				•																			
Employment/Labor																							•	•		
Energy								•		•			•													
Environment								•		•	•	•	•	•	•											
Finances																										
Food/Nutrition	•			•																						
Foreign Aid																										
Forestry/Wildlife							•	•		•	•	•		•												
Funding															•											
Health	•	•	•	•	•																					
Historic Preservation														•												
Immigration																		•								
Import/Export																										
Information																										
Insurance																										•
Intelligence																	•									
International Affairs																										
Law Enforcement											•			•		•	•	•	•							
Law/Justice																	•			•	•					
Libraries				•																						
Low Income/Elderly/Youth Assistance						•																		•		
Maritime Activities																										
Marketing																										
Materials/Facilities																										
Military Affairs																										
Mining								•					•		•										•	
Minorities							•																			
National Security		•																								
Native Americans					•		•																			
Nuclear Energy																										
Postal Service																										
Printing																										
Recreation								•			•	•		•												
Safety		•													•										•	
Scholarly Research																										
Scientific Research	•	•	•						•				•	•												
Social Services																										
Statistics			•																			•				
Taxes/Revenue													•													
Technology																										
Trade																										
Transportation																										
Veterans																										
Volunteers																										
Wages/Prices/Rates																							•			
Waterways								•		•																
Weapons																										

AGENCY NAME

AGENCY MISSION

Federal Dept.	Labor		Navy										State	Transportation									Treasury				
Page No.	411	413	426	428	431	433	435	438	430	440	445	442	448	465	459	466	470	473	476	478	455	472	480	482	484	488	490	495
Agency Mission	PBGC	VETS	SECNAV	NAVAIR	NAVFAC	NAVSEA	NSWCDD	NUWCD	NAWCAD	NWC	MILSEA	SPAWAR	STATE	TSA	FAA	FHWA	FRA	MARAD	NHTSA	RSPA	COAST	TRANSIT	BATF	PRINT	DEBT	FMS	IRS	OTS
Agriculture																												
Arts																								•				
Auditing			•																						•	•	•	
Aviation/Space				•				•				•			•													
Banking																												
Budget/Economic Policy			•																									
Business	•																											
Communications																								•				
Consumer Protection																												
Defense								•																				
Disaster Assistance																			•		•	•						
Discrimination																												
Education																												
Employment/Labor		•																										
Energy																												
Environment					•																							
Finances																												•
Food/Nutrition																												
Foreign Aid																												
Forestry/Wildlife																												
Funding																					•							
Health																												
Historic Preservation																												
Immigration													•															
Import/Export																												
Information																												
Insurance	•																											
Intelligence																												
International Affairs													•															
Law Enforcement																					•		•					•
Law/Justice																												
Libraries																												
Low Income/Elderly/Youth Assistance																												
Maritime Activities					•	•	•					•						•			•							
Marketing																												
Materials/Facilities			•								•																	
Military Affairs			•	•	•	•	•	•	•	•	•	•	•								•							
Mining																												
Minorities																												
National Security													•	•							•							
Native Americans																												
Nuclear Energy																												
Postal Service																												
Printing																								•				
Recreation																												
Safety															•	•	•		•	•	•							
Scholarly Research																												
Scientific Research				•		•	•	•	•	•		•			•				•	•								
Social Services																												
Statistics																												
Taxes/Revenue																								•		•	•	
Technology																												
Trade																		•										
Transportation											•			•	•	•	•	•	•	•	•	•						
Veterans		•																										
Volunteers																												
Wages/Prices/Rates																												
Waterways																		•			•							
Weapons				•		•	•	•		•		•																

AGENCY NAME

AGENCY MISSION

Federal Dept. Page No. / Agency Mission	Treasury OCC 498	CUSTOMS 485	MINT 493	Veterans SECRET 496	VETERANS 501	NATSERV 263	AID 254	CIA 258	CFTC 261	EPA 271	EXIMBANK 276	FCC 278	FDIC 280	FEC 282	FEMA 284	FLRA 286	ART/HMN 310	FMC 288	FMCS 289	FRS 299	FTC 291	GSA 293	ITC 296	SSA 349	MSPB 297	NASA 301	NARA 306	NCUA 308
Agriculture						•																						
Arts																	•											
Auditing													•															•
Aviation/Space																										•		
Banking	•		•										•							•								
Budget/Economic Policy									•																			
Business																												
Communications												•																
Consumer Protection													•								•							
Defense								•																		•		
Disaster Assistance															•													
Discrimination																												
Education																	•											
Employment/Labor				•															•							•		
Energy																										•		
Environment										•																		
Finances																												
Food/Nutrition																												
Foreign Aid																												
Forestry/Wildlife										•																		
Funding															•	•												
Health				•	•																			•				
Historic Preservation																	•					•					•	
Immigration																												
Import/Export	•																						•					
Information																												
Insurance				•									•										•					•
Intelligence								•																				
International Affairs	•						•	•			•												•					
Law Enforcement	•	•						•														•						
Law/Justice																•												
Libraries																											•	
Low Income/Elderly/Youth Assistance																												
Maritime Activities																		•										
Marketing			•									•									•							
Materials/Facilities																						•						
Military Affairs																												
Mining																												
Minorities																												
National Security								•																		•		
Native Americans																												
Nuclear Energy																												
Postal Service																												
Printing																												
Recreation																												
Safety																					•							
Scholarly Research																											•	
Scientific Research										•																•		
Social Services					•																			•				
Statistics																												
Taxes/Revenue	•																											
Technology													•															
Trade											•							•					•					
Transportation																										•		
Veterans				•																								
Volunteers						•																						
Wages/Prices/Rates																			•									
Waterways																			•									
Weapons																												

AGENCY NAME

Agency Mission	Independent															Legislative & Judicial						
Page No.	312	314	317	319	323	325	329	335	340	342	353	356	365	330	337	384	417	415	419	423	385	421
	NLRB	NSF	NTSB	NRC	OPM	PEACE	POST RAT	RRB	SBA	SMITH	TVA	POLICE	EEOC	POSTAL	SEC	COURTS	CBO	CRS	GAO	LIBRARY	SUPREME	GPO
Agriculture						•					•											
Arts										•												
Auditing															•				•			
Aviation/Space			•																			
Banking																						
Business	•								•				•		•							
Budget/Economic Policy																	•					
Communications																				•		
Consumer Protection																						
Defense																						
Disaster Assistance																						
Discrimination										•			•									
Education		•				•				•												
Employment/Labor	•				•								•									
Energy											•											
Environment			•								•											
Finances																						
Food/Nutrition																						
Foreign Aid						•																
Forestry/Wildlife																						
Funding		•																				
Health																						
Historic Preservation																						
Immigration																						
Import/Export																						
Information																						•
Insurance								•					•									
Intelligence																						
International Affairs																						
Law/Justice	•															•			•		•	
Law Enforcement												•										
Libraries										•										•	•	
Low Income/Elderly/ Youth Assistance																						
Maritime Activities			•																			
Marketing																						
Materials/Facilities																						
Military Affairs																						
Mining																						
Minorities									•				•									
National Security																						
Native Americans																						
Nuclear Energy				•							•											
Postal Service							•							•								
Printing																						•
Recreation											•											
Safety			•																			
Scientific Research		•								•												
Scholarly Research										•								•		•		
Social Services																						
Statistics																						
Taxes/Revenue																						
Technology																						
Trade																						
Transportation			•					•														
Veterans																						
Volunteers						•																
Wages/Prices/Rates							•															
Waterways											•											
Weapons																						

AGENCY NAME

LOCATION

Federal Dept. groupings — Agriculture (AMS–NRCS), Air Force (LOGISTICS), Army (TRADOC, AUDIT, CECOM, CORPS, TANKAUTO, TRAFFIC)

Location	AMS (99)	ARS (101)	FSA (111)	APHIS (105)	ERS (109)	CSREES (107)	RHS (141)	GIPSA (116)	FNS (117)	FSIS (120)	FAS (122)	FOREST (124)	RMA (137)	NASS (130)	RBS (139)	RUS (142)	NRCS (135)	LOGISTICS (145)	TRADOC (153)	AUDIT (148)	CECOM (151)	CORPS (149)	TANKAUTO (157)	TRAFFIC (155)
Alabama																							●	
Alaska												●												
Arizona																					●			
Arkansas									●															
California	●	●							●	●		●								●		●		
Colorado	●								●	●		●												
Connecticut																								
Delaware																								
Florida																								
Georgia	●	●							●	●		●								●		●		
Hawaii																								●
Idaho																								
Illinois	●	●							●	●													●	
Indiana		●																						
Iowa										●														
Kansas		●								●												●		
Kentucky																								
Louisiana												●												
Maine																								
Maryland	●									●												●		
Massachusetts									●															
Michigan										●													X	
Minnesota		●								●		●												
Mississippi	●	●																						
Missouri		●																				●		
Montana		●										●												
Nebraska										●														
Nevada																								
New Hampshire																								
New Jersey								●														X	●	
New Mexico												●												
New York										●														
North Carolina		●							●			●												
North Dakota																								
Ohio										●								X						
Oklahoma		●																		●	●			
Oregon									●			●												
Pennsylvania	●								●			●										●		
Rhode Island																								
South Carolina																								
South Dakota																								
Tennessee																								
Texas		●							●	●										●	●		●	
Utah		●										●								●				
Vermont																								
Virginia								●										X	X	●				X
Washington		●																						
Washington DC	X	X	X	X	X	X	X	X	X	X	X	X	X	X	X	X	X					X		
West Virginia																								
Wisconsin									●	●														
Wyoming																								
Puerto Rico												●												
Nationwide			●			●	●	●	●					●	●	●	●						●	●
Overseas											●											●	●	●

*   An "X" indicates the agency's headquarters location.

**   The Nationwide category indicates that there are regional offices located throughout the U.S., sometimes one per state.

AGENCY NAME

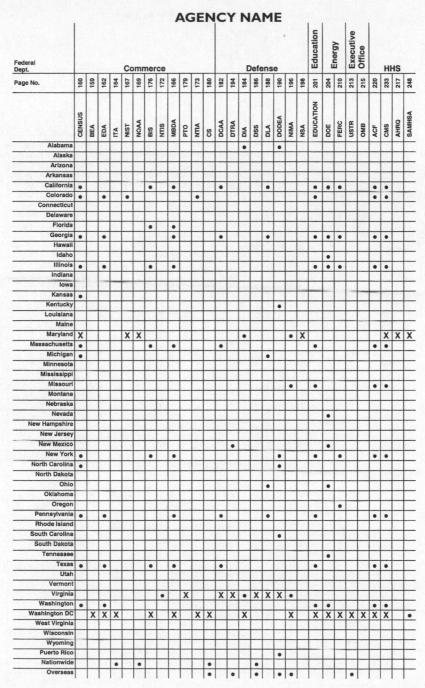

LOCATION

Federal Dept.	Commerce												Defense								Education	Energy		Executive Office		HHS			
Page No.	160	159	162	164	167	169	176	172	166	179	173	180	182	194	184	186	188	190	196	198	201	204	210	213	215	220	233	217	248
	CENSUS	BEA	EDA	ITA	NIST	NOAA	BIS	NTIS	MBDA	PTO	NTIA	CS	DCAA	DTRA	DIA	DSS	DLA	DODEA	NIMA	NSA	EDUCATION	DOE	FERC	USTR	OMB	ACF	CMS	AHRQ	SAMHSA
Alabama															•			•											
Alaska																													
Arizona																													
Arkansas																													
California	•				•		•		•				•				•				•	•	•			•	•		
Colorado	•		•	•					•												•					•	•		
Connecticut																													
Delaware																													
Florida							•		•																				
Georgia	•		•						•				•				•				•	•	•			•	•		
Hawaii																													
Idaho																							•						
Illinois	•		•				•		•												•	•	•			•	•		
Indiana																													
Iowa																													
Kansas	•																												
Kentucky																		•											
Louisiana																													
Maine																													
Maryland	X				X	X									•				•		X						X	X	X
Massachusetts	•						•		•				•								•					•	•		
Michigan	•																•												
Minnesota																													
Mississippi																													
Missouri																			•		•					•	•		
Montana																													
Nebraska																													
Nevada																						•							
New Hampshire																													
New Jersey																													
New Mexico															•							•							
New York	•						•		•										•		•		•			•	•		
North Carolina	•																		•										
North Dakota																													
Ohio																	•					•							
Oklahoma																													
Oregon																							•						
Pennsylvania	•		•				•		•				•				•				•					•	•		
Rhode Island																													
South Carolina																			•										
South Dakota																													
Tennessee																						•							
Texas	•		•				•		•				•								•					•	•		
Utah																													
Vermont																													
Virginia								•	X				X	X	•	X	X	X	•										
Washington	•		•																			•	•				•	•	
Washington DC		X	X	X			X		X	X	X	X			X					X	X	X	X	X	X	X	X	X	•
West Virginia																													
Wisconsin																													
Wyoming																													
Puerto Rico																		•											
Nationwide			•	•									•				•												
Overseas													•		•			•	•					•					

AGENCY NAME

LOCATION

Federal Dept.	HHS					Housing	Interior									Justice						Labor					
Page No.	230	237	226	244	238	251	258	361	372	364	367	370	374	377	381	392	395	397	399	390	388	401	405	404	407	410	408
	FDA	HRSA	CDC-ATSDR	NIH	IHS	HUD	BIA	BLM	NBS	RECLAIM	FWS	USGS	MMS	NPS	OSM	DEA	FBI	INS	MARSHAL	PRISONS	ATTNY	BLS	ESA	ETA	MSHA	PWBA	OSHA
Alabama															•												
Alaska		•			•		•	•			•		•	•													
Arizona				X			•	•								•											
Arkansas																											
California	•	•			•	•	•	•	•		•	•	•	•		•		•		•		•	•	•		•	•
Colorado		•	•			•		•	•	X	•	•	•	•		•							•	•			•
Connecticut																											
Delaware																											
Florida	•															•											
Georgia	•	•	X			•						•		•		•				•		•	•	•		•	•
Hawaii																											
Idaho								•			•																
Illinois	•	•				•								•		•						•	•	•		•	•
Indiana														•													
Iowa																											
Kansas	•																										
Kentucky														•											•		
Louisiana	•												•			•											
Maine																											
Maryland	X	X		X	X														•								
Massachusetts	•	•				•								•		•						•	•	•		•	•
Michigan	•															•											
Minnesota	•				•		•							•													
Mississippi																											
Missouri	•	•				•										•						•	•	•		•	•
Montana					•		•	•			•																
Nebraska															•												
Nevada											•																
New Hampshire																											
New Jersey	•															•											
New Mexico				X			•	•			•					•											
New York	•	•				•										•						•	•	•		•	•
North Carolina																											
North Dakota																											
Ohio	•		•													•											
Oklahoma								•								•											
Oregon					•			•	•		•																
Pennsylvania		•				•								•	•					•		•	•	•		•	•
Rhode Island																											
South Carolina																											
South Dakota					•		•																				
Tennessee	•					•										•											
Texas	•	•				•												•		•		•	•	•			
Utah								•		•																	
Vermont																			•								
Virginia								•	•			X		•											X		
Washington	•	•				•				•						•	•							•	•		•
Washington DC						X	X	X		•	X		X	X	X	X	X	X	X	X	X	X	X	X		X	X
West Virginia			•						•											•	•						
Wisconsin																											
Wyoming								•							•												
Puerto Rico	•																		•								
Nationwide	•													•				•	•	•					•		
Overseas																•	•	•									

AGENCY NAME

LOCATION

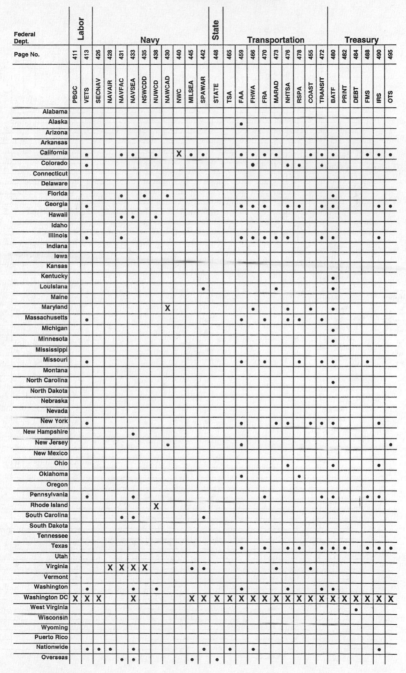

Federal Dept.	Labor		Navy										State	Transportation									Treasury					
Agency	PBGC	VETS	SECNAV	NAVAIR	NAVFAC	NAVSEA	NSWCDD	NUWCD	NAWCAD	NWC	MILSEA	SPAWAR	STATE	TSA	FAA	FHWA	FRA	MARAD	NHTSA	RSPA	COAST	TRANSIT	BATF	PRINT	DEBT	FMS	IRS	OTS
Page No.	411	413	426	428	431	433	435	438	430	440	445	442	448	465	459	466	470	473	476	478	455	472	480	482	484	488	490	495
Alabama																												
Alaska															•													
Arizona																												
Arkansas																												
California		•			•	•			•	X	•	•			•	•	•	•			•	•	•			•	•	•
Colorado																•			•	•			•					
Connecticut																												
Delaware																												
Florida					•		•			•													•					
Georgia		•													•	•	•	•			•	•				•	•	•
Hawaii					•	•				•																		
Idaho																												
Illinois		•			•										•	•	•	•	•		•	•					•	
Indiana																												
Iowa																												
Kansas																												
Kentucky																							•					
Louisiana												•						•					•					
Maine																												
Maryland										X						•		•		•			•					
Massachusetts		•													•	•		•	•				•					
Michigan																							•					
Minnesota																							•					
Mississippi																												
Missouri		•													•	•		•			•	•				•		
Montana																												
North Carolina																							•					
North Dakota																												
Nebraska																												
Nevada																												
New York		•													•		•	•		•	•		•				•	
New Hampshire						•																						
New Jersey										•					•													•
New Mexico																												
Ohio																	•						•				•	
Oklahoma															•					•								
Oregon																												
Pennsylvania		•			•													•					•	•		•	•	
Rhode Island								X																				
South Carolina					•	•							•															
South Dakota																												
Tennessee																												
Texas															•		•	•		•	•	•	•	•		•	•	•
Utah																												
Virginia			X	X	X	X					•	•					•				•							
Vermont																												
Washington		•				•	•								•					•			•	•				
Washington DC	X	X	X			X				X	X	X	X	X	X	X	X	X	X	X	X	X	X	X	X	X	X	X
West Virginia																										•		
Wisconsin																												
Wyoming																												
Puerto Rico																												
Nationwide		•	•	•		•							•	•		•											•	
Overseas				•		•					•		•															

AGENCY NAME

Treasury: OCC (498), CUSTOMS (485), MINT (493), SECRET (496) · **Veterans:** VETERANS (501) · **Independent:** NATSERV (263), AID (254), CIA (258), CFTC (261), EPA (271), EXIMBANK (276), FCC (278), FDIC (280), FEC (282), FEMA (284), FLRA (286), ART/HMN (310), FMC (288), FMCS (289), FRS (299), FTC (291), GSA (293), ITC (296), SSA (349), MSPB (297), NASA (301), NARA (306), NCUA (308)

LOCATION

Location	OCC	CUSTOMS	MINT	SECRET	VETERANS	NATSERV	AID	CIA	CFTC	EPA	EXIMBANK	FCC	FDIC	FEC	FEMA	FLRA	ART/HMN	FMC	FMCS	FRS	FTC	GSA	ITC	SSA	MSPB	NASA	NARA	NCUA
Alabama																										•		
Alaska																											•	
Arizona		•																										
Arkansas																												
California	•	•	•						•	•	•	•	•		•	•		•		•	•	•		•	•	•	•	•
Colorado			•							•		•			•	•						•		•	•		•	
Connecticut																												
Delaware																												
Florida		•								•		•						•								•		
Georgia	•	•								•		•	•		•	•				•	•	•		•	•		•	•
Hawaii																												
Idaho																												
Illinois	•	•							•	•	•	•	•		•	•				•	•	•		•	•		•	•
Indiana																												
Iowa																												
Kansas																								•				
Kentucky				•																								
Louisiana		•										•															•	
Maine																												
Maryland		•										•												X		•	•	
Massachusetts		•								•		•	•			•				•		•		•	•		•	
Michigan		•								•		•																
Minnesota							•													•								
Mississippi																										•		
Missouri	•									•		•	•							•		•		•			•	
Montana																												
North Carolina												•																
North Dakota																												
Nebraska																												
Nevada												•																
New York	•	•	•						•	•	•	•	•		•			•		•	•	•		•	•	•	•	•
New Hampshire																												
New Jersey																												
New Mexico																										•		
Ohio												•								•	•						•	•
Oklahoma																												
Oregon																												
Pennsylvania			•							•		•			•					•		•		•	•		•	
Rhode Island																												
South Carolina																												
South Dakota																												
Tennessee														•														
Texas	•	•							•	•	•	•	•		•	•		•		•	•	•		•	•	•	•	•
Utah																												
Virginia		•				X														•				X		•		X
Vermont																												
Washington		•								•		•			•						•	•	•	•	•		•	
Washington DC	X	X	X	X	X	X	X	X	X	X	X	X	X	X	X	X	X	X	X	X	X	X	X	X	X	X	X	X
West Virginia																												
Wisconsin																												
Wyoming																												
Puerto Rico		•																•										
Nationwide				•	•	•						•						•										
Overseas				•			•	•																				

AGENCY NAME

LOCATION

Federal Dept. Page No.	312	314	317	319	323	325	329	335	340	342	353	356	365	330	337	384	417	415	419	423	385	421
	\ \ \ \ Independent \ \ \ \															Legislative & Judicial						
	NLRB	NSF	NTSB	NRC	OPM	PEACE	POST RAT	RRB	SBA	SMITH	TVA	POLICE	EEOC	POSTAL	SEC	COURTS	CBO	CRS	GAO	LIBRARY	SUPREME	GPO
Alabama	•				•						•		•						•			
Alaska	•		•																			•
Arizona	•									•			•									
Arkansas																						
California	•		•		•	•			•				•	•					•			•
Colorado	•		•		•	•			•				•	•					•			•
Connecticut	•																					
Delaware																						
Florida	•									•			•	•								
Georgia	•		•	•	•	•							•	•					•			•
Hawaii	•				•																	
Idaho																						
Illinois	•		•	•	•	•	X		•				•	•					•			•
Indiana	•																					
Iowa	•																					
Kansas	•																					
Kentucky																						
Louisiana	•												•									•
Maine																						
Maryland	•		X							•			•									
Massachusetts	•				•	•			•	•				•					•			•
Michigan	•				•								•									
Minnesota	•				•	•																
Mississippi																						
Missouri	•				•				•				•						•			•
Montana																						
North Carolina	•				•								•									
North Dakota																						
Nebraska																						
Nevada	•			•																		
New York	•					•			•	•			•	•								•
New Hampshire																						
New Jersey	•		•																			
New Mexico	•												•									
Ohio	•				•								•						•			•
Oklahoma	•																					•
Oregon	•																					
Pennsylvania	•		•	•					•				•	•								•
Rhode Island																						
South Carolina																						•
South Dakota																						
Tennessee	•		•								X		•									
Texas	•		•	•	•	•							•	•					•			•
Utah														•								
Virginia		X			•					•									•			•
Vermont																						
Washington	•		•		•								•						•			•
Washington DC	X		X		X	X	X		X	X		X	X	X	X	X	X	X	X	X	X	X
West Virginia																						
Wisconsin													•									
Wyoming																						
Puerto Rico	•				•																	
Nationwide								•	•					•							•	
Overseas						•						•